TRUTH AND KNOWLEDGE IN AN EMPTY WORLD

TRUTH AND KNOWLEDGE IN AN EMPTY WORLD

STUDIES IN INDIAN AND TIBETAN BUDDHISM

TRUTH AND KNOWLEDGE IN AN EMPTY WORLD

Essays in Conversation with Tom Tillemans

Edited by Sara McClintock

Wisdom

Wisdom Publications
132 Perry Street
New York, NY 10014 USA
wisdom.org

Library of Congress Cataloging-in-Publication Data
Names: McClintock, Sara L. editor
Title: Truth and knowledge in an empty world: essays in conversation
    with Tom Tillemans / edited by Sara McClintock.
Description: First edition. | New York: Wisdom Publications, 2026. |
    Series: Studies in Indian and Tibetan Buddhism |
    Includes bibliographical references.
Identifiers: LCCN 2025046988 (print) | LCCN 2025046989 (ebook) |
    ISBN 9798890700322 paperback | ISBN 9798890700377 ebook
Subjects: LCSH: Emptiness (Philosophy) |
    Truth—Religious aspects—Buddhism | Mādhyamika (Buddhism)
Classification: LCC BQ4275 .T78 2026 (print) | LCC BQ4275 (ebook)
LC record available at https://lccn.loc.gov/2025046988
LC ebook record available at https://lccn.loc.gov/2025046989

ISBN 979-8-89070-032-2   ebook ISBN 979-8-89070-037-7

30 29 28 27 26
5 4 3 2 1

Cover and interior design by Gopa & Ted2. Interior typeset by Kristin Goble.

Printed on acid-free paper that meets the guidelines for permanence and durability of the Production Guidelines for Book Longevity of the Council on Library Resources.

Printed in the United States of America.

Please visit fscus.org.

Publisher's Acknowledgment

The publisher gratefully acknowledges the generous help of the Hershey Family Foundation in sponsoring the production of this book.

Contents

Preface

THERE is no philosophy without conversation and no conversation without friends. The origins of this book can be found, therefore, in conversations among friends. Such conversations are too many to count, too many to recall. But we know that it is only by virtue of our exchanges with others that we become who we are, that we see things as we do. When those exchanges take place between friends, they become conversations. Whether our conversations are temperate or heated, probing or predictable, sustained or spontaneous, they offer opportunities for growth and the transformation of even our most cherished notions. When the person with whom we converse is Tom Tillemans, we can be sure that even our most tightly sealed up opinions and arguments will be cracked open to let new light stream in to reveal new questions, new possibilities, new angles, and new ideas. The articles in this volume all emerge from scholars whose ideas have been shaped through conversations with others, including each other and, most decisively, with Tom.

To honor a teacher, a colleague, and a friend and to thank them for their contributions over a long career, it is traditional to offer a Festschrift on some special occasion. Usually, the former students of the honoree will collect, in secret, many short articles from their mentor's admirers, publishing the work as a surprise to be presented at a retirement party, conference, or other event. When John Dunne and I first discussed how to put together a volume to honor Tom, we realized that while a book would be a wonderful outcome, what really mattered were the conversations that would lead to that publication. And we could not conceive of having those conversations without Tom being part of them.

We decided, therefore, to take a different route, involving Tom from the beginning. We settled on the idea of a small workshop where we could delve into a few of the many core themes that have interested Tom over the years and that would lead eventually to a book. It was Tom who came up with the title for the project, *Truth and Knowledge in an Empty World*, and John and I readily agreed that it was a fitting designation for what we hoped would be a stimulating set of continuing conversations both in person and in print. John and I agreed to divide the labor, with John doing a masterful job of organizing the workshop at the University of Wisconsin-Madison and hosting the participants over several days. My part came later, collecting and editing the papers, and writing this preface and the introduction. I should also mention here the invaluable help of our sagacious editor at Wisdom, David Kittelstrom, of our talented copy editor, Sarah Fleming, and of our rigorous production editor at Wisdom, Ben Gleason.

Among the highlights of the workshop, of course, were the many conversations that took place, whether at the conference venue, the Center for Healthy Minds, the excellent restaurants where we gathered in the evenings, or at the home of John and Anna Dunne, who graciously hosted us on the final night. Most of the papers engaged with or referenced Tom's work directly or otherwise touched on themes central to his writings on truth, epistemology, and the nature of philosophy. The ensuing conversations were passionate, playful, and illuminating. There was much laughter woven among the inevitable disagreements, but most of all, there was joy. This book is both the fruit of those conversations and their continuation. We trust that the articles here will further stimulate new questions, new possibilities, and new ideas. To all of our readers, including the many colleagues and friends we could not include in this volume, you also are part of these conversations, and your contributions are felt keenly throughout.

John and I would also like to acknowledge the staff at the Center for Healthy Minds as well as the very capable Tiantian Cai and her fellow doctoral students, Jeremy Manheim, Ajita Raghavendra, and Carlos Recarte. Without their help, the workshop would not have been possible.

Truth and Knowledge in an Empty World Workshop Group Photo
Madison, Wisconsin, May 18–21, 2023

Participants L to R: Constance Kassor, Mark Siderits, Kenneth Liberman, David Higgins, Georges Dreyfus, Jan Westerhoff, John Dunne, Dan Arnold, Tom Tillemans, Jay Garfield, Vincent Eltschinger, Birgit Kellner, José Cabezón, John Taber, Sara McClintock, David Kittelstrom

Introduction: Conversations with Tom Tillemans

ANYONE who spends time with Tom Tillemans will soon realize that he is a wonderful conversation partner. Whether telling stories about his mother's experiences in the Dutch resistance, his stint on a Canadian oil rig, or his attempts to learn Cree, an indigenous language spoken across much of northern Canada, his talk is always entertaining, illuminating, and punctuated by hearty laughs. If you happen to be a philosopher or even just a person with philosophical inclinations, a conversation with Tom is sure to induce a wide range of expressions across your face. One moment you may find yourself with furrowed brow, puzzling over some deep, previously unnoticed conundrum that Tom has brought to your attention, while another moment may see a broad grin spread across your visage as you recognize the brilliance of one of his many insights or inquiries. If you happen to be a scholar of Buddhist philosophy or Asian intellectual history, you no doubt will be tempted to ask many questions of this profoundly learned yet approachable professor with an avuncular air. And if your curiosities run more toward language and philology, Tom will again not disappoint, as he reflects with erudition on the foibles and rewards of translation and the persons we become when we inhabit diverse linguistic worlds.

The contributors to this volume are among the many lucky ones who have had the opportunity to converse repeatedly with Tom. We come together to honor this productive engagement through which our own scholarly work has been so greatly enriched. We are delighted that Tom has agreed to continue these conversations by offering a contribution of his own. This confirms that while the present *liber amicorum* is ostensibly a celebration of the life and work of the Buddhist philosopher and philologist Tom Tillemans, it is even more so a celebration of the friendship that has allowed so many conversations to flourish and change us.

The authors in this book have come to know Tom Tillemans in a variety of ways, each one of us encountering him through his person or his works at particular, often memorable, moments in our lives. I count myself among the extremely fortunate who have had occasion to talk shop with Tom uncountable times, and this introduction is first and foremost an homage to those conversations and the friendship they have nurtured and implied. In a bit, I will attempt to give a taste of some of the conversations that Tom and I conducted recently over Zoom as I was preparing to write this introduction. But first, for those who have yet to meet Tom or who are less familiar with his story, it is appropriate to give a short introduction to his life and works.[1] His unlikely and propitious career has brought him to live and work on several continents and to collaborate broadly across several disciplines. Seemingly without thought for personal advancement or fame, driven primarily by his relentless philosophical appetite, Tom has been drawn to any person who could provide him with food for thought and to any place where he could find minds that would challenge his own. As he has said about himself, "I was one of these peculiar people that never really had any doubt about what they wanted to do in life. It was simply a question of *how* to do it. And, of course, who was going to finance it." Most of the story of his life is thus about his doing some sort of philosophy, sometimes in far-flung places or unconducive contexts, and, of necessity, the search for the means to somehow continue doing it.

Life

Early formation in Canada and India

Tom was born to Dutch parents in the Netherlands on December 21, 1950, but moved as a very young child to Dawson Creek, a municipality in northern British Columbia that marks the beginning of the Alaska Highway. He remembers the mud, the extreme cold, and the bewildering incongruity with the life he had led up to that time in Holland. Apparently his parents had naively envisioned life on the northern prairies to be a bit more romantic than it turned out to be, and his family found themselves moving progressively southward until finally settling in Vancouver. It was here that Tom completed his secondary education and eventually entered college. It was also here that Tom had his first taste of philosophy, which came around age fourteen while on a hike with his father, an intellectual whose expertise ranged broadly

---

1. The material and quotations attributed to Tom in this introduction are drawn from online conversations I held with Tom from October 2023 through January 2024 and from his recorded interview with the Oral History of Tibetan Studies Project at Oxford University. See https://oralhistory.iats.info for more about the project. A full list of Tom's published works can be found at the end of this introduction.

from classics to English literature and later to child psychology and special education. Tom remembers his father explaining Plato's *Republic*, including the problem of universals, various controversies between Plato and Aristotle around the reality or unreality of the Forms, and a fair dose of metaphysics with a political turn. The conversation immediately sparked a passion in Tom. He recalls that his father subsequently slipped him a copy of G. H. Sabine's *History of Political Theory* (1937), not exactly a page-turner for a teenager, and that he devoured it as best he could, often not having a clue how to pronounce names like Hegel and Hobbes. He soon began to read whatever philosophy he could digest, sneaking Bertrand Russell's *History of Western Philosophy* onto his lap in school during otherwise rather boring classes. He liked Russell's irreverence. When it was time to study at the University of British Columbia, there was never any question as to what would form the focus of his learning.

At university, Tom studied the basics of philosophy, following his teacher's advice that "You have to learn to walk before you can run." The University of British Columbia at that time used a tutorial system, modeled on the system at Oxford and Cambridge, in which a student would meet with a teacher weekly to present and defend a paper. No doubt the philosopher who impressed him most there was Jonathan Bennett, rightly well known for his penetrating use of analytic philosophy to understand arguments in key texts in the history of philosophy. This methodology would influence Tom throughout his own career. He followed Bennett's courses on Kant avidly and had a memorable weekly tutorial with him on Wittgenstein.

Tom cites these years as the period in which he learned to think and write analytically, and indeed the emphasis of his philosophical training in Vancouver was in analytic philosophy, logic, and philosophy of language. The philosophers he read most intensively at this point were heirs to the tradition of logical positivism, authors who were often highly skeptical of the metaphysical claims of traditional philosophy—thinkers like Carnap, Ayer, Wittgenstein, Strawson, and Quine. Tom muses that his lack of technical acumen in mathematics and science may have driven him toward a more informal approach such that he became interested in the more basic problems about philosophical thinking, about what we are doing when we argue, and about what we are doing when we hold a metaphysical thesis. He was exposed, too, to Austin, Ryle, and the ordinary language philosophy that was then à la mode. Driving questions became, and remain, what one can and should do with philosophy and where it goes wrong, becoming a particular type of nonsense.

In the process, Tom became intrigued with Buddhist philosophy and studied elementary Sanskrit under Ashok Aklujkar. He had considered going on to do a doctorate in philosophy right away. But he quickly determined that at age twenty-two, he needed to get out and experience the world more first. He worked for a while in construction, as a chokerman in the forest industry, and on an oil rig in southern Alberta. While working off and on as a longshoreman in the port of Vancouver, he used to go in his free time to the recesses of the UBC library to study Sanskrit and Tibetan. Sometime around 1973, while in the stacks of the old library, he discovered the world of Zen Buddhism through a volume of Sonja Arntzen's translations of the poet Ikkyū Sōjun. His interest would be further deepened when he met Jōshū Sasaki Rōshi, an intriguing, unfathomable Rinzai master.

Tom's exposure to Tibetan thought began in the early 1970s when he followed Kalu Rinpoche's teachings in Vancouver. His attraction to Buddhist philosophy was growing, and by now he had concluded that he really needed to get serious about learning the necessary languages. After saving some money, Tom and his wife, Shelley, set off for India. Tom initially hoped to study with Kalu Rinpoche in Darjeeling, but as they encountered problems obtaining a permit, they ended up going to Dharamsala instead. It was there that Tom learned basic spoken Tibetan, first by engaging in all sorts of daily-life talk with his cook, Wangchuk, and then by learning to debate in Tibetan with a geshé named Tashi Wangyal who worked at the Library of Tibetan Works and Archives. In Dharamsala, Tom also learned from Geshé Tamdin Rabten (1921–86), a monastic scholar and former tutor of the Fourteenth Dalai Lama known especially for his incisive teaching of Tibetan logic and Madhyamaka. In Dharamsala, Tom also encountered Shunzō Onoda, a scholar of Tibetan monastic debate, who was to become a lifelong friend.

Reasoning philosophically in Tibetan was intriguingly odd and different from anything he had done before. Thus began Tom's long history of wrestling with linguistic relativism, or perhaps the incommensurability of certain conceptual schemes, insofar as he found that he was unable to explain adequately or even paraphrase in English certain aspects of the logic and reasoning that seemed very intelligible to him and his teachers in Tibetan. Questions about whether Tibetan debate logic did not recognize certain classical theorems, or whether the philosophical positions expressed in it were largely language-dependent and inexplicable in the terms of the analytic philosophy in which Tom had been trained, became increasingly paramount for Tom. These are issues that have continued to absorb him through the present.[2]

---

2. See his *Views from Tibet* (2022), 114ff.

Moving to Switzerland

After a couple of years in Dharamsala, around 1976, Tom and Shelley decided to go to Switzerland, where they could continue their study of Tibetan philosophy under Geshé Rabten, who had moved there to serve as the second abbot of the Tibet Institute Rikon, a monastery built by a Swiss industrialist for the Tibetan refugee community in Zell-Rikon im Tösstal in the canton of Zurich. At Rikon and subsequently from 1978 in Mont-Pèlerin, overlooking Lake Geneva, Tom joined a number of other seekers and scholars interested in learning from Geshé Rabten, including Alan Wallace, Stephen Batchelor, and Shunzō Onoda, and spent a number years studying debate, logic, and other traditional Tibetan philosophical topics. It was in Switzerland, too, that Tom first met Georges Dreyfus, then an ordained Buddhist monk on his way to becoming the first Western *lharampa* geshé, the highest monastic degree available in the Geluk tradition. As Tom recalls, Georges could weave masterfully back and forth among topics from Abhidharma to Madhyamaka to epistemology. Tom learned a great deal from him—and still does.

Initially in Rikon and then in Mont-Pèlerin, Tom had contact with the Buryat lama Geshé Ngawang Nyima (1907–90), who had been the abbot of Drepung Gomang Monastery in India. This playful debater had walked from Buryatia via Ulaanbaatar to Lhasa in 1923. After years of study in Tibet, he made his way to India in 1959 and eventually to Europe, where he spent six years in Leiden working with David Seyfort Ruegg. Tom recalls that Geshé Ngawang Nyima would never give you the answer. His pride and joy was his debate-trick book, *Bsdus grwa brjed tho* ("Mnemonic Notes on the Collected Topics"), a hundred photocopied pages full of his handwritten memories of debates, definitions, and sophisms, a few of which he had supposedly invented himself and introduced into the Lhasa milieu. After an exhausting, winding debate, he would eventually say, "Ah, now I've got you doubting things (*da the tshom za gi 'dug*)!" Quirky arguments in Tibetan—many of which can never be translated into English—have always interested Tom. Sometimes he would say that their attraction was ludic and aesthetic, a bit like that of the architecture of Friedensreich Hundertwasser: no straight lines going anywhere, and all the more interesting for it. He later came to respect the perspective of the twentieth-century Dutch logician Evert W. Beth, who taught that logic and philosophical reasoning regularly make substantive advances via analyses of imaginative sophistry.[3] That seems to Tom to be an important truth, not just with regard to Greece but also India, Tibet, and China.

3. See Tillemans 1991a, 403 and n1.

This period began Tom's connection with several Japanese scholars of Indian and Tibetan philosophy. In addition to Onoda, who had come along to Mont-Pèlerin from Rikon and with whom Tom enjoyed speaking in Tibetan, Katsumi Mimaki was also around during this period. Tom recalls that it was from Mimaki-san that he first learned the necessity of precision in philology. As a philosopher, Tom had up to that time been rather flippant about fastidious discussions of textual readings. But through his contact with Mimaki (who became a professor at the University of Kyoto and later a member of the Japan Academy), he came to have a much deeper appreciation for the importance of attending to every linguistic element when reading and translating texts and of not allowing errors and misunderstandings to compound. Attention to detail has been a defining feature of Tom's work ever since, and philological precision is a value he has consistently endeavored to pass along to his students.

Along with Mimaki, another person Tom met during this time who would turn out to play an outsized role in his development as a scholar was Jacques May, a philosophically gifted Indologist and scholar of Buddhism who had trained in Paris under such giants as Louis Renou, Marcelle Lalou, Jean Filliozat, Paul Mus, and Paul Demiéville. May held a chair *ad personam* of Buddhist philology at the University of Lausanne. Tom recounts that it was the two of them, Mimaki and May, who persuaded him of the value of being an Indologist, of really knowing Sanskrit and being able to read the Indian texts independently of the Tibetan commentarial tradition. He came to feel that to do justice to Tibet, you had to be able to stand outside it. Only by means of a thorough understanding of the Indian texts on their own terms is one able to really appreciate the Tibetan contributions in interpreting them. From this point on, Tom attempted to see Tibetan Buddhist philosophical texts stereoscopically, knowing that they reflect not simply a continuation of the Indian tradition but also a genuine creativity and innovation that can be difficult to appreciate in the absence of Indological training.

Tom had already unofficially resumed his study of Sanskrit in the Department of Oriental Languages and Cultures at the University of Lausanne under both Jacques May and Heinz Zimmerman. But around this time, he began to run seriously low on funds. Therefore, to support himself, his wife Shelley, and their young daughter, Tom now officially enrolled in the University of Lausanne, primarily to obtain a Swiss work permit that would allow him to do various jobs, including hauling sacks of wheat in a grain mill and harvesting grapes in vineyards. It was during one of those harvesting stints that a friend, Geneviève Billeter, mentioned to Tom that her brother was a professor of Chinese at the University of Geneva. She soon introduced Tom to Jean-François Billeter and his wife Cui Wen, and Tom began his study of modern and classical Chinese with them. In this way Chinese became another branch of his university studies, leading him to eventually obtain a *licence ès lettres* (*mention très bien*) degree in Sanskrit, Chinese, and philosophy from the universities of both Lausanne and Geneva in 1983.

May had a bit of a cult following. He was old school, had a bowl haircut, thick glasses, a long cigarette holder, and often paced around the room like a caged tiger. He attracted auditors from outside the university who would come to listen to the eccentric professor speak eloquently not only on Buddhist philosophy but also on a range of Mahāyāna sūtras and narrative literature, often spending an entire lecture unpacking the literary, philosophical, and philological resonances of a Sanskrit term. Between 1985 and 1990, May delivered a five-year-long course on the *Mūlamadhyamakakārikā* of Nāgārjuna, the notes for which have now been edited and published by Jérôme Ducor and Henry W. Isler, two of May's students who were present during this time.[4] Tom remembers that although May did not call himself a philosopher, he did have a highly developed philosophical perspective, one that was both original and synthetic, influenced greatly by his reading of Hegel and Kant. May was also well versed in French literature, with a particular affinity for the poetry of Stéphane Mallarmé. He could quote Nāgārjuna and Vasubandhu in Sanskrit, knew Pāli, Tibetan, Chinese, and Japanese, and took inspiration from Zen Buddhism. Tom was May's first doctoral student to finish and defend a thesis in Lausanne.

Becoming a scholar

The early 1980s marked the beginning of Tom's professional career as a scholar, seeing his initial publications and participation in international Indological and Buddhist studies conferences. In 1981, Tom embarked for Vienna, where he gave his first academic paper at the Csoma de Kőrös Symposium. His article, "The 'Neither One nor Many' Argument for *Śūnyatā* and Its Tibetan Interpretations," was later published in the conference proceedings. At the symposium, Tom met many scholars who would become lifelong colleagues and conversation partners, including Leslie Kawamura, Lambert Schmithausen, David Seyfort Ruegg, Ernst Steinkellner, Helmut Tauscher, Michael Torsten Much, János Szerb, Zoltán Horváth, and Paul Williams. Tom recounts

---

4. Jacques May, *Les vers didactiques fondamentaux sur la doctrine de la voix du milieu (Mūla-Madhyamaka-kārikā) de Nāgārjuna*, edited by Jérôme Ducor et Henry W. Isler, foreword by Tom J. F. Tillemans (Geneva: Librairie Droz, 2024).

fondly that, although Steinkellner understandably does not remember it, it was he who fronted Tom much-needed money for his train ticket back to Lausanne at the end of the conference.

Next came the first of Tom's many appearances at an International Association of Buddhist Studies conference, the fifth congress of the IABS held at Oxford University in 1982, where he had been invited to participate on a panel on Buddhist logic and epistemology organized by Bimal Krishna Matilal. His paper, on identity and referential opacity, was eventually published in a book edited by Matilal, and it was Tom's first explicit attempt to put Indian and Tibetan Buddhist philosophical theories into direct conversation with ideas in analytic philosophy. In the paper, Tom seeks to show that it was "a problem similar to that of referential opacity" as articulated by W. V. Quine that "motivated Buddhist logicians to devise a pan-fictional and highly intensional theory of language."[5] This would be just the beginning of Tom's long career of bringing these two philosophical worlds to bear upon one another.

At Oxford, in addition to Matilal, Tom met another host of scholars of Indian and Buddhist philosophy, many of whom became valued friends and interlocutors, including José Cabezón, David Eckel, Brendan Gillon, Richard Hayes, Shōryū Katsura, and Mark Siderits. Tom made a particularly strong connection with Katsura, who had himself been a student of Jacques May years earlier in Kyoto. Katsura arranged for Tom to get a Monbushō scholarship to study in Hiroshima, a timely rescue, since Tom's funds were again about to run dry. While in Japan, Tom continued his study of Sanskrit texts with Katsura, working especially on the fourth chapter of Dharmakīrti's *Pramāṇavārttika*. They also read some of Xuanzang's Chinese translation of Dharmapāla's commentary on Āryadeva's *Catuḥśataka*, a text that would become central to Tom's doctoral dissertation and his eventual monograph, *Materials for the Study of Āryadeva, Dharmapāla and Candrakīrti* (1990). Tom also began his study of Tibetan grammatical traditions, reading some important *sum rtags* texts with Katsura and the linguist Derek Herforth, who was also in Hiroshima at that time. This collaboration subsequently also resulted in a book, *Agents and Actions in Classical Tibetan* (1989). Tom's prolific publishing career was taking off.

Returning to Lausanne with Shelley and his young daughter, Tom contributed to the support of his family by teaching English in Swiss secondary schools while continuing to work on his dissertation and struggling to understand the Chinese translations of Dharmapāla's lost Sanskrit text. Dharmapāla's commentary on Āryadeva is not part of the Tibetan monastic

---

5. Tillemans 1986b, 216.

curriculum, nor does it continue to be studied by Chinese Buddhists. As such, Tom found there were no scholars who could help identify the moves, protagonists, and antagonists in the abundant dazzling arguments in the text. Eventually, though, Tom realized that by learning to decode Xuanzang's translation practices, he could gain some facility in dimly discerning the Sanskrit that must have lain behind the Chinese text. Tom rented a little room where he would go each day with his briefcase in tow to buckle down, write, and think. In comparison to translating Dharmapāla's commentary on Āryadeva's *Catuḥśataka*, Tom remembers, translating Candrakīrti's commentary on the same text was easy.

During this time, Tom also continued to work on translations from the fourth chapter of the *Pramāṇavārttika*, publishing small slices in the *Wiener Zeitschrift für die Kunde Südasiens*. This work, too, eventually resulted in an impressive and enormously valuable contribution to Buddhist studies, his book *Dharmakīrti's Pramāṇavārttika: An Annotated Translation of the Fourth Chapter (parārthānumāna)* (2000).

Tom publicly defended his doctorate thesis in 1989, formally receiving his *doctorat ès lettres* (D.Litt.) in Buddhist studies from the University of Lausanne in 1990 when the two volumes of *Materials for the Study of Āryadeva, Dharmapāla and Candrakīrti* were published in Steinkellner's series in Vienna—at that time, publication in a decent academic series was a condition for the conferral of the degree. Not long after this, Tom was invited by Lambert Schmithausen to serve as a short-term replacement for David Seyfort Ruegg, who had abruptly retired from the University of Hamburg. With Tom's family established in Switzerland, he commuted for this stint, cramming all his classes into sixteen periods over two long days every second week. (He recalls that Schmithausen at one point told him "If you can do this, you can do anything.") At Hamburg he met other interesting people who were to become friends and interlocutors, including the eccentric and brilliant Claus Oetke, who occasionally sat in on Tom's class on a text by Alasha Ngawang Tendar and then sent him postcards filled with symbolic logic.

At Hamburg, Tom taught, among other things, a course on Tsongkhapa's Madhyamaka, focusing especially on the *Eight Difficult Points of the Mūlamadhyamakakārikā (Rtsa shes dka' gnad/gnas brgyad kyi zin bris)*, a set of lecture notes on Tsongkhapa's core teachings on Prāsaṅgika Madhyamaka written by Tsongkhapa's disciple Gyalstab Darma Rinchen. Schmithausen sat in on the class, and Tom recalls that it was from him that he learned something of the art of how to discern which variants are interesting and which are not when editing a text. As Tom put it, "To this day, I think that a lot of times, the best critical editions are done by people who know what to leave out as insignificant. The maniacal or almost obsessive listing of all variants . . . actually makes an edition often impossible to use. What's really important is to *see* what's significant and not overburden a reader with trivia." Tom says that he also learned from his good friend Helmut Krasser, who similarly advocated this kind of discernment. Although Tom never officially studied in Vienna, he felt like he did because he visited frequently and kept up a strong relationship with the circle of scholars there.

Becoming a professor

Not long after Tom's Hamburg stint, when Jacques May retired in 1992, Tom was appointed to take his teacher's place and painlessly became a full professor at the University of Lausanne. Tom points out that the unanticipated rapidity of his rise was just how things could work in Switzerland in those days. Needless to say, he counts himself extremely lucky to have largely dodged the usual process of applying for various jobs, getting promoted with tenure, and so on. And, seemingly miraculously, his good fortune continued. Not long after his appointment at Lausanne, Tom learned that a Dutch woman named Elisabeth de Boer, who had practiced Zen for many years in the monastery in Japan with which Jacques May had been connected during his work with the École française d'Extrême Orient, had willed a very large sum of money to the chair of Buddhist studies at the University of Lausanne. As Tom says, "That happened to be me." The terms of her will ensured that Buddhist studies would continue in Switzerland, as she had stipulated that her gift was conditional upon Lausanne having a chair in Buddhist studies financed by the Swiss state. Lausanne University, whether interested or not in the subject matter, would not want to give up such an impressive resource. Tom realized that, besides a lot of money, he now had job security.

This astonishing turn of events also meant that Tom was now able to sponsor a wide range of scholarly activities, including organizing conferences, hosting researchers, underwriting travel for students and other academics, and supporting doctoral students. It would not be an exaggeration to say that all the scholars contributing to this volume have benefitted from the Fonds de Boer in some fashion over the course of their careers. Among the significant things Tom was able to do was to arrange to appoint Cristina Scherrer-Schaub, another of Jacques Mays's former students, as a professor at the University of Lausanne. He further was able to collaborate with his colleague at Lausanne, the scholar of Indian philosophy and intellectual history Johannes Bronkhorst, to organize conferences on topics like Sāṃkhya philosophy. He brought a number of students to Tibet, including some who were to go on to become leading figures in Buddhist studies, and he sponsored others to attend international conferences. He organized and funded research stays in Lausanne by diverse international scholars, including Takashi Iwata, Sadananda Das, Heidi Köppl, Georges Dreyfus, Jiří Holba, Donald Lopez, Ken Liberman, Chizuko Yoshimizu, Hideyo Ogawa, Martin Adam, Denise Lo (Lo Weitzu), Raynald Prévéreau, Naomi Sato, Kenneth Zysk, Mark Siderits, Koji Tanaka, and Bronwyn Finnigan.

Starting in the mid to late 1990s, Tom generously sponsored and supervised a number of doctoral students, starting with John Dunne and myself, who came from the United States for two years and ended up persuading Tom to be the director of our dissertations after the passing of our original advisor at Harvard, Masatoshi Nagatomi. Two Swiss scholars who are now leaders in their fields, Vincent Eltschinger and Pascale Hugon, both studied under Tom, focusing on Indian and Tibetan epistemology, respectively. Tom's good friend Mimaki sent his student Tōru Tomabechi from Kyoto to work on Indian Buddhist tantric materials and also to collaborate with Tom in the study of one of Tibet's most independent thinkers, Shākya Chokden. Tom's friend and teacher Katsura sent Ryusei Keira, a scholar of Kamalaśīla who had studied with Yasunori Ejima in Tokyo. Later, Tom met and then invited David Higgins to come from Canada to do a doctorate. David was one of Herbert Guenther's last students and had a great deal of knowledge of the Tibetan Great Perfection (*rdzogs chen*) traditions. Tom also brought Thomas Doctor, a Danish student of the Kagyü-Nyingma teacher Chökyi Nyima Rinpoché, to work on early Tibetan Madhyamaka.

During this period, Tom became increasingly involved with the International Association of Buddhist Studies, serving for eight years (1998–2006) with Cristina Scherrer-Schaub as co-editor of the *Journal of the International Association of Buddhist Studies*, organizing the association's twelfth congress, held at the University of Lausanne in 1999, and eventually assuming the role of the association's general secretary (2002–10). Working alongside Jérôme Ducor, who served as the association's treasurer, and Danielle Feller, who provided indispensable aid, the Lausanne team helped to revitalize the association. Tom was becoming increasingly disinterested in the ways Buddhist studies was represented in the American Academy of Religion and was convinced of the need for a place for exchange among scholars who possessed the kind of philological training and instincts that were, and continue to be, the backbone of his own philosophical investigations relating to Buddhist thought. This led him to devote significant energy and resources to the association. In this vein, too, Tom agreed to become the editor for a new academic series at Wisdom Publications, Studies in Indian and Tibetan

Buddhism, which allows philologically rigorous Buddhist philosophical studies to reach a wider audience. The series was launched with the publication of Tom's *Scripture, Logic, Language: Essays on Dharmakīrti and His Tibetan Successors* (1999) to establish the series' commitment to textually informed scholarship.

Starting in the early 2000s, through his connection with Thomas Doctor and Heidi Köppl, Tom began to travel regularly to the Rangjung Yeshe Institute in Kathmandu to teach and attend annual conferences on Buddhist studies arranged by Chökyi Nyima and his students. The conferences became a kind of hub for philosophers interested in questions of Buddhist epistemology and logic, often including scholars like Klaus Dieter-Mathes, John Dunne, Jonardon Ganeri, Jay Garfield, and others. After some years, these meetings culminated in a group of scholars getting together and calling themselves the Cowherds—a nod to the stock Madhyamaka phrase *gopālāṅganā*, meaning "cowherds and women," used to indicate ordinary, uneducated persons who do not possess much in the way of philosophical learning. In addition to Tom, the Cowherds were Georges Dreyfus, Bronwyn Finnigan, Jay Garfield, Guy Newland, Graham Priest, Mark Siderits, Koji Tanaka, Sonam Thakchoe, and Jan Westerhoff. Together they produced a polygraph, *Moonshadows: Conventional Truth in Buddhist Philosophy* (2011), an indispensable resource for anyone wishing to understand the range of Madhyamaka positions on conventional truth.

In the following years, Tom was involved with a number of highly specialized conferences, some of which led to the publication of top-notch edited volumes. In 2005, he attended a three-day Buddhism in Logic and Analytic Philosophy conference at Westminster College at Cambridge University, organized by the set theorist and philosopher Thomas Forster and sponsored by the Saint Luke's Institute. This gathering eventually resulted in a book, edited by Tom together with Mario D'Amato and Jay Garfield, *Pointing at the Moon: Buddhism, Logic, Analytic Philosophy* (2009). The volume is one of the first to seriously put Buddhist philosophers in conversation with experts in modern non-classical logics.

In 2006, Tom drew on the Fonds de Boer to sponsor a four-day conference at Crêt Bérard, a retreat center in the hills of Lausanne, where a wide range of scholars gathered to think about and discuss the problem of the Buddhist nominalist theory of *apoha*. This group consisted some of Tom's teachers, students, and longtime interlocutors: Arindam Chakrabarti, Amita Chatterjee, Georges Dreyfus, John Dunne, Jonardon Ganeri, Brendan Gillon, Bob Hale, Pascale Hugon, Shōryū Katsura, Parimal Patil, Prabal Kumar Sen, Ole Pind, and Mark Siderits. The fruit of this conference came some years later in the form of a book, edited by Tom along with Mark Siderits and Arindam Chakrabarti, *Apoha: Buddhist Nominalism and Human Cognition* (2011). The volume remains a seminal collection of articles on one of Indian Buddhist philosophy's most intriguing contributions to theories of language, epistemology, and metaphysics.

Retirement

In 2011, Tom made the decision to take an early retirement at age sixty. Things were changing in the Swiss universities in the wake of the Bologna reforms, particularly for his Department of Oriental Languages and Cultures, and not for the better in his estimation. Gene Smith, the legendary textual preservationist and founder of the Tibetan Buddhist Resource Center in New York, approached Tom with the idea to become the chief editor for 84000, a nonprofit project dedicated to the massive task of publishing online translations of the entire Tibetan Buddhist canon starting with the Kangyur, the collection of Tibetan translations of Indian works considered to be *buddhavacana* or "words of the Buddha," after which they would continue with the Tengyur, the collection of translations of treatises penned by Indian authors subsequent to the Buddha. The Kangyur represented new territory for Tom, who had spent most of his time until then focused on the philosophical texts found in the Tengyur, but he leaned into it, realizing how much there was to learn. Tom took on the role and remained in it through 2019, leading the 84000 project through a crucial formative period and simultaneously developing his own knowledge of the scriptural canon. As part of this project, Tom led a course at the University of Vienna in Buddhist translation studies in 2014, supervising a translation by the students of the *Sūtra on Wisdom at the Hour of Death* (Tōhoku catalog 122) that was published online in 2016. He later contributed his own translation of a longer sūtra, *Questions Regarding Death and Transmigration* (Tōhoku 308). This text, which may have been known to Nāgārjuna,[6] both refutes various ancient non-Buddhist Indian notions of the afterlife and presents an account of how there can be rebirth in the absence of any actual transmigration (*saṃkrama*) of a real entity. Tom's philosophical interests were evident.

Moving back to British Columbia with Shelley, Tom settled on Gabriola Island, where he has continued his relentless appetite for research, writing, and learning languages. He has published articles on an impressive range of topics. These include a substantive entry on Dharmakīrti for *The Stanford Encyclope-*

---

6. See the introduction, §i.9, at https://read.84000.co/translation/toh308.html.

dia of Philosophy (revised 2021) and numerous contributions to a host of felicitation and other edited volumes, encyclopedias, handbooks, and journals. A collection of some of his most important writings on Madhyamaka, *How Do Mādhyamikas Think? And Other Essays on the Buddhist Philosophy of the Middle*, appeared in 2016. More recently, he produced a hefty volume showcasing the range of his erudition, *Views from Tibet: Studies on Tibetan Buddhist Logic, the Philosophy of the Middle, and the Indigenous Grammatico-Linguistic Tradition* (2022). Traveling abroad frequently to visit his two daughters in Switzerland, as well as internationally for conferences, Tom remains active as a scholar and perpetual student, continuing his exchanges both remotely and in person with his mentors, friends, and past students around the world.

Given that I count such conversations with Tom among the most highly rewarding and pleasurable activities of my adult life, it was with great eagerness that, following the wonderful workshop in Madison organized by John Dunne, I proposed to Tom that he and I conduct a series of conversations online to help prepare me to write this introduction. He agreed, and over several months, we met regularly so I could hear not only some of the details related above about his life and career but also something of how his thoughts have developed over the years, especially in relation to the key topics of this volume: truth, knowledge, and an empty world. Physically located on opposite sides of the North American continent, with Tom on Gabriola Island and me in Atlanta, Georgia, we took a series of meandering conversational strolls through topics both philosophical and personal, at times delving into the dense thickets of technical analysis, at other times emerging to survey some broad vista of philosophical life. In the following section of this introduction, I attempt to convey some of these conversational highlights, after which I will reflect a bit on the articles in this volume, which are all very much a part of this larger conversation among friends.

Thought

My conversations with Tom

Back when I was a doctoral student conducting research in Lausanne, I remember struggling to wrap my head around where Tom stood on one particular issue. Tom had introduced me to the study of truth theories, and I was eager to get his take on how to apply these theories to Buddhist philosophy, especially in the contexts of Madhyamaka's two truths and the epistemological theories of the *pramāṇa* tradition. The cafeteria of the University of Lausanne, with the outline of the French Alps across the lake in view in the windows, was a common place for such conversations to unfold. I remember that Tom astonished me one day by floating the idea that perhaps Dharmakīrti did not actually *have* a theory of truth. (He developed this idea more fully in the introduction to his *Scripture, Logic, Language*.) I'm not sure why this surprised me so much. I suppose at the time I just assumed that if a philosopher speaks about truth, they must have a *theory* about what truth is. But Tom was far ahead of me in his recognition that such need not be the case. I learned from that comment, and I have continued learning about truth from Tom ever since.

Now, a quarter century later, I thought I had a pretty good understanding of Tom's philosophical positions and general outlook. But in the course of our recent conversations, Tom again managed to upend some of the perspectives I had come to take for granted. Our talks unfolded over four or five sessions. For the most part, my role was to ask questions, giving Tom ample time and space to respond while I sought clarifications here and there. When our conversations were complete, I wrote up an account based on my notes. Tom then gave substantial feedback, reworking some sections to better reflect the nuances of his thinking and to fill in some gaps that we had not covered orally. I returned to the document and made some more edits for clarity. What follows, therefore, is not so much a transcript of our discussions as it is a collage designed to give a sampling of Tom's wide-ranging knowledge and unique way of thinking. Not surprisingly, a great deal has been left out. Tom and I both thought it best to stick mainly to the topics that form the subject of this book. I hope, nevertheless, that what remains can give a tantalizing taste of the kinds of insights that inevitably arise when one is lucky enough to sit down for an extended conversation with Tom.

Where philosophy goes wrong

Truth was a key topic of our conversations, one to which we repeatedly returned. I opened our first meeting with an invitation for Tom to tell me more about what interests him about truth, what attracts him to a deflationist model, and how he thinks about Buddhist philosophy in this regard. Tom reflected that he thinks he was always some kind of budding quietist. He recalls being interested from a young age in the question of what philosophy is for, what one can legitimately do with it, and where and how it might go wrong—where, that is, philosophy might become nonsense. His study of analytic philosophers like Carnap, Ayer, and Wittgenstein had gotten him interested in problems of thinking: What are you doing when you argue? What are you doing when you hold a metaphysical thesis? These are questions that continue to preoccupy him today.

Tom told me he is a person who by temperament appreciates differences more than identities. He has been mostly disinterested in quests for such things as universally held ethical principles, immutable laws of thought, absolute religious unities, and so on, as these often seem to him frustratingly vague and contrived. Instead, Tom values deeper and more precise exploration of differences—those places where things do not line up so easily—especially those that open up new horizons and destabilize received ideas. No wonder, then, that as a young man Tom would be attracted to Wittgenstein's interest in difference, disunity, and the idea that we should "look and see" the complexity of things. It resonated with Tom to read that philosophies go wrong when they claim to find essences of grammar, knowledge, truth, goodness, or necessity. As he put it much later, seeking such unities seemed to him largely akin to engaging in a "science of Tuesdays."[7]

But while Tom was and is put off by the cheap unities and rash essentialism that sometimes appear under the aegis of comparative philosophy, he is in no way averse to the cosmopolitan and judicious use of the tools of all kinds of philosophy to better penetrate some of the many ways philosophers have of going astray. For example, Wittgenstein in the *Philosophical Investigations* had importantly seen philosophy as being under the sway of certain underlying pictures that hold philosophers (and others) captive. One such image is the idea that there must be something like what the *Investigations* terms "superlative facts" to guide and ground our thought. These supposed "facts of the matter" are abstractions similar to what John McDowell called the "ethereal Platonic rails" that philosophers imagine guiding and validating our language usage and claims of truth. Here, the captivating picture (from which it can be exceedingly difficult to escape) is that the non-arbitrariness of truth claims and of logical necessity requires a kind of metaphysical realism according to which there exists a definite totality of all real objects, some properties of which are intrinsically possessed. Additionally, this metaphysically realist picture entails that there can be a view *sub specie aeternitatis*, a God's-eye view or "sideways on" perspective concerning how that totality exists in itself. This is a much stronger type of realism than the harmless, even indispensable, variety conveyed by maxims like not everything we believe is in fact so, and other such common-sense ideas about reality and truth—a subtle and elusive

7. See Tom's article in this volume.

distinction that Tom reminded me had been deftly probed by Cora Diamond in her justly famous article "Realism and the Realistic Spirit."[8]

The point, Tom told me, was that metaphysicians typically *do* try to build systems on their visions of the totality of the real, systems that they inevitably think *can* capture how the totality actually is in itself, with probative arguments being the bridge between how things appear and how they really are. Such metaphysicians believe we can attain a vantage point from which we can see how our thinking as a whole matches up with how things are in themselves. Indian and Tibetan Buddhist writers of the realist epistemological school, for example, speak of the need for contact (*sparśa*) between the knower and the known, and of a substantive, natural relation (*svabhāvapratibandha*) that makes thought reach (*prāpaka*) the real. But is such a vantage point, and hence the view from it in which such entities and relations are ascertained, actually available? Tom maintains there is no such meaningful perspective, and thus the task, whether for a Buddhist philosopher who aims at thesislessness or for a Wittgensteinian who aims at undoing metaphysical seductions, is to tease out the pervasive misapprehensions that lurk in our seemingly innocent ways of knowing. Such is the spirit in which he embraces both the Tibetan idea of the importance and elusiveness of the "recognition of what is to be denied" (*dgag bya ngos 'dzin*) and much of Wittgenstein's therapeutic, quietist goals of gaining the ability to no longer advance or reject philosophical theses and, ultimately, of stopping to do philosophy as it has hitherto been practiced.

When one destabilizes philosophers' quests for a special perspective—an Archimedean point from which to evaluate things, or superlative facts by which to ground things—their elaborate theories about the probativeness and non-arbitrariness of reasoning are destabilized, too. I asked Tom what then remains of truth, the real, and reason. He responded that just as we have deflationary truth and innocuous realism without the guidance of superlative facts, so, too, good reasoning demands nothing further, nothing completely extra-human, no underlying rails that guarantee non-arbitrariness and necessity. So what does Tom make of the logical theory of the Buddhist realist thinker Dharmakīrti with its demands for a "natural relation" or a "logical nexus" (*avinābhāvaniyama*) that is present in intrinsically existing reality and that underlies the capacity for people to articulate definitive proofs and to correctly say when and why a good reason is good? Perhaps surprisingly, Tom holds that in the end there is not actually much meaningful to be gained by

---

8. The essay is the first chapter in Diamond's book *The Realistic Spirit: Wittgenstein, Philosophy, and the Mind* (The MIT Press, 1991).

such theories. It turns out that the specter of arbitrariness as imagined by realist thinkers like Dharmakīrti is not and never really has been a genuine problem at all.

The seduction of argument

I confess, it was a bit of a revelation to me to discover just how far Tom goes in his dismissal of definitive proofs. Although I knew about his interest in quietism and deflationism, and I understood his worries about metaphysical underpinnings for truth claims and logic, I had also always seen him as someone with a genuine passion for more formal kinds of argumentation and logic, as would seem evident from his many writings on these topics. So I asked him about that. He explained that his interest in logic and systems of argumentation is partly about knowing what's going on in the opposing camp and partly about exploring the myriad ways of constructing arguments. But that's not the whole story. Rather, he tells me, you have to know the seduction that underlies this kind of thinking. You need to see how various philosophical ideas and theories—universals, facts of the matter, nominalism, realism, antirealism, and so on—can get their grip on you. You need, that is, to do something similar to the Tibetan doxographical tenets study tradition (*grub mtha'*). There, you study a wide range of philosophical views not just so you can better defeat them but, even more profoundly, so that you can understand what is really at stake when you commit to a particular philosophical position. You need to understand the attraction of a given position, why an intelligent person might be seduced by it. And to understand the seduction, you need to be seduced yourself, at least to some degree.

Tom emphasized that philosophical argumentation is very different from formal logical reasoning for theorems that, once understood, will clinch disputed issues. Formal logic has no doubt yielded remarkable results in the foundations of mathematics or computer science, and there is no reason to doubt its value. The force and autonomy of philosophical arguments, on the other hand, tends to be oversold by traditional Buddhists and modern philosophers alike. Philosophical arguments involve a complex mix of human factors such as competing visions, mindsets, imagery, adoption of new language, and so on.[9] For Tom, the persistent idea that proper philosophical argumentation *stands or falls on its own*, that it has and must have independence or autonomy (*svātantrya*), is an oversimplification. Even worse, it is an illusion. Get-

9. On metaphysical argumentation as mastery of new language, see Tom's recent article "Is Metaphysics Madness? A Sixth-Century Polemic Unpacked" (2023b).

ting out from under the grip of that captivating picture is a lot harder than one might think but is necessary if our ideas of truth and reality are not to become pinned down under the metaphysical weight of intrinsic existence and necessity.

I asked Tom for an example of how philosophical arguments can lead us astray, and he offered the example of Nāgārjuna's fivefold analysis of wholes and parts.[10] Tom emphasized that he thinks it is a mistake to take this analysis, as many do, to stand on its own as a proof of mereological nihilism—that is, the position that *any* part-whole relation is contradictory such that there can never be any partite thing. Nāgārjuna's analysis begs far too many important questions to ever clinch the issue for those, like Naiyāyikas or modern mereologists, who hold a very different reasoned vision of things. But beyond that, Tom further thinks there are many Mādhyamikas, Tsongkhapa chief among them, who do not take Nāgārjuna's analysis to lead inexorably to mereological nihilism. Instead, such Mādhyamikas grant sanguinely that the mere notion of a composite like a cart is *not* contradictory, and they certainly do not think that the mere existence of parts, wholes, and composition should be refuted by a series of *reductio ad absurdum* arguments. Tom is thus critical of attempts to use the Madhyamaka "neither one nor many" arguments (*ekānekaviyogahetu*) to prove the unreality of composites.

Rather, he feels the most crucial thing here, as elsewhere in Madhyamaka, is to use the analysis to recognize the compelling attraction of metaphysical realism to see more clearly how philosophical problematics, like part-whole problems, are in its grip. The broad lines of the argumentation can then be directed to show various possible difficulties concerning intrinsically existing objects—meaning those objects imagined via an inflated conception of truth/reality (*satyābhimāna*). When one understands a little better what one was pursuing all along, then *that* might indeed turn out to be impossible. But ordinary tables, chairs, and carts, along with their components, are themselves neither inconsistent nor unreal.[11] There is little point in devising ever more elaborate technical arguments to show that they are.

10. See, e.g., Nāgārjuna's *Mūlamadhyamakakārikā* 10.14–15 and 16.2.

11. A cart is not, for example, like Russell's impossible barber who shaves all and only people in his village who do not shave themselves. See Tom's recent article "Reversing Śāntarakṣita's Argument: Or Do Mādhyamikas Derive Part-Whole Contradictions in All Things?" (2021b) for different Indo-Tibetan positions on the concepts/things themselves being inconsistent.

Quietism

Summarizing the import of all this, Tom pointed out that a frequent way Madhyamaka has been interpreted—both traditionally and in modern times—is that it gets beyond realism to an all-encompassing antirealism. He then explained that he sees *that* kind of Madhyamaka as proceeding crucially on the assumption that one *can have* a clear perspective on what it would be for a given thing to exist fully really in the first place, such that one then *can show* that nothing satisfies the criteria for such fully real existence. That's one way to go. It leads Buddhists to negative ontologies and global error theories: that the world is itself unreal and only superficially thought to exist; that everything an unenlightened being might think or seem to know must actually be erroneous; or, if one goes the idealist route like Dharmapāla, that belief in an external world is an error and only the mental is real. These are various historically attested antirealist readings of Madhyamaka texts. But another way to go is to say that Madhyamaka helps us to recognize that we actually *do not have* the type of clear view that would be needed to make any definitive positive or negative determinations concerning what intrinsic reality would be or must be like. We have only the deep-seated illusion of such a clear perspective, so that all that *seems* to be established in light of such a perspective or vision, whether positive or negative, is actually quite unintelligible. This way leads to quietism.

For Tom, as a quietist Buddhist himself,[12] antirealism is just as problematic as metaphysical realism, no more, no less. On Tom's quietist reading, Mādhyamika thinkers may be understood to be suggesting that an inflated conception of truth/reality (*satyābhimāna*) or, what is equivalent, the subtle action of grasping at truth/reality (*satyagraha, bden 'dzin*) confusedly requires that things must be existent or nonexistent in the strong sense demanded by metaphysical realism. That is, *satyābhimāna* is itself a kind of Buddhist sideways-on, or *sub specie aeternitatis*, view. When *satyābhimāna* is not taken as an *actual* perspective but more like an insidious confusion or a kind of masquerade of a rational vision, then a thoroughgoing negative ontology can be no better founded than its realist counterpart. The recurring point in Madhyamaka texts is that any genuine intelligibility of a negation depends on the genuine intelligibility of its positive counterpart—in effect, if some would-be attribution is nonsensical, then the denial of that nonsensical attribute remains nonsense, too, and in the same way.[13] Neither the realist nor the anti-

---

12. Tom lays out his understanding of himself as a Buddhist in his recent article "Why I Am a Buddhist" (2022a).

13. Cf. Nāgārjuna *Madhyamakakārikā* 13.7: *yady aśūnyaṃ bhavet kiṃ cit syāc chūnyam iti kiṃ*

realist has a clear idea of what they want, despite thinking that they do, and they poison their thinking accordingly. Quietism in the face of unintelligibility is not a philosophical position; it is a type of vigilance.

The dismal slough

We will see in this book that a lot of the contributors engage with a term Tom coined: the "dismal slough." Tom uses this term critically to characterize what he calls the "typical" Prāsaṅgika Madhyamaka global error theory, and he rejects that interpretation of Madhyamaka in favor of one that is "atypical." As we saw above, there is a frequent approach in the study of Madhyamaka, in both traditional and modern exegesis, according to which ideas about the world are intelligible but actually false. This is the typical Prāsaṅgika error theory. Tom reads their formula *blo 'khrul ba'i ngor yod pa* ("things exist [only] in the view of mistaken minds") starkly: they hold that the only "truths" (in scare quotes) are what some or perhaps all people mistakenly agree to be true. Tom holds that while this is a quite natural reading of Candrakīrti's texts, it nevertheless leads to various unpalatable—shall we say, "dismal"—consequences. This is especially so given Candrakīrti's recurring principle that this mistaken truth, or more exactly customary truth (*saṃvṛtisatya*), is no other than precisely what is established by the world (*lokaprasiddha*).

As Tom and I discussed this problem, we became aware that John Newman, in a recent article examining some of Tom's earlier publications, has ably shown that Candrakīrti does *not* just uncritically reproduce as worldly truth all that the lowest common denominator of the populace holds. Instead Candrakīrti admits and advocates "a hierarchy of knowledge within knowledge that is established by ordinary people in the world."[14] Tom readily conceded this point. There is room for experts in Candrakīrti's world and for the revision of beliefs. The worst-case scenario that Tom had feared in earlier publications, in which worldly truth was always and only decided by unnuanced populism, is not something Candrakīrti himself advocated. But even in those earlier publications, Tom recognized that Candrakīrti thought he could promote needed revisions by pitting some beliefs and attitudes against others

cana / na kiṃ cid asty aśūnyaṃ ca kutaḥ śūnyaṃ bhaviṣyati // "If there were something that was non-empty [i.e., intrinsically existent], there would be something empty. Now there is nothing whatsoever that is non-empty. How could anything ever be empty?"

14. John Newman, "Candrakīrti on *Lokaprasiddhi:* A Bad Hand, or an Ace in the Hole?" *Journal of Indian Philosophy* 52 (2024): 73–99. See especially p. 95.

and pointing out misapplications of well-known epistemic standards.[15] Tom's point, however, was that one way or another, Candrakīrti and his followers would not get very far, and not nearly far enough, if that was all they could do.

Tom clarified to me that one problem with positing a hierarchy within *lokaprasiddha* is that doing so still does not allow us to handle the more difficult cases within or across societies and their elites. Popular opinions vary significantly in diverse places and times, as do those of elites, as do epistemic procedures and standards even within a single society. Whether we adopt a global error theory and equate truth with the opinions of ordinary people, or we limit truth to expert opinions, holding it to be that which conforms to the epistemic procedures and standards of experts within a society, we will still have to contend with a large number of conflicting truth claims. Many such claims, including those concerning odd cosmologies and various traditional beliefs about physics, psychology, or medicine, will remain unacceptable for a rational person. Some will be unintelligent and retrograde. And some—for example, those emerging from elaborate justifications of slavery or female genital mutilation—will be utterly repugnant. But countering all these irrational and repugnant claims is neither easy nor obvious. For example, Tom explained to me, when it comes to metaphysics, Candrakīrti *thought* he could counter belief in God and enduring entities via what generally was *lokaprasiddha* in his surroundings. But he underestimated how intelligent theists in very different cultures would make their case using their own experts and their own, divergent standards. Arriving at what Mādhyamikas call the "correct customary truth" is not just the straightforward enterprise of plumbing the beliefs and standards one happens to observe.

I pushed back on Tom to question whether it might not be the case that when truth claims appear unintelligent or rationally unacceptable, this could be due to the divergent epistemic procedures and standards we have inherited and with which we have become accustomed to assessing the world. Might it not be that our rejection of seemingly irrational claims is due primarily to the picture of reality that currently captivates us and the notions of truth and reality in whose grip we are currently held? Might we not, in other words, be in the thrall of our own truthiness? Tom felt I had missed the mark. The problem here is that if we suggest that truth and acceptability are simply relative to actual contexts and epistemic standards, then we enervate these concepts by taking off their important corrective edge. We rob truth of its normativity. For

---

15. For Tom's position, see his book *How do Mādhyamikas Think?* (2016, 54). See also his recent contribution on Āryadeva in the *The Routledge Handbook of Indian Buddhist Philosophy* (2023a) for examples of Candrakīrti using rational arguments to reform customary truth.

what do we mean by "truth" if it is not that which people *should* aim for and if it does not involve correction and censure when people get it wrong? Substituting descriptions of what some or all people *de facto* happen to think, or have thought, or would think following their particular societies' lights significantly weakens or misses that robust normativity. The typical Prāsaṅgika Madhyamaka position is, in Tom's eyes, a descent into this kind of philosophical swamp—the dismal slough—where, for metaphysical reasons, philosophers of various stripes downgrade truth to a kind of ignorant consensus, or they construe ". . . is true" relativistically as a disguised two-place relation ("x is true for y"), or they minimize normativity so that saying something is true is little more than an endorsement or a profession of solidarity. In effect, they confusedly lessen the force of vital, practical norms because of their attachment to antirealism.[16]

On the other hand, if you are a quietist rather than an antirealist, you can better avoid that kind of relativistic slough. Norms concerning truth are not held hostage to anything about the totality of the real or to a God's-eye perspective in Buddhist garb. For Tom, we can continue to seek *resolutions* to conflicts rather than just changes in adversaries' opinions. Often we will find some deeper form of agreement, or perhaps it will become clear that the conflict in question was merely verbal, two parties using language differently. But there will also be many occasions when we should not shy away from showing that certain propositions that a given person, group, or society (including perhaps our own) claim to be true by their lights have never been true at all. The issue that Tom explores in the final essay in this book is whether the Mādhyamika accepts that there are genuine sources of knowledge, or *pramāṇas*, justifying truth claims. The typical Prāsaṅgika position is that there cannot be such robust, normative *pramāṇas*, because there is no grounding of truth claims in intrinsically existing reality. The atypical position, which Tom finds in Tsongkhapa's Madhyamaka philosophy and develops further using modern resources, like deflationary truth theories, is that there *are* genuinely normative *pramāṇas*, even though they have no such metaphysical grounding. What keeps Tom up at night are the numerous bogus moves in current thinking that look uncomfortably similar to typical Prāsaṅgika in denigrating truth in favor of solidarity with opinions, standards, and interests of groups. That slip-

---

16. Richard Rorty, for example, defended relativism and a view of truth as endorsement and solidarity. See his "True to Life: Why Truth Matters," *Philosophy and Phenomenological Research* 1 (2005): 232: "I use 'true' as a term of endorsement, as a name for the property preserved in valid inference, and in various other ways, but not as the name of a relation to a mysterious entity called 'the world,' nor as the name of a deeply normative property."

page had consequences in both India and Tibet, and it does so now, too, both intellectually and in matters of practical life. Tampering with the normativity in the concept of truth—or worse, abandoning truth more or less outright—whether in religion, politics, or elsewhere, is devastating.

For Tom, engaging in comparative philosophy allows us to stretch concepts in ways that are helpful in opening or destabilizing our subjectivities or worlds. We start to see some of how we have been seduced by our prior ideas, and we can begin to experiment with other forms of seduction on the way to becoming a bit more free from confusion. When it comes to Buddhist philosophy, Tom tells me he is not much of a reductionist. He's not really attracted to the impersonal perspective that the Abhidharma promotes, nor to a Madhyamaka-style mereological nihilism, according to which *any* part/whole relationship would be fraught with contradictions. He is more interested in the idea that Tsongkhapa promotes according to which whole entities like pots, cars, and people do exist and are established by *pramāṇa*s. What is needed is for us to come to understand what precisely it is that should be denied (*dgag bya ngos 'dzin*), or in other words, where we go wrong when an indispensable, innocuous conception of truth and reality turns into the inflated conception. This discrimination is not to be obtained through ever more subtle and involved argumentation operating in a vacuum. The important insight from Tsongkhapa is that argumentation between Mādhyamikas and realists does not stand on its own but depends upon and fleshes out competing, direction-giving visions, be they clear or confused. Tom sees that as a kind of methodological lesson. The crucial role of direction-giving visions is not just limited to this one specific debate, in Tom's opinion, but can be extended widely to major philosophical arguments, East or West. Instead of more of the usual salvos of sophisticated arguments, we may well do better to seek a deeper and less technical recognition of what is at stake in the competing visions—that is to say, what is actually being envisaged and what is being denied.

When our conversations were finished, although I still felt Tom was a bit of a mystery, I now could see better how his rejection of relativism and his commitment to truth sit really quite well with his deflationism about truth and his quietism about metaphysics. Although the universe may be entityless, with no lonely objects—no objects that would be what they are even if nothing else existed—this does not mean that every statement turns out to be false. Norms of truth can remain robust. And for those difficult cases in philosophy, ethics, or religious thought where truth is, and may well remain, highly contested? There's only one thing you can do—keep talking and be interested in what the other person is saying. Tom by inclination rejects quests for certainties and attainments. He values movement and likes to cite his compatriot Leonard Cohen: "There is a crack, a crack in everything. / That's how the light gets in." The great danger is that you stop the conversation. Don't stop an honest dialogue between truth seekers.

With that injunction from Tom to carry on assiduously, I felt even more joyful than I already had at the prospect of bringing forth this book of conversations by some of Tom's many friends. I think it will not be lost on readers that quite a few of the contributors in the volume felt emboldened to take on some of Tom's strongest arguments about the nature of truth and knowledge in an empty world. I take this as an excellent sign indicating that Tom has cultivated a body of work and a circle of friends that are not afraid to seek out the cracks in everything. Let us hope that our work together succeeds in uncovering ever more flaws to let the light get in. Perhaps we will one day find our way out of the need to do philosophy anymore. But until then, we continue our impassioned conversations.

With that, I now turn to a summary of the contributions. In keeping with the friendly nature of this volume, I will in what follows refer to the contributors after first mention by their given names, just as we did during our workshop in Madison.

Interlocutors

Four conversations about truth

Our book begins with a contribution by Jay Garfield, who very appropriately starts by imagining a conversation with Tom at a bar. The topic of their bar talk concerns the hairs that appear to be floating in Jay's field of vision and the status of those hairs. Tom says they are not real, but when Jay asks his ophthalmologist, she takes him at his word that the hairs are there and asks only about their quantity. Who is right? Jay hopes to provide a philosophical answer that would satisfy a Mādhyamika, and he deploys the rubric of the tetralemma to argue that the Mādhyamika's two truths, represented in his example by the floating hairs understood as nonexistent by Tom and as existent by the ophthalmologist, are both, in fact, *truths*, even though neither one alone reveals the whole story. The rest of Jay's paper is taken up with pushing back on Tom's reading of Candrakīrti as a global error theorist, the position that Tom has referred to as the "dismal slough" of a thoroughgoing relativism. Jay shares with Tom an admiration for Tsongkhapa's philosophical acumen and skepticism about the arguments advanced by one of Tsongkhapa's fiercest critics, Taktsang. Nevertheless, Tom and Jay differ insofar as Jay holds Tsongkhapa's reading of Candrakīrti to be more exegesis than critique, and Jay sees Candrakīrti not as a global error theorist but as someone who embraces a nonfoundational epistemology capable of rendering correct judgments about what is and is not true. Like Tom, Jay wants to preserve the possibility for our ordinary standards of truth and falsity to apply to ordinary, conventional knowledge. Their main disagreement, it would seem, is the degree to which Candrakīrti might be thought to agree with the two of *them*.

After Jay, we get another contribution from one of Tom's longtime interlocutors, Mark Siderits. Mark endorses Tom's understanding of Madhyamaka as entailing a deflationist account of truth and a soteriology rooted in metaphysical quietism. He also thinks it's important to leave space for Mādhyamikas to employ analysis to distinguish true from false and to avoid becoming mired in the dismal slough of popular opinion. Conceding that Candrakīrti himself has signaled that analysis should be avoided—given that there is nothing of substance for such analysis to find—Mark nevertheless charts a way forward via a very specific understanding of what analysis does in a Buddhist context. Mark maintains that Buddhist analysis is reductive insofar as it seeks to analytically decompose composite entities with the aim of finding the elements that explain the facts about them. To reject all such analysis (as Candrakīrti seems to recommend) is to head straight into the dismal slough. So what is a Mādhyamika to do if they are not to abandon their foundational claim that nothing has intrinsic nature, that analysis does not terminate in ultimately real entities? Mark suggests that they adopt a radical semantic contextualism, according to which the meaning of a sentence is partly determined by the context of utterance—where the context will include facts about the aims of the interlocutors. Only when we ignore this fact about linguistic meaning do we end up thinking that analysis will inevitably lead to a demand for things with intrinsic natures to serve as the grounds of everything else. After laying out how all this might work, he concludes that analysis can be safely engaged in by Mādhyamikas.

Dan Arnold continues the conversation by challenging the idea that Candrakīrti would accept the beliefs of cowherds to be conventionally normative, a portrayal he attributes to Tom and sees as a caricature of Candrakīrti's more sophisticated take. Indeed, Dan rebuts what he calls Tom's dim view of Madhyamaka's options for avoiding the dismal slough when Candrakīrti is at the helm. But Dan also dismisses Tom's turn toward Tsongkhapa, whose reading of Candrakīrti Dan sees as a bit off the mark. That is, for Dan, Candrakīrti accepts neither a populist account of the conventional nor the technical tools of the Buddhist epistemologist (the move Dan understands Tsongkhapa to make) even when these tools are confined to the conventional realm. Instead,

Dan holds that Candrakīrti clearly endorses conventional norms for truth even as he wholly rejects any epistemic grounding for them. As evidence for this, Dan joins Mark in pointing out that Candrakīrti regularly uses the normative discourses of both Abhidharma and the Sanskrit grammatical tradition to gradually deepen what he holds to be genuine conventional truths, notably such Buddhist doctrines as impermanence and no-self. But the grounding for this conventional discourse is not to be found in Dignāga's *pramāṇa*s, perception and inference. Rather, Dan understands Candrakīrti to advance something like a pragmatic-transcendental argument, according to which norms for truth are *always already* at play due to the intersubjective and dependently arisen nature of language and reasoning.

Thus far, the conversations have tended toward a somewhat firm yet genteel rehabilitation of Candrakīrti in the face of Tom's vigorous criticisms. Now, however, with the entrance of Sonam Thakchoe, the gloves come off. Here, for the first time, we encounter a sustained critique of Tom's distinction between typical and atypical Prāsaṅgika-Mādhyamikas. Previously, Jay had already mildly rebuked the distinction; now Sonam makes it the main object of negation. On Sonam's reading of Tom, what makes Tsongkhapa an atypical Prāsaṅgika is his deflationism about truth, while Candrakīrti is seen as more typical due to his adherence to a global error theory or panfictionalism. Sonam responds by highlighting Candrakīrti's tripartite theory of conventional truth, arguing that Candrakīrti is not in fact a panfictionalist but has a strong commitment to distinguishing truth from error even at the conventional level. At the same time, Sonam maintains that, like Tsongkhapa, Candrakīrti is also a deflationist about truth. Relying on a passage from the *Śūnyatāsaptativṛtti* that he calls a first smoking gun, Sonam shows that while Candrakīrti did accept *pramāṇa*s, he emphatically denied their metaphysical foundation. With his second smoking gun, from the same text, he argues that while Candrakīrti sees conventional truth as deflationary for the wise, it is actually *inflationary* for ordinary beings who still engage in reification. While Sonam offers a strong alternative reading of Candrakīrti to that of Tom, a lingering question does remain: does the fact of different truths for different folks bring us back again to the dismal slough, at least so long as there are no exalted beings around? That is, if conventional truths are keyed to different kinds of knowers, with their diverse sense and cognitive faculties, how does one draw the line between truth and error in the conventional realm? On Sonam's reading, Candrakīrti has an answer: not all ordinary beings are naïve inflationists. There are wise ordinary beings who understand the deflationary nature of conventional truth and are thus able to distinguish truth from error without relying on the epistemic authority of exalted beings.

Eight conversations about knowledge

After these four initial conversations about truth, talk now turns to the topic of how truth can be known. Here, numerous thorny problems of epistemology occur, and many voices clamor to be heard. We begin with the voice of José Cabezón, another longtime friend and interlocutor, who asks an intriguing question: Can emptiness be understood philosophically? This query gets at the heart of what Buddhist philosophy even *is*, insofar as it asks whether comprehending Buddhist ideas of emptiness, no-self, and so on can even take place when their study is purely theoretical, or whether such comprehension requires contemplative or other soteriological practice. José draws on Tsongkhapa's innovative idea that the correct identification of the so-called object of negation (*dgag bya*) or—in Tom's words—"what is to be denied" is crucial for a correct initial inferential understanding of emptiness to arise. In an inference establishing emptiness, the object of negation is true or inherent existence, and not to understand this means that one will also misunderstand emptiness because one will negate either too much or too little. The trouble, though, is that we as sentient beings are all saddled with a beginningless innate ignorance (*ma rig pa lhan skyes*) that causes us erroneously to see things *as if they did* possess true or inherent existence. And the most significant manifestation of innate ignorance is the sense of "I" that seems to accompany us throughout our lives. Taking inspiration from the Fifth Dalai Lama, who builds on Tsongkhapa's insights, José paints a picture according to which the identification of this sense of "I," which is the core object of negation for a full comprehension of emptiness, cannot take place without the aid of quiescence (*śamatha*) and other meditative states. Even though understanding emptiness does require the correct application of inference, that application is not possible if one is unable to identify the object of negation, and that identification requires, according to Tsongkhapa and his followers, some—perhaps even a considerable—degree of contemplative practice.

A similar theme is now advanced by Jonardon Ganeri, who draws on the work of several contemporary philosophers to think through Buddhist conundrums concerning self, no-self, and the processes by which craving and clinging can be overcome. Jonardon introduces the work of Akeem Bilgrami, who argues that the intentional states of beliefs and desires are transparent, or known to those who possess them, at least when agency is in play. This transparency extends even to dispositions, and much of Jonardon's paper is devoted to an exploration of how Buddhists understand the possibility of undoing the harmful disposition of clinging. He notes that an assertion that one has a particular experience (of suffering or desire, for example) is, for Buddhists, not a claim to *ownership* of that experience; instead it is simply a claim to an experience within a stream. There is thus a kind of agency without an agent, and this allows for the transparency that Bilgrami also asserts. Recognizing one's desires and especially one's clinging as deeply problematic, a Buddhist may generate and even cultivate disgust toward them as a step toward an experience of dispassion in which the boundaries of the person disappear and there is no further space of identification. So it is an emotional response that leads to transformation as much as any critical or rational analysis. Jonardon's contribution may be seen in part as a response to Tom's work on *akrasia*, or weakness of the will.

The conversation now moves from the psychological to the logical with an analysis by Shōryū Katsura of Bhāviveka's proof formulation (*prayoga*) in light of Dignāga's theories of inference. This contribution pays homage to Tom's philologically precise studies of the logical structures of the Indian Buddhist epistemologists. The main goal here is to see how Bhāviveka is using Dignāga's proof formulation to inferentially establish emptiness and other key Madhyamaka doctrines. By a careful analysis of several different proof formulations, Shōryū concludes not only that Bhāviveka knew Dignāga's system and that he generally followed it, but also that in proposing a *negative* Madhyamaka proposition (e.g., color-form is not substantially real), Bhāviveka innovates by introducing the qualifier "ultimately" (*paramārthataḥ*). Shōryū speculates about the influence of Yogācāra thought on Bhāviveka, who perhaps wanted to ensure that there would be some continuity between the conventional and ultimate truths even while continuing to use the tools of the epistemological tradition. Using inferential reasoning, one establishes the "true conventional" (*tathyāsaṃvṛti*), which then serves as a "staircase" (*sopāna*) on which one may ascend to eventually directly realize the ultimate (*tattva*).

Chizuko Yoshimizu picks up on this same theme in her article on the Tibetan Madhyamaka commentator Gyamarwa Jangchup Drak, who, like Bhāviveka, also defends the notion of a stairway to the ultimate truth. Chizuko guides us through Gyamarwa's reading of Jñānagarbha's text, the *Satyadvayavibhaṅga*, showing how Gyamarwa's reading echoes the philosophical positions of Śāntarakṣita and Kamalaśīla. Here again, we find an argument for the utility of the Buddhist epistemological tools for honing one's correct conceptual understanding of emptiness prior to the production of a direct yogic perception of that ultimate reality. As Chizuko points out, however, for Jñānagarbha and Śāntarakṣita, the absence that is emptiness must be conventional insofar as it is merely a negation of what does not ultimately exist, since negations still belong to the realm of discursive proliferation (*prapañca*), and it is only through the calming of such proliferation that one may realize the ultimate truth. In the end, a Mādhyamika realizes the ultimate truth through "nonseeing" (*adarśana*). Arising in this connection are the statuses of reasoning and its object. Are they conventional or are they ultimate? Jñānagarbha's text is ambiguous, and the commentary, attributed by some to Śāntarakṣita, seeks to resolve the problem with the introduction of the idea of a figurative ultimate. Gyamarwa, however, insists that the object of reasoning is the nonfigurative ultimate, because insight endowed with reasoning reveals the nonfigurative ultimate truth by eliminating all proliferations. Although Gyamarwa worked in the time prior to the introduction of the Svātantrika-Prāsaṅgika distinction by Patsab Nyima Drak, it is clear that the question of the role and capacity of reasoning in relation to the ultimate was already a topic of contention in Tibet. Gyamarwa's position was later strengthened by his disciple Chapa Chökyi Sengé.

Continuing the metaphor of a staircase or ladder illustrating the gradual refinement of knowledge from the conventional to the ultimate, we come now to John Dunne's contribution on the topic of levels in Madhyamaka. Here, John sets out to demonstrate how diverse Indian Mādhyamikas from Nāgārjuna to Sahajavajra have embraced this theme, which he places in the middle of a continuum from Candrakīrti's seemingly "pessimistic" assessment of the validity of conventional knowledge to Tsongkhapa's more "optimistic" one. For those espousing this form of gradualism, although language and reason remain tainted by ignorance, they nevertheless can be carefully used to lead one up and out of ignorance toward enlightened, nonconceptual wisdom. To ponder more deeply this seeming paradox, John attends to some key verses in Śāntideva's *Bodhicaryāvatāra*, which he reads alongside Prajñākaramati's commentary. In doing so, John discovers that progression along the ladder of reasoning may not be quite so easy for the Mādhyamika to defend as initially imagined. Indeed, when asked for a foundation for knowledge, Śāntideva resorts to the idea of what is commonly accepted—the baseline for what Tom refers to as "dismal" relativism—and rejects that knowledge must be grounded by a *pramāṇa*. Prajñākaramati, in contrast, then tries to rescue the *pramāṇa*s, casting them as merely conventional, at least up until one has refined one's perception to the point of it consisting in mere reflexive awareness. John concludes that the ladder of reasoning proposed by many Mādhyamikas may best be understood as yielding contemplative insight rather than rational certainty.

No matter the ultimate status of reasoning, however, there can be no doubt that many influential Mādhyamikas have been inspired by their reading of the Buddhist logician-epistemologists. In the next contribution, Birgit Kellner expands the conversation with an innovative look at one of the most widespread Madhyamaka arguments, the NONMA, or the neither-one-nor-many argument, which was developed using standards of reasoning originating with Dharmakīrti. Examining some varieties of this basic structure, which Tom had earlier studied extensively in the works of both Śāntarakṣita and Tsongkhapa, Birgit ends up distinguishing NONMAs and NINDAs—that is, neither-identical-nor-different arguments. Much depends on the interpretation of the key terms *eka* and *aneka*, which can indicate both "one and many" and "identical and different." Drawing on Tom's earlier work, Birgit correlates this distinction to a difference between monadic (one/non-one) and dyadic (identical/not-identical) predicates. She investigates prominent historical and modern interpreters who have read Dharmakīrti as advancing a NONMA, assessing whether and how they may figure into a system of "levels of analysis," as presented elsewhere by John Dunne.[17] Her conclusion is that when Dharmakīrti analyzes the status of the multiplicity presented in a single moment of awareness, he does not use a NONMA but rather puts forward a NINDA. Here the reality of consciousness is not questioned; rather, it is only the reality of its contents that is refuted. She further suggests that it might be conspicuous that Dharmakīrti in both cases formulates seeming NONMA-type arguments as conclusions to preceding and more extensive argumentations, indicating that it might be worthwhile to look at such arguments also as hermeneutic and rhetorical devices and not just in terms of their logical function and philosophical import.

Kenneth Liberman now picks up the thread of the conversation about the structures of Buddhist philosophical argumentation with a contribution on negative dialectics in Tibetan Madhyamaka debate practices. He reminds us that contemplative practices can go beyond meditation to include also analysis, argumentation, logic, and debate. Connecting the Buddhist critique of reification to the modern critique of alienation, Ken seeks to explore the negative dialectics of Madhyamaka not only at the cognitive and rational levels, but at the sociological and anthropological levels as well. Negative dialectics, whether among European or Tibetan thinkers, works against the fetishization of certainties and often leads to perspectives in which philosophizing itself must eventually cease. Ken considers the role of the formalization of thought in logic and otherwise, how it is a necessity for communication and collaboration, and how it also need not be fetishized as fully objective to be useful. He then goes through some typical moves in Tibetan philosophy: projection, reductio ad absurdum, public debate, cultivation or habituation, and practices

17. See John Dunne, *Foundations of Dharmakīrti's Philosophy* (Boston: Wisdom Publications 2004), 53–64.

of nonabiding. At the end of the day, Ken argues, Madhyamaka negative dialectics are designed to pull the rug out from under us, both in our profound and our mundane thinking. As such, they are a key tool in our arsenal for combatting our rampant self-delusion.

As the final voice in this long section of conversations about knowledge, we have the contribution of Jan Westerhoff, who explores symmetric existential dependence relations in Madhyamaka. Given that a key object of refutation in Madhyamaka, *svabhāva*, is defined in part by its lack of participation in any relation of dependence, an exploration of such relations is one way to deepen our understanding of the Madhyamaka doctrine of emptiness. Jan identifies various kinds of dependence relations analyzed by Nāgārjuna and others. First, there are conceptual dependence relations in which two concepts, for example, short and long, mutually require one another to make sense. Jan stipulates that this kind of dependence relationship is also existential insofar as the two concepts require one another to exist at all. There are also causal and mereological symmetric dependence relations. Here, the symmetry is more difficult to see, since one might imagine that a cause could exist even if it never gave rise to its effect or parts might exist even if they never came together to form a whole. Jan proposes that the symmetry is discovered through parametrization. That is, the form of dependence differs for each of the two relata. The son's very *existence* depends on his father, while the father's *description* as a father depends on his son. The symmetry, however, best comes out when even these causal and mereological relations are seen to be, at the end, conceptual. Yet this conceptual dependence is also existential insofar as Madhyamaka entails a kind of structuralism in which individuals are products of networks of relations. In such networks, when any entity is shown to lack ultimate existence, any other entity that depends on it necessarily will lack such existence also.

Three conversations about the world

Having now conversed about the topics of truth and knowledge, it is time to consider the world in which these are found. The first person to enter the conversation here is myself, Sara McClintock, with a contribution that asks about whose world the Mādhyamika invokes when using phrases like "established for the world" (*lokaprasiddha*). My interest is in drawing attention to the socially constructed nature of the world, particularly as this impinges not only on customary truth but also on moral reasoning. The paper begins with a close reading of Tom's work surrounding the questions of whether and how a Mādhyamika can reform customary truth or justify ethical actions. After surveying some of Tom's major contributions, I point to a potential limitation in the way Tom has approached Madhyamaka theories of truth. That is, while the Sanskrit term *satya* can be applied to propositions and beliefs, the traditional truth-bearers of analytic philosophy, it also can describe existentially real states of affairs or things. As Tom deliberately chooses to exclude this second aspect of truth in Madhyamaka thought, the remainder of my paper asks what is lost in making this move, with my conclusion being that doing so tends to exclude attention to the social practices that allow the world to consider a given set of propositions and beliefs to be candidates for truth in the first place. That is, there is a historical *a priori* that we need to consider when examining what is established for the world, and this makes the matter of reforming or even identifying customary truths inescapably a matter of deep ethical concern. We have to ask whose world is in play when exploring what is and what is not true, as well as what is and is not ethically right. The paper concludes with some reflections on the disadvantages of using the method of rational reconstruction to read Buddhist texts. I argue that such a method risks imposing too much of our own world on Buddhist authors and can profitably be relinquished.

Continuing with the theme of the world, Pascale Hugon now enters the conversation with an in-depth analysis of a precursory early Tibetan debate on what it means for a Mādhyamika to "follow the world," meaning to simply go along with what is established for the world rather than subscribing to a philosophical tenet system. The participants in this debate are late eleventh-to-twelfth century scholars whose views are presented in Gyamarwa Jangchup Drak's *Dbu ma de kho na nyid rnam par dpyod pa*. Pascale focuses on a section of the text devoted to the distinction between correct and mistaken conventionals, where she identifies the main participants in the debate, apart from the author himself, as Gyamarwa's teachers Khyung Rinchen Drak and Gangpa Sheu Lodrö Jangchup. In the passage, Gangpa and Gyamarwa are seen to criticize Khyung for holding that a Mādhyamika should simply follow the world in determining conventional truth and error. They also cry foul when Khyung is seen to vouch for valid cognition while refusing to adopt the framework of a specific tenet system, having refuted each of them in turn. Although Khyung counters with a proposal to define distinct contexts (*skabs*)—a Pramāṇa context and a Madhyamaka one—where different rules would apply, the critics have none of it. No matter how the world is defined, whether in terms of cowherds versus philosophers or in terms of common appearances, the world by itself is not enough to determine truth from falsity. Pascale concludes her paper with some reflections on the sources for Khyung's position, gesturing toward the distinction between "following tenets" and "following the world" as found in the *Bden gnyis spyi bshad*, an eleventh-century work that reports the teachings of Atiśa on the two truths. The question of whether Khyung may have been directly or indirectly influenced by Candrakīrti's ideas thus remains open.

Our conversation now enters a distinctly tantric domain with the contribution by David Higgins on the topic of the unity of the two truths. While the title of David's paper suggests it might better be placed in the section containing conversations about truth, the topic of the inseparability of the two truths as explored by Nyingma and Kagyü thinkers more strictly touches on the totality of all that is. David's contribution is thus better classified as a conversation about the world, even if the concept "world" is not explicitly theorized. Drawing on works from Dzogchen and Mahāmudrā figures like the eleventh-century Rongzompa, the fourteenth-century Longchenpa, the sixteenth-century Mikyö Dorjé, and others, David shows how Tibetan tantric theorists enlist Nāgārjuna's equation of emptiness and dependent arising in support of their position that all distinctions between appearance and reality are fundamentally flawed. Emphasizing that the unity of the two truths should in no way be taken as an ontological ground, David guides us to see how these unified truth theorists understand the difference between the two truths to be a matter not of kind of but of degree. Seeing the two truths as a useful phenomenological distinction and not a distinction about reality itself thus helps to heal the rift that may be inadvertently introduced by Mādhyamikas with their emphasis on the misleading nature of ordinary appearances. As David puts it, this "two worlds" theory collapses under the unity doctrine in which there is only one world that is increasingly clearly encountered when conceptual overlays and distortions are removed.

Tom's response and the science of Tuesdays

Appropriately, after listening to all the speakers at the workshop and now reading their contributions in this volume, Tom has shared with us a response. In the first part, he defends his vision of two kinds of Prāsaṅgika Madhyamaka, a typical and an atypical type. He takes some time to argue on philological grounds for reading Candrakīrti as an error theorist and for his position that Tsongkhapa is offering an innovative new take on the Madhyamaka thought he inherited from India even as he and his followers present themselves as providing nothing more than a straightforward exegesis. No doubt one of Tom's more provocative positions is that Tsongkhapa not infrequently made Candrakīrti into a better philosopher than he actually was.

To work through the themes of typical versus atypical Prāsaṅgika, Tom turns to the debate that the Sakya thinker Taktsang Lotsāwa Sherab Rinchen had with Tsongkhapa on the topic of the *pramāṇa*s. The key takeaway for Tom is that Tsongkhapa had the promising insight that our understanding has right and wrong parts (*cha*), which appear mixed and inseparable to ordinary people. Those with discernment, however, can learn to sift out the right from the wrong by zeroing in on what is to be denied (*dgag bya*)—namely, metaphysical realism, in its gross and subtle forms. Tom then takes a step outside of Buddhist philosophy to reflect on the notion of warranted assertibility as a criterion for truth, seeing this as what a sophisticated typical Prāsaṅgika would end up espousing. Tom sees Tsongkhapa, however, as holding out for a stronger version of truth, one more strongly normative along the lines of Huw Price's idea of truth as providing friction and involving censure when people get truth wrong. All this results in Tom falling in with Tsongkhapa's and Price's commitment to a strong norm of truth and truth-telling and rejecting both typical Prāsaṅgika and warranted assertibility. But what grounds truth for Tsongkhapa? Tom argues it was not some substantive truth-making property. Even though Tsongkhapa defers to the *pramāṇa*s, he does so without Dharmakīrti's metaphysical grounding in particulars and correspondence. Nor, for Tom, need Tsongkhapa seek any substantive theory. The quest for such theories is arguably a quest for a misguided type of understanding, a "science of Tuesdays." Just because there is no single, unifying explanation for why certain events have occurred on a Tuesday and not another day, it does not mean that there are no explanations at all for why the respective events occurred when they did. Likewise, truths can be explained individually. And this is the case in the absence of any substantive theory of truth.

Tom J. F. Tillemans's List of Publications and Doctoral Theses Directed

Monographs and Essay Collections

1989   With Derek D. Herforth. *Agents and Actions in Classical Tibetan: The Indigenous Grammarians on Bdag and Gźan and Bya Byed Las Gsum.* Wiener Studien zur Tibetologie und Buddhismuskunde 21. Vienna: Arbeitskreis für Tibetische und Buddhistische Studien Universität Wien.

1990   *Materials for the Study of Āryadeva, Dharmapāla and Candrakīrti: The Catuḥśataka of Āryadeva, Chapters XII and XIII, with the Commentaries of Dharmapāla and Candrakīrti: Introduction, Translation, Sanskrit, Tibetan and Chinese Texts, Notes.* 2 vols. Wiener Studien zur Tibetologie und Buddhismuskunde 24. Vienna: Arbeitskreis für Tibetische und Buddhistische Studien Universität Wien. Reprinted in one volume by Motilal Banarsidass Publishers, Delhi, 2008.

1993   *Persons of Authority: The sTon pa tshad ma'i skyes bur sgrub pa'i gtam of A lag sha Ngag dbang bstan dar: A Tibetan Work on the Central Religious Questions in Buddhist Epistemology.* Tibetan and Indo-Tibetan Studies, University of Hamburg. Stuttgart: Franz Steiner Verlag.

1999   *Scripture, Logic, Language: Essays on Dharmakīrti and His Tibetan Successors.* Studies in Indian and Tibetan Buddhism. Boston: Wisdom Publications.

2000   *Dharmakīrti's Pramāṇavārttika: An Annotated Translation of the Fourth Chapter (parārthānumāna). Volume 1 (k. 1–148).* Vienna: Verlag der Österreichischen Akademie der Wissenschaften.

2016   *How Do Mādhyamikas Think? And Other Essays on the Buddhist Philosophy of the Middle.* Studies in Indian and Tibetan Buddhism. Somerville, MA: Wisdom Publications.

2022   *Views from Tibet: Studies on Tibetan Buddhist Logic, the Philosophy of the Middle, and the Indigenous Grammatico-Linguistic Tradition.* Beiträge zur Kultur- und Geistesgeschichte Asiens 106. Vienna: Austrian Academy of Sciences Press.

Edited Volumes and Special Journal Issues

1992   With Johannes Bronkhorst and Katsumi Mimaki. *Études bouddhiques offertes à Jacques May. Asiatische Studien / Études Asiatiques* 46.1.

1995   Editor of *Asiatische Studien / Études Asiatiques* 49.4. [Proceedings of the Panel on Indo-Tibetan Buddhism at the International Association of Buddhist Studies Congress, Mexico City, 1994.] Preface by Tom J. F. Tillemans.

2008   With Georges Dreyfus. *Argumentation* 22 [Volume on Buddhist Argumentation]. Amsterdam: Springer Verlag.

2009   With Jay L. Garfield and Mario D'Amato. *Pointing at the Moon: Buddhism, Logic, Analytic Philosophy.* New York: Oxford University Press.

2011   With Mark Siderits and Arindam Chakrabarti. *Apoha: Buddhist Nominalism and Human Cognition.* New York: Columbia University Press.

2011   As part of the Cowherds. *Moonshadows: Conventional Truth in Buddhist Philosophy.* Oxford: Oxford University Press.

Articles

1982   "The 'Neither One nor Many' Argument for *śūnyatā* and Its Tibetan Interpretations: Background Information and Source Materials." *Études de Lettres: Revue de la Faculté des Lettres de l'Université de Lausanne* 1982.3: 103–28.

1983   "The 'Neither One Nor Many' Argument for *śūnyatā* and Its Tibetan Interpretations." *Contributions on Tibetan and Buddhist Religion and Philosophy: Proceedings of the Csoma de Kőrös Symposium held at Velm-Vienna, Austria, 13–19 September 1981,* vol. 2, edited by Ernst Steinkellner and Helmut Tauscher, 305–20. Vienna: Arbeitskreis für Tibetsiche und Buddhistische Studien, Universität Wien.

1984a "On a Recent Work on Tibetan Buddhist Epistemology." *Asiatische Studien / Études Asiatiques* 38.1: 59–66.

1984b "Sur le *parārthānumāna* en logique bouddhique." *Asiatische Studien / Études Asiatiques* 38.2: 73–99.

1984c "Two Tibetan Texts on the 'Neither One nor Many' Argument for *śūnyatā*." *Journal of Indian Philosophy* 12.4: 357–88.

1986a "Dharmakīrti, Āryadeva and Dharmapāla on Scriptural Authority." *Tetsugaku* 38 (felicitation volume for Profs. A. Uno and K. Ogura): 31–47.

1986b "Identity and Referential Opacity in Tibetan Buddhist *apoha* Theory." In *Buddhist Logic and Epistemology: Studies in the Buddhist Analysis of Inference and Language*, edited by Bimal K. Matilal and Robert D. Evans, 207–27. Dordrecht: D. Reidel.

1986c "*Pramāṇavārttika* IV (1)." *Wiener Zeitschrift für die Kunde Südasiens* 30: 143–62.

1986d With Masahiro Inami. "Another Look at the Framework of the *Pramāṇasiddhi* Chapter of *Pramāṇavārttika*." *Wiener Zeitschrift für die Kunde Südasiens* 30: 123–42.

1987 "*Pramāṇavārttika* IV (2)." *Wiener Zeitschrift für die Kunde Südasiens* 31: 141–61.

1988a "On *bdag* and *gzhan* and Related Notions of Tibetan Grammar." In *Tibetan Studies: Proceedings of the 4th Seminar of the International Association for Tibetan Studies*, edited by Helga Uebach and Jampa L. Panglung, 491–502. Munich: Kommission für Zentralasiatische Studien, Bayerische Akademie der Wissenschaften.

1988b "Some Reflections on R. S. Y. Chi's *Buddhist Formal Logic*." *Journal of the International Association of Buddhist Studies* 11.1: 155–71.

1989a "Indian and Tibetan Mādhyamikas on *Mānasapratyakṣa*." *The Tibet Journal* 14.1: 70–85.

1989b "Formal and Semantic Aspects of Tibetan Buddhist Debate Logic." *Journal of Indian Philosophy* 17: 265–97.

1990 "On *sapakṣa*." *Journal of Indian Philosophy* 18: 53–79.

1991a "Dharmakīrti on Some Sophisms." In *Studies in the Buddhist Epistemological Tradition: Proceedings of the Second International Dharmakīrti Conference Vienna, June 11–16, 1989*, edited by Ernst Steinkellner, 403–18. Österreichische Akademie der Wissenschaften, Philosophisch-Historische Klasse, Beiträge zur

Kultur- und Geistesgeschichte Asiens 8. Vienna: Verlag der Österreichischen Akademie der Wissenschaften.

1991b   "gSer tog Blo bzang tshul khrims rgya mtsho on Tibetan Verbs."
In *Tibetan History and Language: Studies Dedicated to Uray Géza
on His Seventieth Birthday*, edited by Ernst Steinkellner, 487–96.
Wiener Studien zur Tibetologie und Buddhismuskunde 26. Vienna:
Arbeitskreis für Tibetische und Buddhistische Studien.

1991c   "More on *parārthānumāna*, Theses and Syllogisms." *Asiatische Studien / Études Asiatiques* 45.1: 133–48.

1991d   "A Note on *bdag don phal ba* in Tibetan Grammar." *Asiatische Studien / Études Asiatiques* 45.2: 311–23.

1992a   "*Pramāṇavārttika* IV (3)." *Asiatische Studien / Études Asiatiques* 46.1
(*Études bouddhiques offertes à Jacques May*): 437–67.

1992b   "La logique bouddhique est-elle une logique non-classique ou dévi-
ante? Remarques sur le tétralemme (*catuṣkoṭi*)." *Les Cahiers de Phi-
losophie* 14: 183–98.

1992c   "Tsong kha pa et al. on the Bhāvaviveka-Candrakīrti Debate." In
*Tibetan Studies: Proceedings of the 5th Seminar of the International
Association for Tibetan Studies, Narita 1989*, edited by Shoren Ihara
and Yamaguchi Zuiho, 315–26. Narita: Naritasan Shinshoji.

1992d   "Amour et religion: Vingt-cinq poèmes tirés d'une nouvelle collection attribuée au sixième Dalai Lama." *Études de Lettres: Revue de la
Faculté des Lettres de l'Université de Lausanne* 1992.4: 125–42.

1993   "*Pramāṇavārttika* IV (4)." *Wiener Zeitschrift für die Kunde Südasiens*
37: 135–64.

1994a   "On *Agents and Actions in Classical Tibetan*: A Reply to Roy A.
Miller." *Indo-Iranian Journal* 37: 121–38.

1994b   "Pre-Dharmakīrti Commentators on Dignāga's Definition of a Thesis (*pakṣalakṣaṇa*)." In *The Buddhist Forum Vol. III: Papers in Honour and Appreciation of Professor David Seyfort Ruegg's Contribution
to Indological, Buddhist and Tibetan Studies*, edited by Tadeusz
Skorupski and Ulrich Pagel, 295–305. London: School of Oriental
and African Studies, University of London.

1995a   "*Pramāṇavārttika* IV (5)." *Wiener Zeitschrift für die Kunde Südasiens*
39: 103–50.

1995b   "Dharmakīrti and Tibetans on *adṛśyānupalabdhihetu*." *Journal of
Indian Philosophy* 23.2: 129–49.

1995c   "On the So-Called Difficult Point of the *apoha* Theory." *Asiatische Studien / Études Asiatiques* 49.4: 853–90.

1995d   With Tōru Tomabechi. "Le *dBu ma'i byuṅ tshul* de Śākya mchog ldan." *Asiatische Studien / Études Asiatiques* 49.4: 891–918.

1995e   "Remarks on Philology." *Journal of the International Association of Buddhist Studies* 18.2: 269–77.

1996   "What Would It Be Like to Be Selfless? Hīnayānist Versions, Mahāyānist Versions and Derek Parfit." *Asiatische Studien / Études Asiatiques* 50.4: 835–52.

1997a   "On a Recent Translation of the *Saṃdhinirmocanasūtra*." *Journal of the International Association of Buddhist Studies* 20.1: 153–64.

1997b   "Dharmakīrti on *prasiddha* and *yogyatā*." In *Aspects of Buddhism: Proceedings of the International Seminar on Buddhist Studies*, edited by Agata Bareja-Starzyńska and Marek Mejor, 177–94. Warsaw: Oriental Institute, Warsaw University.

1997c   "Où va la philologie bouddhique?" *Études de Lettres: Revue de la Faculté des Lettres de l'Université de Lausanne* 1997.4: 3–17. [Inaugural lecture given at Lausanne, October 27, 1993.]

1998a   With Donald S. Lopez Jr. "What Can One Reasonably Say about Nonexistence? A Tibetan Work on the Problem of *āśrayāsiddha*." *Journal of Indian Philosophy* 26.2: 99–129.

1998b   "A Note on *Pramāṇavārttika*, *Pramāṇasamuccaya* and *Nyāyamukha*: What Is the *svadharmin* in Buddhist Logic?" *Journal of the International Association of Buddhist Studies* 21.1: 111–24.

1998c   "Issues in Tibetan Philosophy." In *Routledge Encyclopedia of Philosophy* 9, edited by Edward Craig, 402–9. London: Routledge.

1998d   "Tsong kha pa blo bzang grags pa." In *Routledge Encyclopedia of Philosophy* 9, edited by Edward Craig, 487–90. London: Routledge.

1999   "How Much of a Proof Is Scripturally Based Inference (*āgamāśritānumāna*)?" In *Dharmakīrti's Thought and Its Impact on Indian and Tibetan Philosophy*, edited by Shōryū Katsura, 395–404. Österreichische Akademie der Wissenschaften, Philosophisch-Historische Klasse Denkschriften 281. Vienna: Verlag der Österreichischen Akademie der Wissenschaften.

2001   "Trying to Be Fair to Mādhyamika Buddhism." The Numata Yehan Lecture in Buddhism, Winter 2001. Calgary: University of Calgary.

2003a   "Metaphysics for Mādhyamikas." In *The Svātantrika-Prāsaṅgika*

Distinction: What Difference Does a Difference Make? edited by Georges B. J. Dreyfus and Sara L. McClintock, 93–123. Studies in Indian and Tibetan Buddhism. Boston: Wisdom Publications.

2003b   "On the Assimilation of Indic Grammatical Literature into Indigenous Tibetan Scholarship." *Asiatische Studien / Études Asiatiques* 57.1: 213–35.

2004a   "Inductiveness, Deductiveness and Examples in Buddhist Logic." In *The Role of the Example (dṛṣṭānta) in Classical Indian Logic*, edited by Shōryū Katsura and Ernst Steinkellner, 251–75. Wiener Studien zur Tibetologie und Buddhismuskunde 59. Vienna: Arbeitskreis für Tibetische und Buddhistische Studien Universität Wien.

2004b   "What Are Mādhyamikas Refuting? Śāntarakṣita, Kamalaśīla et alii on Superimpositions (samāropa)." In *Three Mountains and Five Rivers: Prof. Musashi Tachikawa's Felicitation Volume*, edited by Shoun Hino and Toshihiro Wada, 225–37. Delhi: Motilal Banarsidass.

2005   "The Slow Death of the *trairūpya* in Buddhist Logic: A Propos of Sa skya Paṇḍita." *Hōrin: Vergleichende Studien zur Japanischen Kultur* 11: 83–93.

2007a   "Trying to Be Fair to Mādhyamika Buddhism." In *Expanding and Merging Horizons: Contributions to South Asian and Cross-Cultural Studies in Commemoration of Wilhelm Halbfass*, edited by Karin Preisendanz, 507–24. Vienna: Verlag der Österreichischen Akademie der Wissenschaften.

2007b   "On *bdag* and *gzhan* and the Supposed Active-Passive Neutrality of Tibetan Verbs." In *Pramāṇakīrtiḥ: Papers Dedicated to Ernst Steinkellner on the Occasion of His 70th Birthday*, edited by Birgit Kellner, Helmut Krasser, Horst Lasic, Michael Torsten Much, and Helmut Tauscher, 887–902. Vienna: Arbeitskreis für Tibetische und Buddhistische Studien.

2007c   "Transitivity, Intransitivity and *tha dad pa* Verbs in Traditional Tibetan Grammar." *Pacific World Journal* [Special Issue: Essays Celebrating the Twentieth Anniversary of the Numata Chair in Buddhist Studies at the University of Calgary, edited by Leslie Kawamura and Sarah Haynes] 3.9: 49–62.

2008a   "Introduction: Buddhist Argumentation." *Argumentation: An International Journal on Reasoning* 22.1: 1–14.

2008b   "Reason, Irrationality and Akrasia (Weakness of the Will) in

Buddhism: Reflections upon Śāntideva's Arguments with Himself." *Argumentation* 22.1: 149–63.

2009a   "How Do Mādhyamikas Think? Remarks on Jay Garfield, Graham Priest and Paraconsistent Logic." In *Pointing at the Moon: Buddhism, Logic, Analytic Philosophy*, edited by Jay L. Garfield, Tom J. F. Tillemans, and Mario D'Amato, 83–99. New York: Oxford University Press.

2009b   "Wie denken Mādhyamikas? Bemerkungen zu Jay Garfield, Graham Priest und parakonsistenter Logik." German translation of 2009a by Birgit Kellner and Sascha Mundstein. In *Denkt Asien Anders? Reflexionen zu Buddhismus und Konfuzianismus in Indien, Tibet, China und Japan*, edited by Birgit Kellner and Susanne Weigelin-Schwiedrzik, 77–98. Göttingen: Vienna University Press, Verlag V&R unipress.

2011a   With Guy M. Newland. "An Introduction to Conventional Truth." In *Moonshadows: Conventional Truth in Buddhist Philosophy*, by the Cowherds, 3–22. Oxford: Oxford University Press.

2011b   With Graham Priest and Mark Siderits. "The (Two) Truths about Truth." In *Moonshadows: Conventional Truth in Buddhist Philosophy*, by the Cowherds, 131–50. Oxford: Oxford University Press.

2011c   "How Far Can a Mādhyamika Buddhist Reform Conventional Truth? Dismal Relativism, Fictionalism, Easy-Easy Truth, and the Alternatives." In *Moonshadows: Conventional Truth in Buddhist Philosophy*, by the Cowherds, 151–65. Oxford: Oxford University Press.

2011d   "Buddhist Epistemology (*pramāṇavāda*)." In *The Oxford Handbook of World Philosophy*, edited by Jay L. Garfield and William Edelglass, 233–44. Oxford: Oxford University Press.

2011e   "How to Talk about Ineffable Things: Dignāga and Dharmakīrti on Apoha." In *Apoha: Buddhist Nominalism and Human Cognition*, edited by Mark Siderits, Tom J. F. Tillemans, Arindam Chakrabarti, 50–63. New York: Columbia University Press.

2011f   "Dignāga, Bhāviveka and Dharmakīrti on Apoha." In *Religion and Logic in Buddhist Philosophical Analysis: Proceedings of the Fourth International Dharmakīrti Conference. Vienna August 23–27, 2005*, edited by Helmut Krasser, Horst Lasic, Eli Franco, and Birgit Kellner, 449–58. Vienna: Verlag der Österreichischen Akademie der Wissenschaften.

2011g   "Dharmakīrti." *Stanford Encyclopedia of Philosophy* [Fall 2011 edition; substantive revisions 2016, 2021]. http://plato.stanford.edu/archives/fall2011/entries/dharmakiirti/.

2011h   "Madhyamaka Buddhist Ethics." *Journal of the International Association of Buddhist Studies* 33.1–2: 353–72.

2011i   "Buddhist Epistemology and Philosophy of Language." In *Philosophische Anthropologie: Themen und Positionen*, edited by Ada Neschke and Hans Rainer Sepp, 149–58. Sprache und Wissenserwerb, Language and Acquisition of Knowledge 5. Nordhausen, Germany: Verlag Traugott Bautz GmbH.

2012   "Zkusme být spravedliví k mádhjamikovému buddhismu." Czech translation of 2001 by Zuzana Vihanová. In *Nágárdžuna Filosofie střední cesty*, edited by Jiří Holba, 80–109. Filosofické interpretace, Svazek 3. Prague: Oikoymenh.

2013a   "Yogic Perception, Meditation and Enlightenment: The Epistemological Issues in a Key Debate." In *A Companion to Buddhist Philosophy*, edited by Steven M. Emmanuel, 290–306. Blackwell Companions to Philosophy Series. Oxford: Wiley-Blackwell.

2013b   "'How Do Mādhyamikas Think?' Revisited." *Philosophy East and West* 63.3: 417–25.

2013c   With Andreas Doctor. "Meditation Revisited." In *Wading into the Stream of Wisdom: Essays in Honor of Leslie S. Kawamura*, edited by Sarah F. Haynes and Michelle J. Sorensen, 351–73. Contemporary Issues in Buddhist Studies. Berkeley: Institute of Buddhist Studies and BDK America, Inc.

2015   "Minds, Dharmakīrti and Madhyamaka." In *The Moon Points Back*, edited by Koji Tanaka, Yasuo Deguchi, Jay L. Garfield, and Graham Priest, 45–66. New York: Oxford University Press.

2016   "Count Nouns, Mass Nouns, and Translatability: The Case of Tibetan Buddhist Logical Literature." In *Comparative Philosophy Without Borders*, edited by Arindam Chakrabarti and Ralph Weber, 35–53. London: Bloomsbury Academic Publishing.

2017a   "Pramāṇavārttika IV, Parārthānumāna (summary)." In *Encyclopedia of Indian Philosophies, Volume 21: Buddhist Philosophy from 600 to 750 A.D.*, edited by Karl H. Potter, 375–402. Delhi: Motilal Banarsidass.

2017b   "Philosophical Quietism in Nāgārjuna and Early Madhyamaka."

In *The Oxford Handbook of Indian Philosophy*, edited by Jonardon Ganeri, 110–32. New York: Oxford University Press.

2018   "Metaphysics and Metametaphysics with Buddhism: The Lay of the Land." In *Buddhist Philosophy. A Comparative Approach*, edited by Steven M. Emmanuel, 87–107. Hoboken, NJ: Wiley-Blackwell.

2019a   "Mādhyamikas Playing Bad Hands: The Case of Customary Truth." *Journal of Indian Philosophy* 47.4: 635–44.

2019b   "The Sūtra *Questions Regarding Death and Transmigration*." [An Annotated Translation.] 84000: Translating the Words of the Buddha. https://read.84000.co/translation/toh308.html.

2019c   "Deflating the Two Images and the Two Truths: Bons Baisers du Tibet." In *Wilfrid Sellars and Buddhist Philosophy: Freedom from Foundations*, edited by Jay L. Garfield, 80–96. London: Routledge.

2021a   "Āryadeva." In *The Encyclopedia of Philosophy of Religion*, edited by Stewart Goetz and Charles Taliaferro. New York: John Wiley.

2021b   "Reversing Śāntarakṣita's Argument: Or Do Mādhyamikas Derive Part-Whole Contradictions in All Things?" In *A Road Less Traveled: Felicitation Volume in Honor of John Taber*, edited by Vincent Eltschinger, Birgit Kellner, Ethan Mills, and Isabelle Ratié, 443–70. Wiener Studien zur Tibetologie und Buddhismuskunde 100. Vienna: Arbeitskreis für Tibetische und Buddhistische Studien Universität Wien.

2021c   "Dharmakīrti." *The Stanford Encyclopedia of Philosophy* [Spring 2021 edition]. https://plato.stanford.edu/archives/spr2021/entries /dharmakiirti/.

2022a   "Why I Am a Buddhist." In *The Rowman & Littlefield Handbook of Philosophy and Religion*, edited by Mark A. Lamport, 349–57. Lanham, MD: Rowman & Littlefield.

2022b   "Methodology: Meditations of a Philosophical Buddhologist." In *Guruparamparā: Studies on Buddhism, India, Tibet and More in Honour of Professor Marek Mejor*, edited by Katarzyna Marciniak, Stanisław Jan Kania, Małgorzata Wielińska-Soltwedel, and Agata Bareja-Starzyńska, 437–50. Warsaw: University of Warsaw Press.

2023a   "Āryadeva: Quietism and Buddhist Ethics." In *The Routledge Handbook of Indian Buddhist Philosophy*, edited by William

Edelglass, Pierre-Julien Harter, and Sara McClintock, 236–51. London and New York: Routledge.

2023b   "Is Metaphysics Madness? A Sixth-Century Polemic Unpacked." In *To the Heart of Truth: Felicitation Volume for Eli Franco on the Occasion of His Seventieth Birthday*, edited by Hiroko Matsuoka, Shinya Moriyama, and Tyler Neill, 277–309. Wiener Studien zur Tibetologie und Buddhismuskunde 104.1. Vienna: Arbeitskreis für Tibetische und Buddhistische Studien Universität Wien.

2025.   "Pramāṇa in Tibet: Debate Traditions (Bsdus grwa)." In *Brill's Encyclopedia of Buddhism Online*, edited by Jonathan A. Silk, Richard Bowring, and Vincent Eltschinger. Brill. https://doi .org/10.1163/2467-9666_enbo_COM_3128.

Short Reviews, Prefaces, Forewords

1990   Review of *The Miscellaneous Series of Tibetan Texts in the Bihar Research Society, Patna* by David P. Jackson. *Asiatische Studien / Études Asiatiques* 44.1: 147–48.

1991   Review of *Tibet: civilisation et société: Colloque organisé par la Fondation Singer-Polignac à Paris, les 27, 28, 29 Avril 1987* edited by Fernand Meyer. *Asiatische Studien / Études Asiatiques* 45.2: 341–43.

1992   "Note liminaire." *Asiatische Studien / Études Asiatiques* 46.1: 9–12.

1993   Review of *The Yogācāra School of Buddhism: A Bibliography* by John Powers. *Asiatische Studien / Études Asiatiques* 47.3: 518–19.

1993   Review of *Tibetan Buddhism: Reason and Revelation* edited by Steven D. Goodman and Ronald M. Davidson. *Asiatische Studien / Études Asiatiques* 47.3: 519–22.

1996   Preface to *The Pañcakramaṭippaṇī of Muniśrībhadra, Introduction and Romanized Sanskrit Text* edited by Zhongxin Jiang and Tōru Tomabechi, ix–x. Schweizerische Asiengesellschaft Monograph 23. Bern: Peter Lang.

2001   Review of *Wisdom, Compassion, and the Search for Understanding: The Buddhist Studies Legacy of Gadjin M. Nagao* edited by Jonathan A. Silk. *The Eastern Buddhist* 33.1: 181–85.

2010   Foreword to *The Buddhist Philosophy of the Middle: Essays on Indian and Tibetan Madhyamaka* by David Seyfort Ruegg, ix–

xi. *Studies in Indian and Tibetan Buddhism.* Boston: Wisdom Publications.

2011   Preface to *Dharmakīrti's Pramāṇaviniścaya, Chapter 3: Critically Edited* edited by Pascale Hugon and Toru Tomabechi, v–vi. Beijing-Vienna: China Tibetology Publishing House, Austrian Academy of Sciences Press.

2024   "Avant-propos." In Jacques May, *Les vers didactiques fondamentaux sur la doctrine de la voie du milieu (Mūla-Madhyamaka-kārikā) de Nāgārjuna,* edited par Jérôme Ducor and Henry W. Isler, vii–viii. Geneva: Librairie Droz.

Doctoral Theses Directed

1999   John D. Dunne. "Foundations of Dharmakīrti's Epistemology: A Study of the Central Issues in His Ontology, Logic and Epistemology with Particular Attention to the *Svopajñāvṛtti*." PhD dissertation, Harvard University.

2002   Sara L. McClintock. "Omniscience and the Rhetoric of Reason in the *Tattvasaṃgraha* and the *Tattvasaṃgrahapañjikā*." PhD dissertation, Harvard University.

2003   Vincent Eltschinger. "Dharmakīrti sur les Écritures et l'Incréation des Vedas: Autour du *Pramāṇavārttika* k. 213–275 et *Svavṛtti*." PhD dissertation, University of Lausanne.

2003   Ryusei Keira. "Madhyamaka and Epistemology: A Study of Kamalaśīla's Method for Proving the Voidness of All Dharmas: Introduction, Annotated Translations and Tibetan Texts of Selected Sections of the Second Chapter of the *Madhyamakāloka*." PhD dissertation, University of Lausanne.

2005   Pascale Hugon. "Trésors du raisonnement: Sa skya Paṇḍita et ses prédécesseurs tibétains sur les modes de fonctionnement de la pensée et le fondement de l'inférence. Édition et traduction annotée du quatrième chapitre du *Tshad ma rigs pa'i gter* et d'une portion de la section initiale du dixième chapitre." PhD dissertation, University of Lausanne.

2006   Tōru Tomabechi. "Étude du *Pañcakrama*: Introduction et traduction annotée." PhD dissertation, University of Lausanne.

2012   Thomas Doctor. "Ornament of Reason: An Annotated English translation of rMa bya Byang chub brtson 'grus's Commentary to the *Mūlamadhyamakakārikā*." PhD dissertation, University of Lausanne.

2012   David P. Higgins. "The Philosophical Foundations of Classical rDzogs chen in Tibet: Investigating the Distinction between Dualistic Mind (*sems*) and Primordial Knowing (*ye shes*)." PhD dissertation, University of Lausanne.

Part 1
Truth

Epistemology for Mādhyamikas:
How Many Hairs Are Falling?

Jay L. Garfield

Suppose that I am developing posterior uveitis but I don't know it. At a meeting of the International Association of Buddhist Studies, I ask Tom Tillemans how many hairs he sees floating through the air in the bar. I ask Tom because he has done more than anyone else in the last hundred years or so to advance our understanding of Madhyamaka metaphysics and epistemology, and so I value his expertise on all matters concerning knowledge and truth. He first thinks that I am making a bad Candrakīrti joke, but after ascertaining that I am serious, he assures me that there are no hairs in this bar. Note: he asserts *correctly* that I see no floating hairs. Tom also suggests that I see my ophthalmologist when I get home.

I do so. The first thing she asks me is, "How many hairs do you see?" I tell her, "About a half dozen." She says, "No big deal then. But if more hairs appear, we need to do something about it." She asks me to make an appointment in six months. When I come back, she asks how many hairs I see, and this time I say, "Over a dozen." She prescribes medication. Note: She presumes that when I said on the first visit that I saw a half dozen hairs and when I said on the second visit that I saw over a dozen, I spoke correctly, and the difference between the number of hairs justified her prescription. She never said, "There are no actual hairs."

So who is right? Tom or my ophthalmologist? There are only four possibilities: (1) Tom, (2) Dr. Rioux, (3) both, or (4) neither. Exploring this tetralemma will give us insight into what epistemology should look like to a Mādhyamika. My account is inspired by how I understand Candrakīrti and Tsongkhapa, but my purpose here is not philological or historical but philosophical. That is, I am *principally* concerned in this essay not with what Candrakīrti actually wrote (although I will defend a reading of his position) but with the philosophical morals that Tsongkhapa and Khedrup Jé drew from Candrakīrti's thought and with the larger question of rational reconstruction: How *should* a Mādhyamika think about *pramāṇa*? This essay emerges from the Cowherds' (2011) project in which Tom participated, from Tom's essay on Wilfrid Sellars and *pramāṇa* (2019), and from the Yakherds' (2021) project, which followed up on the Cowherds' work. There is a strain of thought in the Tibetan Sakya and Kagyü traditions, sometimes taken up by contemporary scholars, that suggests that Buddhist epistemology is the exclusive province of the Pramāṇavāda tradition of Dignāga and Dharmakīrti and that it has no place in Madhyamaka thought. Geluk scholars strongly disagree, and I think that they are right to do so. So while I will disagree with Tom's own reading of Candrakīrti, I will defend and extend his thoughts about how Prāsaṅgika epistemology *should* look.

I will begin by asking just who is right about the hairs and then explore what the grounds of such correctness might be. In that context, I will first ask how Candrakīrti sees things and then ask how a Mādhyamika *should* see things. I will conclude with a full-throated defense of epistemology as central to the Madhyamaka project and of the claim that that same epistemology demands and vindicates the reality of the conventional world.

Who's Right? Epistemology and the Catuṣkoṭi

Let's get back to my vision. Is Tom right when he denies that there are any hairs, or is Dr. Rioux right when she notes that there are now even more of them than there were before and we need to do something about them?

Well, it could be Tom. There is a reason why floaters are considered illusory and why Candrakīrti takes the nonperception of floaters as an analogy for the perception of emptiness. First, when we see that there are no floaters, we don't see something positive; we see a mere absence, like the absence of intrinsic nature. But second, and more importantly for our purposes, when we perceive emptiness, we see the actual, final nature of things; the world is actually devoid of falling hairs. So it sounds like Tom gets things right. There are no hairs; not a half dozen; not a dozen; none at all.

But it could also be Dr. Rioux. She knows her stuff, and in particular, she knows that the difference between seeing a few floaters and seeing a lot of them is clinically significant. So when she notes that I saw only a few on my first visit and lots on my second, I don't go to Tom Tillemans for a second opinion or remonstrate with her that there is nothing to worry about because there really are no hairs falling. Instead, I fill the prescription, knowing that since there is a difference between seeing a few and seeing many hairs, the fact that I now see many hairs in my visual field is significant, regardless of what might be the case in the visual fields of others.

Now, some might respond at this point that to take Dr. Rioux's part at this stage is to be guilty of an epistemologically significant equivocation on what it means *to see*, as well as an ontologically significant equivocation on what it means *to exist*. That is, to the extent that we read *to see* in a factive sense, Tom is right and Dr. Rioux is wrong; to the extent that we read it as synonymous with *appears to*, she is right and he is wrong. *Mutatis mutandis* for *to exist*. To the extent that *exists* means to be part of a mind-independent reality, Tom seems right; to the extent that it means *is an object of knowledge of consciousness*, Dr. Rioux has it right. So, this line of thought goes, it is only by an illicit relativization to a particular cognitive perspective that we make the second *koṭi* plausible.

As Mādhyamikas, though, I think that we should resist this attempt to deprecate Dr. Rioux's perspective. This point is best made with reference to the denizens of different realms of saṃsāra. Let's just stick with animals for present purposes. Consider the difference between how a bee sees a calla lily and the way I see it. The bee sees in the infrared and ultraviolet ranges, and I do not. I see a uniformly white flower. The bee sees a big, bright bullseye in the center of the flower and a set of dark stripes leading to it. So who is right, and who is wrong? Is the lily white or variegated? The moment one asks this question, one sees how stupid it is. The lily in my world is white; the lily in the bee's world is variegated; and even to ask what the lily *really* looks like, independent of our visual faculties, is simply nonsense. There is a way a lily looks to me, a way it looks to a bee, and so on, but no way that it simply looks, *tout court*.

To think that there is a way that it simply *looks* is to take it to exist intrinsically, to deny its emptiness and the relativity of its nature to the minds that apprehend it. Now, let us apply the analogy to the case of the floaters in my visual field. Dr. Rioux's point is this: we must relativize our claim regarding the color of lilies to the visual faculties of their perceivers. So, just as there is no fact of the matter about what lilies look like independent of those faculties, we must relativize our claim regarding the existence of falling hairs to the faculties of different perceivers. And this means that there is no fact of the matter about how many hairs there are independent of those faculties. In my visual field, she concludes, there are hairs, and it is her job as a clinician to interrogate how many there are.

This observation takes us straight to the third *koṭi*. Since we have good reason to say that Tom is right and good reason to say that Dr. Rioux is right, it follows that we have good reason to say that *both* of them are right. Tom is right that there are no hairs in the world inhabited by those not suffering from posterior uveitis, and Dr. Rioux is right that there are hairs in my visual field. Each of them can appeal to appropriate *pramāṇa*s to vindicate their respective views, and in each case, we can explain the difference between truth and falsity. This seems like a nice irenic compromise.

Serious Mādhyamikas, however, know that the third *koṭi* is unstable and takes us straight to the fourth: neither of them is correct. Tom says that there are no hairs, but my ophthalmologist confirms that there are a determinate number of them; she says that there are hairs, but Tom confirms that in reality there are none. They are both wrong. And we can do all of this in the negative mood as well: We should not say what Tom says, as it denies what is important clinical information. We should not say what Dr. Rioux says, as it implicates the existence of hairs outside of the context of my own pathology; we should not say that both of these are correct, since we should not say either one; and we should not say that neither of them is correct, or we have no way at all of talking about posterior uveitis. Each, we might say, is said only for practical purposes.

Alternatively, we might say that we assert that there are floaters to explain the patient's experience; we assert that there are none to explain to the patient that they are ill; we assert both to distinguish the patient's experience from that of everyone else; and we assert neither because each is misleading. Anyone familiar with Nāgārjuna's various deployments of the *catuṣkoṭi* in *Fundamental Verses on the Middle Way* (*Mūlamadhyamakakārikā*) and with Candrakīrti's and Tsongkhapa's commentaries will recognize these patterns of reasoning. And the third and fourth *koṭi*s set our agenda: We need to understand why the conventional truth and the ultimate truth are equally *truths*, and thus *objects of knowledge*. But we also need to understand why neither of them alone can be the whole story; neither can *exhaust* the truth, and to grasp only one is not to have knowledge in the full sense.

Geluk Readings of Madhyamaka Epistemology: Reading Candrakīrti

In "How Far Can a Mādhyamika Buddhist Reform Conventional Truth? Dismal Relativism, Fictionalism, Easy-Easy Truth, and the Alternatives" (Tillemans 2011), Tom presents a reading of Candrakīrti according to which conventional truth amounts to leaving us all mired in what Tom memorably calls "the dismal slough." He characterizes that as the view that "nothing the world ever endorsed could be criticized or rejected and that, on the conventional at least, a Mādhyamika's principal epistemic task [is] just to passively acquiesce and duplicate" (152). As he points out:

Most of us would agree that the potential flattening of the normative roles of truth and knowledge that such duplication brings is indeed quite dismal. It is a trivialization of the idea of truth to think that we could somehow settle what *is* true by periodically taking inventories of what people believe to be true at given times and places. (Tillemans 2011, 152)

And following Kamalaśīla, Tom suggests that this may well have been Candrakīrti's position (Tillemans 2011, 153–55). Tom concludes that Tsongkhapa's reconstruction of Candrakīrti's position as involving a distinction between conventional truth and conventional falsity and as allowing the use of conventional *pramāṇa*s to distinguish between truth and falsity and to correct conventional error is not so much faithful exegesis of Candrakīrti's own position as creative philosophy that vamps on Candrakīrti. That is, while Tom ends up endorsing Tsongkhapa's view, he does so as an implicit *critique* rather than as an *exegesis* of Candrakīrti. I disagree. So, first, I want to defend Candrakīrti and Tsongkhapa's exegesis. I will then consider Taktsang's own critique of Tsongkhapa's exegesis and defense of wallowing in the dismal slough. I will show that he is wrong as well. This will set the stage for a broader look at Madhyamaka epistemology.

To buttress the dismal reading of Candrakīrti's attitude to epistemology, Tom relies on Candrakīrti's citation in his commentary on Nāgārjuna's *Fundamental Verses on the Middle Way* 18.8 of the following well-known passage from the Ratnakūṭa collection of sūtras:

The world argues with me. I don't argue with the world. What is agreed upon in the world to exist, I too agree that it exists. What is agreed upon in the world to be nonexistent, I too agree that it does not exist. (*Trisaṃvaranirdeśaparivarta*, quoted in Tillemans 2011, 151)

But the context in which this passage is cited does not support the dismal reading. Here Candrakīrti is glossing the verse:

Everything is real, is not real,
is both real and unreal,
and is neither unreal nor real.
This is the Lord Buddha's teaching. (*Fundamental Verses* 18.8)

And he is reading this as an exposition of progressive teaching: the Buddha first teaches a kind of realism—providing a deeper but still realistic analysis of ordinary phenomena—because that is where ordinary people start; they need to move from a naïve realism about the world to a more sophisticated view in which the entities they take for granted are analyzed in terms of causal processes, dharmas, and other fundamental phenomena, in preparation for an analysis in terms of emptiness. The Ratnakūṭa quotation in this context is intended only to justify the first phase of this graduated set of teachings, the teachings to beginners or to ordinary people: the idea is that the Buddha begins by taking for granted what they take for granted and uses this as a platform on which to build his pedagogy.

We can get a much better sense of how Candrakīrti thinks about the status of conventional truth from remarks like this one in the *Commentary on Āryadeva's Four Hundred Verses* (*Catuḥśatakaṭīkā*), commenting on 15.10:

> What arises does not come into existence,
> and similarly that which ceases does not go out of existence.
> Since this is how things are, how could
> it not all be like a magician's illusion?

> When the production of dependently originated things is seen this way, they are regarded as like a magician's illusions. But they are not like the son of a barren woman. If they *were* analyzed like that, the existence of all arisen things would be refuted. And if that were the case, we could not say that the production of compounded phenomena is like a magician's illusion, and we *would* explain using examples such as the son of a barren woman. But since we wish to avoid the absurd consequence that dependently arisen phenomena are nonexistent, we do not use these analogies. Instead, so as not to contradict the existence of dependent origination, we compare the production of things to analogies such as a magician's illusion. (Candrakīrti 2007, 369)

Analogies matter. Here, Candrakīrti distinguishes two different analogies often used in Madhyamaka treatises. The son of a barren woman is an analogy for something that does not exist at all—conventionally or ultimately— and that simply makes no sense; it signifies something incoherent. The magical illusion, however, is not like that. It exists; if it did not, nobody would attend magic shows. It is dependently originated, brought about by the magician. If it were not, even I could produce the illusion. And finally, while it does exist, it does not exist as it appears; its mode of existence and mode of appearance are discordant. When the magician chants "Abracadabra" over a pile of sticks, he produces a *real* illusion that appears to be, but is not, a real elephant. Once again, if the illusion were not real, or if the elephant were, nobody would pay to see this magician.

Candrakīrti is therefore explicitly denying that he (or Āryadeva) rejects the reality of conventional truth: it is *not* like the son of a barren woman. *Instead,* it is like the magical illusion: it exists, but in a way that is different from its appearance. Conventional truth is real but only conventionally real; it appears to us to exist intrinsically, but it does not. Conventional phenomena appear to be independent, but like the illusion, they are only dependently arisen. This is an *affirmation*, not a *denial*, of the reality of the conventional. But, one might wonder, what does this say about the *epistemology* of the conventional? Here we turn to Candrakīrti's commentary *Clear Words* (*Prasannapadā*). Here, Candrakīrti is responding to one who would argue that to be only conventionally real is to be *unreal* and that only ultimate truth counts as *truth*:

> Since you don't understand ultimate and conventional truth, you don't use appropriate analyses, and so you completely destroy any understanding of the conventional. Since we understand how to think about the conventional, we adhere to mundane ways of thinking about it. So, like experienced participants in mundane practices, we use those practices to dispel the position you defend and to refute your position regarding the conventional. (Candrakīrti 2003, 50)

The important point here is not simply that the conventional truth is important and must be understood but also that mundane epistemic standards can be used to evaluate and to reject other standards. This is an appeal to the recursive and self-correcting character of conventional epistemological practices. We use our epistemic instruments not only to determine what our objects of knowledge are like but also to calibrate and to assess other epistemic standards. For example, I use the *testimony* of my ophthalmologist to determine whether my vision is good; I use my *inferential* understanding of the status of the conventional to compare the *analogies* of the son of a barren woman and a magical illusion; and I use my own *perception* and inference to validate the testimony that led me to trust my eyes in the first place. The *pramāṇa*s form an interdependent web, itself supported by the *prameya*s, the reliable objects of those epistemic instruments, just as Nāgārjuna repeatedly says it should go in *Replies to Objections* (*Vigrahavyāvartanī*) (Garfield 2015; Westerhoff 2010).

This is the basis of Nāgārjuna's and Candrakīrti's attack on foundationalism and endorsement of a coherentist epistemology (Garfield 2011; Garfield and Thakchoe 2025; Westerhoff 2010). And this is why it is so important for Candrakīrti to distinguish *within the conventional* the conventionally true (that which is delivered by a properly functioning epistemic instrument) and the conventionally false (that which is delivered by poorly functioning instruments). Conventional epistemic instruments work because they serve our purposes well, including the purpose of improving our epistemic practices (Newland 2011). This is no dismal slough; instead, it is a steady uphill path into fresh air and light.

Tsongkhapa follows Candrakīrti closely in this regard. In the *Great Exposition of the Stages of the Path* (*Lam rim chen mo*) he writes:

> Candrakīrti repeatedly allows that these conventionalities, such as forms and sounds, do exist. However, they are not in the least established by reasoning that analyzes reality—that is, analyzes whether they have intrinsic nature. (Tsongkhapa 2002, 157)

Tsongkhapa here, and throughout his discussion of the epistemology of the conventional in the *Great Exposition*, insists that Candrakīrti's analysis of conventional phenomena as empty of any intrinsic identity not only is *consistent* with their conventional reality but in fact *presupposes it*. Candrakīrti and Tsongkhapa are in clear agreement that the two truths are two *truths* and that the illusory nature of conventional truth does not undermine its status as a truth. Khedrup Jé puts this point nicely in the *Great Digest* (*Stong thun chen mo*):

> It is not contradictory that, on the one hand, it be an object that deceives insofar as, within the consciousness that takes it as its object, the way in which it appears does not accord with the way it exists, and that, on the other hand, this valid cognition is undeceived in regard to the phenomenon insofar as it establishes that phenomenon as it is in a positive way. (Cabezón 1992, 371)

The sense in which conventional phenomena are deceptive is this: they appear to be more than merely conventional. But just as we may be wrong in believing that a rabbit was conjured from an empty hat while right that the magician has produced an illusory rabbit and not a wombat, we may be wrong in thinking that a pot is ultimately real while being right that the conventionally real thing in front of us is a pot. And we are right because our ordinary epistemic instruments are working properly.

While Tom is right that Tsongkhapa and his followers extend Candrakīrti's analysis in their own commentaries, this extension is not a fanciful riff on Candrakīrti—Tsongkhapa is not, as Tom puts it, turning Candrakīrti into a "significantly better philosopher than he actually was" (Tillemans 2011, 165). Instead, he is presenting a careful exegesis and rational reconstruction of Candrakīrti's position. But Tom is not the first to think that Tsongkhapa is distorting Candrakīrti in an attempt to integrate epistemology into Madhyamaka. We now turn to a medieval Tibetan version of this charge. Attention to this critique of Tsongkhapa helps us to see better what is at stake.

Defending Geluk Epistemology: The Taktsang Debates

Among the most trenchant critics of Tsongkhapa's interpretation of Candrakīrti and of his epistemology on its own terms was Taktsang Sherab Rinchen (1405–??). In chapter 5 of his *Freedom from Extremes through the Comprehensive Knowledge of Philosophy* (*Grub mtha' kun shes nas mtha' bral sgrub pa*, Yakherds 2021, 2:8–148), he levels eighteen distinct charges against Tsongkhapa, both hermeneutical and philosophical in character. The philosophical critique focuses on three principal issues: (1) knowledge makes no sense in the context of pervasive illusion, since to know is to be free from deception; (2) knowledge requires foundations, because if there are no foundations, there is no source of justification; and (3) knowledge makes no sense in the conventional world, because the entities in the conventional world do not exist, and so there is no truth regarding them to know.

On the problem of pervasive illusion, Taktsang writes:

> Consider an ordinary visual cognition that is generally regarded as nonerroneous: because it is an erroneous cognition of visible form, it could not be an epistemic warrant for visual form. Don't even try to prove the opposite; you have already explicitly accepted the premise—that cognition is mistaken with regard to visible form because cognition is distorted by apprehending things as real. (Yakherds 2021, 2:34)

Taktsang immediately quotes Candrakīrti's *Commentary on Āryadeva's Four Hundred Verses* as authority for this:

> [T]o . . . think that sensory cognitions function as epistemic warrants for their objects is utterly indefensible. From a mundane perspective, an epistemic warrant is regarded as a nondeceptive cognition. The Blessed One has taught that cognition is a conditioned phenomenon and therefore is false and deceptive, just like an illusion. Being false, deceptive, and illusory, it cannot be nondeceptive, because things appear to it in a way that is different from the way that they actually are. Therefore it is not reasonable to regard such a cognition as an epistemic warrant because then all cognitions would end up being epistemic warrants. (Yakherds 2021, 2:34)

Taktsang's point is pretty clear: since—as Candrakīrti points out—our senses and cognitive capacities are known to be deceptive, they cannot function as warrants, because to be an epistemic warrant is by definition to be nondeceptive. He therefore faults Tsongkhapa and his tradition both on their Candrakīrti exegesis and on their epistemology.

This point is connected directly to Taktsang's foundationalist critique of Geluk epistemology:

> [O]ur opponents claim on the one hand that objects have no nature or essence whatsoever, and on the other that such things as fire's having the function of burning are not just mere mental imputations but perform their functions in a nondeceptive, foundational way, albeit merely conventionally. For this reason, they say, the conventional and ultimate natures of phenomena must be used in tandem to produce ascertainment . . . [T]his is the principal contradiction to which they fall prey. This is because for the Great Madhyamaka there is absolutely no object of negation—viz., nature—beyond the idea that the functioning world has an objective, foundational, nature.
>
> They might reply that they do not accept foundations. But not being foundational contradicts being epistemically warranted; for to be epistemically warranted means to be nondeceptive, and being nondeceptive means nothing more than being foundational. (Yakherds 2021, 2:25)

Taktsang here directly connects warrant to foundations, arguing that Tsongkhapa is trying to have his coherentist cake by talking of convention and interdependence while eating its foundations, since without foundations, no claim can rise to the status of knowledge.

Finally, regarding the status of conventional reality and the possibility of knowledge of it, Taktsang writes:

> In the Prāsaṅgika's own system, one indeed realizes that the relative truth is false. Therefore it is contradictory to hold on the one hand that all relative objects are false and on the other hand that the cognitions that are their subjects can be nondeceptive and epistemically warranting. (Yakherds 2021, 2:33)

Knowledge, in other words, is always knowledge of real things. But the phenomena of the relative, or conventional truth, Taktsang argues, are false—nonexistent. Therefore any awareness of them is the awareness of a nonexistent phenomenon and so cannot be knowledge.

These are serious critiques both of Geluk readings of Candrakīrti and of Geluk epistemology on its own terms. And while Taktsang Sherab Rinchen and Tom Tillemans disagree about whether the dismal slough is a fit place in which to dwell, they agree that that is where Candrakīrti leaves us: for Taktsang that is a feature; for Tom, a bug. Nonetheless, I think that we can see why this reading of Candrakīrti is incorrect and why the Geluk approach to epistemology is superior to any that rejects the possibility of conventional knowledge.

Despite the clarity and precision of Taktsang's analysis, it fails both as a reading of Candrakīrti and as an epistemological position. Seeing why helps us to understand Candrakīrti's program better and to see how a Mādhyamika (or anyone, really) ought to think about knowledge. Let us begin with the hermeneutical side. We have already considered some statements from Candrakīrti—some of those cited by Tsongkhapa—to defend reading Candrakīrti as endorsing the reality and the knowability of conventional truth. We could have included others, such as *Entering the Middle Way* (*Madhyamakāvatāra*) 6.23:

> One understands the two natures of all objects
> by seeing that all phenomena are both real and unreal.
> Reality is the object of the perception of truth.
> That which is seen falsely is called the conventional truth.
>   (2009, 213)

In the commentary to this verse, Candrakīrti says, "It has been shown that each phenomenon has its own two natures—a conventional and an ultimate nature" (2009, 214). Here and in the subsequent commentary, Candrakīrti plainly endorses the view that the conventional truth is an actual nature of objects, and that there is a way to see it. Candrakīrti doubles down in verses 6.24 and 25:

> We explain that there are two ways to perceive falsely:
> one's sense faculties may function properly or be impaired.
> When contrasted with properly functioning faculties,
> that which is perceived through impaired faculties is regarded
>   as false. (2009, 220)

> We ordinarily say that that which is delivered
> by unimpaired sense faculties is true.
> We ordinarily say that all the rest
> is taken by everyone to be false. (2009, 221)

It is hard to escape the conclusion that Candrakīrti takes conventional truth very seriously, arguing not only that the conventional truth constitutes one of the natures of every object but also that within the conventional we can distinguish between conventional truth and conventional falsity, a point that looms large both in epistemology and ophthalmology!

But what should we say about passages such as that from the *Commentary on Āryadeva's Four Hundred Verses* that Taktsang adduces in favor of the dismal reading of Candrakīrti? I think that it is easy to defang that citation: in verses from *Entering the Middle Way* we must understand *false* to mean *deceptive*, and we must understand *false perception* to be perception that represents empty, conventionally real things to be intrinsically real and ultimately existent. *Mutatis mutandis*, we should read the passage in the *Commentary on the Four Hundred* in the same way. When Candrakīrti says that ordinary perception is "false, deceptive, and illusory," it is deceptive regarding the ultimate nature of things; so when he concludes that it is not a warrant, he concludes that it is not a warrant with regard to that nature. This is not an arbitrary interpretation, not a cherry-picking of favorable passages. Instead, this reading allows us to read the passage from the *Commentary on the Four Hundred* as consistent with those regarding the two truths in *Clear Words* and in *Entering the Middle Way*.

When we come back to the ground of epistemology, things are, if anything, even clearer and easier. Let us take the three points we noted above in order. First, we can make perfect sense of epistemic warrant in the context of illusion or deception. This is because one can be deceived about one aspect of an object of knowledge without being deceived about *every aspect*. A colorblind person might be deceived about the color of an apple but be perfectly capable of distinguishing apples from peaches. Such a person might know that there is an apple on the table without knowing whether it is a Granny Smith or a Gala.

Second, foundationalism is a terrible epistemological position, not only because nobody has ever been able to identify any plausible candidate for the foundations of knowledge but also because the project is self-undermining. If the search for foundations is driven by the ideas that every item of knowledge must be justified and that self-justification would be question-begging, then one is forced to conclude that the foundations one finds are not themselves known and so can hardly serve the epistemic role they are supposed to serve. The Buddhist metaphor of mutual support, like that provided by sheaves of grain stacked *against* each other, is far better than the metaphor of independent foundations. And we can know all of this (and more), so there has to be knowledge that lacks foundations. This point was made eloquently in the twentieth century by Wittgenstein and Sellars centuries after Candrakīrti realized it.

Finally, as should now be clear, the idea that the conventional world is nonexistent is at odds both with Madhyamaka thought as articulated by Candrakīrti and with common sense. Conventional existence is not an *alternative* to existence; it is an *explanation* of the only mode of existence that anything can have, which is interdependent existence. And so, since to exist conventionally is to be real, it is to be knowable; therefore there must be conventional *pramāṇa*s. This is why Candrakīrti and Tsongkhapa endorse them. Recognizing this fact takes us out of the dismal slough and back into reality.

Why This Matters: Knowledge in the Context of Massive Illusion

One way of capturing what it is for a thing to be real is to say that there is a difference between getting it right and getting it wrong regarding that thing—in other words, that we can distinguish truth and falsity with respect to it. And one way of capturing what it is to know an object is to say that there are accepted ways of justifying one's claims regarding it. This is why the insight that Candrakīrti expresses in *Entering the Middle Way* 6.24–25 and in the autocommentary to those verses is so important. Even if I mistakenly take the apples on my table to exist intrinsically, it is one thing to believe that there are six of them there and another to believe that there are a dozen. If one is right, the other is wrong; the fact that we can get it right or wrong means that they are real; and the fact that I can get it right by looking shows that vision, however metaphysically deceptive it might be, is a *pramāṇa* in the context of counting apples.

And what goes for apples goes for floaters: even though there are no hairs falling through the space around me, there is a real difference between seeing two or three of them and seeing hundreds, a difference that makes a great difference to Dr. Rioux, however much Taktsang and Tom might assert that they are entirely nonexistent. Just as they are nonexistent in one sense but existent in another, my perception of them is deceptive in one sense but warranting in another. It is deceptive regarding their mode of existence but warranted regarding their numerosity (and my posterior uveitis).

There is another perhaps more important insight lurking in this discussion, one toward which Candrakīrti gestures in his talk of what ordinary people say and know in 6.23–25 of *Entering the Middle Way* and in the discussion of the four *pramāṇa*s in *Clear Words*, but with which Tsongkhapa runs and which Hume and Wittgenstein make explicit in *A Treatise of Human Nature* and in *On Certainty*, respectively (Garfield 2019, 3): to come to know is to engage in a conventional practice, a practice governed by mundane conventions. It is *not* simply to aim our senses or conceptual apparatus at an object. Seeing is only knowing if I have independent reason to know that my vision is good; inference only gets me knowledge if I have learned how to distinguish sound from unsound reasoning; and so on.[1] Only once we have learned *how to justify* can we become knowers. (See also Sellars 1997.)

This means that all knowing *presupposes* conventions and the conventional world. Even coming to know the ultimate is to engage in epistemic practices. This is why Tsongkhapa insists that even direct nonconceptual insight into emptiness achieved in meditative equipoise must be grounded in a premeditative, conceptual, inferential understanding of emptiness and that this insight only rises to the level of *knowledge* when it is confirmed by post-meditative reflection. That is, a conceptualized (*rnam grangs*) understanding of the ultimate is a necessary condition of a nonconceptual (*rnam grangs ma yin pa*) apprehension. This insight follows on Nāgārjuna's insistence in *Fundamental Verses* 24.8–10 that conventional truth is the necessary means for knowing the ultimate (Garfield 2020). For this reason, to deny the possibility of knowledge of the conventional, or the utility of conventional *pramāṇa*s, is simply incoherent.

Moreover, if as Mādhyamikas we take seriously not only the distinction between the two truths but also their identity—and this is very much Candrakīrti's Madhyamaka—we must recognize that to deprecate the conventional is to deprecate the ultimate. Even emptiness, because it is empty,

---

1. Thurman (1980) makes much the same point, arguing that what distinguishes Candrakīrti's understanding of meaning and of epistemology is akin to Wittgenstein's: it is non-egocentric and relies on our participations in joint conventions.

exists only conventionally. So if we were to take Taktsang's side in this debate, not only would we lose knowledge of the conventional and the reality of conventional phenomena; we would also lose the possibility of knowledge of the ultimate and the reality of emptiness. And as Nāgārjuna reminds us at 24.10 of *Fundamental Verses*:

> Without depending on the conventional truth,
> the meaning of the ultimate cannot be taught.
> Without understanding the meaning of the ultimate,
> nirvāṇa is not achieved.

For all of these reasons, epistemology is a Madhyamaka concern. The Madhyamaka system requires an account of knowledge and how it is to be achieved. The doctrine of the two truths demands that epistemology account for conventional knowledge as well as the knowledge of emptiness. And that account must be one that recognizes knowledge as grounded in mundane convention, even if it can flower into a transcendent insight. To their credit, Candrakīrti and Tsongkhapa recognize that fact and develop a sophisticated account of epistemic practice. And Tsongkhapa's reading of Candrakīrti— despite Tom's reading of it as "atypical"—succeeds precisely because he sees and respects the critique of foundationalism in epistemology; Taktsang's fails because he presupposes a foundationalist epistemology. While Candrakīrti's position may not always be entirely clear, and while competing readings of Candrakīrti may appear to be exercises in comparative cherry-picking, it should be clear that he is no foundationalist. And therefore it should be clear that he is a coherentist and a conventionalist regarding knowledge. He leads us not into a dismal slough but into clarity about our epistemic practices.

So when I visit my ophthalmologist and she checks on my floaters, I can count them and feel secure that in doing so, not only am I in accord with the mundane practice of my culture, but I am also consistent with the teachings of the Prāsaṅgika Madhyamaka tradition. I am sure that Tom would disagree with none of the epistemology; I hope that now he sees that the Buddhist tradition owes that epistemology to Candrakīrti.

Bibliography

Cabezón, José. 1992. *A Dose of Emptiness: An Annotated Translation of the sTong thun chen mo of mKhas grub dGe legs dpal bzang.* Albany: State University of New York Press.
Candrakīrti. 2003. *Dbu ma rtsa ba'i 'grel pa tshig gsal.* Sarnath: Gelukpa Student Welfare Committee.

————. 2007. *Bzhi brgya pa'i rnam bshad legs bshad snying po*. Sarnath: Gelukpa Student Welfare Committee.

————. 2009. *Dbu ma la 'jug pa'i rgya cher bshad pa dgongs pa rab tu gsal ba*. Sarnath: Gelukpa Student Welfare Committee.

Cowherds, the. 2011. *Moonshadows: Conventional Truth in Buddhist Philosophy*. New York: Oxford University Press.

Garfield, Jay L. 2011. "Taking Conventional Truth Seriously: Authority Regarding Deceptive Reality." In *Moonshadows: Conventional Truth in Buddhist Philosophy*, by the Cowherds, 23–38. New York: Oxford University Press.

————. 2015. *Engaging Buddhism: Why It Matters to Philosophy*. New York: Oxford University Press.

————. 2019. *The Concealed Influence of Custom: Hume's Treatise from the Inside Out*. New York: Oxford University Press.

————. 2020. "Thinking Beyond Thought: Tsongkhapa and Mipham on the Categorized Ultimate." *Philosophy East and West* 70.2: 1–16. Also in *Buddhist Minds and Bodies: Essays in Honor of José Ignacio Cabezón*, edited by Vesna Wallace and Rory Lindsay (Wisdom, 2026).

Garfield, Jay L., and Sonam Thakchoe. 2025. *By the Light of the Moon: Candrakīrti's Prāsaṅgika Madhyamaka*. New York: Oxford University Press.

Newland, Guy Martin. 2011. "Weighing the Butter, Levels of Explanation, and Falsification: Models of the Conventional in Tsongkhapa's Account of Madhyamaka." In *Moonshadows: Conventional Truth in Buddhist Philosophy*, by the Cowherds, 57–72. New York: Oxford University Press.

Sellars, Wilfrid. 1997. *Empiricism and the Philosophy of Mind*. Cambridge, MA: Harvard University Press.

Thurman, Robert A. F. 1980. "Philosophical Nonegocentrism in Wittgenstein and Candrakīrti in Their Treatment of the Private Language Problem." *Philosophy East and West* 30.3: 321–37.

Tillemans, Tom J. F. 2011. "How Far Can a Mādhyamika Buddhist Reform Conventional Truth? Dismal Relativism, Fictionalism, Easy-Easy Truth, and the Alternatives." In *Moonshadows: Conventional Truth in Buddhist Philosophy*, by the Cowherds, 151–66. New York: Oxford University Press. Reissued in *How Do Mādhyamikas Think?*, 47–63 (Wisdom, 2016).

————. 2019. "Deflating the Two Images and the Two Truths: Bons Baisers du Tibet." In *Wilfrid Sellars and Buddhist Philosophy: Freedom from Foundations*, edited by Jay L. Garfield, 80–96. London: Routledge.

Tsongkhapa. 2002. *The Great Treatise on the Stages of the Path to Enlightenment*, vol. 3. Translated by the Lamrim Chenmo Translation Committee. Ithaca: Snow Lion.

Westerhoff, Jan. 2010. *Dispeller of Disputes: Nāgārjuna's Vigrahavyāvartanī*. New York: Oxford University Press.

Yakherds, the. 2021. *Knowing Illusion: Bringing a Tibetan Debate into Contemporary Discourse*, 2 vols. New York: Oxford University Press.

Candrakīrti on the Couch:
Why Mādhyamikas Need Analysis

Mark Siderits

How, now, to help the cow out of the dismal slough? And is that a gnu ambling through the dismal slough? The slough in question is one that Tom Tillemans first alerted us to in his work for the Cowherds (Tillemans 2011). At the Kathmandu Cowherd Conclave in 2009, the meeting out of which *Moonshadows* (Cowherds 2011) developed, there was some discussion concerning the correct pronunciation of *slough*. This was triggered by Tillemans's use of the apt expression "dismal slough" for the problematic view of truth that some have seen in Candrakīrti. Tillemans himself pronounced *slough* to rhyme with *through*. Other Cowherds, though, insisted on pronouncing it to rhyme with *bough*. For my own part, I wrongly thought that the noun *slough* was pronounced like the verb *slough*, which rhymes with the American pronunciation of *cough*. Having been corrected, I now wish to declare my allegiance to Team Bough.

But I knew Tom long before that Kathmandu discussion. We first met at a symposium on Buddhist logic and epistemology organized by B. K. Matilal in conjunction with the Fifth International Association of Buddhist Studies Congress held at Oxford in 1982. At the time, we were both working on the *apoha* theory, but our shared interests in a wide variety of other topics in the Buddhist philosophical tradition would lead to many more interactions. Perhaps the most consequential for my own philosophical development came when, in 2003, he arranged for me to present a series of lectures in Lausanne on the topic of truth in Madhyamaka. Among the participants in those Lausanne conversations were Georges Dreyfus, Pascale Hugon, Jiří Holba, Koji Tanaka, and Bronwyn Finnigan; Tom even managed to arrange a visit by Arindam Chakrabarti.

When I came to Lausanne, I had already written the chapter on truth in Madhyamaka that would appear in the first edition of *Empty Persons* (Siderits

2003). But I had begun to sense that in writing that chapter, I had followed Michael Dummett into some very dark waters. My interactions with Tom that spring helped me see two things about Madhyamaka: that its account of truth is deflationist, and that its soteriology runs through metaphysical quietism. What he said about the slough at the Cowherd Conclave in 2009 mostly concerned the first point, the trap we may fall into when we embrace a purely conventionalist account of truth. The central claim of Madhyamaka is that all dharmas are devoid of intrinsic nature (*svabhāva*). If, as Ābhidharmikas claim, the only entities that might be ultimately real are precisely the things with intrinsic nature (the dharmas), then if Madhyamaka is right about emptiness, the only sort of truth there can be is conventional truth. And as Tillemans pointed out, it is not just certain modern scholars who suspect that this stance leads in the end to a form of relativism about truth; Kamalaśīla was equally horrified by this seeming consequence of full-bore antirealism. Tillemans himself thought a Mādhyamika like Candrakīrti could find their way out of such a bog. The version of the slough I want to discuss, though, is the one that results from the intersection of Tom's two insights: the one about truth and the reading of Madhyamaka as metaphysical quietism. My focus will be on Candrakīrti's Madhyamaka. The question I will address is whether his account of truth is compatible with a Buddhist soterial project.

Conventional Truth

For Candrakīrti, conventional truth is "what is known even to cowherds and women."[1] By this he seems to mean how things appear to ordinary folk, the common-sense truths about the world shared by all—for instance, that fire is by nature hot or that things are subject to arising and dissolution.[2] And such commonly accepted beliefs are, Candrakīrti tells us, ones that he will find no fault with. He quotes a passage in which the Buddha proclaims that while the world may dispute his claims, he does not disagree with the world concerning what it affirms and what it denies. Do all agree that fire is hot and water is wet? Then far be it from Candrakīrti to disagree. He of course adds that the world is fundamentally deluded, that its views concerning such things as fire and water are no better than the beliefs of those with myodesopsia (*timira*) about the hairs they see floating in the sky. Conventional truths are really no kind of truth at all. But this is not to say that the beliefs of the folk are to be replaced

---

1. PP 260 ad MMK 15.1.

2. PP 418 ad MMK 21.10.

by a better set of convictions that come closer to representing how things really are by looking more deeply into reality.

Tillemans suggests that Candrakīrti may have strayed into this dismal slough simply because he was dealt a bad hand. The Mahāyāna scriptural source (possibly *Trisaṃvaranirdeśaparivarta*) that Candrakīrti cites in his explication of what it means for a statement to be conventionally true, and how one should regard conventional truths, makes what seems to be a significant omission. The passage Candrakīrti quotes at *Madhyamakāvatāra* 6.81 lacks an important qualification found in the Pāli parallel of his Mahāyāna source. What is missing from the Sanskrit version quoted by Candrakīrti but present in the Pāli is mention of "the wise" (*paṇḍita*) as arbiters of what is established in the world (*lokaprasiddha*).[3] This omission feeds directly into Candrakīrti's characterization of conventional truth as what is agreed to "even by cowherds and women." Conventional truth is, on this account, just that about which there is consensus, how things seem to ordinary folk. The omission of "the wise" suggests that the received folk wisdom is not subject to correction by expert critique. And since for Madhyamaka the very idea of the ultimate truth is incoherent so that the only sort of truth there can be is conventional truth, it follows that our understanding of how things are is simply to be read off the surface of what most people say most of the time.

Tillemans finds fault with this account (beyond its classism and sexism) in its also ruling out the sorts of epistemic improvement that play so large a role in our lives today: "technical subjects like logic, linguistics, and economics, not to mention physical science, would be impossible and would be eliminated in favor of oh-so-readily-understandable common sense" (2011, 161). Had "the wise" been brought into the account, room might have been made for the role of expertise in the progressive refinement of our collective understanding of the world. But even if this approach can be made to work, there is still a problem: on Candrakīrti's approach to conventional truth, it is not at all clear how the central goal of Buddhist practice, dissipation of the "I" sense, is to be achieved. Where Tillemans thinks Candrakīrti is merely doing his best to play the bad hand he was dealt, I suspect Candrakīrti thought that for Buddhist purposes, what he'd been dealt were winning cards.

The bluff I suspect Candrakīrti was trying to play has to do with the gap between his stance toward conventional truth and the professed Buddhist aim of achieving the cessation of existential suffering. I begin with conventional truth. If Madhyamaka is right in its core claim that nothing has intrin-

3. I first learned this from Tom, who says he learned it in turn from Stephen Batchelor (Tillemans 2016, 58–59).

sic nature, and we also accept the Abhidharma claim that only things with intrinsic nature could be ultimately real (i.e., real independently of the concepts we happen to use), it follows that there is nothing for ultimate truths to be true of. This is the result that may be put, somewhat cryptically, as "The ultimate truth is that there is no ultimate truth." There being no such thing as ultimate truth, there is just conventional truth. The aspiration to discover how things are independently of the mind's constructive activity is simply not going to pan out.

I am now persuaded that Tillemans is right to characterize the result as a distinctively Madhyamaka form of deflationism. For a deflationist, there is no more to truth than what is captured in the T-schema:

"S" is true if and only if S.

A statement's being true consists in nothing more than its assertion conditions. It has nothing to do with the statement's picturing how things are, or its cohering with what one holds true, or its facilitating successful practice. Truth is just what all would agree in saying about some matter. This fits quite well with one thing Candrakīrti says about conventional truth: that it is what is established for the world (*lokaprasiddha*) or what the world acknowledges. Naturally, he is well aware that universal agreement cannot be required. The person with the eye disorder of myodesopsia (*timira*) will not agree with us in saying what is seen when looking at the sky on a clear day: where we see uniform blue, they see hairs floating on the firmament. But conventional truth contains resources with which to iron these things out. Through judicious use of (conventional) epistemic instruments (*pramāṇa*s), we can correct for erroneous appearances and achieve consensus.[4] So conventional truth—i.e., truth—need not include such clear falsehoods as that the earth is flat or that the sun, planets, and stars revolve around the earth.

Analysis

Something else Candrakīrti says about conventional truth may prove harder to digest. This is that conventional truth dissolves under analysis (*vicāra*), something to which the world does not resort. At *Madhyamakāvatāra* 6.35, for instance, he claims that since analysis shows nothing can originate, whether from itself or from something distinct, to hold the common-sense view that

---

4. Newland (2011) attributes this corrective move to Tsongkhapa, but it seems perfectly compatible with what Candrakīrti says on the subject of conventionally established *pramāṇa*s.

things undergo origination one must simply set aside the question whether origination is from the originated or from something else (or from both or from neither). Likewise, in his *Prasannapadā* critique of Bhāviveka's reconstruction of the argument of *Mūlamadhyamakārikā* 1.1, Candrakīrti claims that Bhāviveka's use of the qualification "ultimately" is pointless, since the world does not engage in the sort of analysis in which the question of identity or distinctness of effect with cause might arise (PP 27). In commenting on *Mūlamadhyamakārikā* 7.32, he denies that the disproof of origination is tantamount to nihilism insofar as worldly establishment is devoid of the sort of analysis that would lead to the result that nothing can exist (PP 172). And in his *Prasannapadā* critique of Dignāga's use of examples like "the head of Rāhu" and "the body of the statue" to support the claim that property-possessor and property may be identical, he points out that common sense could not function if the question of identity and distinctness were allowed to be raised—that is, if one conducted analysis in terms of this distinction (PP 67). Similar claims occur throughout chapter 6 of the *Madhyamakāvatāra*, e.g., at *Madhyamakāvatāra* 6.170, where he equates the claim that the Mādhyamika has no dispute with the world (made at 6.81) with the claim that worldly categories function in the absence of analysis. But perhaps his clearest articulation of the point is at *Madhyamakāvatāra* 6.35:

> Since these things underlying their ultimate intrinsic nature [of neither arising nor ceasing], when subjected to analysis, do not obtain the state [of arising and ceasing], so analysis is not to be carried out with regard to conventional truth as commonly understood.[5]

This raises two questions. First, what does Candrakīrti mean by "analysis"? And second, why does he think that the conventional world simply disappears when subjected to it? A survey of occurrences of the term *vicāra* in the *Prasannapadā* and *Madhyamakāvatāra* shows it to denote a wide array of argumentative strategies familiar from the works of Nāgārjuna, Āryadeva, Buddhapālita, and the like. The contact/noncontact dilemma is called an analysis.[6] The three-times argument against proximate conditions is called an analysis.[7] The fivefold examination of the self that Nāgārjuna employs in

---

5. MAv 6.35: *arvāṅ na tattvātmakarūpato 'mī sthitiṃ labhante pravicāryamāṇāḥ / yataḥ padārthā na tato vicāraḥ kāryo hi lokavyavahārasatye //*.

6. PP 151–55 ad MMK 7.8–11; MAv 6.169–75.

7. PP 86 ad MMK 1.9.

the *Mūlamadhyamakārikā* is described as an analysis.[8] This examination concerns possible relations a self might bear to the psychophysical constituents: identity, distinctness, *skandha*s as locus of self, self as locus of *skandha*s, and self as possessor. Candrakīrti adds two more in his sevenfold analysis of ways that a chariot might be related to its parts: collection and arrangement.[9] In each of these cases, the point of the examination is to show that if the entity in question is taken to be something ultimately real, something with intrinsic nature, then it cannot fulfill some necessary condition for its standing in the right relation to the world. For instance, a cause, understood as an ultimately real entity, cannot occur before its effect, after its effect, or simultaneous with its effect.

Candrakīrti does concede that there is an innocent use of the term *svabhāva* in worldly discourse, as when people say that a lotus, but not quartz, is intrinsically red, or that fire but not water is essentially hot.[10] The idea here is that the redness of quartz or the heat of water depends on some extraneous element, such as the presence of iron or proximity to fire, whereas the lotus is just naturally red and fire is just intrinsically hot. But this usage encounters difficulties once one reflects on the fact that lotus and fire are thought to arise in dependence on causes, and prior argumentation[11] has supposedly demonstrated that nothing can ultimately be said to arise. So in our everyday commerce with the world, we may distinguish between intrinsic and extrinsic natures, but the moment one begins to engage in serious ontological reflection, the distinction loses all purchase: nothing may be said to have intrinsic nature. That the world does not engage in analysis is crucial to there being anything at all for the world to talk about.

The resemblance of some of the procedures that Candrakīrti calls *analysis* to the standard Abhidharma technique for determining the ontological status of an entity will be obvious. Vasubandhu, for instance, tells us that something is ultimately real only if its concept still applies after separation and qualitative analysis.[12] When bowl and neck are separated, the concept *pot* no longer applies. A particle of water that is too small to allow for spatial separation still allows for a sort of conceptual division: as an aggregate of occurrences of its most fundamental properties, such as color and wetness, neither of which

8. PP 433 ad MMK 22.1.

9. MAv 6.151.

10. PP 260 ad MMK 15.1.

11. E.g., MMK chap. 1, MAv 6.8–119.

12. AKB ad AK 6.4.

could be taken to be bits of water. Substances such as pots and water particles are thus shown to be mere conceptual fictions, aggregates of more basic entities, things that are in our folk ontology only because our common discourse employs such concepts as *pot* and *water particle*. The natures that make such things be the sorts of things they are, are borrowed from other entities. The pot borrows its shape from the bits of clay from which it is built up. The water particle borrows its color and tangible nature from the color and tangibility tropes of which it is composed. The natures of pot and particle are not intrinsic; they lack *svabhāva* and so are not ultimately real. Candrakīrti would agree.

A word is in order at this point concerning how best to understand the source of these ontological scruples. In both sorts of cases the idea seems to be that aggregation is ontologically suspect, but why should that be? Why should the fact that a concept captures the concomitance of two or more things be taken to show that its application represents a superimposition on the world? If those things are in fact invariably concomitant, then why would their being bundled together in a single conceptual package not be a way of representing how things are independently of the concepts we happen to employ? The answer has it that this bundling is a concession to our interests and cognitive limitations and so is seen as not guaranteed to reflect how things objectively are. Taking our cue from the nun Vajirā, we should understand the term *chariot* to be a mere convenient designation, a way to denote wheels, axle, felly, and so on when assembled in a certain way, a single term that saves us the bother of having to designate each part individually and then indicate their mode of assembly.[13] Use of the *chariot* concept is thus more efficient and so has utility.

The anti-substance bias of Abhidharma metaphysics might initially seem puzzling. We do after all quite naturally think of whatever we take to be the elementary particles of the material world as entities in their own right. There is the particle, and then there is its mass, its charge, and so on as the properties that it has. As is so often the case, Nyāya-Vaiśeṣika does a good job of reflecting common sense when it classifies substances and tropes or property particulars as distinct categories. The question intimated by Vasubandhu's procedure of conceptual division is this: Just what is this thing, the particle itself, as distinct from the properties it is thought to bear? What the idea of an enumerative term reminds us of is that our puzzlement at this question might be explained

13. Tillemans questions this understanding of the genesis of our conventional ontology as motivated by considerations of efficiency (2017, 123 and 131n6; 2016, 10). My response is that such usage is said to involve enumerative expressions (*saṅkhā*; see MP 64) like *pair* or *dozen*, terms that are clearly used because they help us avoid unnecessary prolixity. The nun Vajirā invokes the chariot metaphor in her conversation with Māra in SN 1:5.10.

as the result of our taking too seriously what is in fact just a way of bundling many things under a single concept—out of a need for efficiency in communication. The entities of our folk ontology are products of *prapañca* or hypostatization, a falsifying tendency to posit referents for what are in fact mere enumerative concepts. Human minds are simply designed to lower the computational load when the cost is not too high. The Buddha's insight was that this cost includes the existential suffering that results from deployment of the "I" sense. Suffering is the result of our acquiescence in the conventional reality of persons. The Abhidharma quest for things that bear intrinsic nature is undertaken to disrupt this hypostatization.

Must Reductive Analysis Be Never-Ending?

Not all cases of what Candrakīrti calls analysis involve a transition from surface-level entities to things thought of as occupying a deeper level. Abhidharma analyses are typically ones that take us from a composite to its underlying constituents, with the composite entity thereby shown to be a merely useful conceptual fiction. For Abhidharma such reductive analyses are undertaken to find things that objectively ground our everyday conceptual practices (with their concessions to our interests and cognitive limitations). Mādhyamikas of course deny the existence of such objective grounding. Candrakīrti thinks that once reductive analysis has begun, it will never end. The Ābhidharmika thinks that we can find things that bear intrinsic natures; a Mādhyamika does not. Some of Candrakīrti's arguments for his conclusion about reductive analysis are more persuasive than others. I will not try to assess them here. What I want to address is what happens if he is right, and the only kind of truth there is turns out to be unanalyzed conventional truth. The price I am concerned a Buddhist must then pay is that there is then no visible escape from the Slough of Despond, existential suffering. To see why, we must revisit Vajirā's conversation with Māra about chariots and persons.

Neither Vajirā nor Māra is particularly concerned about the ontological status of chariots. What they care about is where persons fit in our scheme. What Vajirā means the example of the chariot to show is that analysis need not lead to utter elimination. While the chariot is not real strictly speaking, we can truthfully say that a chariot *just is* wheels, axle, felly, and so on assembled in the right way. Our common-sense belief in the reality of chariots is vindicated by their reduction. This is why statements about chariots can be conventionally *true*. When we believe there are such things as chariots, we're just looking through the wrong end of the microscope. *Chariot* is our way of accommodating our interests and cognitive limitations, but that accommodation has a ground in how things actually are. Now apply this lesson to *person*. If its analysis in terms of causally connected sets of psychophysical elements is to likewise yield vindication and not elimination, we must acknowledge not only the cognitive limitations (or, less politely, error) behind its introduction but also its utility. Yes, the "I" sense is the source of existential suffering, but is the use of the concept an unmitigated disaster? Clearly not. Prudential rationality requires it, as does the moral practice of assigning praise and blame to the actions of ourselves and others. Since we have an interest in seeing to it that our fellow creatures develop concern for their own long-term self-interest and for the interests of others, it is eminently understandable that we should deploy just such a concept.[14] It's just that we end up taking persons too seriously. Māra wants us to retain our single-minded fixation on them, since Māra delights in the suffering of others. Vajirā wants us to instead see through them—as fictions, yes, but fictions that are often useful. And to pull that off, she thinks we must suppose that analysis ends somewhere, that there are real truth-makers to be found. The neither-identical-nor-distinct argument against the ultimate reality of chariots tells us what those truth-makers must be like: they must bear their natures intrinsically. The chariot is not ultimately real precisely because all its properties are extrinsic—borrowed from the properties of its parts. And for Vajirā's strategy to work, there must be things whose properties are their own. Analysis must end somewhere; it must be reductive.

I claim that the dismal slough yawns before us if we hold that analysis does not end where it must, in things with intrinsic natures, and that their absence would mean that we must acquiesce in conventional truth as the only sort of truth there can be. Acquiescing means doing nothing to dispel the "I" sense. And that in turn means no cessation of existential suffering. Yes, Candrakīrti says that persons are a myth, an illusory magic show. But he says exactly the same thing not only about chariots, pots, forests, and the like but also about *skandhas*, *āyatanas*, *dhātus*, *svalakṣaṇas*, atoms, and so on. So either they all go, or we keep them all. And if we keep them all, we are not to inquire about how they stand with respect to one another. Do not ask how the pot stands with respect to its constituent atoms, how the forest stands with respect to the trees, how the person stands with respect to the psychophysical elements. And now I ask: How is the "I" sense to be dispelled if we cannot say that a person is merely a causal series of psychophysical elements?[15]

Of course, Candrakīrti is well aware of the trap here. In his refutation of

---

14. The "ownerless suffering" argument of BCA 8.90–103 can be seen as indirectly making precisely this point about prudential rationality.

15. I confess that I may have Tillemans entirely wrong here, and he may in fact take the goal of

the personalist (*pudgalavāda*) view, Candrakīrti points out that merely refuting the existence of the sort of simple, eternal self posited by philosophers of a Nyāya or Sāṃkhya persuasion will not bring about the cessation of suffering. But this is precisely what he sees personalists as saying when they claim that the Buddha merely meant to deny the existence of the philosophers' self and not the existence of the person. Candrakīrti compares this to someone who, having seen a snake in the walls of their house, tries to allay their fears by rejoicing at the absence of an elephant inside (MAv 6.141). Belief in the philosophers' self is a mere surface manifestation of a problem that runs much deeper. Its source is not philosophical elaborations of common sense but common sense itself. What his "no analysis" stipulation seems to guarantee, however, is that the problem can only be addressed by wholesale rejection of the project of truth-seeking.[16]

A Contextualist Path Forward?

I find persuasive Tillemans's characterization of the Madhyamaka project as quietist. He is, I think, quite right to say that the task of Nāgārjuna and his followers is to help us overcome the urge to engage in serious ontology. This is what I take Nāgārjuna to be indicating when he says in the dedicatory verse of the *Mūlamadhyamakārikā* that the goal is "the auspicious cessation of hypostatization" (*prapañcopaśamaṃ śivam*).[17] What is it about doing metaphysics, though, that makes it not just a source but *the* source of existential suffering? If dispelling the "I" sense is the goal, then it is not clear why one should have to become convinced that the pursuit of ontological grounding is futile to achieve that end. Indeed Candrakīrti himself seems to be of two minds about this. In his debate with the personalists, he has them quote the Buddha to the effect that the self is the *skandhas* to defend their view that the person is real. He then replies that since the Buddha elsewhere denies that the *skandhas* constitute the self, his intent in this passage is simply to deny that there is anything more to the person than the *skandhas* (MAv 6.132). And tellingly,

Buddhist practice to be something other than extirpation of the "I" sense. He did once describe a state lacking the "I" sense as "pathological" (Tillemans 1995, 8).

16. Or, as some Mādhyamikas seem to have thought, making ultimate truth something inexpressible and available only to the fully enlightened. Candrakīrti himself seems to gesture in this direction at MAv 6.28–29. It is unclear, though, what a deflationist could make of a truth that is inexpressible.

17. McClintock (2023, 337) puts this as the point that "relinquishing grasping at existence and nonexistence and cultivating a resolute positionlessness stops the arousal of afflictive emotions, as well as harmful views and the arguments they engender."

Candrakīrti describes the Buddha's teaching as an instance of corrected conventional truth (*aviparītasaṃvṛttisatya*). But how is conventional truth being corrected here? Clearly, by means of analysis. A person, the Buddha is here understood as saying, is nothing over and above a causal series of sets of psychophysical elements.[18] Persons are reducible to *skandha*s. This move bears all the marks of reductive analysis.

And yet at the same time, Candrakīrti believes he has arguments showing that *skandha*s, as things that purportedly originate, could not have *svabhāva*. Is it that it's permissible for buddhas to engage in reductive analysis but not for us ordinary worldlings? Is it that buddhas know to stop at the level of *skandha*s and not go on to show that these are no more ultimately real than chariots, armies, or pots? There may in fact be something to this idea of knowing when to stop, and we will return to it. But there is nothing obvious about the difference between the enlightened and those still mired in ignorance and error that would explain why only the former can safely engage in Abhidharma-style reductive analysis. Buddhas do, after all, tailor their teachings to the unliberated to help them attain the cessation of suffering. So if their teachings include a version of conventional truth that has been subjected to analysis, one would think we unenlightened folk should be able to follow them in their reasoning. Otherwise, why would it be helpful?

Candrakīrti has interesting things to say about any sort of analysis that sets out to discover the ultimate truth. It fosters, he says, love of one's own view and anger toward the view of one's opponent. For this reason, it is not conducive to liberation; indeed, it seems to reinforce the defilements and thus keep one mired in suffering. One should instead practice the sort of analysis that Mādhyamikas recommend, the deflationary sort that brings about a quietist cessation of hypostatization (MAv 6.119). And there may be some truth to the claim that engaging in the sort of ontological theorizing that is at the heart of Abhidharma-style analysis might only strengthen the "I" sense. This would, of course, be perverse, since the point of the practice is supposed to be just the opposite. But for precisely that reason, the practitioner of such analysis might well be blind to the deleterious effects of their practice, pounding the table over the nonexistence of a self. So one can see how the Abhidharma practice of reductive analysis might seem incompatible with a Buddhist project. Still, very few of the unenlightened engage in the practice of serious ontology, so this can hardly be the principal cause of suffering.

So let's return to the idea of knowing when to stop (or, better, pause)

---

18. This "nothing over and above" seems equivalent to what McClintock (this volume) calls the REALLY operator.

analysis. The slogan "The ultimate truth is that there is no ultimate truth" was meant to capture the idea that liberation from suffering is achieved through the cessation of *prapañca*. We have just seen how odd this seems, but perhaps the idea is simply that reductive analysis is necessary but not sufficient for attaining the liberating insight, that it must eventually be succeeded by the sort of analysis Candrakīrti favors, the sort that undermines the very idea of ultimate truth. Consider in this light Nāgārjuna's investigation of the self, *Mūlamadhyamakārikā* chapter 18. In verses 1–5, Nāgārjuna presents the orthodox Abhidharma understanding of nonself and the path to its realization. But then in the next six verses he argues that it is insight into the emptiness of all dharmas that is required for liberation. Why might this be? What I would suggest is that the metaphysical theorizing necessary to fully grasp the idea of nonself can itself pose a subtle obstacle to genuine liberation from the "I" sense. Liberation requires that one first become a serious ontologist and then use the analytical tools of serious ontology to undermine that very enterprise. This will raise the suspicion that the teaching of nonself is actually false, with a consequence unacceptable to the Buddhist: that at least some of the Buddha's teachings are deceptive. Nāgārjuna responds by claiming that the Buddha employs a technique of "graded teaching" (*anuśāsana*), using assertions tailored to meet the pedagogical needs of the audience in question (MMK 18.8). But to put these suspicions fully to rest, a Mādhyamika might need to deploy a contextualist semantics. This will allow us to say that what the Buddha taught when he taught the Abhidharma was not in fact false.

We are familiar with terms whose reference varies in dependence on facts about the context of utterance, such as personal pronouns ("you," "they") and indexicals ("here," "now"). For statements containing such terms, we would agree that to know what is said by the utterance of such a statement, we must know the context in which the statement is uttered. A radical semantic contextualism claims this is true of all statements. One reason for saying this is that at least one relevant factor in a context of utterance concerns what will count as truth-makers for an assertion. A Mādhyamika will immediately object that invoking truth-makers is deeply problematic in that it quickly leads to the metaphysical realist notion of grounding in an objectively determinate reality. But the radical semantic contextualist will reply that the truth-makers they have in mind are quite innocent. Here is how. In the case of assertions, a given context of utterance will involve two or more interlocutors engaged in a joint project of problem-solving: exchanging information and engaging in joint reasoning concerning what is to be done. If their exchange is to be productive, there needs to be tacit agreement about how disputes are to be resolved.[19] Sometimes this will not involve questions of the level of analysis. If I assert that the bridge is unsafe and you question my assertion, we might agree that the issue can be settled in terms of properties of the bridge itself: when we look, we just see that it is shaky. It is, we might then say, just intrinsically shaky. In other cases, though, we might need to move to the level of the constituent parts and examine those of their properties relevant to questions of structural soundness. Or we might feel we must descend yet one level further, to the chemical constituents of the structural members and seek the answer there. We can imagine possible contexts of utterance for each of these scenarios, depending on the needs, interests, and cognitive limitations of the parties to the speech context. A semantic contextualist could then claim that since the truth-makers for what we thought of as a single assertion ("The bridge is unsafe") differ from one case to the next, these are actually different assertions in the different cases. (Compare "It is warm in here" uttered in the distinct contexts of the sauna and the malfunctioning walk-in cooler.) Now to treat some states of affairs as truth-makers for certain assertions is to invoke intrinsic natures. If we are satisfied that we need go no deeper than the level of the bridge's structural members to assess its safety, we are then committed to taking the properties of those members as intrinsic (and the bridge's being either stable or unstable as extrinsic). A Mādhyamika will point out that this agreement is contingent on facts about our interests and cognitive limitations as they impact on this specific context. That we agree to stop at this level of analysis does not show that we have in fact found the intrinsic natures that explain everything at this and all higher levels of analysis. This formulation of semantic contextualism thus shows that natures deemed intrinsic are not intrinsic across all contexts. This is how the truth-makers invoked by the radical semantic contextualist are innocent. At the same time, though, the Buddha did not lie when he claimed that the person is just a causal series of sets of *skandha*s. His commitment to dharmas with their own *svabhāva*s is not contradicted by his saying elsewhere, in a different context of utterance, that all dharmas are devoid of *svabhāva*. Being a skilled pedagogue, the Buddha knew where analysis would stop for his interlocutors in a given context. What he then said was (conventionally) true.

I do not pretend that Mādhyamikas actually embraced radical semantic contextualism. Still, it is true that a kind of contextualism may be seen already in the precursor to the distinction between ultimate and conventional truth—

---

19. To call the agreement tacit is to say that it need not be any more than dispositions on the part of the participants: if they disagreed over the truth value of some assertion, here are the sorts of states of affairs they would take as settling the matter.

namely, the distinction between texts that are fully explicated (*nītārtha*) and those requiring interpretation (*neyārtha*). The latter distinction has to do with the sort of audience the Buddha was addressing when he delivered the discourse in question. So semantic contextualism does have a Buddhist pedigree. What a radical form would do for Madhyamaka is allow for an innocent use of reductive analysis in its refutations of the views of metaphysical realists. For a radical form shrinks the world (*loka*) of "acknowledged by the world" (*lokaprasiddha*) down to a specific context of utterance. What count as truth-makers, things with intrinsic nature, vary in accordance with the background beliefs and needs of the speaker and audience being addressed. The uninstructed individual, someone who implicitly accepts our common folk ontology, will agree, when asked, that questions about personal identity can be answered in terms of facts about *skandha*s, *dhātu*s, and *āyatana*s. An external-world realist Ābhidharmika may be made to agree that questions about physical dharmas are to be settled in terms of facts about sensory cognition and so on. This does not represent progress toward the metaphysical realist dream of apprehending how things ultimately are. The point is strictly soteriological: weakening the "I" sense of a specific audience with particular interests and cognitive limitations. Reductive analysis practiced under this understanding also redeems a place for the sort of worldly expertise of "the wise" that uses reductive analysis. The ophthalmologist can cure myodesopsia precisely because ophthalmology reduces the eye to its constituents of lens, retina, and vitreous. (The problem plaguing the *taimirika* is in the vitreous.) A Madhyamaka embrace of radical semantic contextualism would allow it to forge a path out of the dismal slough. Analysis is not so bad after all for Mādhyamikas. Perhaps Candrakīrti should consider seeing a therapist.

Abbreviations

AK	*Abhidharmakośa* of Vasubandhu. See Pradhan 1975.
AKB	*Abhidharmakośabhāṣyam* of Vasubandhu. See Pradhan 1975.
BCA	*Bodhicāryāvatāra* of Śāntideva. See Vaidya 1960.
MAv	*Madhyamakāvatāra* of Candrakīrti. See Li 2015.
MMK	*Mūlamadhyamakakārikā* of Nāgārjuna. See La Vallée Poussin [1903–13] 1970.
MP	*Milindapañha*. See Heim 2025.
PP	*Prasannapadā* of Candrakīrti. See La Vallée Poussin [1903–13] 1970.
SN	*Saṃyutta Nikāya*. See Feer 1884–98.

Bibliography

Cowherds, the. 2011. *Moonshadows: Conventional Truth in Buddhist Philosophy.* New York: Oxford University Press.

Feer, M. Leon. 1884–98. *Saṃyutta Nikāya.* 5 vols. London: Pali Text Society.

Heim, Maria, trans. and ed. 2025. *The Questions of Milinda.* Murthy Classical Library of India. Cambridge, MA: Harvard University Press.

La Vallée Poussin, Louis de, ed. (1903–13) 1970. *Mūlamadhyamakakārikās (Mādhyamikasūtras) de Nāgārjuna, avec la Prasannapadā Commentaire de Candrakīrti.* Bibliotheca Buddhica 4. Osnabrück: Biblio Verlag.

Li Xuezhu, ed. 2015. "*Madhyamakāvatāra-kārikā* Chapter 6." *Journal of Indian Philosophy* 43: 1–30.

McClintock, Sara. 2023. "Six Verses from Nāgārjuna's Lost Treatise Establishing the Transactional." *Journal of Indian Philosophy* 51: 319–41.

Newland, Guy Martin. 2011. "Weighing the Butter, Levels of Explanation, and Falsification: Models of the Conventional in Tsongkhapa's Account of Madhyamaka." In *Moonshadows: Conventional Truth in Buddhist Philosophy,* by the Cowherds, 57–72. New York: Oxford University Press.

Pradhan, Prahlad, ed. 1975. *Abhidharmakośabhāṣyam of Vasubandhu.* Patna: Jayaswal Research Institute.

Siderits, Mark. 2003. *Personal Identity and Buddhist Philosophy: Empty Persons.* Aldershot, UK: Ashgate. (Rev. ed., 2015.)

———. 2011. "Is Everything Connected to Everything Else? What the Gopīs Know." In *Moonshadows: Conventional Truth in Buddhist Philosophy,* by the Cowherds, 167–80. New York: Oxford University Press.

Tillemans, Tom J. F. 1995. "What Would It Be Like to Be Selfless? Hīnayānist Versions, Mahāyānist Versions and Derek Parfit." *The Numata Yehan Lecture in Buddhism 1995.* Calgary: University of Calgary.

———. 2011. "How Far Can a Mādhyamika Buddhist Reform Conventional Truth? Dismal Relativism, Fictionalism, Easy-Easy Truth, and the Alternatives." In *Moonshadows: Conventional Truth in Buddhist Philosophy,* by the Cowherds, 151–65. New York: Oxford University Press.

———. 2016. *How Do Mādhyamikas Think? And Other Essays on the Buddhist Philosophy of the Middle.* Studies in Indian and Tibetan Buddhism. Somerville, MA: Wisdom Publications.

———. 2017. "Philosophical Quietism in Nāgārjuna and Early Madhyamaka." In *The Oxford Handbook of Indian Philosophy,* edited by Jonardon Ganeri, 110–32. New York: Oxford University Press.

Vaidya, P. L., ed. 1960. *The Bodhicāryāvatāra of Śāntideva with the Commentary Pañjikā of Prajñākaramati.* Dharbanga: Mithila Institute.

Materials for the Study of Cowherds:
Are Their Beliefs Normative for Candrakīrti?

Dan Arnold

Honoring Tom Tillemans

I spent more time with Tom's two-volume *Materials for the Study of Āryadeva, Dharmapāla, and Candrakīrti* (1990) than with anything else I studied as a doctoral student. With its austerely philological title and unadorned bright yellow covers (hallmarks of Indological publications from Vienna), this work was astounding for its singular expertise in philology and philosophy alike, showing that the methodological imperatives of these disciplines are not, as often supposed, mutually exclusive. At the same time, it showed—as I particularly appreciate only now that I have been consulting it for decades—that being adequate to both disciplines at once takes a lot of work; these volumes are to be admired as much for their authoritative translations and critical editions (from Sanskrit, Tibetan, *and Chinese*) as for cogently showing that the likes of Āryadeva, Dharmapāla, and Candrakīrti debated questions that make contact with questions centrally at issue, as well, for the likes of Wilfrid Sellars. Both volumes are among the most heavily annotated books in my library.

I have continued learning from Tom ever since, so it culminated decades of conversation when contributors to the present volume gathered, in May 2023, to workshop their contributions in Madison, Wisconsin. There, I realized how directly Tom's work has suffused my intellectual life but also how many other intellectual relationships that matter to me likewise implicate Tom. Recalling, in particular, a 2006 workshop that Tom convened for an Amsterdam conference of the International Society for the Study of Argumentation, I realized that virtually everyone gathered in Madison for the present volume had likewise been in Amsterdam in 2006 discussing "argumentation in Buddhist philosophy"; no wonder I remember that as a favorite academic event.[1] Tom's involvement has sustained the flourishing of many of the scholarly conversations to which I am party, and it's a great pleasure to offer this essay as expressing my appreciation of that; notwithstanding its critical assessment of one aspect of Tom's reading of Candrakīrti, this essay honors the impossibility of my having developed any worthwhile ideas on the subject without having spent decades learning from Tom.

Are the Beliefs of Cowherds Normative for Candrakīrti?

It has lately become commonplace to worry that Candrakīrti's Madhyamaka is a "dismal slough" of relativism, as suggested by an essay Tom Tillemans first published in 2011 (henceforth cited in a 2016 reprint).[2] As that essay's subtitle clearly indicates, Tillemans takes a dim view of Madhyamaka's options when it comes to making philosophical sense of conventional truth (*saṃvṛtisatya*): "Dismal Relativism, Fictionalism, Easy-Easy Truth, and the Alternatives." Taking Candrakīrti's view to epitomize the dismal alternative, Tillemans represents that view as "an extreme conservatism" about conventional truth: "a Mādhyamika's principal epistemic task," he says of this, "is just to passively acquiesce and duplicate" whatever ordinary people take for true (2016, 47). Later elaborating this reading, Tillemans compares a scriptural passage in Sanskrit that Candrakīrti often cites in support his idea of conventional truth—a Mahāyāna passage "of unspecified provenance," Tillemans emphasizes (2022, 225)[3]—with a parallel passage from the Pāli canon. In Candrakīrti's version, the Buddha is represented as deferring to *everyone* (*loka*, "the world"), whereas the Pāli text has the Buddha defer only to those *with expertise* (those whom the world calls *paṇḍita*).[4] That Candrakīrti favors the former when he could (presumably) have quoted something like the Pāli, Tillemans suggests, would seem to confirm that Candrakīrti upheld a "populist" conception of conventional truth, adequacy to which demands only

1. Published in *Argumentation* 22.1 (2008), the conference papers represent most of the present volume's contributors.

2. Tillemans 2011, 152; as reprinted, "dismal slough" becomes "dismal position" (2016, 47).

3. Earlier (Tillemans 2016, 58n1) he had suggested the version cited by Candrakīrti may be from the *Trisaṃvaranirdeśaparivarta* chapter of the Ratnakūṭa collection of sūtras.

4. See Tillemans 2022, 224–27. Expanding the circle of parallel texts considered, Newman (2024) cogently challenges Tillemans's characterization of Candrakīrti's favored proof-text; see, as well, Salvini 2019. Both Newman and Salvini provide illuminating discussion of this and other ideas central to this essay.

"acquiescing, across the board, in the actually attested opinions of the lowest common denominator" (2022, 230).

On Tillemans's reading, that is what Candrakīrti means whenever he invokes the example of things familiar to "everyone from cowherds on up"—familiar, that is, to persons whom Candrakīrti takes to be of "unrefined" intellect,[5] hence to Tillemans's lowest common denominator. According to Tillemans, Candrakīrti thus takes the example of cowherds as integral to a definition of conventional truth (*saṃvṛtisatya*), which consists, on this definition, merely in what unrefined persons believe. Following Paul Boghossian's discussion of reductionist accounts of normativity (1989), we might say the view Tillemans attributes to Candrakīrti amounts to a *communitarian* conception of *saṃvṛtisatya*; on such a view, the normative status of conventional truth makes sense only with reference to a community of actors bound by its norms, as there is no way "to define a distinction, at the level of the individual, between correct and incorrect dispositions" (Boghossian 1989, 535). *Norms*, that is, constitutively involve the possibility of deviations therefrom, and a communitarian account identifies that with the possibility of an individual's deviation from a community. The problem, Boghossian comments, is that a *community* of language users can still be "disposed to call both horses and deceptively horsey looking cows on dark nights 'horse'"—but a communitarian account "cannot call the[se] *mistakes*, for they are the community's dispositions," so the original difficulty is just "duplicated at the level of the community" (1989, 536). To that extent, reference to a community cannot by itself account for normativity.

If an account of *saṃvṛtisatya* cannot distinguish any candidate instances as possibly mistaken, it cannot make sense of *saṃvṛtisatya* as any kind of *truth*; I concur with Tillemans in thinking the conception of conventional truth he attributes to Candrakīrti is problematic. The question is whether that really is Candrakīrti's view. Here, in Tillemans's translation, is the passage he adduces as expressing the "dismal" view he takes for Candrakīrti's:

> Why should we analyze it when [a fact such as] the production
> of sprouts and the like being conditioned by seeds and so forth is
> just simply acknowledged by everyone from cowherds on up? Judi-
> cious people should not analyze in order to ascertain the natures
> of entities, because [if they did,] it would follow that there would
> be no end [to such analysis] and it would follow that it would not
> be judicious.[6]

5. On the general characterization "unrefined," see Li 2019, 69; cf. note 17 below.

6. Tillemans 2016, 49; here and subsequently, the bracketed items are original to the translations

Clearly, this passage rejects the idea that proponents of Madhyamaka owe us a philosophical analysis of causation (of "the production of sprouts and the like"). Much less clear, I think, is whether anything here suggests that conventional truth just is what is "acknowledged by everyone from cowherds on up"; indeed, the passage doesn't actually say anything about *saṃvṛtisatya* per se.

But here's the thing: *the foregoing passage is not by Candrakīrti*. What Tillemans adduces as epitomizing Madhyamaka's dismal option is actually a passage from Kamalaśīla,[7] who is here stating the view (without attribution) as a foil for his own. To be sure, Tillemans is right that "important aspects" of the foregoing passage suggest Kamalaśīla "might have been thinking of the sixth-century Prāsaṅgika-Mādhyamika philosopher Candrakīrti"—but Tillemans sensibly qualifies that, immediately adding, "or at least (to be even less committal) someone like him" (2016, 49). Nonetheless, Tillemans represents Kamalaśīla's critique of this view—which identifies much the same problem distilled above from Boghossian's treatment of normativity—as counting against Candrakīrti. Responding to the foregoing passage, Kamalaśīla thus says, "it is possible that what is [generally] acknowledged is wrong"; absent that possibility, Kamalaśīla adds, nobody could be wrong about anything.[8] Tillemans commends Kamalaśīla for thus recognizing "the needed normativity in the concept of truth" and for showing "the populist alternative as rationally disastrous" (2022, 232).

Tillemans's "populist" alternative is indeed a problematic conception of truth. However, appropriate caveats about whether this is *Candrakīrti's* alternative have vanished as Tillemans's assessment has hardened into received wisdom, reflected in the declaration that begins the main section of Mark Siderits's contribution to the present volume: "For Candrakīrti, conventional truth is 'what is known even to cowherds and women.'"[9]

quoted, which in this case is that of Tillemans (from which, however, I have omitted Tillemans's parenthetic provision of Tibetan and Sanskrit terms).

7. In particular, from his *Sarvadharmaniḥsvabhāvasiddhi*, extant only in Tibetan; for the text, see Tillemans 2016, 59–60n6.

8. Tillemans 2016, 49. As reflected by my last clause, I take Kamalaśīla's "otherwise" (presumably Sanskrit *anyathā*) differently than Tillemans, who thus translates the whole response: "it is possible that what is generally acknowledged is wrong. Otherwise [if analysis using *pramāṇa* were unnecessary], no one who applied himself to what he had himself acknowledged would ever end up being unreliable about anything at all" (2016, 49; bracketed insertion original).

9. See above, page 68.

Analyses That Are Normative for Candrakīrti

In fact, Candrakīrti says no such thing. The idea that conventional truth is just what cowherds believe is a caricature of Candrakīrti's thought, and it badly misrepresents the significance of his appeals to the example of things familiar to the unrefined. To be sure, such appeals figure centrally in Candrakīrti's discussions of the two truths, wherein Candrakīrti is often concerned to emphasize respects in which *saṃvṛtisatya* is basically deficient. Candrakīrti is also concerned, though, to clarify why conventional truth must remain intelligible; although it "comes into being as projected through mere error" (*viparyāsamātrāsāditātmabhāvasattākā*), he says in the *Prasannapadā*, *saṃvṛtisatya* is nonetheless the "basis of accumulating the roots of merit conducive to liberation."[10] Indeed, Candrakīrti's Madhyamaka is distinguished by his way of emphasizing that conventional truth remains intelligible in the wake of Madhyamaka critique, and Candrakīrti's project must therefore make sense as *recuperating* conventional truth. Before examining passages in which Candrakīrti appeals to what is understood by the unrefined, it thus behooves us first to appreciate that Candrakīrti understood *saṃvṛti* to have, as thus specified in the *Prasannapadā*, at least these three senses:

> *Saṃvṛti* is completely concealing (*varaṇam*); this is because ignorance, insofar as it completely delimits the reality of all the basic categories of existence, is explained as concealing that those are without self. Alternatively, *saṃvṛti* is mutually dependent occurrence (*parasparasaṃbhavana*), in the sense that one thing depends upon another. Finally, *saṃvṛti* is customary agreement (*saṃketa*), meaning everyday commerce (*lokavyavahāra*)—and that is distinguished by things like words and referents, cognition and cognizables, and so on.[11]

---

10. Translated from La Vallée Poussin 1970a, 68.7–69.1 (unless otherwise noted, all translations are my own); cf. Arnold 2005, 176–77.

11. Translated from La Vallée Poussin 1970a, 492.10–12; cf. Shenghai Li 2019, 50 et passim. Reading the same passage, Tillemans (2022, 227) attributes Candrakīrti's three senses entirely to uncertainty about the underlying verbal root, commenting that Candrakīrti "seems to have been unable or unwilling to decide, and thus gave us three choices." I think it unlikely that Candrakīrti's philosophical position is driven by what a Sanskrit text or word form demands or allows; as well versed in the Sanskrit grammatical tradition as Candrakīrti is, his exploitation of lexical ambiguities is more likely to be philosophically motivated than the other way around.

How any particular discussion of *saṃvṛtisatya* is to be understood will vary, surely, depending on which of these ideas is to the fore. The influential presentation early in the *Madhyamakāvatāra*'s sixth chapter, for example, begins with Candrakīrti's introducing *saṃvṛtisatya* (at 6.23) as salient for its "concealing" how things really are. While that is clearly to emphasize the basically deficient character of *saṃvṛtisatya*,[12] the next three verses take pains to clarify that the deficiency is not such as to vacate *saṃvṛtisatya* of normative significance. As Candrakīrti will contend at *Madhyamakāvatāra* 6.26, then, even according to his conception of it as basically "concealing" reality, conventional truth nonetheless affords resources sufficient to judge some views wholly mistaken:

> Even for customary usage (*lokataḥ*), of course, there is no reality in
> what is variously posited by idolaters (their heads nodding with the
> sleep of ignorance) or in what is imagined in case of phantoms and
> mirages and the like.[13]

We will return to this verse below, when we examine passages in which Candrakīrti invokes the example of things familiar to the unrefined and where our last example will be from Candrakīrti's prose commentary on this verse. For now, I just want to emphasize that the contention of *Madhyamakāvatāra* 6.26 could make sense only if Candrakīrti's account is not, in fact, without normative resources. Tillemans represents Candrakīrti's account of *saṃvṛtisatya* as utterly lacking in this regard; if we are to appreciate the sense it makes for Candrakīrti to contend otherwise, we should first note that Tillemans's misgivings really have to do only with Candrakīrti's refusal of demands especially for *epistemological* warrant.

In this regard, Tillemans follows the Tibetan philosopher Tsongkhapa

---

12. Here, as at the outset of the foregoing passage from the *Prasannapadā*, it is also to exploit the sense of the verbal root √*vṛ*.

13. MA 6.26, translated from the Sanskrit in Li Xuezhu 2015, 7. Regarding the admittedly questionable translation of *tīrtha* as "idolater," see note 42, below. As I have discussed elsewhere (Arnold, forthcoming), "variously" here renders the indeclinable *yathāsvam*; most modern translations, perforce done from the Tibetan translation (until recently the only extant), read as La Vallée Poussin took the Tibetan to suggest: "Les conceptions imaginaires des hérétiques (*tīrthikas*) troublés par le sommeil de l'ignorance, – **comme l'*ātman* . . .**" (1910, 302; bold emphasis added). Taking the Tibetan to represent Sanskrit *yathâtma*, this reads the phrase as adducing the *self* (*ātma*) as exemplifying things posited by non-Buddhists. La Vallée Poussin had misgivings about that reading, however, and the now-available Sanskrit text confirms his suspicion: "La traduction proposée ne me satisfait que médiocrement, – *Peut-être = yathāsvam = chacun à sa manière, chacun pour soi . . .*" (1910, 302n3; emphasis added).

(1357–1419), whose influential appropriation of Candrakīrti's Madhyamaka is distinguished chiefly by its introduction of the tools of epistemology (*pramāṇaśāstra*)—in particular, by Tsongkhapa's appropriation of the generally empiricist epistemology elaborated by Dharmakīrti (ca. 600–660), which Tsongkhapa took to bolster Candrakīrti's account of conventional truth. Tsongkhapa's case for that idea is not straightforward, at least not exegetically; while Candrakīrti didn't know Dharmakīrti's works (the two were roughly contemporaneous), Candrakīrti advanced a cogent critique of the epistemology of Dignāga (ca. 480–540), whose project was carried on by Dharmakīrti. The upshot of Candrakīrti's critique is that Dignāga's epistemology not only fails to disclose reality but fails *even as an account of conventional truth*.[14] That would seem to foreclose Tsongkhapa's contention that epistemology, for Candrakīrti, is innocuous so long as its scope is limited to conventional truth.

Of course, Tsongkhapa may have had reasonable philosophical motives for overriding Candrakīrti on this point—but it may also be that Tsongkhapa was motivated by considerations having more to do with his contemporaneous Tibetan interlocutors than with anything at issue for Candrakīrti.[15] In any case, a regrettable upshot of Tsongkhapa's influential reading of Candrakīrti has been to lend credence to the idea that Candrakīrti's conception of conventional truth (*saṃvṛtisatya*) requires epistemological grounding if it is to make sense as any kind of truth. If, as I would contend, that is just the presupposition Candrakīrti's critique of epistemology targets, it clearly begs the question to judge his critique deficient for its refusal to adduce epistemological warrant. In fact, we will see that in his discussions invoking the example of cowherds, Candrakīrti suggests lines of argument that make sense of his rejection of epistemology as first philosophy; before turning to these passages, however, it behooves us first to appreciate that despite his uncompromising rejection of Dignāga's epistemology, Candrakīrti readily invokes other sorts of analyses as normative.

In the first place, Candrakīrti regularly invokes typically Ābhidharmika analyses as normative. Candrakīrti himself emphasizes Abhidharma's

14. Dignāga's views, which epitomize "epistemology" for Candrakīrti, are the subject of a lengthy critique in chapter 1 of the *Prasannapadā*, as discussed in Arnold 2005. On Candrakīrti's contention that Dignāga's approach fails to be adequate to conventional truth, see especially Arnold 2005, 175–83 and 280n32.

15. John Newman comments, for example, that Tsongkhapa contended chiefly with Tibetan philosophical opponents who were "anti-rationalist and nihilistic" interpreters of Candrakīrti (at least "in his opinion, in one way or another"); Candrakīrti instead targeted "'realist' essentialists," i.e., "Buddhists like Dignāga, Dharmapāla, and Bhāviveka, who, in Candrakīrti's opinion, all advocated some degree of essentialism (*sasvabhāvabhāvavāda*)" (Newman 2022).

significance as target of Madhyamaka critique,[16] so it is easy to forget that that critique was never proposed as showing Ābhidharmika categories or analyses as *false*; what Madhyamaka purports to show, rather, is just that even Abhidharma's systematic analyses cannot make sense as more than conventionally true. However, insofar as the upshot of Madhyamaka critique is that nothing could ultimately make sense as more than conventionally real, Madhyamaka's deflation of Ābhidharmika analyses does not undermine the intelligibility or utility thereof. There is no contradiction in Candrakīrti's framing Madhyamaka critique as targeting typically Ābhidharmika presuppositions, even as he repeatedly invokes characteristically Ābhidharmika analyses in all sorts of contexts. Indeed, Candrakīrti's works include a *Treatise on the Five Aggregates* (*Pañcaskandhaprakaraṇa*), "the only such treatise written by a Madhyamaka author in India," as Shenghai Li comments (2019, 67). According to its opening verse, this treatise defines and contextualizes Ābhidharmika categories "in order to expand the intelligence of those whose intelligence is unrefined."[17]

Notwithstanding his own emphasis on Abhidharma as a target of Mādhyamika critique, then, Candrakīrti nonetheless commends Abhidharma as capable of *deepening* conventionally true understanding. Indeed, Ābhidharmika analyses are not just conventionally true on Candrakīrti's view but are *normative* for his idea of conventional truth. As Mattia Salvini explains to similar effect, Candrakīrti takes Abhidharma's impersonal analyses to be "only one step removed from the final step of analysis," whereas common-sense entities (paradigmatically, *persons*) are "several steps removed from that finer step"; thus, assent to common-sense entities fails "even [to] match the 'selflessness of persons,' the level at which one speaks of causal processes but not anymore of personal identities" (Salvini 2023, 410–11). Candrakīrti allows, in other words, that persons and other conventionally real entities do indeed admit of redescription in Abhidharma's reductionist terms, and insofar as such analyses deepen the understanding of the selflessness of persons, he urges, they are to be cultivated—even as Madhyamaka critique remains concerned to show the emptiness not just of *persons* but also of the *dharmas* of Ābhidharmika analyses.

Madhyamaka critique culminates, Salvini thus says, when "the analysis will have to shift to a mode unavailable to the Abhidharma, revealing that

16. Cf. note 38 below.

17. Translated from Lindtner 1979, 95; cf. Shenghai Li (2019, 69), who notes that the term I've here translated as "unrefined" (*sbyangs pa med pa*) is redolent of another Tibetan expression (*ma byang ba*) used in translating Candrakīrti's characterization of people like cowherds; exploring the range of these expressions (which Li takes to suggest "unpracticed, unlearned, untrained, unrefined, and not purified"), Li says the upshot of this opening verse is thus to commend Abhidharma as beneficial for "people not schooled in the way of the conventional" (2019, 69).

the atom is untenable: analysis has exhausted itself in not finding the initial object of analysis anywhere" (2023, 411). This shift in analytic perspective can come about, however, only if Ābhidharmika analysis really has exhausted itself; there is no point in Madhyamaka's emphasizing the emptiness *of dharmas* unless "persons" have first been redescribed as consisting in those. And while proponents of Abhidharma "may not be willing to continue the analysis until the very ideas of 'perception' and 'entities' are shown to be illusory," Salvini says, "in some sense they have, according to Candrakīrti, done half of the Madhyamaka job."[18]

Salvini has also focused on the significance of Sanskrit disciplines of grammar and linguistic analysis (the tradition of *vyākaraṇa*) in the works of Nāgārjuna and, especially, Candrakīrti.[19] It makes sense that Candrakīrti would take his bearings from the grammatical tradition because "familiarity to everyone" (*lokaprasiddhi*) is, for Candrakīrti, a major constraint on philosophical reason (although *how* this constrains philosophical reason remains to be discussed below). As often noted, grammatical and linguistic analysis were as axiomatically normative for Indian philosophy as geometry was for Greek, so Candrakīrti could reasonably take these analyses as epitomizing widely prevailing norms. More significantly, Candrakīrti's "usage of grammar to uncover presuppositions" (Salvini 2023, 408) reflects what strike me as philosophically principled commitments. In fact, Candrakīrti's orientation to these norms—evident in predilections akin to P. F. Strawson's ordinary language philosophy—is the basis of his aforementioned critique of Dignāga's epistemology, which Candrakīrti frames in terms of just one question: Can Dignāga's epistemology make sense, as claimed, as accounting merely for "ordinary affairs involving epistemic norms and their objects" (*pramāṇaprameyavyavahāro laukiko*)?[20] This cannot be maintained, Candrakīrti argues, precisely because Dignāga's epistemology is oriented by its tendentious definitions of ordinary words (especially *pratyakṣa* and *svalakṣaṇa*); to the extent that Dignāga's peculiarly technical usage of epistemic terms cannot be made consistent with their ordinary usage, his epistemology cannot claim to offer practically significant answers to questions of conventional truth.

What is more, Candrakīrti's clearly pragmatic-transcendental stance is arguably consistent with—indeed, demanded by—Madhyamaka's orienting

---

18. Salvini 2023, 411. For discussion of a passage from Candrakīrti that suggests much the same idea, see Arnold 2005, 178–79.

19. Cf. Salvini 2011, 2014, and 2019. See, too, Newman 2024.

20. From La Vallée Poussin 1970a, 58.14–15; cf. Arnold 2005, 151; MacDonald 2015, 220.

idea.[21] Insofar as Mādhyamikas most want to show, in other words, that all beings and occurrences are "empty" just insofar as they are dependently originated, what is salient about conventional usage of epistemic terms is precisely that these always already exhibit dependent origination.[22] This is just as Salvini suggests in summarizing the significance that grammatical and linguistic analysis have for Candrakīrti:

> Candrakīrti appeals to expressive cogency, that is, to the necessary coherence between what the linguistic forms presuppose and what they are intended to express. This principle of linguistic coherence relies directly on his view that whatever exists can exist only in relation to something else. (Salvini 2023, 408)

As I similarly concluded based on a close reading of Candrakīrti's critique of Dignāga, Candrakīrti readily invokes the conventionally normative discourse of Sanskrit grammatical analysis "because the content of his metaphysical claim requires that he do so" (Arnold 2005, 182). That's because his metaphysical claim is precisely that nothing at all could have an intrinsic nature; since that is just to say that nothing can be more than conventionally real, our conventions therefore cannot themselves be ultimately *explained*, though they are usefully *described* by the grammatical tradition.

Why Then Does Candrakīrti Invoke the Example of Things Familiar to Cowherds?

Candrakīrti thus had no compunction about appealing to Ābhidharmika and grammatico-linguistic analyses as normative for rightly understanding conventional truth; indeed, it is in light of just such norms that Candrakīrti judges Dignāga's epistemology incoherent, and we will presently see that Candrakīrti also invokes these norms in the passages referring to cowherds. It therefore cannot be right that Candrakīrti's account of *saṃvṛtisatya* gives up on normativity altogether. To that extent, it must be supposed that Candrakīrti considered it important to reject *epistemology*, in particular, as normative for conventional truth. If that is right, then it begs the question to fault Candrakīrti's account just for its eschewing provision of epistemo-

---

21. On Candrakīrti's approach as demanding a rejection of epistemology (and on this as reflecting a basically "transcendental" orientation), see Arnold 2005, 203–4. For more on my understanding of "pragmatic-transcendental," see Arnold 2021a.

22. See La Vallée Poussin 1970a, 75.10–12; cf. Arnold 2005, 182.

logical warrant. A charitable reading of him demands that we consider what could make it reasonable for Candrakīrti to resist the idea of epistemology as first philosophy.

Candrakīrti's appeals to things familiar to the unrefined perhaps complicate efforts at reading him charitably; if these appeals are meant as *defining* what is conventionally true—as demanding (Tillemans says) our "acquiescing, across the board, in the actually attested opinions of the lowest common denominator"—it would seem that Candrakīrti's account, notwithstanding his critique of Dignāga, might after all benefit from some epistemological sophistication. But Candrakīrti does not, in fact, appeal to the beliefs of the unrefined by way of defining what counts as "true"; indeed, the upshot of the discussions involving these appeals is generally quite to the contrary. As we now turn our attention to several such discussions, it is important that we follow each to its conclusion, quoting extensively from Candrakīrti to ensure that nothing is taken out of context. Doing so, we will find that these passages are not at all concerned with defining *saṃvṛtisatya*; instead, they concern the very different question of what, in the first place, can reasonably be thought to require explanation.

Prasannapadā on Mūlamadhyamakakārikā 15.1

We begin with the passage included (as indicated by inverted commas) in the declaration, quoted above, that frames Mark Siderits's contribution to this volume: "For Candrakīrti, conventional truth is 'what is known even to cowherds and women.'"[23] Siderits quotes from Candrakīrti's comments on *Mūlamadhyamakakārikā* 15.1, where the expression "familiar to people like cowherds and women" (*gopālāṅganājanaprasiddham*) is indeed to be found.[24] This reference figures, however, in an *objection* anticipated by Candrakīrti: "But surely it is well known to cowherds and women that heat is the distinguishing feature (*svabhāva*) of fire."[25] Here at issue is whether it makes sense for Madhyamaka critique to target the notion of *svabhāva*, given that that word has a familiar sense in ordinary usage, denoting the not obviously problematic idea of "defining characteristic" or (as I've translated) "distinguishing feature." How, then, can Candrakīrti claim that Mādhyamika critique leaves conventional truth intact when the principal target thereof is an idea that actually has a respectable place in ordinary usage?

23. See note 9 above.

24. See La Vallée Poussin 1970a, 260.14.

25. La Vallée Poussin 1970a, 260.14.

The objection is thus to the effect that Candrakīrti *fails*, in this case, to defer to conventional truth. In response, Candrakīrti acknowledges the familiar sense of the word *svabhāva* and proceeds to explain that Madhyamaka really targets something other than that sense:

> We do not say it isn't well known; rather, we say that it does not have a claim to be an **intrinsic nature** (*svabhāvo bhavitum arhati*), because it lacks the characteristic of **existing by itself** (*svabhāvalakṣaṇaviyuktatvāt*).[26]

Candrakīrti's point—brought out (as indicated above in bold) by exploiting the underlying lexemes of the word *svabhāva* as meaning "existent (*bhāva*) by (or *as*) itself (*sva-*)"[27]—is that Madhyamaka just rejects the idea that anything's defining characteristics could make sense as *independently* or *intrinsically* existent. The question remains, though, of what could entitle the Mādhyamika to target a conception of *svabhāva* seemingly at odds with the conventional sense of that. In this regard, Candrakīrti explains that the idea of a thing's distinguishing features, if innocuous in itself, insidiously fosters the habituated self-grasping that is the real target of Madhyamaka critique:

> Because they are in thrall to error born from ignorance, however, everyone conceives what has come into existence (*bhāvajātam*), though that is without intrinsic nature, as being endowed with intrinsic nature (*sasvabhāvatvena*). Those with cataracts, for example, are because of the cataracts preoccupied with the distinguishing feature (*svabhāva*) of hairs (although those are quite nonexistent), which are taken as endowed with intrinsic nature (*sasvabhāvatvena*). Likewise the immature, the sight of their judgment afflicted by the cataracts of ignorance, fixate on what has come into existence (which is without intrinsic nature) as having intrinsic nature.[28]

Nothing is said here about how we are to conceive *saṃvṛtisatya*. Moreover, it here becomes clear that the beliefs of unrefined people like cowherds are significant precisely as requiring normative correction. Thus Candrakīrti

26. La Vallée Poussin 1970a, 260.14–15; bold added for emphasis.

27. La Vallée Poussin 1970a, 260.4–5.

28. La Vallée Poussin 1970a, 261.1–4.

concludes the discussion by suggesting how Abhidharma's tools, although constitutively limited, can facilitate the needed correction:

> And in the Abhidharma, the Buddha propounded only the specific nature (*svarūpam*) that is conventional (*sāṃvṛtaṃ*) for these, according merely to what is familiar to immature people (*bālajanaprasiddhyā*). What things have in common, however—being impermanent, first of all—he explained as their general characteristics.[29]

Far from ratifying the beliefs of the unrefined as criterial for conventional truth, this discussion shows why it makes sense for Candrakīrti to emphasize that Abhidharma's analyses, although conventionally (not ultimately) true, can nonetheless help in undermining habituated self-grasping. As Shenghai Li explains, the discussion thus advances Candrakīrti's thought that "the classification of unique and common characteristics of things [represents] the main contents of Abhidharma texts" (2019, 68). While Abhidharma's individuation of dharmas by their *svabhāva* ("distinguishing features") represents a concession to beings in thrall to reification, Ābhidharmika analyses nonetheless advance the understanding at least that existents are *generally* characterized by their impermanence. To that extent, Ābhidharmika analyses make sense as capable of improving conventionally true understanding, even as Candrakīrti emphasizes, in concluding, why none of the characteristics identified by such analyses could have any claim to be an "intrinsic nature": Those "who do not apprehend the *svabhāva* constructed by the minds of immature people (which is like the vision of hairs in the experience of one with cataracts)" recognize that what Abhidharma analysis yields "is not the intrinsic nature of entities."[30]

Prasannapadā on Mūlamadhyamakakārikā 21.11

Candrakīrti again invokes beliefs held by the unrefined a few chapters later, in commenting on *Mūlamadhyamakakārikā* 21.11. Here, as in the foregoing instance, the example is adduced by way of objection to the Mādhyamika's point. In this case, the objection is to Nāgārjuna's preceding argument (that of MMK 21.10), which was to the effect that arising and dissolution (*saṃbhava* and *vibhava*) ultimately make no sense, whether as distinct from one another or as unitary. Candrakīrti anticipates a common-sense objection to that:

29. La Vallée Poussin 1970a, 261.5–7.
30. La Vallée Poussin 1970a, 261.7–9.

> What is the point of this hairsplitting? After all, insofar as everyone
> from cowherds and women on up observes occurrence and dissolu-
> tion, there do exist both occurrence and dissolution; it is just sons
> of childless women that cannot be seen.[31]

Nāgārjuna's arguments, this objection suggests, could not be good grounds to
doubt what even unsophisticated people understand. But this objection gets
no traction, Candrakīrti explains in response, in the first place because "it is
not the case that there is existence of whatever is apprehended by everyone."[32]
Candrakīrti here explicitly rejects the idea (attributed to him by Tillemans
and Siderits) that "being familiar to the unrefined" is what defines conventional truth. Indeed, what is here salient about "everyone from cowherds and
women on up," Candrakīrti elaborates, is precisely that they believe lots of
things acknowledged by ordinary usage as unreal:

> That is, people including even cowherds and women see even non-
> existent things—celestial cities, apparitions, dreams, wheels of fire,
> water in mirages, and so on—because of impaired faculties.[33]

The fact that occurrences of all sorts are widely experienced, then, does not
count against Nāgārjuna's critique of "arising" and "dissolution" because this
fact is consistent with Madhyamaka's main contention, here pithily expressed
by Nāgārjuna in the concluding half-verse (MMK 21.11cd) introduced by
Candrakīrti's foregoing comment: "Both arising and dissolution are observed
just because of delusion."[34] Despite having argued at *Mūlamadhyamakakārikā*
21.10 that the very idea of "arising" cannot be made coherent, Nāgārjuna can
thus acknowledge that occurrences of all sorts are widely experienced. For the
upshot of Madhyamaka critique is just that *all* intelligible occurrences, in the
final analysis, ultimately have the same status that conventional truth attributes only to certain illusions (apparitions and dreams and the like). And this
is the case insofar as anything at all that can show up for experience depends,
like apparitions and dreams, in part on the "impaired faculties" of the living
beings for whom they show up.[35]

31. La Vallée Poussin 1970a, 418.12–15.

32. Or "whatever is apprehended by a world" or "according to ordinary usage" (*yad yal
lokenôpalabhyate*) (La Vallée Poussin 1970a, 419.2).

33. La Vallée Poussin 1970a, 419.2–4.

34. La Vallée Poussin 1970a, 419.6.

35. On the dependence of occurrences on the capacities of the beings to which they manifest,

That is nothing if not a normative conclusion, and Candrakīrti recognizes that it will thus be asked how it can be ascertained that even what is experienced "by the world in its multitudes" (*vāralokena*) misleads everyone. Unfazed, Candrakīrti says this is ascertained by *reasoning* (*yukti*), immediately proceeding to sketch the argument of Nāgārjuna's subsequent verse (21.12).[36] The particulars of that argument do not matter here; I would merely emphasize the alacrity with which Candrakīrti embraces reasoning as appropriate to the task of disclosing what is obscured by conventional truth.

Commentary on Madhyamakāvatāra 6.26

Let us now turn to the last of our passages referencing cowherds, which comes in Candrakīrti's prose comments on *Madhyamakāvatāra* 6.26, a verse we saw already above. The verse caps an influential presentation of the two truths launched by *Madhyamakāvatāra* 6.23, and it is worth noting that the objection that occasions that whole presentation is the same as the one motivating the previously considered discussion. Likewise following a Madhyamaka critique of an eminently familiar phenomenon—in this case, causation as "arising from another" (*parata utpāda*)[37]—the objection here is expressed by *Madhyamakāvatāra* 6.22:

> What, pray tell, could be accomplished by the reasoning here described? Since everyone (*lokaḥ*) is attached to their own experience (*svadṛśi*) as authoritative, and everyone surely understands dependence (*parabhāva*) as based on another (*parataḥ*), what then is the point of arguing whether origination is from another?[38]

If nobody doubts that causation is relation with "others," and if Abhidharma's systematization of "causes and conditions" (*hetu* and *pratyaya*) therefore was

see Salvini 2014.

36. La Vallée Poussin 1970a, 419.6–10.

37. That is, the arguments of MA 6.14–21, where the stakes are high; for the idea of causation as "arising from another" would seem to be just what Buddhists affirm as "dependent origination" (*pratītyasamutpāda*). Recognizing that Madhyamaka's critique of the idea thus amounts to refutation of a seemingly Buddhist view (i.e., Abhidharma's theorization of "causes and conditions," *hetu* and *pratyaya*), Candrakīrti develops this objection at length in comments introducing MA 6.14; see La Vallée Poussin 1970b, 87.15–89.3; cf. La Vallée Poussin 1910, 285–86.

38. MA 6.22; translated from Li Xuezhu 2015, 7.

not called for in the first place, what then could be the point of Madhyamaka's critique?

It is in response to this objection that *Madhyamakāvatāra* 6.23 introduces the two truths. In doing so, Candrakīrti first emphasizes what must be said about conventional truth just insofar as his is finally a *Buddhist* account; to that extent, the account must make sense of the thought that all beings are basically misled by the habituated self-grasping from which the Buddhist path promises release. That means *saṃvṛtisatya* must be conceived as somehow reinforcing the problem to be overcome, which is reflected, Candrakīrti says, in the lexically basic sense of the verbal form *saṃ-√vṛ* as denoting "obscuration" or "concealment":

> Reality (*tattva*) is what is within range of those who see rightly (*samyagdṛśāṃ yo viṣayaḥ*); for those who see falsely, there is said to be truth that conceals (*saṃvṛtisatya*).[39]

Thus having saddled himself with the challenge of explaining how this "concealing" could yet be a kind of *truth*, Candrakīrti dedicates the next six verses (6.24–29) to clarifying that conventional truth still affords normative resources for the improvement of understanding. Conventional truth already distinguishes, for example, between "those whose faculties are intact and those whose faculties are defective." And while views typical of the first sort of people are true "just customarily" (*satyaṃ hi tal lokata eva*), views that reflect defective faculties are "false according to the very same custom" (*lokata eva mithyā*).[40]

Of course, if Candrakīrti acknowledges as false only what conventional truth *already takes as such*, his would be the kind of communitarian account that cannot, as I have agreed, by itself make sense of the normativity *saṃvṛtisatya* must have if it is to be any kind of truth. We have seen, however, that Candrakīrti readily appeals to Ābhidharmika analyses as advancing the understanding of conventional truth; despite Madhyamaka's critique of Abhidharma's concessions to habituated reification, Ābhidharmika analyses advance the understanding at least that everything is *impermanent*, whereas non-Buddhist thinkers instead compound the habituated errors of conventional truth, doubling down on them and *theorizing* ideas of "self" that even conventional truth can show to be deluded. That, finally, is just the point made by *Madhyamakāvatāra* 6.26, which as we saw above contends that despite its

39. MA 6.23cd, from Li Xuezhu 2015, 7.

40. MA 6.25cd, from Li Xuezhu 2015, 7.

basically "concealing" dimension, *saṃvṛtisatya* affords resources for judging Buddhist philosophical accounts alone as rightly oriented—for judging, as the verse says, that "there is no reality in what is variously posited by idolaters (their heads nodding with the sleep of ignorance)."[41]

In his prose comments on *Madhyamakāvatāra* 6.26, Candrakīrti once more invokes an example familiar even to the unrefined, thus explaining that the verse's idolaters have no claim even to conventional truth because of their "idolizing"[42] the very presupposition that is targeted by Madhyamaka critique: that *conventionally* real is not "real" enough.

> Intent on penetrating reality, these idolaters aim at achieving utmost certainty in determining, accurately and without error, matters such as production and destruction, which are familiar to unrefined people like cowherds and women. Like a tree climber who lets go of a lower branch without grabbing a higher one, they will drop with a great fall into chasms of insidious views; lacking discernment of the two truths, they will reach no fruit, so what is posited by them—[Sāṃkhya's] three constituents of nature and so on—does not, according to conventional truth, exist at all.[43]

It should again be emphasized that it is not, in the first place, *conventional truth* that is here called "familiar to unrefined people." What is familiar to the unrefined, rather, is matters that philosophers typically purport to explain. Thus it is not truth criteria that are here at issue but a more basic question: Can "matters such as production and destruction" reasonably be considered in need of philosophical explanation?

Answering this, Candrakīrti's analogy suggests a pragmatic-transcendental argument to the effect that the intelligibility of practical reason—of all that Candrakīrti means by "worldly commerce" (*lokavyavahāra*)—always already presupposes some grasp of matters like production and destruction.[44] Insofar as philosophical inquiry itself is an instance of worldly commerce, its intelligibility shares that presupposition. It cannot coherently be maintained, therefore, that philosophical inquiry is uniquely capable of substantiating the

---

41. See note 13 above.

42. It is with this "idolizing" in mind that I have all along been translating *tīrtha[ka]* as "idolater," notwithstanding the Christian theological baggage that makes this a problematic translation.

43. Translated from La Vallée Poussin 1970b, 105.13–106.1. La Vallée Poussin's translation (1910, 302) seems to me to miss the point of the analogy.

44. On my understanding of "pragmatic-transcendental," see Arnold 2021a.

same matters, and it makes no sense to think such substantiation is required.[45] Candrakīrti particularly rejects speculative entities (like the three *guṇas* of Sāṃkhya cosmology) posited as affording privileged understanding—as affording "utmost certainty," that is, on matters whose intelligibility is already presupposed by any pursuit of understanding.

The problem, on Candrakīrti's view, is not just that such speculative entities are practically meaningless; more insidiously, for philosophers to capitulate to foundationalist demands for certainty is just to encourage precisely the habituated self-grasping to be uprooted by Buddhist practice. Notwithstanding Abhidharma's concessions to the same habits (even as it reaches more refined levels of analysis), Abhidharma's analyses do at least emphasize that all entities are impermanent—non-Buddhist accounts instead double down on the problematic predilections, veritably idolizing the intrinsic nature criterion targeted by Madhyamaka critique. To suppose that our epistemic practices do not make sense unless provided with irrefragable philosophical grounding, however, is to let go of the only branch we could be standing on, with no others reachable.

Conclusion: Why It Makes Sense That Candrakīrti Eschews Epistemology

In fact, one upshot of Madhyamaka critique is that any "branch" that can be reached by a tree climber could only be conventionally real; no other kind could, *ipso facto*, admit of relation. It thus makes no sense to persist in demanding achievement of an altogether different kind of foothold—an imperishable limb, perhaps, so far above all the others as to secure the foundationalist's aim at "utmost certainty." This is not, however, to deny that *tree climbing* makes sense, or that tree climbers may vary in the heights they can achieve—which is to say that Candrakīrti's conception of *saṃvṛtisatya* has, in fact, resources for capturing its normative character as a sort of *truth*. Not without reason, then, does Candrakīrti contend that it is not Madhyamaka critique that imperils the intelligibility of practical reason; that is imperiled, rather, by philos-

---

45. Candrakīrti offers much the same line of argument in concluding his analysis (at MA 6.151–57) of all the ways in which a *chariot* could relate to the *parts* thereof. Having shown that none of these ultimately withstands scrutiny, Candrakīrti invites the objection that Madhyamaka critique thus renders unintelligible what is practically incontrovertible (i.e., much ordinary discourse unproblematically refers to *chariots*). Turning the tables, Candrakīrti responds: "This is a problem only for you. A chariot does not make sense when sought according to the above-described sevenfold method, and yet *you* remain intent on rigorously demonstrating its existence" (La Vallée Poussin 1970b, 276.18–277.4).

ophers' persistence in thinking that nothing conventionally taken as "real" could count as such without philosophical substantiation.

I would emphasize, moreover, that one can in the first place suppose that the intelligibility of ordinary epistemic practices (or the possible truth of Madhyamaka's claims) is imperiled by Madhyamaka critique only if one persists in presupposing just what Candrakīrti denies. Though quoting *Kamalaśīla's* summary of the "dismal" view, Tillemans persists in thinking *Candrakīrti's* Madhyamaka deficient. As I read him, this is because Tillemans presupposes that a "philosophically more promising stance" must recognize "the need for *strong* normativity," and he thus thinks it obvious that it would behoove Candrakīrti to acknowledge that "there are *pramāṇa*s and hence *robustly right* answers about them."[46] As betrayed by the qualifiers I have italicized ("*strong* normativity," "*robustly right* answers"), Tillemans's worry presupposes the possibility of achieving precisely what Candrakīrti argues is unachievable. What could it mean that the normativity of Candrakīrti's *saṃvṛtisatya* is not "strong" enough, and that "robustly right" answers to epistemological questions must therefore be acknowledged, if not that *conventionally* right answers are not "robust" enough? To persist in presupposing that, however, is to deny just what Candrakīrti would have us understand.

If we are to avoid thus begging the question, we must suppose that Candrakīrti's rejection of epistemology is philosophically well motivated. This involves acknowledging that Candrakīrti has much to say, as we have seen, about the norms he readily invokes, and about the sense these make (despite what they "conceal" just in virtue of being conventional) as advancing conventionally true understanding. In concluding, I want to suggest a way of understanding Candrakīrti's idea that recuperating conventional truth demands rejecting the project of epistemology. Candrakīrti's predilections reflect, I suggest, basic misgivings about epistemology's methodological presumption of *individual subjects* as the obvious units of analysis. Insofar as epistemology was exemplified for Candrakīrti by Dignāga's project, Candrakīrti could reasonably suppose the problems with epistemology are epitomized by Dignāga's account of perception—in particular, by Dignāga's idea of perception as centrally involving self-awareness (*svasaṃvitti*), a conception that does not make sense, Candrakīrti argued, even as conventionally true. Candrakīrti's uncompromising critique of self-awareness can, I think, be reasonably challenged,[47] but his stance looks more interesting if taken to reflect a commitment to conceiving *norms* as intersubjectively available. That is, if thought itself makes

---

46. Tillemans 2022, 6; emphasis added.

47. For thoughts on this, see Arnold 2016, 2021.

sense only relative to a shared space of reasons—only, as Candrakīrti would have it, relative to the kinds of linguistic norms that are "well known" (*prasiddha*) to all competent language-users—that is good reason to question the normative significance of self-awareness, which instead directs our attention inward.

That this is Candrakīrti's view is evident, I think, in his basically grammatical orientation to philosophical analysis. The intersubjective character of normativity is paradigmatically evident in language, and the project of the Sanskrit grammarians was to derive rules in virtue of which uses of language can be "generally intelligible" (*lokaprasiddha*). Candrakīrti's eschewal of epistemology, I thus suggest, reflects a principled finding: philosophers should reject psychologistic analyses of epistemic justification, instead taking their bearings from linguistic analysis of intersubjectively intelligible *meaning*. The significance of this insight can be brought out with reference to Charles S. Peirce, whose orienting commitments involve much the same idea. Thus, Peirce was oriented by a *semiotic* conception of thought, a conception that he considered badly distorted by William James's influential appropriation of his (Peirce's) pragmatism.[48] Succinctly characterizing the difference between Peirce's project and James's, Vincent Colapietro comments that for James, "the most fundamental feature of personal consciousness is the irreducible fact of privacy," whereas what mattered for Peirce was "the ubiquitous possibility of communication"—indeed, Colapietro says, Peirce thought "the distance between two minds, rather than being the most absolute breach in nature, is the most fordable stream in this domain."[49] We are apt to think otherwise, Peirce argued, insofar as we wrongly suppose that the most salient feature of *thought* is its being immediately present to a subject. Even a solitary thinker, however, is intelligible as *thinking*, Peirce says, only insofar as a person is not "absolutely an individual"—insofar, that is, as their *thoughts* consist in what thinkers "say" to themselves over time, which means (among other things) that "all thought whatsoever is a sign, and is mostly of the nature of language."[50]

I think Candrakīrti takes his bearings from much the same idea, similarly contending that when it comes to *understanding*, there can be no explaining the socially constituted norms that must suffice; any explanation offered must presuppose just such norms if it is to make sense. That strikes me as

48. I here take my bearings from Peirce's late essay "What Pragmatism Is" (1905), which clarifies what Peirce took James and others to have misunderstood about Peirce's earlier proposals. For my reading of Peirce vis-à-vis James, see Arnold 2021a and 2021b.

49. Colapietro 1989, 78.

50. Peirce 1905, 170.

a philosophically interesting position, and there is reason to think, with Candrakīrti, that it is also a position demanded by Madhyamaka analysis. Whether or not that is right, charitably interpreting Candrakīrti's arguments requires entertaining the possibility that on questions of epistemic justification, his Madhyamaka shifts the burden of proof. It is, then, time we stopped fretting about whether Candrakīrti's position makes sense as possibly true and seriously entertained his own contention: that the intelligibility of truth is undermined not by Madhyamaka critique but precisely by epistemological objections to that.

When it comes to the question of whether Candrakīrti's Madhyamaka undermines the grounds of its own possible truth, I would thus contend that Tom Tillemans's influential reading begs the question. It is no less true, however, that I cannot have arrived at that idea without having spent years engaging Tom's work, and I offer this essay as honoring that fact.

Bibliography

Arnold, Dan. 2005. *Buddhists, Brahmins, and Belief: Epistemology in South Asian Philosophy of Religions*. New York: Columbia University Press.

———. 2016. "The Buddhist Challenge." *Los Angeles Review of Books*. November 16.

———. 2021a. "Pragmatism as Transcendental Philosophy, Part 1: Peirce in Light of James's Radical Empiricism." *American Journal of Theology & Philosophy* 42.1: 50–103.

———. 2021b. "Pragmatism as Transcendental Philosophy, Part 2: Peirce on God and Personality." *American Journal of Theology & Philosophy* 42. 2: 3–71.

———. 2021c. "Should Mādhyamikas Refute Subjectivity? Thoughts on What Might Be at Stake in Debates on Self-Awareness." In *Buddhist Philosophy of Consciousness: Tradition and Dialogue*, edited by Mark Siderits, Ching Keng, and John Spackman, 154–88. Leiden: Brill-Rodopi.

———. Forthcoming. "Candrakīrti on What Is Unreal Even for Conventional Truth: The Significance of a Prevalent Misreading of *Madhyamakāvatāra* 6.26." In *Buddhist Minds and Bodies: Essays in Honor of José I. Cabezón*, edited by Vesna Wallace and Rory Lindsay. Studies in Indian and Tibetan Buddhism. New York: Wisdom Publications.

Boghossian, Paul A. 1989. "The Rule-Following Considerations." *Mind*, New Series, 98.392: 507–49.

Colapietro, Vincent. 1989. *Peirce's Approach to the Self: A Semiotic Perspective*. Albany: State University of New York Press.

Dreyfus, Georges. 1997. *Recognizing Reality: Dharmakīrti's Philosophy and Its Tibetan Interpreters*. Albany: State University of New York Press.

Garfield, Jay L. 1995. *The Fundamental Wisdom of the Middle Way: Nāgārjuna's Mūlamadhyamakakārikā*. New York: Oxford University Press.

La Vallée Poussin, Louis de. 1910. "*Madhyamakāvatāra*: Introduction au Traité du milieu de l'Ācārya Candrakīrti, avec le commentaire de l'auteur, traduit d'après la version tibétaine [6.1–6.80]." *Le Muséon* 11: 271–358.

La Vallée Poussin, Louis de, ed. (1903–13) 1970a. *Mūlamadhyamakakārikās (Mādhya-mikasūtras) de Nāgārjuna, avec la Prasannapadā Commentaire de Candrakīrti*. Biblio-theca Buddhica 4. Osnabrück: Biblio Verlag.

———. (1907–12) 1970b. *Madhyamakāvatāra par Candrakīrti: Traduction tibétaine*. Bibliotheca Buddhica 9. Osnabrück: Biblio Verlag.

Li, Shenghai. 2019. "Dimensions of Candrakīrti's Conventional Reality." *Journal of Indian Philosophy* 47: 49–72.

Li, Xuezhu, ed. 2015. "Madhyamakāvatāra-kārikā Chapter 6." *Journal of Indian Philosophy* 43: 1–30.

Lindtner, Christian, ed. 1979. "Candrakīrti's *Pañcaskandhaprakaraṇa*: I. Tibetan Text." *Acta Orientalia* 40: 87–145.

MacDonald, Anne. 2015. *In Clear Words: The Prasannapadā, Chapter One. Vol. II: Annotated Translation, Tibetan Text*. Vienna: Verlag der Österreichischen Akademie der Wissenschaften.

Newman, John. 2022. Review of *Knowing Illusion: Bringing a Tibetan Debate into Contemporary Discourse by the Yakherds*. H-Buddhism. https://www.h-net.org/reviews/showrev.php?id=58306.

———. 2024. "Candrakīrti on *lokaprasiddhi*: A Bad Hand, or an Ace in the Hole?" *Journal of Indian Philosophy* 52: 73–99.

Peirce, Charles S. 1905. "What Pragmatism Is." *The Monist* 15.2:161–81.

Salvini, Mattia. 2011. "*Upādāyaprajñaptiḥ* and the Meaning of Absolutives: Grammar and Syntax in the Interpretation of Madhyamaka." *Journal of Indian Philosophy* 39: 229–44.

———. 2014. "Dependent Arising, Non-Arising, and the Mind: MMK1 and the Abhidharma." *Journal of Indian Philosophy* 42.4: 471–97.

———. 2019. "Etymologies of What Can(not) Be Said: Candrakīrti on Conventions and Elaborations." *Journal of Indian Philosophy* 47: 661–95.

———. 2023. "Candrakīrti: Gardener of Sky-Flowers." In *The Routledge Handbook of Indian Buddhist Philosophy*, edited by William Edelglass, Pierre-Julien Harter, and Sara McClintock, 404–20. New York: Routledge.

Tillemans, Tom J. F. 1990. *Materials for the Study of Āryadeva, Dharmapāla and Candrakīrti: The Catuḥśataka of Āryadeva, Chapters XII and XIII, with the Commentaries of Dharmapāla and Candrakīrti: Introduction, Translation, Sanskrit, Tibetan and Chinese Texts, Notes*. Wiener Studien zur Tibetologie und Buddhismuskunde 24, parts 1–2. Vienna: Arbeitskreis für Tibetische und Buddhistische Studien.

———. 2011. "How Far Can a Mādhyamika Reform Customary Truth? Dismal Relativism, Fictionalism, Easy-Easy Truth, and the Alternatives." In *Moonshadows: Conventional Truth in Buddhist Philosophy*, by the Cowherds, 151–66. New York: Oxford University Press.

———. 2016. "How Far Can a Mādhyamika Reform Customary Truth? Dismal Relativism, Fictionalism, Easy-Easy Truth, and the Alternatives." In *How Do Mādhyamikas Think? And Other Essays on the Buddhist Philosophy of the Middle*, 47–66. Boston: Wisdom Publications.

———. 2022. *Views from Tibet: Studies on Tibetan Buddhist Logic, the Philosophy of the Middle, and the Indigenous Grammatico-Linguistic Tradition*. Vienna: Austrian Academy of Sciences Press.

Candrakīrti's Tripartite Theory
of Conventional Truths:
A Case Against Typical/Atypical Readings[1]

Sonam Thakchoe

IMUST EXPRESS my deepest admiration for Professor Tom J. F. Tillemans, whose outstanding career has been one of remarkable accomplishments and contributions to the field. It was a great and humbling experience to have worked with Professor Tillemans on the book *Moonshadows* as one of his fellow Cowherds, providing a rare opportunity to observe him closely and learn from his expertise in blending philosophical, philological, and linguistic skills in a creative and rigorous style. Possessing such a rare combination of skills and such high standards of excellence remains for me a dream. His approach bridging Western analytical philosophy and Buddhist thought has revolutionized the study of Buddhist philosophy. Deeply grateful for his contributions, I wish him a fulfilling retirement.

In some of his later works, Tom Tillemans presents two different ways to interpret Candrakīrti's Madhyamaka, including in his book *How Do Mādhyamikas Think?* These are the atypical Prāsaṅgika and the typical Prāsaṅgika readings. Tillemans refers to the atypical Prāsaṅgika interpretation of Candrakīrti as the "deflationist approach," while he calls the global error theory or revolutionary fictionalist approach the typical reading of Candrakīrti.

A deflationist approach, often called *deflationism*, is a position in the philosophy of language and truth that seeks to "deflate" or simplify specific complex philosophical issues, particularly relating to truth, meaning, and reference. In the context of truth, deflationary theory holds a very basic understanding. There, the concept of *truth* is not substantive or deep, requiring elabo-

---

1. My deep gratitude to Sara McClintock and David Kittelstrom, whose careful, detailed, and insightful critiques of the draft significantly improved this paper.

rate philosophical analysis. It simply denies the existence of any substantial properties—anything that can withstand specific types of analysis or have intrinsic causal efficacy. The term *deflationism* or "deflationary theory" is used in contrast with the term *inflationism* or "inflationary theory." According to deflationism, truth, reference, meaning, and other related concepts involve deflationary properties in that they have no discoverable natures, no reality beyond what is conveyed in ordinary claims. Candrakīrti, as a deflationist, holds a basic sense of *truth* that rejects such substantive properties. He believes that, for instance, "The cat is sitting on the mat" is true just because the cat is sitting on the mat, nothing more.[2]

In contrast, the inflationary approach seeks to "inflate" or complicate issues relating to truth, meaning, and reference. Inflationism posits the existence of theoretically significant, substantive properties such as discoverable natures and causal efficacy beyond what are conveyed in ordinary claims. Inflationists hold a realist sense of *truth* that corresponds to facts, withstands specific types of analysis, is verifiable, and has intrinsic causal efficacy. They believe, for example, that "the table exists" is true if and only if the table is intrinsically causally effective—in that it performs its functions independent of any and all other factors, including extrinsic factors such as the needs of those who make the assertion that "the table exists." Candrakīrti rejects inflationism.[3]

Tillemans attributes a deflationist reading of Candrakīrti to Tsongkhapa (Tsong kha pa Blo bzang grags pa, 1357–1419). According to this interpretation, Candrakīrti is considered a competent philosopher because he possesses robust epistemology for both ordinary and exalted individuals through the use of reliable sources of knowledge. However, according to Tillemans's view of Tsongkhapa's interpretation, Candrakīrti is regarded as a poor philologist—in the sense that Tsongkhapa's interpretation of Candrakīrti fails to provide sufficient textual evidence to support this interpretation.[4]

In the typical reading of Candrakīrti that Tillemans describes, Candrakīrti holds a position that Tillemans calls global error theory, which is an epistemic antirealist position that claims there are no objective epistemic facts and all epistemic claims are fundamentally erroneous or based on false presuppositions. In simpler terms, epistemological claims are impossible. Epistemological error theorists argue that when people make epistemic assertions, such as "The perception of blue is true," they are making claims about objective epistemic facts that do not exist as such. Candrakīrti is an error theorist because he argues

2. Båve 2006, 9–12.

3. Båve 2006, 9–12.

4. Tillemans 2011, 151–65; Tillemans 2019, 642.

that epistemic language contains an inherent "error" in that it presupposes the existence of objective epistemic facts and values that do not exist. Candrakīrti does not deny that people have epistemic beliefs and use warrants, but he claims that these beliefs are based on a mistaken understanding of the world.

Tillemans also claims that Candrakīrti adopts a revolutionary fictionalist or panfictionalist approach toward ordinary discourses and language. According to the fictionalist approach, discourse is literally false but still worth uttering in certain contexts because the pretense that such claims are true serves various theoretical and practical purposes. Being fictionalist about a particular discourse means that, in our naïve attitude, we slip into fictional talk, which is in one sense wholly incorrect and—at best—only halfway correct. We may be justified in using singular terms to refer to particular objects, but we are wrong if we think that they actually succeed in referring to them.[5]

Tillemans describes this latter approach as the "typical Prāsaṅgika" reading of Candrakīrti, and he attributes it to Jayānanda (late eleventh century) and Taktsang Lotsāwa (Stag tshang lo tsā ba, 1405–77).[6] On this reading, Candrakīrti emerges as a decent philologist—providing sound textual evidence to support his claims—but a hopeless philosopher: an epistemological nihilist, global error theorist, and panfictionalist,[7] stuck in a "dismal slough," as Tillemans puts it,[8] in which truth is only ever fiction or error (*bhrānta* = *'khrul ba*).[9]

This "typical" reading of Candrakīrti, Tillemans argues, rejects any commitment to truth or reality by assuming a "pretense or make-believe" position.[10] Even the term *right understanding* has no more purchase than as a "seeming to be right" that satisfies "widespread acceptance by the deluded world."[11] On this reading, moreover, Candrakīrti appeals to whatever the world of deluded beings acknowledges (*lokaprasiddha*), an *argumentum ad populum*, endorsing

---

5. In his argument, Tillemans refers to Steven Yablo's (1998, 200) oracle argument, which presents a scenario where an all-knowing oracle informs us that abstract entities do not exist. If we were to accept this verdict, we would no longer believe in the existence of abstract entities. However, our use of descriptive sentences to refer to these entities would remain unchanged. We would continue to describe them in the same way as before without feeling any difference. For more on fictionalism see also Szabó 2001 and Nolan, Restall, and West 2005.

6. Tillemans 2011, 151–65; 2019, 642.

7. Tillemans 2016, 5.

8. Tillemans 2016, 4; 2019, 640.

9. Tillemans 2016, 52.

10. Tillemans 2016, 53.

11. Tillemans 2016, 4.

everything whatsoever "the world" says or believes to be true as indeed true—
at least conventionally.[12] Tillemans describes this "typical" approach to truth
as a "dismal position," a "trivialization of the idea of truth," "dumbed-down
truth," "easy-easy truth," and "hopelessly dismal" truth.[13] He further claims
that Candrakīrti radically shuns "any and all deeper questions about what
there actually is," finding satisfaction in whatever the world acknowledges.[14]
Candrakīrti is thus a destructive nihilist and a global skeptic according to
whom things are just false appearances (*ābhāsa* = *snang ba*) that lack any genuine existence and exist purely from the point of view of "mistaken minds"
(*blo 'khrul ba'i ngor yod pa*).[15]

In what follows, I will not only show why this "typical" reading of
Candrakīrti is flawed, I will also present an alternative to the "atypical" reading that Tillemans attributes to Tsongkhapa, doing so based on a more holistic
reading of Candrakīrti's Madhyamaka works. I will show that Candrakīrti is
an astute and systematic thinker who delivers both philologically sound textual analyses and philosophically consistent deflationist metaphysics, according to which things are nothing more than thoroughly relational, illusory, and
empty of essence and self. I will argue that his deflationist epistemology is perfectly compatible and complementary with his core deflationist metaphysics,
and it requires only a minimalist *pramāṇa* system at play, not the "full-fledged
pramāṇas" of the Pramaṇavādins, as Tillemans claims.

Candrakīrti emerges, on *my* atypical reading, as a pluralist and pragmatist
about truth, a philosopher for whom truth is deflationary—episodic, plastic,
and dynamic. Truth unfolds as events with epistemic, semantic, and/or moral
significance. The key to my interpretation lies in making sense of what is for
Candrakīrti a tripartite theory of conventional truth, one that is invariably
context sensitive, deeply embedded in linguistic conventions that provide the
tools to corroborate its own truth or falsity.

Candrakīrti's Madhyamaka works talk about three levels of epistemic
conventions:

1. Conventions *not* of the world (*alokasaṃvṛti* = *'jig rten ma yin
   pa'i kun rdzob*), associated with defective epistemic instruments.
   Defective epistemic instruments, despite their name, are reliable

---

12. Tillemans 2016, 47; Siderits 2016, 32.

13. Tillemans 2016, 47.

14. Tillemans 2016, 5.

15. Tillemans 2016, 4.

(*pramāṇa*) with respect to the conventions that are not of the world because they satisfy the epistemic standards of those conventions, resulting in the conventional truth *not* of the world (the first-order conventional truth).

2. Conventions of the world (*lokasaṃvṛti* = *'jig rten gyi kun rdzob*), associated with healthy epistemic instruments. The healthy epistemic instruments of ordinary beings are likewise reliable with respect to their respective conventions because they satisfy the epistemic standards of those worldly conventions, resulting in the conventional truth of the world (the second-order conventional truth).

3. Conventions of exalted beings, associated with an ārya's healthy epistemic instruments. Healthy epistemic instruments of āryas are reliable with respect to ārya conventions, resulting in the conventional truth of exalted beings (the third-order conventional truth).

To unpack Candrakīrti's arguments underlying his tripartite theory of conventional truth, we need to understand the dual-order epistemic error theory he deploys to articulate the distinctions among them. According to this dual-order error theory, the causes of epistemic error are of two kinds: adventitious and innate. Candrakīrti maintains that adventitious causes of epistemic error undermine the epistemic conventions of the conventional truth, while the innate causes undermine the epistemic conventions of the ultimate truth.

Conventional Truth Not *of the World Versus Conventional Truth of the World*

Candrakīrti introduces these two types of epistemic conventions (*vyavahāra*) in his *Prasannapadā* when commenting on *Mūlamadhyamakakārikā* 24.8, the oft-cited verse where Nāgārjuna affirms the necessity of relying on conventional truth. In his commentary, Candrakīrti identifies several meanings of the word *convention* (*saṃvṛti*). This much is well known. But then, while analyzing "convention of the world" (*lokasaṃvṛti*), he introduces, via a rhetorical question, the idea of a convention *not* of the world (*alokasaṃvṛti*). He says:

> "Convention of the world" (*lokasaṃvṛti*) means a convention in/ for the world. [Question:] But is there then also some convention *not* of the world (*alokasaṃvṛti*) from which the convention of the world is distinguished? [Reply:] This [*lokasaṃvṛti*] conveys (*anuvāda*) how things are established—uncritically [that is, without analysis]. However, those not of the world (*aloka*) are those

who see falsely due to having distorted sense faculties—via a visual disorder, jaundice, and the like. The convention not of the world is their convention. It is from this that the "convention of the world" is distinguished.[16]

Candrakīrti uses a rhetorical question to distinguish the convention of the world from the convention not of the world. The convention of the world he says serves two epistemic functions. (1) It presents how things are established based on how they conventionally appear to healthy sensory cognitions. (2) It does not broach deeper critical analysis; healthy sensory cognitions function to enact conventional truths strictly non-analytically and non-philosophically. These two epistemic functions are necessary to meet the standard of conventional reliability (*pramāṇa*), the epistemic conventions of healthy sensory cognitions.

In other words, any epistemic instrument that does not satisfy these two criteria cannot meet the conventional *pramāṇa* standard and, thus, does not constitute the epistemic conventions of the world. If cognition fails to satisfy the second epistemic function and engages in deep critical analysis, it will be classified as analytical cognition, which sets the *ultimate pramāṇa* stan-

---

16. Candrakīrti, *Prasannapadā* ad *Mūlamadhyamakakārikā* 24.8. La Vallée Poussin 1970, 215: *loke saṃvṛtir lokasaṃvṛtiḥ / kiṃ punar alokasaṃvṛtir apy asti yata evaṃ viśiṣyate lokasaṃvṛtir iti yathāvasthitapadārthānuvāda eṣa / nātraiṣā cintāvatarati / atha vā / timirakāmalādyupaha tendriyaviparītadarśanāvasthānas te 'lokāḥ / teṣāṃ ya saṃvṛtir asāv alokasaṃvṛtiḥ //*; D 3860, 163ab: *'jig rten gyi kun rdzob ni 'jig rten gyi kun rdzob bo zhes 'jig rten kun rdzob ces gang las de ltar khyad par du byed pa 'jig rten ma yin pa'i kun rdzob kyang yod dam zhe na / 'di ni dngos po ji ltar gnas pa rjes su brjod pa yin gyi / 'dir dpyad pa de mi 'jug go // rnam pa gcig tu na / rab rib dang ling thog sngon po dang / mig ser la sogs pas dbang po nyams pas mthong ba phyin ci log las gnas pa de dag ni 'jig rten ma yin te / de dag gi kun rdzob gang yin pa de ni / 'jig rten kun rdzob bden pa ma yin pas / 'jig rten kun rdzob bden pa dang / zhes de las khyad par du byas so //.* Interestingly, when Jayānanda paraphrases this passage in his *Madhyamakāvatāraṭīkā* (ad *Madhyamakāvatāra* 6.1), he dismisses Candrakīrti's notion of *alokasaṃvṛti*, thus rejecting his distinction between *lokasaṃvṛti* and *alokasaṃvṛti*: "*Convention of the world* (*lokasaṃvṛti*) means the defining characters of objects of knowledge, which constitutes convention in/for the world. [Question:] Since you declare convention in/for the world, is there then also a convention *not* of the world? [Reply:] No, there is not. [The expression] simply conveys (*rjes su brjod pa*) how things are established and does not constitute critical analysis. Those who see falsely due to having sense faculties damaged by a visual disorder, jaundice, and so on, they [also] constitute convention for/in the world. Therefore *convention of the world* is so termed." D 3870, 108b: *gal te 'jig rten gyi kun rdzob ces brjod pas 'jig rten ma yin pa'i kun rdzob kyang yod dam zhe na ma yin te / ji lta ba gzhin du gnas pa'i dngos po rnams la rjes su brjod pa tsam yin pas / 'dir rtag pa 'de lta bu 'jug pa ma yin no // yang rab rib dang / mig ser ba la sogs pas nye bar bcom pa'i dbang po phyin ci log to mthong ba'i gnas skabs ni 'jig rten pa'i kun rdzob yin pas de rnams las khyad par du bya ba'i phyir 'jig rten kun rdzob ces bya ba smos pa yin no //.*

dard, not the conventional, which is what we are concerned with here. If cognition fails to satisfy the first epistemic function and does not accord with how things are established conventionally, it will not meet the conventional *pramāṇa* standard and will be relegated to the epistemic conventions *not* of the world.

The convention *not* of the world, Candrakīrti explains, consists of the epistemic conventions belonging to those whose sense faculties are damaged. This line of explanation corresponds to another passage from the *Prasannapadā*, discussed below, where Candrakīrti explicitly differentiates the epistemic procedures of the convention of the world and of the convention *not* of the world based on the absence or presence of sensory defects. Adventitious causes of epistemic error consist of malfunctioning epistemic instruments—the sensory faculties. The defective sensory cognitions produce fictitious objects that appear to them as objective facts; hence with respect to these fictions, the defective cognitions are *pramāṇas*—nondeceptive in relation to these fictive objects—in that they warrant the truths of those fictions, making them conventional truths not of the world.

However, the epistemic convention of the world can easily falsify all the defective epistemic instruments as errors for reifying and wrongly apprehending fictitious appearances as objective facts. The convention not of the world consists only of fictions according to Candrakīrti's epistemology.[17] Thus the conventional truth of the world rises to the challenge of recognizing that the objects of defective sensory faculties—the conventional truths not of the world—are completely fictional and erroneous.

On this view, healthy sensory cognitions of all cognitive agents—ordinary beings, Mādhyamikas, arhats, ārya bodhisattvas, and buddhas—are *pramāṇas*, conventionally true epistemic warrants. To the extent that they are free from the adventitious causes of epistemic error, they all satisfy the epistemic standards of the convention of the world and can successfully deliver the two primary epistemic functions of conventional truths. By the same logic, defective sensory cognitions of cognitive agents are, alike, conventionally false epistemic warrants by virtue of failing to meet both basic epistemic criteria, and thus they are all relegated to the conventional truth *not* of the world, irrespective of the cognitive agent in question. Both an ordinary beggar and a Mādhyamika monk seeking alms can be right about the fact that the food they visually perceive can satiate their hunger; both can also be wrong thinking that the piles of magical sticks they perceive in the hands of a magician can satiate their hunger

17. See Candrakīrti's *Pañcaskandhaprakaraṇa*, D 3866, 240–41 and 266a, Thakchoe 2012, and Garfield and Thakchoe 2025, 33–72, for his positive *epistemology* of perception.

or that a mirage can satisfy their thirst. These distinctions of right and wrong belong to the domain of conventional truth of the world, where even cognitive agents with healthy sense faculties sometimes make erroneous judgments.

But things are more complex when it comes to people whose sensory faculties are diminished by adventitious defects. In the *Prasannapadā*, Candrakīrti makes a crucial distinction by way of an example:

> The double moon and so on are not *pratyakṣa*—perceptible—with respect to cognition of those without the disorder (*timira*), even though they are *pratyakṣa* with respect to cognition of those with the disorder and so on.[18]

In Candrakīrti's theory of perception, *pratyakṣa*, which can mean both perception and what is perceptible, is one of four nondeceptive epistemic instruments (*pramāṇas*). The passage cited above is part of Candrakīrti's concluding discussion on *pratyakṣa*, stressing his unique account of *pratyakṣa* as a *pramāṇa* in which even a conventionally mistaken epistemic process (e.g., cognition of the double moon) constitutes *pratyakṣa*, contrary to the Dignāga-Dharmakīrtian approach, which excludes such cognitions altogether from the *pratyakṣa* category. This statement about the double moon is clear proof that, despite Tillemans's criticism that Candrakīrti takes everything on face value without analysis, Candrakīrti does indeed make a subtle distinction when it comes to his epistemology of perception, including cognitions of fictional entities caused by visual impairment such as a double moon or hair-like filaments falling from the sky. He argues that the double moon is not *pratyakṣa* with respect to the conventional truth of the world—that is, of someone who has healthy vision—and therefore, healthy vision is not *pramāṇa* with respect to a double moon. The reason is that the visual cognition of the double moon fails to meet the first criterion of conventional *pramāṇa*. That is, cognition of the double moon may be said to engage with its object nonanalytically, meeting the second criterion, but it mistakenly apprehends that there are two moons, failing to apprehend the object's conventional reality.[19] At the same time, he also argues that insofar as the double moon *is* seen by those with an eye disorder, it therefore *is* a kind of *pratyakṣa* in the sense of being a perceptible entity.

18. Candrakīrti, *Prasannapadā* ad *Mūlamadhyamakakārikā* 1.3; La Vallée Poussin 1970, 26: *dvicandrādīnāṃ tu ataimirikajñānāpekṣayā apratyakṣatvam, taimirikādyapekṣayā tu pratyakṣatvam eva //.*

19. For detailed discussions of subtle distinctions Candrakīrti undertakes in his epistemology of perception, see Thakchoe 2012, and Garfield and Thakchoe 2025, 33–72.

While the cognition of a double moon may not be a conventional *pramāṇa* for the world, it is a *pramāṇa* for those not of the world (i.e., those who do not participate in the same cognitive world as those with healthy sense faculties).

Thus Candrakīrti's first-order error theory concerning adventitious causes of epistemic defects allows him to justify the distinction between conventional truth of the world and conventional truth *not* of the world. Whereas the conventional truth of the world consists of true concepts that are free from extraneously defective cognitive processes, the conventional truth *not* of the world consists of false concepts, those born of extraneously defective cognitive processes. On Tillemans's theory, Candrakīrti's discussion would end here because according to his reading, Candrakīrti is a panfictionalist who holds the view that asserts conventional truth is only fiction or error (*bhrānta* = 'khrul ba*) produced by ignorance and rejects any commitment to truth or reality by "adopting a type of pretense or make-believe" position.[20] But Candrakīrti is very clear that this distinction alone cannot be the whole story when it comes to perceiving fictional entities such as a double moon. While there is only one moon, some people nevertheless have visual experiences of a double moon and floating hairs, for which a Mādhyamika must have an explanation. So what is the causal explanation behind such experiences? Again, Candrakīrti argues that despite the impaired visual faculty, the double moon is a *pratyakṣa*, and therefore the same cognition with the visual disorder is epistemic warrant—*pramāṇa*—with respect to the double moon. His reasoning is that the double moon is real in terms of cognition with that visual disorder since the false cognition (grasping that the double moon is real) and the false concept (the double moon exists) both arise from the same disorder. Thus the cognition of a double moon is a *pramāṇa* with respect to conventional truth *not* of the world, even though that same cognition of the double moon is false with respect to conventional truth of the world.

Why might this matter? Consider that for Candrakīrti certain fictional entities such as Īśvara (God) exist as truths *not* of the world from the perspective of defective epistemic processes that are impaired by extraneous causes of mental defects. From a healthy conventional standpoint, the concept of God is a pure falsehood, a fiction, a speculative belief, and an imaginary idea formulated due to defective thought processes. Yet this conceptual fiction is true for the respective defective mental cognition that experiences Īśvara, because even though the concept is pure fiction, the erroneous thought process that arises from having this fictional concept as its intentional object is a genuine causal

20. Tillemans 2016, 52.

cognitive process.[21] Making room for this kind of conventional truth *not* of the world allows one to take seriously the experiences of others, even when the Mādhyamika recognizes the defects in the sense faculties—including defects of the mind (*manas*)—that have produced the perceptions and conceptions that the Mādhyamika knows are false from the point of view of the conventional truth of the world. Allowing for and explaining this experience is useful for teaching others about the mistakes in their thinking and perceiving that are preventing them from seeing the conventional truth of the world and are keeping them stuck in the conventional truth not of the world.

With careful distinction among the three types of conventions, I argue, Candrakīrti makes a robust and explicit move away from Tillemans's revolutionary or panfictionalism (which he identifies with global error theory), the view that asserts conventional truth is only fiction or error and that rejects any commitment to truth or reality by assuming a type of "pretense or make-believe" position[22]—directly undermining his accusations that Candrakīrti is a panfictionalist or global error theorist. If Candrakīrti is a panfictionalist or a global error theorist, we should have evidence of Candrakīrti dumbing down conventional truths globally, equating them with fictional truths not of the world. Tillemans's panfictionalism argument may be able to account for the status of fictional concepts as being true, as make-believe or pretense with respect to the defective sensory cognition (even though they are entirely false), which is also Candrakīrti's position.

But it is not clear how such a panfictionalism could ever differentiate between entirely fictional concepts (such as Īśvara) and the genuine beliefs—the actual cognitive processes and ideas—these fictional concepts both arise from and give rise to. Īśvara does not exist according to Candrakīrti because Īśvara is a purely fictional concept, and there is no conventionally true epistemic instrument that warrants its truth. But what about the contents of the beliefs of those who imagine and believe in Īśvara's existence? Don't they have cognitive processes such as beliefs that arise from grasping such fictional concepts? Whether or not Īśvara exists, beliefs in Īśvara's existence are cognitive processes with robust causal efficacies, argues Candrakīrti. I doubt panfictionalism can handle this distinction, although it matters greatly to Candrakīrti's epistemology and psychology.[23] True, he does not consider Īśvara as part of

---

21. Garfield and Thakchoe, 2025, 33–72.

22. Tillemans references Steven Yablo's (1998, 200) oracle argument. See note 5 above.

23. See Garfield and Thakchoe 2025, 8–33, for a comprehensive analysis of why Tillemans's typical or panfictionalist interpretation of Candrakīrti is fundamentally committed to error theory and is ensnared in the "dismal slough."

his ontological categories, but the cognitive and phenomenological processes induced by belief in Īśvara do form a part of Candrakīrti's psychological causal dependence explanation.[24]

We may thus draw the following conclusions: it is crucial to understand that Candrakīrti's epistemology is not confined to the first-order error theory. His contribution to epistemology stresses the importance of rising above both first-order error theory and second-order error theory to develop and appreciate his unique accounts of Madhyamaka epistemology based on the epistemic convention of the world and conventional truth of the world, the epistemic convention of the exalted and conventional truth of the exalted.[25]

Conventional Truth of the World Versus Exalted Conventional Truth

Thus far, I have argued that Candrakīrti pursues important distinctions between epistemic convention *not* of the world and epistemic convention of the world, as well as conventional truths *not* of the world and conventional truths of the world based on the first-order epistemic error as their differentiating criteria. However, there is also the issue of the second-order epistemic error resulting from innate ignorance (*avidyā*), which, Candrakīrti maintains, causes cognitive distortions concerning epistemic judgments about the epistemic conventions of the world and the conventional truth of ordinary beings, thus limiting the scope, accuracy, and efficacy in the delivery of the exalted conventional truth (and exalted ultimate truth). The innate cause of epistemic error—deluded ignorance—functions as the criterion that allows Candrakīrti to articulate epistemic distinctions between the worldly conventional truth of ordinary beings and the exalted conventional truth indicated by the Mādhyamikas. Candrakīrti claims that whereas ignorance as the innate cause of epistemic error underpins the naïve realistic worldly conventional truth of ordinary beings, entirely unbeknownst to them, epistemic instruments of exalted beings operate free from the innate causes of epistemic error, hence defining exalted conventional truths of the Mādhyamikas (the second-order error theory).

In what follows, I turn to Candrakīrti's *Śūnayatāsaptativṛtti*, which addresses the distinction between the inflationary approach and the deflationary approach. Here the *inflationary approach* (*sgro btags pa'i don rig pa*) is the reifying epistemic convention of naïve ordinary beings, who operate under

24. Candrakīrti, *Madhyamakāvatārabhāṣya* ad *Madhyamakāvatāra* 6.114, D 3862, 249a.

25. See Garfield and Thakchoe 2025, 33–72, for a detailed discussion on how Candrakīrti, on our reading, escapes fictionalism and error theory.

the influence of the innate confusion (*moha, avidyā*) with its reifying tendencies to presupposing persons and things in inflationary terms as absolutes; as having objective, intrinsic natures (*svabhāvas*) or inherent characteristics (*svalakṣaṇas*); and as enduring, independent, and persistent selves (*ātmans*). Operating under the sway of ignorance, the worldly epistemic approach carries out its inflationary epistemic judgments based on how things naïvely appear, without critical analysis. This inflationary approach sets the dual epistemic standard for the worldly epistemic convention—*pramāṇa*—in inflationary terms because it (1) presents *saṃvṛtisatya* not as conventional truth but as an ultimate (*paramārtha*), and it does so (2) uncritically, without analysis. Candrakīrti explains that according to worldly epistemic convention, there is a lack of true understanding of reality, and hence it can only metaphorically assert that something is *saṃvṛti*, not fully comprehending its deeper deflationary implications. Even though some ordinary beings may have some conceptual or rational understanding, the epistemic convention of ordinary beings only has an inflationary understanding of what *saṃvṛti* implies—that is, its being deceptive, illusory, and false—since it invariably experiences *saṃvṛti* as factual, genuine, and true.

This is not, however, the case with exalted epistemic convention. "It constitutes an insight into reality, and it is this epistemic convention that understands reality in deflationary terms; there alone lies the ultimate truth (*don dam pa'i bden pa kho na*)."[26] It can genuinely express the insight that things are *saṃvṛti* with full conviction of its deeper deflationary implications. This is Candrakīrti's signature deflationary approach of the exalted epistemic convention. By *deflationary approach (sgro ma btags pa'i don rig pa)*, he specifically means nonreifying epistemic convention of ārya beings, who understand the reality of things and persons in deflationary terms as thoroughgoing relations or dependent originations (*pratītyasamutpāda*), impermanence (*anityatā*), emptiness (*śūnyatā*), and nonself (*anātman*). Operating under the sway of the perspicacious gaze of wisdom, being free from ignorance, the deflationary approach sets the dual epistemic standard (*pramāṇa*) of āryas in deflationary terms: the ārya (1) correctly apprehends things as they are, strictly in terms of their conventional truth, as illusory, empty of *svabhāvas* and *svalakṣaṇas*, and dependently originated, and (2) correctly engages with them nonanalytically without making any assumptions of metaphysical substances.

Candrakīrti endorses four types of deflationary *pramāṇas*—direct per-

---

26. Candrakīrti, *Śūnayatāsaptativṛtti*, D 3867, 268a: *gang du bden pa'i don mi snang ba ma yin la sgro ma btags pa'i don rig pa'i tha snyad la / de la 'di ni don dam pa kho na'o zhes rnam par 'jog go //.*

ception, inference, testimony, and analogy—that are nondeceiving epistemic warrants with respect to their deflationary truths. Defining each of them individually, Candrakīrti is unequivocal in the *Prasannapadā* about the deflationary character of the four *pramāṇa*s and their objects, the *prameyārtha*s, of exalted beings when he says,

> We explain that worldly objects can be apprehended by means of the four *pramāṇa*s, all of which exist by virtue of being mutually dependent upon each other. Where there is *pramāṇa*, there also exists *prameyārtha*; where there exists *prameyārtha*, there also exists *pramāṇa*. The duo—*pramāṇa* and *prameya*—are *absolutely not* intrinsic natures (*svabhāva*). Therefore the world consists of precisely the mode in which things are observed. More can be elaborated on this.[27]

Here is the first philological smoking gun against both of Tillemans's readings, typical and atypical. It is against the typical reading of Tillemans because it categorically denies Candrakīrti *any* account of *pramāṇa* in virtue of his denial of the foundationalist *pramāṇa* theory of the Pramāṇavāda;[28] it is against the atypical reading because it presupposes the absolute truth of the typical reading, which rules out any talk of *pramāṇa* in Candrakīrti's system and presupposes that Tsongkhapa is responsible for imposing the Pramāṇavāda's foundationalist theory of *pramāṇa* on his nonfoundationalist metaphysical system. Nothing could be further from the truth, and nothing could be clearer than the above passage's articulation of the deflationary character of *pramāṇa* and *prameya* as "absolutely not intrinsic natures," completely synchronizing with Candrakīrti's deflationary metaphysics.[29]

In contrast, inflationary *pramāṇa* defines the normative epistemic

27. Candrakīrti, *Prasannapadā* ad *Mūlamadhyamakakārikā* 1.3; La Vallée Poussin 1970, 26: *tāni ca parasparāpekṣayā sidhyanti satsu pramāṇeṣu prameyārthāḥ, satsu prameyeṣvartheṣu pramāṇāni / no tu khalu svābhāvikī pramāṇaprameyayoḥ siddhir iti / tasmāl laukikam evāstu yathādṛṣṭam ity alaṃ prasaṅgena //*; D 3860, 25b: *de'i phyir de ltar tshad ma bzhi las 'jig rten gyi don rtogs par rnam par 'jog pa yin no // de dag kyang phan tshun ltos pas 'grub par 'gyur te / tshad ma dag yod na gzhal bya'i don dag tu 'gyur la / gzhal bya'i don dag yod na tshad ma dag tu 'gyur gyi / tshad ma dang gzhal bya gnyis ngo bo nyid kyis grub pa ni yod pa ma yin no // de'i phyir mthong ba ji lta ba bzhin du 'jig rten pa nyid yin la rag ste / spros pas chog go /.*

28. Tillemans 2019, 641, and Tillemans 2022, 231.

29. For more detail, see Candrakīrti, *Pañcaskandhaprakaraṇa*, D 3866, 180a, for some of the most illuminating discussions on the role of rational analysis in deflationary metaphysics and epistemology of wisdom/knowing (*prajñā* = *shes rab*).

convention of ordinary beings, which takes for granted naïve realism, the folk belief that persons and things are enduring selves, *svalakṣaṇas, svabhāvas*, intrinsic natures, substances, and essences—all under the sway of ignorance. In the *Prasannapadā*, Candrakīrti describes ignorance as "unknowing" (*ajñānaṃ*), "darkness" (*tamo*), and "the concealer (*pracchādakaṃ*) of reality as it is (*yathābhūtārtha*)"—a consciousness that superimposes substances by virtue of which ordinary beings become attached to things.[30] It is the insidious cause of epistemic defects that constitute deep-rooted phenomenological, cognitive, and psychological distortion and confusion. The epistemic problems arising from innate confusion are much subtler when compared to the causes of adventitious epistemic defects, entirely beyond the scope of ordinary, worldly epistemic convention and conventional truth. Ordinary epistemic convention does not even register ignorance as a cause of epistemic defect at all. Rather, ordinary epistemic convention is invariably inflationary, built upon the unquestioned absolute truths of worldly epistemic practices, decisively representing objective truths as epistemically warranted by the *pramāṇa*s.

It is on this ground that Candrakīrti makes it plain, in his commentary on the *Śūnyatāsaptati* of Nāgārjuna, that the exalted convention is primarily responsible for supplying the critical two truths definitions and distinctions.

> Things consist of two truths by virtue of reifying cognition and nonreifying cognition. The epistemic convention of āryas defines (*'phags pas tha snyad mdzad*) them, respectively, as the conventional truth and the ultimate truth. But it is not only exalted beings who employ the convention of defining the two truths. Among ordinary beings are experts in the matters of worldly convention who can do so as well.[31]

This statement from Candrakīrti—the second smoking gun against the so-called typical reading—turns on its head the claim that ordinary beings run the two truths show and determine their definitions and distinctions in

---

30. Candrakīrti, *Prasannapadā* ad *Mūlamadhyamakakārikā* 26.1; La Vallée Poussin 1970, 230: *tatra avidyā ajñānaṃ tamo yathābhūtārthapracchādakaṃ stimitatā /*; D 3860, 182b: *ma rig pa ni mi shes pa ste / mun pa dang yang dag pa ji lta ba la sgrib par byed pa'o /.*

31. Candrakīrti, *Śūnyatāsaptativṛtti*, verse 1, D 3867, 268a: *'dir dngos po rnams phyin ci log dang phyin ci ma log pa'i shes pa'i dbang gis bden pa gnyis te / kun rdzob kyi bden pa dang don dam pa'i bden pa zhes bya bar 'phags pas tha snyad mdzad la / 'phags pa 'ba' zhig kho na bden pa gnyis rnam par 'jog par mdzad pa ma yin te / 'jig rten pa 'jig rten gyi tha snyad la mkhas pa rnams kyang bden pa gnyis kyis tha snyad byed do //.*

Candrakīrti's Madhyamaka. On Tillemans's typical Prāsaṅgika interpretation of Candrakīrti, Mādhyamikas, buddhas, ārya bodhisattvas, and arhats
with their exalted conventions take a backseat as passive observers, simply
endorsing *lokaprasiddha*—the worldly epistemic convention set out by ordinary beings, because the latter set the epistemic standard for the former.[32] But
here, we see Candrakīrti himself directly discredits that interpretation, asserting the exact opposite. The exalted epistemic convention is the key player in
the business of making the two truths distinction alongside some philosophically sophisticated ordinary beings. The worldly epistemic convention of ordinary beings in general is not an authority in making two-truths distinctions
because it operates under the influence of the second-order epistemic defects
of ignorance and does not have the epistemic credentials to rise to the level of
ontologically and epistemically deflating the inflationary—nonillusory and
substantially real—implications of what the term *saṃvṛti* in *saṃvṛtisatya*
entails. Invariably presupposing and reifying *saṃvṛti* to be ontologically
inflationary—as consisting in nonillusory, nonempty objective facts that are
real, unchanging substances—the worldly epistemic convention is not up to
the task of fully understanding the implications of *saṃvṛti* and hence cannot
define with conviction "This is the *saṃvṛti*" (*'di ni kun rdzob pa'o*).[33] This is
because the term *saṃvṛti* means "unreal," "false," and "illusory," and for ordinary beings to fully understand its deeper implications, they would have to
be liberated from their attachment to reality of things and persons, in which
case they would become āryas, not naïve realists attached to their reality. The
ability to deflate the inflationary implications of *saṃvṛti* as unreality, illusory,
fictional nature, however, requires a much higher level of epistemic sophistication and confidence, and ordinary beings, says Candrakīrti, simply lack that
level of insight. Āryas, on the other hand, "understand the deflationary meaning of *saṃvṛti*, and they can confidently assert that things can only be conventionally real and nothing whatsoever can be ultimately real, defining with
conviction 'This alone is *paramārtha* (*don dam pa*).'"[34]

It turns out this realization of the ultimate truth is a necessary condition to
be able to realize the deflationary meaning of *saṃvṛti* effectively; hence only an
exalted epistemic convention can rise to that challenge. Indeed, Candrakīrti

---

32. Tillemans 2022, 231.

33. Candrakīrti, *Śūnyatāsaptativṛtti*, D 3867, 268a: *'di ltar bden pa'i don ni mi snang la sgro btags
pa'i don rigs par tha snyad byed pa la 'di ni kun rdzob pa'o zhes tha snyad byed do //.*

34. Candrakīrti, *Śūnyatāsaptativṛtti*, D 3867, 268a: *gang du bden pa'i don mi snang ba ma yin
la sgro ma btags pa'i don rig pa'i tha snyad la / de la 'di ni don dam pa kho na'o zhes rnam par 'jog
go //.*

explicitly warns us against the typical reading of the error theorist in order "to avoid misrepresenting *saṃvṛti* to mean the perspective of the ordinary beings, for that would," he says, "require committing to the assumption that ordinary beings have the knowledge that the objects are unreal (*mi bden pa'i don*)."[35] However, global error theory or panfictionalism operates on the assumption that the worldly convention of ordinary beings has complete and total control of *saṃvṛtisatya* as fictional or "easy-easy" truth. But Candrakīrti is unequivocal in denying that ordinary epistemic convention can have direct knowledge of *saṃvṛti* as deflationary truth; the so-called easy-easy truth is, in fact, not so easy for ordinary beings to get their heads around, for they are invariably bogged down by the innate grasping at all objects of their experience as inflationary truths, with ultimate and objective reality. "Such objective reality does not exist from the perspective of exalted beings, much like a name assigned to an entity that does not exist. Exalted beings, therefore, take those same objects to be only conventionally real, according to the ordinary convention."[36]

Turning on its head the typical panfictionalist interpretation, according to which *saṃvṛtisatya* is reducible to epistemic errors of ignorance and thus wholly fictional and not true from the perspective of ordinary beings,[37] Candrakīrti argues that only an ārya's epistemic convention has the credibility to understand *saṃvṛtisatya* in purely fictionalist terms as unreality or illusory (*brzun pa nyid*).[38] Since the inflationary epistemic convention of ordinary beings does not withstand Madhyamaka analysis, it "does not exist as objective reality (*yang dag pa'i don*); therefore exalted beings define worldly convention as *saṃvṛti*," in deflationary terms, with a firm epistemic confidence.[39]

Candrakīrti affirms this deflationism in *Yuktiṣaṣṭikāvṛtti* when he says: "It is just so! Since saṃsāra is also a concept (*rtog pa*), nirvāṇa too must be a concept; both exist as worldly conventions." He goes on to cite the Prajñāpāramitā

---

35. Candrakīrti, *Śūnyatāsaptativṛtti*, D 3867, 268a: *re zhig gang la 'di kun rdzob ces tha snyad byed pa de la mi bden pa'i don 'jig rten pas khong du chud pa nyid kyis de'i yul la bsam pa gtang bar mi bya'o //*.

36. Candrakīrti, *Śūnyatāsaptativṛtti*, D 3867, 268a–b: *gang yang 'jig rten gyi tha snyad la bden par 'dod pa de yang 'phags pa rnams 'jig rten kun rdzob kyi bden par bzhed de / med pa'i don la tha snyad 'dogs pa ltar don med pa nyid du brjod do //*.

37. Taktsang 2007, 272.

38. Candrakīrti, *Śūnyatāsaptativṛtti*, D 3867, 268b: *de yang brdzun pa nyid du rtogs par byed pa / 'phags pa nyid kyis 'chad par 'gyur ba'i 'jig rten pa rab tu grags pa'i rigs pa nyid kyis nye bar ston par mdzad de / de ni rab tu grags pa'i dpes ma grags pa'i don rtogs pa'i phyir ro //*.

39. Candrakīrti, *Śūnyatāsaptativṛtti*, D 3867, 268b: *de ni 'dir 'jig rten gyi tha snyad la rnam par dpyad na/ yang dag pa'i don ma grub pa'i phyir 'phags pas 'jig rten gyi tha snyad la kun rdzob ces gsungs so //*.

sūtra in which Śāriputra asks Venerable Subhūti, "Do you claim that even nirvāṇa is like an illusion, like a dream?" to which Subhūti replies, "Śāriputra, even if there were a truth that surpasses nirvāṇa, I would still say, 'This is like an illusion.' If nirvāṇa were not dependent on the concept saṃsāra, it would not be like an illusion. But it is dependent on saṃsāra, so even nirvāṇa must be conceptualized as a conventional truth."[40] From the deflationary standpoint of the exalted epistemic convention, saṃsāra and nirvāṇa stand or fall together; both are ontologically equally deceptive and illusory according to the *Madhyamakāvatāra* on the ground that "the two truths have no intrinsic natures."[41]

In Candrakīrti's deflationism—the view according to which the ultimate truth is that there is no ultimate reality, or the view that there is only conventional reality and there is a natural symmetry between exalted conventional truth and its ultimate truth—nirvāṇa is still the ultimate truth. This is true both epistemically and psychologically but not metaphysically. Nirvāṇa means the culmination of the final knowledge, the realization of the ultimate soteriological goal of the Mādhyamika: achieving the true freedom from psychological conditioning of attraction, repulsion, and confusion caused by the innate epistemic error of ignorance, but it does not stand outside the laws of dependent origination and emptiness that also characterize saṃsāra.

This is directly contrasted with the view of worldly conventional truth, which assumes saṃsāra and nirvāṇa are ontologically hierarchical, with the presumption that nirvāṇa is ontologically superior as ultimately real, whereas saṃsāra is ontologically lesser and merely conventionally real. Candrakīrti states his distinctions between the two approaches carefully and concisely:

> Thus the term *saṃvṛti* is not synonymous with the term *vyavahāra* for ordinary beings. The term has its basis instead in the convention of the *saṃvṛti-paramārtha* distinction, which constitutes two counterparts, of which the term *saṃvṛti* linguistically captures

---

40. Candrakīrti, *Yuktiṣaṣṭikāvṛtti*, D 3864, 7b: *ci mya ngan las 'das pa yang kun rdzob kyi bden pa yin nam / de de bzhin te / 'khor bar yongs su rtog pa yod na mya ngan las 'das par yongs su rtog ste / de gnyi ga yang 'jig rten gyi tha snyad yin pa'i phyir ro // de bas na bcom ldan 'das ma las gsungs pa / tshe dang ldan pa rab 'byor mya ngan las 'das pa yang sgyu ma lta bu rmi lam lta bu'o zhes smra'am / sh'a ri'i bu mya ngan las 'das pa bas ches lhag pa'i chos shig yod na yang sgyu ma lta bu'o zhes kho bo smra'o zhes 'byung ngo // gal te de 'khor bar rtog pa la ltos pa ma yin na de sgyu ma lta bur mi 'gyur ro // de bas na mya ngan las 'das pa yang kun rdzob kyi bden par yongs su brtags pa yin no /.* Cf. Candrakīrti, *Śūnayatāsaptativṛtti*, D 3867, 319a.

41. Candrakīrti, *Madhyamakāvatāra* 6.37–38, D 3861, 206a: *bden pa gnyis su'ang rang bzhin med pa'i phyir //.*

one.[42] The term *saṃvṛti* amounts to the ordinary convention but not reality, as ordinary beings presuppose. It is logical, then, that *exalted beings are exclusively entitled to assert the proposition that saṃvṛti is not reality.* The two terms—*vyavahāra* and *saṃvṛti*—are, for the exalted being, synonymous, and thus there is no inconsistency there.[43]

Here Candrakīrti is emphatic in stating that exalted beings are exclusively capable of fully comprehending the implications of the *saṃvṛti*, ruling out this possibility for ordinary beings. This is the third smoking gun against the typical, panfictionalist reading of Candrakīrti, according to which Candrakīrti allegedly identifies *saṃvṛtisatya* with the deluded epistemic convention of ordinary beings. It is also against Tillemans's atypical reading, which takes for granted that the typical reading has better textual support and that Tsongkhapa's reading of Candrakīrti is unsupported. Believe it or not, Candrakīrti is not introducing anything out of the ordinary here. He is just continuing the standard and orthodox tradition of the Mahāyāna sūtras, such as the *Saṃvṛtiparamārthasatyanirdeśa* (D 179), in which the distinctions are always laid out as "the two noble truths" (*dvayāryasatya*) and likewise as "four noble truths" (*caturāryasatya*) precisely from the perspective of the ārya. Mādhyamikas, according to Candrakīrti, are the ones who came up with the definitions of the two truths in the context of three epistemic conventions; it makes sense that the two truths equally represent, in the context of exalted conventional truth, the ontological and epistemological deflationism of the Madhyamaka. But not so from the perspective of the worldly conventional truth of ordinary beings, where even the term *saṃvṛtisatya* always carries inflationary metaphysical and epistemological baggage.

Conclusion

The discussions I have presented from Candrakīrti's *Prasannapadā* and *Śūnyatāsaptativṛtti* thus shift the burden of proof on Tillemans's typical and atypical readings of Candrakīrti. The philological and philosophical foun-

42. Candrakīrti, *Śūnyatāsaptativṛtti*, D 3867, 268b: *kun rdzob kyi sgra ni 'jig rten pa'i tha snyad kyi rnam grangs ma yin te / kun rdzob dang don dam pa'i dbye bas de ni rnam pa gnyis su gnas pa'i phyir dang tha snyad kyi phyogs gcig la kun rdzob kyi sgras brjod pa'i phyir ro //.*

43. Candrakīrti, *Śūnyatāsaptativṛtti*, D 3867, 268b: *rigs pa'i stobs kyis 'di'i don ni gang zhig 'jig rten gyi tha snyad la kun rdzob kyi sgras brjod la / de ni 'di ltar gang 'jig rten gyi tha snyad 'di ni 'jig rten kun rdzob ste / de ni de kho na nyid ma yin no zhes 'phags pa kho na gsungs par rigs la / tha snyad dang kun rdzob kyi sgra dag kyang rnam grangs nyid de / de la skyon med do //.*

dations on which stand Tillemans's error theory or global fictionalism is the claim that Madhyamaka's two truths distinctions arise from the worldly convention of ordinary beings and that conventional truth is wholly reducible to falsifying inflationary ordinary beliefs. Candrakīrti makes his objection to this reading pointedly in his commentary on Nāgārjuna's *Śūnyatāsaptati* when he says, "It makes no sense to claim that ordinary perception should replace the exalted insight into reality as it is."[44] Thus conventionally true epistemic instruments, or *pramāṇa*s, of ordinary beings cannot supersede the function of conventionally true epistemic instruments of exalted beings. In fact, the exalted conventional truth revises and improves the worldly conventional truth and brings it in line with how things really are: constantly changing events arising and passing away in dependence upon ever-changing causes and conditions, eliminating all unsubstantiated metaphysical presuppositions and beliefs.

We can conclude by remarking: (1) The conventional truths not of the world are *pramāṇa*s with respect to the fictitious objects of defective epistemic instruments because they arise from the defective sensory cognitions. However, these are just epistemic errors, and their objects are mere fictions, hallucinations from the epistemic standard of the worldly conventional truth of healthy epistemic instruments. Therefore we can describe the second-order conventional truth as an error theorist or fictionalist about the first-order conventional truth. (2) The conventional truth of the world is free from such adventitious causes of epistemic defects and therefore is *pramāṇa* with respect to its inflationary—intrinsically real—objects. This worldly conventional truth is also not the final truth; it operates under the pathology of cognitive ignorance as the second-order epistemic error and hence mistakenly reifies conventional truth in inflationary terms as ultimate and objective. Those same inflationary conventional truths of ordinary beings, however, are deflationary truths from the perspective of exalted epistemic convention. (3) The exalted conventional truth is free from the pathology of the second-order causes of epistemic defects and therefore is *pramāṇa* with respect to its objects existing as merely conventional realities. And since there is nothing that can falsify the third-order, exalted conventional truth of the Mādhyamikas, according to Candrakīrti, it not only successfully delivers Madhyamaka's pragmatic conventional epistemic tasks but also satisfies the ultimate epistemic standard of the ultimate truth—that is to say, the realization that the ultimate truth is

---

44. *Śūnyatāsaptativṛtti*, D 3867, 202b: *'jig rten pa'i mthong pas de kho na mthong ba gsal ba rigs pa'ang ma yin te | de ni 'jig rten kho na las tshad ma nyid yin pa'i phyir dang | des dmigs pa'i don yang rdzun pa bslu pa'i chos can nyid du bsgrubs pas phyir ro |.*

that there is no ultimate reality and that there is only conventional reality. This is the trademark of the Prāsaṅgika's enlightened deflationism, which is the direct outcome of its deflationary approach to truth, a far cry from the error theory, according to which Candrakīrti's fictionalism emerges from the ignorance of ordinary beings.

Bibliography

Båve, Arvid. 2006. *Deflationism: A Use-Theoretic Analysis of the Truth-Predicate.* Stockholm Studies in Philosophy 29. Stockholm: Almqvist & Wiksell International.

Candrakīrti. *Catuḥśatakaṭīkā* (*Rgya cher 'grel pa*). D 3865, dbu ma, *ya*, 30b6–239a7.

———. *Madhyamakāvatāra* (*Dbu ma la 'jug pa*). D 3861, dbu ma, *'a*, 201b1–219a7.

———. *Madhyamakāvatārabhāṣya* (*Dbu ma la 'jug pa'i bshad pa*). D 3862, dbu ma, *'a*, 220b–348a.

———. *Pañcaskandhaprakaraṇa* (*Phung po lnga'i rab tu byed pa*). D 3866 dbu ma, *ya*, 239b1–266b7.

———. *Prasannapadā* (*Tshig gsal*). (1) D 3860, dbu ma, *'a*, 1b1–200a. (2) For Sanskrit, see La Vallée Poussin 1970.

———. *Śūnyatāsaptativṛtti* (*Stong nyid bdun cu pa'i 'grel pa*). D 3867, dbu ma, *ya*, 267a1–336b7.

———. *Yuktiṣaṣṭikāvṛtti* (*Rigs pa drug cu pa'i 'grel pa*). D 3864, dbu ma, *ya*, 1b1–30b6.

Garfield, Jay L., and Sonam Thakchoe. 2025. *By the Light of the Moon: Candrakīrti's Prāsaṅgika Madhyamaka.* New York: Oxford University Press.

Jayānanda. *Madhyamakāvatāraṭīkā* (*Dbu ma la 'jug pa'i 'grel bshad*). D 3870, dbu ma, *ra*, 1b–365a.

MacDonald, Anne. 2015. *In Clear Words: The Prasannapadā, Chapter One.* 2 vols. Beiträge zur Kultur- und Geistesgeschichte Asiens 86. Vienna: Verlag der Österreichischen Akademie der Wissenschaften.

Nāgārjuna. *Śūnyatāsaptati* (*Stong pa nyid bdun bcu pa*). D 3827, dbu ma, *tsa*, 24a–27a.

Nolan, Daniel, Greg Restall, and Caroline West. 2005. "Moral Fictionalism Versus the Rest." *Australasian Journal of Philosophy* 83: 307–30.

La Vallée Poussin, Louis de. 1970. *Mūlamadhyamakakārikās* (*Mādhyamikasūtras*) *de Nāgārjuna, avec la Prasannapadā Commentaire de Candrakīrti.* Bibliotheca Buddhica 4. Osnabrück: Biblio Verlag.

Saṃvṛtiparamārthasatyanirdeśa. Kun rdzob dang don dam pa'i bden pa bstan pa'i mdo. D 179, mdo sde, *ma*, 244b–266b.

Siderits, Mark. 2016. *Studies in Buddhist Philosophy.* New York: Oxford University Press.

Szabó, Zoltán. 2001. "Fictionalism and Moore's Paradox." *Canadian Journal of Philosophy* 31: 293–308.

Taktsang Lotsāwa Sherab Rinchen (Stag tshang Lo tsā ba Shes rab rin chen). 2007. *Grub mtha' kun shes nas mtha' 'bral sgrub pa zhes bya ba'i bstan bcos rnam par bshad pa legs bshad kyi rgya mtsho.* Taktsang Lotsawa Sherab Rinchen's Collected Works First Recorded in Tibet, 1:150–362. Beijing: Krung go'i bod rig pa dpe skrung khang.

Tillemans, Tom J. F. 2011. "How Far Can a Mādhyamika Buddhist Reform Conventional Truth? Dismal Relativism, Fictionalism, Easy-Easy Truth, and the Alternatives." In

Moonshadows: Conventional Truth in Buddhist Philosophy, by the Cowherds, 151–65. Oxford: Oxford University Press.

———. 2016. *How Do Mādhyamikas Think? And Other Essays on the Buddhist Philosophy of the Middle*. Studies in Indian and Tibetan Buddhism. Somerville, MA: Wisdom Publications.

———. 2019. "Mādhyamikas Playing Bad Hands: The Case of Customary Truth." *Journal of Indian Philosophy* 47.4: 635–44.

———. 2022. *Views from Tibet: Studies on Tibetan Buddhist Logic, the Philosophy of the Middle, and the Indigenous Grammatico-Linguistic Tradition*. Vienna: Austrian Academy of Sciences Press.

Thakchoe, Sonam. 2012. "Candrakīrti's Theory of Perception: A Case for Non-Foundationalist Epistemology in Madhyamaka." *Acta Orientalia Vilnensia* 11.1: 93–124.

Yablo, Stephen. 1998. "Does Ontology Rest on a Mistake?" *Proceedings of the Aristotelian Society, Supplementary Volumes* 72: 229–61.

PART 2
KNOWLEDGE

Can Emptiness Be Understood Philosophically?

José Ignacio Cabezón

Lfred North Whitehead famously claimed that European philosophy is a series of footnotes to Plato. Tom Tillemans's contributions to Madhyamaka philosophy are so extensive that, especially in a volume in his honor, it is difficult to choose a topic that is not a mere footnote to one of his papers. This chapter elaborates on a topic, innate ignorance, that is only briefly treated in one of Tillemans's footnotes. Although it is but a footnote to one of Tillemans's footnotes, this author nonetheless hopes that the chapter sheds new light on some of questions that have been central to Tom Tillemans's work on Madhyamaka.

Academic Buddhist philosophers—the types of scholars who are included in this book—take as axiomatic the view that their enterprise is independent of Buddhist practice. No Buddhist moral, psychological, or contemplative prerequisite is required to understand, analyze, and make judgments about Buddhist doctrines. You don't have to be saintly to understand or assess the claims found in Buddhist texts, nor does this require expertise in any contemplative practice, any access to extraordinary cognitive states, or any commitment to the Buddhist soteriological project. Buddhist philosophers of old did not posit preconditions for understanding or responding to their views. It is therefore perfectly reasonable to assert that the study of Buddhist philosophy is independent of any form of mental cultivation or meditation. In taking this position, academic Buddhist philosophers are simply positioning themselves on the hither side of the famous emic hearing-reflection-meditation triad and leaving questions of meditation and salvation to others. Surely, that is perfectly appropriate, isn't it?

For a number of years, I have pondered whether it is possible to treat Buddhist philosophical questions divorced from Buddhist practice and soteriology—or rather, whether it is possible to do so without seriously misrepresenting the object of our study. What is lost when Buddhist views of the mind, language, knowledge, and the self are considered freestanding theories distinct from the psychological, therapeutic, and soteriological nexus in which they are enmeshed? What might be gained by properly contextualizing them within the tradition of Buddhist practice? What would it mean, for example, to see *apoha* "as part of the Buddhist program of emancipating people from the clutches of attachment," as Pradeep Gokhale has suggested (2013, 605)? What would it mean to do philosophy in a way that acknowledges the polysemy of the term *reasoning* (*yukti*), which, according to Richard Nance (2007), is (in some sources at least) inextricably linked to one-pointedness of mind or to the acquisition of gnosis?

No doubt, it is sometimes possible to decontextualize Buddhist ideas—to treat them apart from psychological, therapeutic, and soteriological concerns. But aren't there cases in which failure to properly attend to the contemplative dimensions of a Buddhist claim distorts it to the point of misrepresentation?

This essay considers one such example, drawn from Tibetan Madhyamaka, that suggests that the Buddhist doctrine of no-self or emptiness *cannot* be understood in strictly conceptual, linguistic terms but instead requires the cultivation of certain inner psychological states. If true—if introspection and meditation are essential to understanding emptiness conceptually—then partitioning Madhyamaka into a strictly philosophical and a strictly contemplative side is impossible. Put another way, if our Tibetan sources are correct, then contemplation is part and parcel of understanding emptiness philosophically.

Tsongkhapa (1357–1419) was one of the most famous advocates of the view that understanding emptiness was as much a contemplative as a rational/conceptual act. He believed that because emptiness is a phenomenon beyond the ken of the senses—because it is "hidden" (*lkog gyur, parokṣa*)—it has to be known inferentially through a syllogism (*sbyor ba, prayoga*), at least initially. The inference involves four steps: (1) identifying the object of negation (*dgag bya, pratiṣedhya*), (2) understanding the syllogism's pervasion (*khyab pa, vyāpti*), (3) understanding that the "reason is instantiated in the subject" (*phyogs chos, pakṣadharma*), and finally (4) understanding the predicate (*sādhyadharma, sgrub bya'i chos*) or conclusion: emptiness, the lack of inherent existence.[1] The importance of the first step—identifying what is to be negated (*dgag bya ngos 'dzin*), or correctly understanding the negandum—is a hall-

---

1. The four points follow the Fifth Dalai Lama's *Revelations of Mañjuśrī* (see below). For Tsongkhapa's wording, see Tsong kha pa, *Dbu ma'i lta khrid*, 886. Later scholars sometimes identify the steps differently—e.g., (1) ascertaining the object of negation (*dgag bya nges pa*), how the self appears to the innate mind; (2) ascertaining the pervasion (*khyab pa nges pa*), that if the self existed as it appears, it would have to be the same as or different from the mind and body; (3) ascertaining that the self is not truly the same (*bden pa'i gcig bral du nges pa*); and (4)

mark of Tsongkhapa's thought, and it is what concerns us here.[2] The negan-dum must be identified or understood for two reasons: first, because it is part of the syllogism proving emptiness. For the syllogism to succeed in yielding knowledge of emptiness, each of its various parts must be understood, and some would say understood not just superficially but in a very strong way: by a valid means of knowledge or *pramāṇa*.[3] Second, since emptiness is a negation—the negation of true or inherent existence—unless the negandum (true existence) is precisely understood, one ends up negating either too much or too little and therefore falls into the extreme of nihilism or eternalism. That, in any case, is Tsongkhapa's position.

Key to identifying the object of negation, says Tsongkhapa, is the notion of innate ignorance (*ma rig pa lhan skyes*, **sahaja/sāhajika avidyā*).[4] All sentient beings suffer from beginningless ignorance that makes everything appear to be truly or inherently existent—to exist from its own side independent of thought and language. The minds of sentient beings assent to this false appear-ance. This causes other mental afflictions like anger to arise, which in turn causes karma, rebirth, and suffering. There are different kinds of ignorance, but the one that is responsible for this cascading series of effects culminating in rebirth and suffering is innate. Innate ignorance exists in all beings, even in the most primitive life forms like insects. If it did not, argues Tsongkhapa, what would cause these creatures to continue to be reborn? Innate ignorance does not involve speech or language. It is therefore subtler than the conceptual forms of ignorance found among humans and other beings (like the gods) who

ascertaining that it is not truly different (*bden pa'i du bral du nges pa*). See e.g., Blo bzang bstan pa rab rgyas, *'Jam dpal zhal lung gi snying po bdud rtsi gser zhun yang gsal sgron me*, 232–34.

2. Tibetan authors before Tsongkhapa—Drolungpa, Chapa, Maja, and so on—also wrote on the negandum, but a comparison of their understanding of the object of negation lies beyond the scope of this essay. While the negandum is an object of inquiry in the works of many earlier Madhyamaka writers, Tsongkhapa's claim that the identification of the negandum requires understanding the object of innate ignorance is, as far as I can tell, unique to him.

3. Hence, when Baso Jé explains this first point in his *Great Instructions on the Madhyamaka View* (*Dbu ma'i lta khrid chen mo*, 12), he calls it "the *pramāṇa* that ascertains the way in which . . . the negandum appears to the innate mind."

4. We do not know when precisely Tsongkhapa came to see the correct understanding of innate ignorance as central to his theory of emptiness. The idea is found in his early Madhyamaka writings like the *Lam rim chen mo*, written in 1402, and persists through to his final Madhyamaka work, the *Illuminating the Intent* (*Dgongs pa rab gsal*), a commentary on Candrakīrti's *Madhyamakāvatāra* written in 1418. Discussion of the innate grasping at the "I" is also found in several sections of Tsongkhapa's commentary to Nāgārjuna's *Madhyamakakārikā*, the *Ocean of Reasoning*. See Tsong kha pa, *Rigs pa'i rgya mtsho*, 26–27, 186–87; Rje Tsong Khapa 2006, 36–37, 244–45.

possess language. Many false ideas about the world require language: the idea that there is a permanent soul or that things have essences. These ideas are not innate to beings. Bugs, for example, do not think about souls or essences. Conceptual constructs like *ātman* are imagined (*kun tu brtags pa, *parikalpita*). People acquire these ideas by being taught them. By comparison to innate ignorance, learned misconceptions—like the idea that the self is permanent, unitary, and independent—are more gross, and taking them as the object of negation means that the negation will not go far enough and therefore that emptiness will not be understood or, worse, will be misunderstood.[5] The world appears incorrectly to both acquired and innate ignorance, and Tsongkhapa believes that the object of both forms of ignorance must be negated but that it is only by negating how things appear to innate ignorance (*ma rig pa lhan skyes la snang ba'i snang tshul*) that we come to a correct understanding of emptiness.[6] As Tsongkhapa states, the false self

> must be identified *within our own mind* and then must be established as nonexistent based on the way that error is actually held *within our own mind.* Contrariwise, philosophy (*dgag sgrub*) that is directed externally leads nowhere; it is like searching for a thief in the meadow when the tracks lead into the woods.[7]

Phabongkha Dechen Nyingpo likewise asserts that studying Madhyamaka philosophy

> may allow one to refute an opponent in debate, but we have not truly recognized the object to be negated until we identify it *within our own experience* . . . It must be identified within the naked experience of our own mind, not just according to others' explanations or in a merely linguistic or conceptual way.[8]

---

5. Phabongkha Rinpoche (1878–1941) suggests that engaging in the act of negation without understanding that the negandum is related to innate ignorance can also result in nihilism. For example, when the vase is seen not to be its spout, base, "belly," and so on, there is a danger that this will lead to the false conclusion that there is no vase at all. Pha bong kha, *Lam rim rnam grol lag bcangs*, 500.

6. This first step in the process of understanding emptiness is considered so important that, according to Jeffrey Hopkins, "some teachers advise watching the I for a week or even months before proceeding to the second step" (1996, 46).

7. Tsong kha pa, *Dgongs pa rab gsal*, 120; Tsongkhapa 2021, 189.

8. Pha bong kha, *Lam rim rnam grol lag bcangs*, 500. My translation benefits from the excellent

However, because innate ignorance is very subtle, understanding it and understanding how the self appears to it—that is, identifying true existence, the object of negation—is said to be extremely difficult and requires extraordinary means. Techniques for gaining access to the innate "I" are elaborated in the supplementary instructions (*man ngag, upadeśa*) on emptiness found in the works of Tsongkhapa but especially in the writings of the later Geluk tradition, to which we now turn.

The Fifth Dalai Lama's (1617–1682) *Revelations of Mañjuśrī: Instructions on the Stages of the Path*,[9] is one of the Geluk tradition's "eight great teachings on the *lamrim*" (*lam rim khrid chen brgyad*). The text provides one of the clearest treatments of how, in practical terms, to identify the negandum.[10] The relevant passage is found in a section of *Revelations* on the no-self of persons (*gang zag gyi bdag med, pudgalanairātmya*). The Fifth Dalai Lama follows Tsongkhapa's four-step scheme to come to an inferential understanding of emptiness. It is the first of these four, the identification of the negandum, that interests us here. This is how the Fifth Dalai Lama begins the discussion:

> The first step is identifying how the innate grasping at the "I" holds the "I." *Buddhapālita's Commentary* states that unless you perfectly identify . . . the object to be negated, the aspect of the self that does not exist, it is like leading an army into battle without knowing where the enemy is, or like shooting arrows without figuring out what the target is . . . Unless the generic image (*don spyi*) of the negandum properly appears to the mind, there is no ascertaining the no-self that is the negation of that object.[11]

translation of Sermey Khensur Lobsang Tharchin and Artemus B. Engle; see Pabongka Rinpoche 2001, 3:276.

9. Ngag bdang blo bzang rgya mtsho, *Lam rim 'jam pa'i dbyangs kyi zhal lung*.

10. The Fifth Dalai Lama states that the bulk of his lamrim lineage descends from Jé Sherab Sengé (Rje Shes rab seng ge, 1385–1445), but the particular instructions on the no-self of persons, he states, is "an experiential teaching that has been transmitted mouth-to-mouth based on the experiences of the great charioteer, the omniscient Norsang Gyatso"; Ngag bdang blo bzang rgya mtsho, *Lam rim 'jam pa'i dbyangs kyi zhal lung*, 197 (translated in Ngawang Losang Gyatso 2022, 360). Mkhas grub nor bzang rgya mtsho (1423–1513) was a student of the First Dalai Lama Gendun Drup (Dge 'dun grub, 1391–1474), from whom he received the lineage of the lamrim teachings. A great adept who spent about forty years of his life in solitary retreat, Norsang Gyatso is counted as the fifty-seventh holder of the lamrim transmission lineage. For a short biography see Cabezón 2017.

11. Ngag bdang blo bzang rgya mtsho, *Lam rim 'jam pa'i dbyangs kyi zhal lung*, 197.

Following Tsongkhapa, the Fifth Dalai Lama defines the negandum as "how the innate grasping at the 'I' holds the 'I'"—that is, the way in which the "I" or self appears to our innate sense of self. Identifying the negandum, he continues, is itself a two-step process: first, becoming aware of our innate sense of self, and second, gleaning how the self appears when that innate sense of self is active within the mind. The latter is the actual identification of the negandum. The negandum itself, he states, is "[the self's] existence under its own power and from its own side, without being imputed by the mind."

To undo innate ignorance requires, first, that the innate sense of self be made vivid within the mind. Tsongkhapa himself implies that this is not straightforward.

> When you analyze how the "I" appears to the mind, if it is unstable (*yor ba'i rnam par snang*), then you have not understood how to analyze the innate "I." It is necessary to ascertain how the "I" appears *at the precise time* that the thought "I" abruptly arises. After that . . . it gets mixed up with other things and cannot be ascertained. To ascertain it, correct your posture, straighten your spine, and making your mind smart and clever . . . first settle into a state of watchful attentiveness (*shes bzhin gyi bya ra*) thinking, "I need to precisely ascertain how the 'I' is appearing." Then, if the thought "I" does not arise on its own, make it intentionally appear. Artificially creating the thought "I," as soon as it abruptly arises, analyze how it appears, and you will then know its own mode of appearance.[12]

Tsongkhapa is outlining a contemplative exercise that leads the adept to understanding how the innate sense of self actually operates within the mind. It is a psychological exercise that involves introspection, attention, and awareness. Tsongkhapa suggests that the process is not easy or straightforward. If the "I" is unstable, it means that the innate self has not fully arisen in the mind. If the innate sense of self remains hidden, he recommends inducing it artificially (*chad du gnyer nas nga'o snyam pa'i blo bcos*), but he does not describe how precisely to do that. The Fifth Dalai, however, explains this very clearly.

> Whether we are asleep or awake, there always exists in our mind a strong sense of "I." But when we encounter things that make us sad or happy, that sense of "I" manifests in an even stronger way. Even when we don't experience such states of joy or pain, it is still

---

12. Tsong kha pa, *Dbu ma'i lta khrid*, 887–88.

present but in a slightly less clear way. Most of those who teach the Madhyamaka view nowadays spout off about the "importance of how the innate sense of 'I' holds the 'I,'" but only as dry words, without analyzing whether such a sense of self is manifest. This is tantamount to pointing at someone whose facial features you only vaguely saw and saying, "That's so-and-so who robbed me yesterday." It's no way to catch the thief. Instead, you must first bring to mind again and again those past instances when you had a clear and self-evident thought of happiness or suffering that was the product of someone truly harming or helping you—for example, when someone falsely accused you of stealing, or when someone gave you something you desired.

In the first case, think, "Never, even in the deepest recesses of my mind, have I had the thought of stealing, but they have accused me of theft!" While experiencing outrage, the "I"—the "I" that is being accused of theft—becomes strong and clear in the middle of your heart, and it appears as vividly as if it could be seen by the eyes and touched by the hand. Likewise, when you think, "These others have helped me in such and such a way," there vividly appears in the center of your heart an "I" that is the beneficiary of their assistance. The mental state that you elicit in dependence on either of these two methods causes other rough conceptual thoughts to become dormant and the innate sense of "I" to become stronger. As this is happening, it is necessary to analyze *how* precisely that mental state is holding the "I."[13]

The Fifth Dalai Lama is here describing the first step to achieve a conceptual understanding of the emptiness of the person: becoming aware of the innate "I," our innate reification of the self. It is important to emphasize that at this point the adept is still on the way to a conceptual understanding of emptiness because the language of the text, filled as it is with instructions about how the self presents itself to the mind and techniques on how to manipulate this, may give one the false impression that it is describing a process that results in a *non*conceptual understanding of emptiness, but that is not the case. The result of all four steps is "the generation of the Madhyamaka view": the conceptual or philosophical understanding of emptiness. A lot of meditation is still required after that to transform that conceptual understanding of emptiness into the direct perception of emptiness that constitutes the first moment of the path of

13. Ngag bdang blo bzang rgya mtsho, *Lam rim 'jam pa'i dbyangs kyi zhal lung,* 198–99.

seeing. But what is being presented here, first by Tsongkhapa and then by the Fifth Dalai Lama, are techniques leading to an understanding of the object being negated via inference. Both authors make it quite clear that without first engaging in such practices, the inference—and hence the conceptual understanding of emptiness—is impossible.

The innate sense of self, the Fifth Dalai Lama states, is always present, but it is stronger and more "visible" when we feel threatened, angry, or happy.[14] It is not possible to identify the negandum—and therefore not possible to proceed to the inference that proves emptiness—without first eliciting an innate sense of self that is clear and vivid. The Fifth Dalai Lama belittles those who pay mere lip service to the psychological process of inducing a vivid sense of the self, comparing them to people who accuse someone of robbing them without really having taken a good look at the thief. He then explains the mental exercises necessary to make the innate sense of self manifest vividly. Once this has been accomplished and that self appears, it is then necessary to analyze *how* it appears—how it reifies the self and grasps it as real. If understanding the innate self is difficult, understanding its "mode of appearance" is even more so.

> It is extremely difficult to analyze both the "I" and *how* the "I" is being grasped simultaneously within a single mental state. When the thought of how it is being grasped is strong, the sharpness of the main object, the "I," becomes unclear and disappears. What is the solution? Quiescence meditation (*zhi gnas, śamatha*) . . . In place of the usual object of quiescence meditation—the visualization of the Buddha's body, for instance—you elicit instead the mental state that thinks "I." While the main part of that mind rests on that "I," a corner of the mind sees, with clear sharpness, how—in what way— it is being grasped. It is said to be like two people walking side by side. While the main part of the eye is looking at the road, the corner of the eye is looking at the companion.
>
> Up to this point you have no real discernment of what the "I" is based on—no discernment apart from its seeming to be in the center of your heart. But from this point forward, as the corner of your mind properly analyzes it, it begins to appear in various ways. Sometimes it seems as though the "I" is based on the body; some-

---

14. Tom Tillemans's suggestion that innate ignorance "might look more to us like unconscious basic biological drives, even a lowest common denominator to life, such as a survival instinct" is consistent with the fact that it manifests (i.e., becomes conscious) when the self is threatened (Tillemans 2016, 46n39).

times it seems to be based on the mind; sometimes it seems to be based on one of the other aggregates. But finally, you will come to see it as based on an undifferentiated whole in which the body and mind appear as if water mixed with milk,[15] and in which the "I" seems to exist, beginninglessly, from its own side—seems to exist inherently and tenaciously. The identification of the "I" as existing in this way is the first of the four points: the ascertainment of what is to be negated. Analyze that until you experience it at a deep level.[16]

Having caused the innate sense of self to appear vividly, it is necessary to then identify *how* it grasps its object since it is in that "how" that the negandum, true existence, will be found. But because it is difficult to hold any object in mind while simultaneously analyzing it, it is necessary at this point to resort to an extraordinary mental state that permits such fine analysis: *śamatha* or quiescence, the fruit of meditation. Here, quiescence is being employed not to deepen the conceptual understanding of emptiness (as it will be later) but rather to identify the negandum, the false, reified quality the mind ascribes to the self, the first step on the way to a conceptual understanding of emptiness. Once the negandum has been identified, the adept then applies one or another form of Madhyamaka reasoning—for instance, the reason of "neither one nor many"—to ascertain its nonexistence. This takes place over the next three steps, culminating in the conceptual ascertainment that there is no inherently existing self.

The last three steps—the ascertainment of *vyāpti*, *pakṣadharma*, and *sādhya*—clearly fall under the rubric of what we understand to be philosophy, but the identification of the negandum, requiring various contemplative

---

15. Khedrup Jé in his *Lamp to Dispel Darkness: Instructions on the View* (*Lta khrid mun sel sgron me*) states, "If you look gently from a corner without losing the consciousness thinking 'I,' there is a separate mode of appearance of I to the consciousness which thinks 'I,' and this appearance is not any of the mental and physical aggregates. The I does not appear to be just a nominal designation, but appears as if self-established. Through holding that the I exists the way it appears, you are bound in cyclic existence." The passage is as translated in Hopkins 1996, 45. A similar claim is made in Tsongkhapa's *Instructions on the View* (Tsong kha pa, *Dbu ma'i lta khrid*, 896): "In general, the aggregates do not appear to the innate mind that apprehends the 'I' ... but appear just prior to it ... In the innate thought 'I' the 'I' appears to be none of the aggregates." The position that the aggregates do not appear to the innate "I" seems to contradict the Fifth Dalai Lama's view that the aggregates appear to it as an undifferentiated whole. Pha bong kha, *Lam rim rnam grol lag bcangs*, 502, adopts the Fifth Dalai Lama's position. How the aggregates appear to the innate "I" is briefly discussed in Hopkins 1996, 46 and 177.

16. Ngag bdang blo bzang rgya mtsho, *Lam rim 'jam pa'i dbyangs kyi zhal lung*, 199–200.

exercises and psychological interventions, seems to fall outside of the scope of philosophy. Can emptiness then be understood philosophically? The answer depends on what one considers philosophy to be. According to Tsongkhapa and his heirs, the doctrine of no-self cannot be understood within any system of philosophy that excludes introspection and deep contemplation from the philosophical project. This precludes most contemporary academic Buddhist philosophy from understanding emptiness. Vice versa, most of the Euro-American analytical tradition would likely be inimical to considering the Gelukpas' process of understanding emptiness to be philosophical.[17]

We'll come back shortly to the question of whether there are *other* forms of Western philosophy that might be more congenial to Tsongkhapa's enterprise. But before we do, we need to consider two other issues. The first is hermeneutical. How idiosyncratic is Tsongkhapa's view? Is it his own creation, or can it be supported by Indian śāstric sources? Why should we think that identifying the object of negation as the object of innate ignorance was a part of the Indian Madhyamaka tradition? Tsongkhapa is clearly aware that this is an issue and quotes various Madhyamaka treatises in support of his view. For example, he quotes Kamalaśīla's *Madhyamakāloka* to demonstrate that all beings hold the world to be inherently real due to their beginningless predispositions for error.[18] Although Kamalaśīla never uses the word *innate*, that this error is innate and not philosophical is arguably inferable from the facts that (a) it is found in all beings and not just in humans and (b) it is caused by karmic predispositions and not acquired through learning.[19] Tsongkhapa also quotes different verses from Candrakīrti's *Madhyamakāvatāra* (6.122cd, 6.124cd, and 6.140–41) that suggest that a permanent soul and other heterodox ideas about the nature of the self cannot be the basis of our sense of self because people have robust notions of self without knowing anything about these philosophical dogmas.[20] To think that one therefore arrives at an understanding of no-self by refuting only such philosophically acquired beliefs is,

---

17. See, however, Georges Dreyfus's (2014, 135–36) remarks concerning the views of Galen Strawson, who believes that "the inquiry into the nature of the self needs to relate to the ways in which we actually conceive of ourselves."

18. The lines from Kamalaśīla's *Madhyamakāloka* are quoted by Tsongkhapa in a discussion of the identification of the negandum in the Svātantrika school. Tsong kha pa, *Dgongs pa rab gsal*, 109–10; Tsongkhapa 2021, 174–75.

19. For an extensive discussion of Tsongkhapa's understanding of this passage, see Yi 2015.

20. Tsongkhapa quotes *Madhyamakāvatāra* 6.122 and 6.124 in Tsong kha pa, *Rigs pa'i rgya mtsho*, 186; Rje Tsong Khapa 2006, 244. The *Madhyamakāvatārabhāṣyā* (on 6.140–41) is quoted in the *Lam rim chen mo*. Tsong kha pa, *Byang chub lam rim che ba*, 645; Tsong-kha-pa 2002, 3:197. Tsongkhapa also obviously comments on all four verses in his commentary on

Candrakīrti states, absurd. While these various passages from Candrakīrti provide some support for Tsongkhapa's theory, nowhere does Candrakīrti explicitly mention innate ignorance, much less techniques for gaining access to an innate sense of self. But despite the lack of robust Indian textual warrants for Tsongkhapa's theory as a whole,[21] one can certainly see how the various views found in Indian texts—that even nonhumans suffer from ignorance, that the sense of self is not learned but derives from predispositions, and that dispelling learned misconceptions about the self does not undermine self-grasping—served as the building blocks for Tsongkhapa's views.

The lack of explicit textual warrants is not the only challenge facing Tsongkhapa's theory. Other problems have even been noted within the Geluk tradition itself. For example, some Geluk Madhyamaka sources suggest that distinguishing between a thing and its inherent existence is extremely difficult.[22] For instance, the conventional self (the basis of negation, *dgag gzhi*) and the inherent existence it appears to have (the object of negation, *dgag bya*) are so intertwined in the mind that they are very difficult to disentangle.[23] Some Geluk sources suggest that the ability to separate a thing's inherent existence from the thing itself does not occur until emptiness has been conceptually understood.[24] This of course presents a problem, for identifying

Candrakīrti's *Madhyamakāvatāra*; Tsong kha pa, *Dgongs pa rab gsal*, 297–99 and 316–17; Tsongkhapa 2021, 425–28 and 448–49.

21. I leave open the question of whether there are other Indian treatises *not* quoted by Tsongkhapa that might lend credence to his views. Several Indian śāstras distinguish between innate and acquired ignorance, or between a self that is innate and one that is acquired (*lhan cig skyes pa'am kun tu brtags pa'i bdag*), usually in the context of discussions of which are abandoned on which paths. Whether any of these texts support Tsongkhapa's views remains to be investigated.

22. On this point, see also Jinpa 2002, 52–53.

23. It is precisely because our cognitions of the conventional world are shot through and through with ignorance that the Sakya scholar Taktsang Lotsāwa (Stag tshang lo tsā ba, b. 1405) went a step further and claimed that enlightenment eliminates not only false appearances but all appearances. He claimed, in other words, that buddhas do not cognize any conventional truths whatsoever, since that would be tantamount to cognizing things that are wholly the creations of ignorance. See Yakherds 2021.

24. Tsongkhapa makes this claim in both the *Lam rim chen mo* and the *Legs bshad snying po*. The topic is discussed in Rdzong dkar 'Jigs med dam chos rgya mtsho, *Drang nges 'jug ngogs*, 578–79: "As [Tsongkhapa states in his *Exposition of*] Insight (*Lhag mthong*), 'Until they understand the view that there is no inherent existence, it is impossible for those individuals to distinguish between *mere existence* and *intrinsic existence*. This means that until the Madhyamaka view has arisen in the mind, innate valid cognitions of conventions (*tha snyad pa'i lhan skyes kyi tshad ma*) cannot be distinguished from valid cognitions that see intrinsic existence (*rang gi ngo bos yod pa 'jal ba'i tshad ma*), and mere existence cannot be distinguished from intrinsic existence . . . But once the view is understood, they can be distinguished."

inherent existence—isolating it as an object distinct from the self—is precisely what the identification of the negandum is all about. We therefore seem to be caught in a vicious circle: the negandum cannot be understood unless one first understands emptiness, and one cannot understand emptiness unless one first identifies the negandum. Gelukpa exegetes attempt to solve this dilemma in different ways. Some claim that when Tsongkhapa said that it was impossible to distinguish between a thing's "mere existence" (*yod pa tsam*) and its inherent existence without prior understanding of emptiness, he didn't mean this to apply to everyone but only to adepts with inferior intellects.[25] Others solve the problem by claiming that the cognition that understands inherent existence is not true knowledge—not a *pramāṇa*—but rather a weaker epistemic instrument called *correct assumption* (*yid dpyod, manaḥparīkṣā*), and thus identifying the negandum doesn't require real knowledge of true existence—something that would be impossible without prior understanding of emptiness—but that identifying the negandum minimally gleans inherent existence; that is, it gleans it enough to proceed to the following steps, its negation through Madhyamaka reasoning.[26]

Some forms of Buddhism—those most suspicious of language, those least bothered by contradiction, and so on—are going to be inimical to the philosophical project from the start. At first blush, Jé Tsongkhapa's Madhyamaka doesn't strike one as being of this type, and for decades Western scholars with a philosophical bent have found in the Geluk tradition a worthy conversa-

---

25. Rdzong dkar 'Jigs med dam chos rgya mtsho, *Drang nges 'jug ngogs*, 579: "The *Ornament to the Lord Father's Thought: A Letter* states that merely through an introduction to the imputed nature of things, the most intelligent disciples, who adopt Prāsaṅgika Madhyamaka philosophy from the start of their spiritual journey, perfectly distinguish between these two—between mere existence and inherent existence—before ascertaining the contours of the negandum. A few intelligent Prāsaṅgikas can distinguish between the two simply by ascertaining the *pakṣadharma* that is, for example, part of ascertaining a subject as being devoid of an essence in the seven ways. Still others find the view by ascertaining the difference between the two through correct assumption (*yid dpyod*) and then go on to fully differentiate them later through a full-fledged *pramāṇa*. Dullards and realists do not understand the difference between the two even through mere assumption, and if they find the view at all, they do so by understanding mere existence and inherent existence individually."

26. For an example of this solution to the problem, see Dga' byang Lha rams pa Bsod nams rgya mtsho, "Dbu ma'i dgag bya ngos 'dzin la dpyad pa," which states: "Since identifying the negandum comes before 'finding the view,' the mind that first ascertains the negandum must be accepted as being an experience of correct assumption that comes about through study (*thos byung*). There are individuals who possess actual knowledge (*tshad ma*) of the object of negation, individuals who possess subsequent knowledge (*bcad shes*) of that, and so on. Thus the mind that identifies the object of negation can be of various types: true knowledge, correct assumption, subsequent knowledge, and so on."

tion partner. But the Geluk theory of the negandum and its views about the lengths to which one must go to understand it should give us pause. For if Tsongkhapa and his followers are right, then philosophy as we know it—as an enterprise that is directed "outwardly" and not at inner cognitive processes— will always fail to understand emptiness *even conceptually*. If understanding emptiness requires one to induce certain emotional states, to engage in deep introspection, and even to have mastered quiescence meditation, as the Fifth Dalai Lama suggests, it would not be surprising if academic philosophers were to take a pass on any Gelukpa invitation to engage in a conversation about emptiness, for who wants to dialogue with someone who considers one's understanding as "leading nowhere . . . as akin to searching for a thief in the meadow when the tracks lead into the woods"?

Not all forms of philosophy, however, are likely to be ill disposed to the Geluk approach. Phenomenology in its broad sense as the study of conscious experience "from the subjective or first person point of view"[27] may well be congenial to it. And emerging fields like the philosophy of meditation will almost certainly be positively predisposed to the possibility of a dialogue with Gelukpa thinkers on this issue. In any case, the goal of this essay was not to plot the way forward but only to show that the path of a meaningful encounter between academic Buddhist philosophy and the traditions that are its objects of study is not nearly as simple and straightforward as we normally take it to be. And if this essay leaves you wondering whether it is possible to understand emptiness in a strictly philosophical way, then that goal will have been achieved.

Bibliography

Ba so Chos kyi rgyal mtshan. *Dbu ma'i lta khrid chen mo.* In *Dbu ma'i lta khrid phyogs bsdebs skad cig tu srid pa hrul por byed pa'i man ngag nges legs nor bu'i mdzod la dbang 'byor pa'i zhi sgo gcig pu,* 2–40. Mundgod: Drepung Loseling Educational Society, 1999.

Blo bzang bstan pa rab rgyas. *Byang chub lam gyi rim pa'i dmar khrid 'jam dpal zhal lung gi snying po bdud rtsi gser zhun yang gsal sgron me.* Blo bzang bstan pa rab rgyas kyi gsung 'bum, 1:119–243. PDF of a xylograph from the Rong po dgon chen blocks dating to 1990–1999. BDRC MW28897.

Cabezón, José I. 2017. "Khedrub Norzang Gyatso." *Treasury of Lives.* https://treasuryoflives .org/biographies/view/Khedrub-Norzang-Gyatso/10168.

Dga' byang Lha rams pa Bsod nams rgya mtsho. "Dbu ma'i dgag bya ngos 'dzin la bod snga phyi'i mkhas pa'i bzhed mtshams la dpyad pa'i gtam rgya mtsho chu thigs." Bod rig pa website. https://bodrigpa.org/archives/3037. Accessed 1/3/2023.

Dreyfus, Georges. 2014. "Self and Subjectivity: A Middle Way Approach." In *Self, No Self?*

27. This is the way phenomenology is defined by Smith 2018.

Perspectives from Analytical, Phenomenological, and Indian Traditions, edited by Mark Siderits, Evan Thompson, and Dan Zahavi. Oxford: Oxford University Press.

Gokhale, Pradeep P. 2013. "An Exclusive Volume on Exclusion." *Philosophy East and West* 63.4: 605–16.

Hopkins, Jeffrey. 1996. *Meditation on Emptiness*. Rev. ed. Boston: Wisdom Publications.

Jinpa, Thupten. 2002. *Self, Reality and Reason in Tibetan Philosophy: Tsongkhapa's Quest for the Middle Way*. London: RoutledgeCurzon.

Nance, Richard. 2007. "On What Do We Rely When We Rely on Reasoning?" *Journal of Indian Philosophy* 35.2: 149–67.

Ngag bdang blo bzang rgya mtsho (Fifth Dalai Lama). *Byang chub lam gyi rim pa'i khrid yig 'jam pa'i dbyangs kyi zhal lung*. In *Lam khrid 'jam dpal zhal lung dang bde lam*, 1–228. Lan kru'u: Kan su'u mi rigs dpe skrun khang, 1999. Translated in Ngawang Losang Gyatso 2022.

Ngawang Losang Gyatso, The Fifth Dalai Lama. 2022. *Words of Mañjuśrī: A Guide to the Stages of the Path*. Translated by Rosemary Patton with Dagpo Rinpoché. In *Stages of the Path and the Oral Transmission*, edited by Thupten Jinpa, 207–382. The Library of Tibetan Classics 6. Somerville, MA: Wisdom Publications.

Pha bong kha Bde chen snying po. *Lam rim rnam grol lag bcangs*. Bylakuppe: Ser smad dpe mdzod, 1998. (Translated in Pabongka 2001.)

Pabongka Rinpoche. 2001. *Liberation in Our Hands, Part Three: The Ultimate Goals*. Translated by Sermey Khensur Lobsang Tharchin with Artemus B. Engle. Howell, NJ: Mahayana Sutra and Tantra Press.

Rdzong dkar 'Jigs med dam chos rgya mtsho. *Drang ba dang nges pa'i don rnam par 'byed pa'i bstan bcos legs bshad snying po'i bsdus don drang nges 'jug ngogs*. Bylakuppe: Ser smad dpe mdzod khang, 2004.

Rje Tsong Khapa. 2006. *Ocean of Reasoning: A Great Commentary on Nāgārjuna's Mūlamadhyamakakārikā*. Translated by Jay L. Garfield and Geshe Ngawang Samten. New York: Oxford University Press.

Smith, David Woodruff. 2018. "Phenomenology." *The Stanford Encyclopedia of Philosophy*, edited by Edward N. Zalta. https://plato.stanford.edu/archives/sum2018/entries /phenomenology.

Tillemans, Tom J. F. 2016. *How Do Mādhyamikas Think? And Other Essays on the Buddhist Philosophy of the Middle*. Studies in Indian and Tibetan Buddhism. Boston: Wisdom Publications.

Tsong kha pa Blo bzang grags pa. *Byang chub lam rim che ba*. Xining: Mtsho sngon mi rigs dpe skrun khang, 1985. Translated in Tsong-kha-pa 2002.

———. *Dbu ma thal 'gyur ba'i lugs kyi zab lam dbu ma'i lta khrid*. In *Rje tsong kha pa'i gsung 'bum*, Bkras lhun par rnying ed., 18: 883–97. Dharamsala: Sherig Parkhang, 1997.

———. *Dbu ma la 'jug pa'i rgya cher bshad pa dgongs pa rab gsal*. Bod kyi gtsug lag gces btus 19. New Delhi: Institute of Tibetan Classics, 2010. Translated in Tsongkhapa 2021.

———. *Dbu ma rtsa ba'i tshig le'ur byas pa shes rab ces bya ba'i rnam bshad rigs pa'i rgya mtsho*. Hunsur: Drepung Gomang Monastery, 2002. Translated in Rje Tsong Khapa 2006.

Tsongkhapa. 2021. *Illuminating the Intent: An Exposition of Candrakīrti's Entering the Middle Way*. Translated by Thubten Jinpa. The Library of Tibetan Classics 19. Boston: Wisdom Publications.

Tsong-kha-pa. 2002. *The Great Treatise on the Stages of the Path to Enlightenment*, vol. 3. Translated by the Lamrim Chenmo Translation Committee. Ithaca, NY: Snow Lion.

Yakherds, the. 2021. *Knowing Illusion: Bringing a Tibetan Debate into Contemporary Discourse*. 2 vols. Oxford: Oxford University Press.

Yi, Jongbok. 2015. "Controversy among dGe lugs pa Scholars about What Is Negated in Emptiness According to the Svātantrika-Mādhyamika School." *Journal of Buddhist Philosophy* 1: 156–92.

Self-Knowledge and Attachment: A View from Madhyamaka

Jonardon Ganeri

Tom Tillemans is one of those rare scholars of Tibetan and Indian Buddhist philosophy for whom the advances in our understanding of logic and language made by twentieth-century analytical philosophers are to be welcomed and not shunned. One finds in his work discussions of fictionalism, paraconsistency, and *akrasia*, as well as referential opacity, mass and count nouns, and intensional contexts (Tillemans 2016 and 2022). He discovers in the work of the Tibetans much that can speak to such topics. Tillemans speaks of an approach that "is also sometimes termed 'fusion thinking,' although," he says, he "would prefer 'cosmopolitan thinking,' as fusion of differing histories, contexts, and views is arguably not a recommendable goal" (2022, 30). I admire him very much for his embrace of this spirit of cosmopolitan thinking, which indeed I regard as key to any future global philosophy. I am very happy to have been invited to contribute to this volume in his honor, and my contribution is intended to be one that embodies the spirit of "cosmopolitan thinking."

Akeel Bilgrami (2006) argues that intentional states—specifically, beliefs and desires—are transparent, meaning that they are, by their very nature, known by their possessors. This is one part of what it means to describe self-knowledge as a constitutive feature of belief and desire. He observes that the notion of an intentional state stands in need of disambiguation: In one sense, an intentional state is simply a disposition—an urge or tendency, for example. But in another sense, intentional states are commitments, states that are normative in that their possession implies that there are things their possessor ought or ought not to do or believe. It is straightforward enough to see that commitments are transparent, for a commitment is the sort of thing one can try and fail to live up to, and "I cannot try and live up to something I do not know I possess" (Bilgrami 2012, 266). Bilgrami argues that dispositions too are transparent, but only in the context of a normative account of agency; that is to say, dispositional beliefs and desires are self-known insofar as they contribute to the rationalization of actions or judgments that can be the object of justifiable reactive attitudes and so fall within the orbit of the normative practices of responsibility. In short, "I am justified in resenting intentional actions (for instance those that cause harm) that flow from someone's dispositions, only if she has self-knowledge of those dispositions" (Bilgrami 2010, 753). Transparency holds for dispositions, given agency. Bilgrami's larger aim is to argue that four different notions—value, agency, intentionality, and self-knowledge—are integrally related. This is what he calls the "integrative strategy."

Peter Strawson, says Bilgrami, argued "that human freedom and agency are not non-normative metaphysical ideas having merely to do with issues about causality. Rather they are constituted by the normative practices surrounding notions of responsibility, such as blame and punishment, and these practices are, in turn, grounded in our normative reactions ('reactive attitudes' such as resentment and indignation) to each other's behaviour" (2010, 752). I will argue that the Buddha—by whom I mean the character depicted in the Buddhist literature rather than a historical individual—agrees in substance with all these claims and that he too pursues an integrative strategy. I will seek to demonstrate this in the context of two intentional states that are the specific focus of Buddhism, craving (*tṛṣṇā*) and clinging (*upādāna*). First, I will argue that that craving is an intentional state of desire-based commitment and that it is sufficient for clinging, which is the appropriation of the craving to oneself. Second, I will argue that the loose category of "constructing activity" (*saṃskāra*) includes dispositional states, and that were they to occur with agency they would fall within the orbit of normative practices. The notion of freedom that the Buddha wishes to defend, however, is not freedom within a normative practice of responsibility but freedom from such forms of attachment as are grounded by that practice. Attachment presupposes self-knowledge: it is in "appropriating" an intentional state to oneself that one becomes attached. So for Buddhism, and especially Madhyamaka, the point of the integrative strategy is that it tells us about the structure of dangers we need to avoid if we are to be free.

"If one craves for p, one clings to one's craving for p."

It is from a stance grounded in the space of norms that the Buddha investigated the moral psychological properties of suffering (*duḥkha*) and craving, which are to be understood within a manifestly normative framework of *wrong* belief or *mistaken* conception (*avijñāna*). These unhealthy ways of being are symptomatic of false moves in the course of a life led well. The false move he identifies, above all else, is that of "taking as one's own" (*upādāna*) what is not, in particular states of pleasure and pain, and in so doing fabricating a false idea of self (*satkāyadṛṣṭi*). A human life is to be thought of in the following way. There are five interwoven sequences of processes, one of which is directly physical (*rūpa*) and the other four more distinctively psychological: felt evaluation (*vedanā*), identificatory labeling (*saṃjñā*), constructing activities (*saṃskāra*), and cognitive world-directedness (*vijñāna*). The picture is strongly anti-substantialist; for example, the body is described as resembling a mass of foam, and affect as being like a bubble. The flow of mental processes is said to be patterned according to a twelve-step chain of dependent origination (*pratītyasamutpāda*) beginning with misconceptions and ending with suffering, aging, and death. One thinks mistakenly that something would be good, imagines it, thinks of oneself as doing or having it. One then experiences it and finds it pleasant; one starts to need it for oneself and is driven by wanting it, and when one does not have it, one suffers.

This description of a complex psychological process uses concepts whose function is to provide or reject justifications. Presented with reasons, one forms a conception of oneself as possibly benefiting from something: this is a fundamental transition into a value-laden first-person perspective. It is a move—for the Buddha invariably a bad one—in the space of reasons, formulated in an idiom that, as I am about to explain, is best interpreted as only surrogately causal, one that does not preclude seeing the transition as involving reason-giving and justification. The final step, too, is described as a transition to a condition of suffering, a value-laden way of making reference to a psychological event. It is thus only using terms whose sense is evaluation-laden that the reference to elements in a causal chain is made. There is no way to describe the causal chains constitutive of the flow of a life in a vocabulary wholly grounded in the realm of natural-scientific law. A certain mental event is picked out with the phrase "suffering" or "distress" (*duḥkha*), and it would be of little relevance to be told to which neurophysiological happening, if any, it is token-identical. What is relevant is that the twelve-step process comes into view when described in normative terms, and that is why the Buddha is able to assert that we should do better in our individual lives by refraining from the transitions it describes.

What generates suffering, above all else, is an intentional state designated *craving*. Craving leads to *clinging*, and clinging is a mode of suffering. Let me follow the analysis of the fifth-century Buddhist philosopher Buddhaghosa: "Felt evaluation experiences the flavour of the object and is a condition for craving; craving lusts after things that solicit lust and is a condition for clinging; clinging clings to things that solicit clinging and is a condition for existence" (*Dispeller*, 195). Here, by a "condition" (*paṭicca*) is meant a sufficient condition. To distinguish craving from clinging, a metaphor is used: "*Craving* is the aspiring to an object that one has not yet reached, like a thief's stretching out his hand in the dark; *clinging* is the grasping of an object that one has reached, like the thief's grasping his objective . . . They are the roots of the suffering due to seeking and guarding"; again, "craving . . . is like the longing for a remedy; clinging . . . is like seizing what is harmful as a consequence of that longing for a remedy . . . as the fish does to the hook through greed for the bait" (*Dispeller*, 196). If bait is a solicitation to the fish, the hook is the cost of accepting it: the world is thus certainly not normatively inert. More formally, the characteristic, function, manifestation, and proximate cause of *craving* are these: being a cause (of suffering), delighting in (having the craved-for object), inability (to surrender it), and how it feels phenomenologically to crave; while those of *clinging* are seizing/grasping, not releasing, strong craving and false view, and craving (*Path*, 528 [17.51]; *Dispeller*, 137). "The meaning of *craving* is a delighting, an engulfing, a current, a creeper, a river, an ocean of craving, and as impossible to fill; the meaning of *clinging* is a grasping, seizing, misinterpreting, adhering, and hard to get by" (*Dispeller*, 198). The types of clinging are enumerated as wrong-view clinging, rites-and-rituals clinging, and self-theory clinging, of which Buddhaghosa says: "What do they theorize about, or to what do they cling? Self. The clinging to theories about self is self-theory clinging. Or: by means of which they cling to a self that is a mere theory about self; thus it is self-theory clinging" (*Dispeller*, 181). I will return to this relation between clinging and self-theory below.

It is past experience of bait that causes the fish to long for it. If one craves to do something, then one's only reason to do it is that one remembers having done it before, a reason that persists as long as one performs the action and does so independently of all other evidence. Craving is wanting to perform an action *only* because one remembers having performed it before. Clinging is a present-tense ongoing but evidence-insensitive occupation in a form of activity or endorsement of a content. Clinging is wanting to continue to perform that activity even in the face of contrary evidence. It is an *evidence-insensitive attachment* to a form of action or a belief. Clinging is doing something only because one has done it before, or believing something only because one has already given one's assent. Often one's attachment to a false belief is grounded only in the fact that one has wanted it to be true, and in this sense clinging is a sort of wish-fulfillment or delusion.

As we distinguish between intention *to* act and intention *in* action, so might we also draw a distinction between desiring *for* and desiring *in*, the former a longing for something that is not yet actual to come about, the latter a wish that something continue to be the case. Craving is a desire-for based solely on past experience, and clinging is a desire-in based solely on craving. The first *selects* a future state of affairs for actualization; the other *sustains* an ongoing commerce with a state of affairs so actualized. Craving is unlike other selective desires in that the only reason one can give for wanting the state of affairs is that one has enjoyed or experienced it before, and this precisely is what makes craving moral-psychologically pernicious. Similarly, clinging is unlike other sustained desires in that the only reason one can give for continuing commerce with the state of affairs is that one craved for it to be the case; and that is what makes clinging a dangerous and delusional psychological state to inhabit.

Cravings are clearly commitments, in Bilgrami's sense. They are desires that one tries to live up to, and the problem with them is that one often succeeds. The norm they express is a norm of attachment: not "make your beliefs accord with the evidence" but "make your beliefs despite the evidence." To redescribe such states as states of clinging is simply to affirm transparency—the craver avows their cravings, "appropriates" them as their own, and is thereby attached to them. There is, then, in the Buddhist theory of the chain of dependent origination an "integrative strategy" at work, affirming a relationship between intentional states and self-knowledge. The loaded terms *craving* and *clinging* are part of a second-order normative vocabulary. They express the thought that these commitments are ones one ought not have—that they embed norms one should not hold oneself accountable to.

Appropriation and Avowal

The endorsement of transparency is related by Mādhyamikas to an expressivist conception of first-person avowal. The meaning of the word *upādāna* in both Pāli and Buddhist Hybrid Sanskrit is "grasping, clinging, addiction, attachment." The same word also means "fuel," and related is the term *upādāya*, whose core meaning is "taking to oneself, assuming," and which is used in both languages in the sense of "on the basis of, making use of, depending on." Related Sanskrit expressions are *upādāna skandha* for the elements of the stream, thought of as the material fuel that sustains the activity of appropriation; *upādāya prajñapti*, the conceptualizing construction that is an appropriating of this fuel; and *upādātṛ*, the appropriator. When this last term is used by Nāgārjuna, he says that it makes no sense to think that one part of the appropriator is destroyed but not another part (*Mūlamadhyamakakārikā* 27.26). Candrakīrti explains that the appropriator is indeed what's called the self, and since it can't be discovered as any of the five types of element, how can one part of it be destroyed but not another? Again, if one part could be destroyed and not another, then one part must be mortal and another part divine. It does not make sense to say that the appropriator either does or does not have parts or limits (*Prasannapadā*, B 590). David Seyfort Ruegg (1981, 40) comments that "It is explained that the relation between fire and fuel is one of appropriator (*upādātṛ*) and appropriated (*upādāna*), which is thus analogous to that between a self (*ātman*) as appropriator and the five psycho-physical groups that are appropriated (*upādāna-skandha*)." Nāgārjuna also said, "Everything expounded in terms of fire and fuel is, without exception, applicable to self and the psychophysical elements" (*Mūlamadhyamakakārikā* 10.15). On this Candrakīrti comments:

> That which is appropriated is the fuel, the five types of appropriated element. That which is constructed in the appropriating of them is said to be the appropriator, the thinker, the performing (*niṣpādaka*) self. In this is generated the activity of "I"-thinking, because from the beginning it has in its scope a sense of self. (*Prasannapadā*, B 212)

This clearly is what Candrakīrti considers the everyday conception of self to consist in: an appropriative act of laying claim to the elements in one's own psychophysical aggregate, an act that does not require there to be any "entity" or "object" that is the self, nor any of the usual apparatus of reference to things:

> And thus the self—dependent on the aggregates, the elements, and the senses as they are in daily life—is thought of as the appropriator of the same; these are the objects appropriated, the self their appropriator. The self is not a real, existent thing, and thus it is not constant, for it has no birth or ending. Attributes like permanence do not apply to it, and it is not, nor is it other than, the aggregates. (*Madhyamakāvatāra* 6.162–63)

In the *Ratnāvalī*, Nāgārjuna plays on another metaphor to describe the relation of dependence between self and stream: "Just as it is said that an image of one's face is seen depending on a mirror but does not really exist, so the conception of 'I' exists dependent on the aggregates, but like the image of one's face the 'I' does not at all really exist" (*Ratnāvalī* 1.31). Candrakīrti's view is that the language of self—use of words like *I, mine, you,* and so forth—is not properly understood as having a representational function. This is an illusion of common sense and surface grammar, an illusion that dissolves on close analytical inspection. Giving up this illusion implies much more than merely giving up the idea of a mental substance; it requires surrender even of a reductionist conception of self. But it does not yet follow that there is no use-explanatory account of the language of self. What, then, is the use of the language of self? The use of "I" serves an appropriative function, to claim possession of, to take something as one's own. The appropriation in question is to be thought of as an *activity* of laying claim to, not the making of an *assertion* of ownership. Grammatical form notwithstanding, the avowal or self-ascription of a mental state, "I have a pain," is not a two-place relation between me and my pain; nor is it like a club's having members or a tree's having roots. When I say "I am in pain," I do not *assert* ownership of a particular painful experience; rather, I *lay claim to* the experience within a stream. This is a performativist account of the language of self, in which "I" statements are performative utterances and not assertions; the function of the term *I* is *not* to refer.

Thus, in Candrakīrti, transparency is seen as conceptually related to an expressivist account of first-person avowal.

Agency and Autonomy

Bilgrami has, as we have seen, argued that dispositions too are transparent, but only given agency. I will now demonstrate that Buddhists make a very similar point. Their objective is to condemn rather than condone the normative practice that this introduces, but what we are interested in is the existence of a conceptual tie. The passage where I find this tie affirmed is one whose exact meaning has been the source of considerable controversy among scholars:

> Constructing activities (Pāli *saṅkhāra*) are nonself. For if, bhikkhus, constructing activities were self, they would not lead to affliction, and it would be possible to have it of constructing activities: "Let my constructing activity be thus; let my constructing activities not be thus." But because constructing activities are nonself, constructing activities lead to affliction, and it is not possible to have it of constructing activities: "Let my constructing activities be thus; let my constructing activities not be thus." (SN iii:67)

I will argue that what "self" refers to in this early text is an exercise of agency. The passage then, plausibly, can be read as stating that an intentional state, even if dispositional, were it to count as an exercise of agency, would be self-consciously determinable by its possessor. Having affirmed that transparency is true only conditionally, the Buddha goes on to deny that the antecedent condition ("given agency . . .") obtains.

Much thinking about the mind has involved a commitment to the existence of agents of mental actions. There is a growing consensus that it is just this view that early Buddhist denials of self were meant to target. Yakupitiyage Karunadasa (2010, 70) speaks of "the Buddhist denial of a self-entity as the agent of experience"; Georges Dreyfus and Evan Thompson (2007, 92) of the denial of a "central controller"; and Karin Meyers (2014, 42) of "the doctrine of non-self (*anātman*), which explicitly denies that actions originate from an agent (*kartṛ*)." Alex Watson (2014, 178) comments that "a notion of an agent standing above the sequence of mental and physical actions is precisely what is denied"; and Peter Harvey (2017, 159) says that "the concept of ultimate agents of action [is] unsupportable . . . That is, there is intending (*cetanā*) but no specific process that is the agent of action, much less a permanent essence that is the agent." The Buddha is presented as agreeing that the first-person concept is individuated by what Christopher Peacocke calls the "thinker-rule," that a use of "I" refers to *x* just in case *x* is "the producer (agent) of that event of thinking" (Peacocke 2014, 83), and as affirming that nothing satisfies this rule. The Buddhist use of the term *self* is thus to refer to something that is an autonomous controlling cause of basic actions including basic mental actions.

What is it, then, for a living human being to exhibit autonomy in action? The work of the philosopher Harry Frankfurt has been extremely influential in recent discussion of these questions. Frankfurt famously defines *autonomy* as being in a position to act on a motivation with which one identifies (Frankfurt 1971 and 1998). There are psychological states that, although they motivate one to act, are in some sense alien to one; examples include the reluctant drug-user, driven to take the drug but disowning their impulse to do so, and more generally cases involving obsessive-compulsive disorders, manias, phobias, and addictions. More severe examples are found in the clinical literature on schizophrenia, where patients report having ideas and desires that are as if inserted in their minds and that they do not regard as being their own, as well as dissociation effects experienced by abuse victims and ownership deficits in the episodic memory of victims of neurological trauma. These are not cases of external coercion but of internal distress and conflict. Frankfurt's concept of identification is the opposite of this notion of alienation: "[A] decision determines what the person *really* wants by making the desire on which he decides fully his own. To this extent the person, in making a decision by which he identifies with a desire, constitutes himself. The pertinent desire is no longer in any way external to him. It is not a desire that he 'has' merely as a subject in whose history it happens to occur, as a person may 'have' an involuntary spasm that happens to occur in the history of his body" (Frankfurt 1998, 170). To identify with a state is, he sometimes says, to be "wholehearted" about it, to "have a stake" in it. Frankfurt adds, though many have disagreed, that willing consists in one's first-order effective desires, and the distinction between willings that are one's own and willings from which one is alienated is explained by the presence or absence of a second-order desire to have the first-order willing.

I want to preserve Frankfurt's valuable theoretical distinction between identification and alienation but dispense with his less convincing higher-order explanation of that distinction, and I will do so through an examination of Buddhist discussion of the topic. A cardinal principle in Buddhist philosophy of mind is the thesis that there is no self as conceived above, a thesis that goes back to the Buddha's celebrated affirmation that it is a mistake to regard as self any of the mental happenings in one's mind:

> Therefore, bhikkhus, any kind of material form whatsoever . . . should be seen as it actually is with proper wisdom thus: "This is not mine, this I am not, this is not my self." Any kind of feeling whatsoever . . . should be seen as it actually is with proper wisdom thus: "This is not mine, this I am not, this is not my self." Any kind of recognition whatsoever . . . should be seen as it actually is with proper wisdom thus: "This is not mine, this I am not, this is not my self." Any kind of constructing activity whatsoever . . . should be seen as it actually is with proper wisdom thus: "This is not mine, this I am not, this is not my self." Any kind of cognitive world-directedness whatever . . . should be seen as it actually is with proper wisdom thus: "This is not mine, this I am not, this is not my self." (MN i:139; SN iii:67)

The aggregate of "constructing activity," in particular, is a broad one. Let me now return to the passage I began this section with:

> Constructing activities are nonself. For if, bhikkhus, constructing activities were self, they would not lead to affliction, and it would be possible to have it of constructing activities: "Let my constructing activity be thus; let my constructing activities not be thus." But because constructing activities are nonself, constructing activities lead to affliction, and it is not possible to have it of constructing activities: "Let my constructing activities be thus; let my constructing activities not be thus." (SN iii:67)

It has been claimed that we find in this passage an analogue of Frankfurt's second-order distinction, for intentions or willings and other processes of executive control including attention belong within the class of constructing activity. Martin Adam says that the Buddha "would probably not have disagreed with the following assertion famously attributed to Schopenhauer: 'A man can *do* what he wants but not *want* what he wants'" (Adam 2010, 251). Notice that transparency does not refer to second-order desires: it does not claim "If one desires p, one desires that one desires p." As such, transparency is formally consistent with the proposition Adam attributes to the Buddha, that "if one desires that p, then one does not desire that one desires that p." Nevertheless, applying Frankfurt's theory, what the Buddha would be saying is that ordinary human beings are alienated from *all* the motivations, preferences, and intentions that move them. That seems highly improbable and suggests that a second-order theory is not the right way to capture the distinction between identification and alienation or the significance of the passage.

Frankfurt's original aim in developing the theory of identification and alienation was to argue against one influential notion of personhood. Peter Strawson's concept of a person is "of a type of entity such that both predicates ascribing states of consciousness and predicates ascribing corporeal characteristics . . . are equally applicable to a single [thing] of that type" (Strawson 1959, 101–2)—that is, as an entity to which both mental predicates and physical predicates can truly apply. Frankfurt rejects this animalist conception, that persons are just animals to whom mental attributes are ascribable, and which in India corresponds to the Cārvāka conception of *puruṣa*, in favor of the view that the concept of a person is rather "designed to capture those attributes which are the subject of our most humane concern with ourselves and the source of what we regard as most important and most problematical in our lives" (Frankfurt 1971, 6). He uses the terminology of identification to speak of these attributes, and, as Richard Moran clarifies, "in the activity of 'identification' someone determines what shall be part of him as a person" (Moran 2002, 214). The boundaries of personhood are thus fundamentally tied to one's profile as a valuing being, with what is important to one as an individual, with what one is committed to in a wholehearted way. Moran says that "it is because their normative structures are so manifestly different from a judgment's requirement of justification . . . that it is worth exploring how [pleasures] can nonetheless be seen as normative responses of this person, in a way that explains why pleasure (like love and caring, and unlike a sensation) is subject to identification and failure to identify, and are thus the expression of the active nature of the person. We can . . . preserve this crucial aspect in which pleasures, like loves and cares, are aspects of the whole person's engagement with the world, without 'rationalizing' or 'intellectualizing' them" (Moran 2002, 210).

Again, we can preserve the distinction between identification and alienation but dispense with a higher-order explanation of that distinction. Frankfurt's analysis of identification in terms of higher-order desire has indeed been found deeply problematic and probably leads to an infinite regress. An improved analysis that seeks to do away with a hierarchy of desires is proposed by Laura Ekstrom. What seems right about Frankfurt's analysis, she claims, is the idea that when we rise above our basic impulses and form attitudes toward them—attitudes, for example, of acceptance or disdain—this is something that requires an active involvement. As Ekstrom puts it, "a desire for having another desire is apparently not the sort of state that arrives unbidden" (2005, 49). Rather than cashing out the idea in a hierarchical manner, though, the new idea is that we allow a role for evaluative reasoning in desire-formation at the ground level. Ekstrom uses the term *preference* for a desire formed in a process of critical evaluation, an evaluation informed by the agent's conception of the good, and the term *acceptance* to mark the mental endorsement of a proposition formed by critical reflection with the aim of assenting to what is true. Her terms *preference* and *acceptance* correspond to the application of Bilgrami's notion of *commitment* in the case of desires and beliefs, respectively.

Normative Reactions

There is a central distinction in Buddhist analysis between those mental processes that are *kuśala*, "wholesome" or "skillful," and those that are *akuśala*, "unwholesome" or "unskillful," where to be wholesome is to be characterized by positive, healthy qualities and to be skillful is to engage in activities that lead to nirvāṇa or awakening (Adam 2005, 64–65). Without doubt, a psychology composed only of *kuśala* motivations is the provisional aspiration of the Buddhist trainee. Something of this distinction seems to be captured by Ekstrom's division of motivations into "preferences" and mere "desires," the former produced by critical reflection in light of the agent's conception of the good. A *kuśala* state might be redescribed in Ekstrom's terms as a preference informed by a conception of the good that consists in activities conducive to nirvāṇa. What is *not* present in the Buddhist account is anything analogous to an evaluative faculty, a conscious capacity to form and reform the designated set of states.

A quite different alternative is articulated in the early Buddhist texts. A passage in the *Mahāli Sutta* seems to describe the mechanism by which the formation of character takes place:

> If, Mahāli, these constructing activities were exclusively pleasur-
> able, immersed in pleasure, steeped in pleasure, and if they were not
> steeped in suffering, beings would not experience revulsion toward
> them. But because constructing activities are suffering, immersed
> in suffering, steeped in suffering, and are not steeped in pleasure,
> beings experience revulsion toward them. Experiencing revulsion,
> they become dispassionate, and through dispassion they are puri-
> fied. This, Mahāli, is a cause and condition for the purification of
> beings; it is thus that beings are purified with cause and condition.
> (SN iii:70)

I read this passage as saying that the process of rejecting alienated desires is
affective rather than reason-driven: One feels repulsed by alienated desires,
the disgust breaks the hold of the desire, and one is eventually freed from
inner conflict. The process is presented as causal rather than judgmental. The
key to understanding the passage, I believe, lies with the word "revulsion" or
"disgust" (Pāli *nibbidā*; Sanskrit *nirvid, nirveda*). Disgust is an emotion elic-
ited by the appraisal of something close at hand as potentially contaminating,
and it manifests in pulling away or aversiveness. The evolution of disgust has
been linked to pathogen avoidance. Though largely involuntary, there would
be no such emotion without an ability to discriminate as potentially contaminating things in one's vicinity. One feels disgust too at one's unwholesome
motivations, and one can feel moral disgust as well, a threatened contamina-
tion of one's orientation toward the good. In describing the unwilling drug-
user, Frankfurt says that he "*hates* his addiction" (1971, 12; my italics), while
Ekstrom says that "the [alienated] desire arrives unbidden, and he finds both it
and its intentional object *disgusting*" (2005, 47; my italics). To find something
disgusting, however, is not to find it wanting in a critical evaluative process,
which can issue at best in the judgment that it is offensive. The *Mahāli Sutta*
passage gets it exactly right: the emotion of disgust and not detached judgment
is what is involved in alienation; one's response to inner conflict and disowned
impulse is not that of soberly detached negative judgment but of revulsion.

Disgust is associated with seeing the constructing activities, including intentions, as danger (*Path*, 650 [21.43]). It is emphasized that with training, the
negative affect of disgust can be ameliorated into a more disengaged turning
away from the object (*Path*, 671 [21.135])—that is, into a kind of disattention.
The fundamental idea is already clearly articulated by the Buddha himself, in
a text that relates the topic with the fundamental theme of attention: "Whatever exists therein of the aggregates he sees those states as impermanent, as
suffering, as a disease, as a tumor, as a barb, as a calamity, as an affliction, as

alien (*parato*), as disintegrating, as void, as not self. He turns his mind away (*paṭivāpeti*) from those states and directs it toward (*upasaṃharati*) the deathless element" (MN i:435–36; cf. AN iv:422). On this last point, Nyanaponika Thera (1977, 17) observes that "when insight is deepened and strengthened, what has been called disgust (in rendering the Pāli term *nibbidā*) has no longer the emotional tinge of aversion and revulsion, but manifests itself as withdrawal"; what starts out as disgust is transformed into something more like disinterest or dispassion. The process described here is one of attention cultivation—specifically now the cultivation of skill in one's capacity to disattend. In terms of our discussion above, what is being cultivated is the control of the attention window, a mechanism of distractor exclusion, a *distractor* being, in the present context, anything labeled as potentially contaminating and therefore felt as disgusting. In a normal human psychology, this process results in an inhibition of states of alienation and the drawing of a boundary that defines a person. There is a suggestion that what is distinctive of the extraordinary psychology of an enlightened buddha is that the ability to disattend is universalized: "Seeing thus, bhikkhus, the well-taught noble disciple experiences disgust toward body, disgust toward feeling, disgust toward recognition, disgust toward constructing activities, disgust toward cognizance. Experiencing disgust, he becomes dispassionate. Experiencing dispassion, his mind is liberated. When it is liberated, there comes the knowledge 'It's liberated.' He understands: 'Destroyed is birth, the holy life has been lived, what had to be done has been done, there is no more for this state of being'" (SN iii:68; MN i:139). In the mental life of a buddha, then, the boundaries that define a person have shrunk to nothing, there is no psychological space of identification, and the person that is a buddha is "empty" (*śūnya*).

So there is indeed, I conclude, a distinction in Madhyamaka Buddhism between identification and alienation, a distinction grounded neither in higher-order desires nor in critical evaluative practice but in informed emotional response. The conception is privative in the sense that there is no positive affect associated with the states one identifies with; this class is simply the exclusion class of the states toward which one feels disaffection. Disgust is thus constitutive of alienation: even the inculcated disgust felt by someone about aspects of their social, ethnic, or sexual identity is an expression of alienation, in this case one that calls for transformation not by *expelling* the alienated attitude but by *endorsing* it, a movement not of contraction but of expansion, with a corresponding transformation in the boundaries of the person. There are two ways to respond to any disgust response: push away the thing one finds disgusting or develop a taste for it.

I therefore propose to understand the Buddhist position as follows. There are states that elicit an attitude of disaffection: one feels disgust. A state not falling into this class is one that one identifies with, where, however, identification has no positive content or phenomenology but consists just in the non-existence of disaffection: that is all there is to being "wholehearted."

Abbreviations

AN	Aṅguttara Nikāya, cited by volume and page of PTS edition
Dispeller	Buddhaghosa 1987–91 (vol. 1)
MN	Majjhima Nikāya, cited by volume and page of PTS edition
Path	Buddhaghosa 1991, with chapter and section number provided in brackets
PTS	Pali Text Society
SN	Saṃyutta Nikāya, cited by volume and page of PTS edition. Translations follow Bodhi 2000.

Bibliography

Adam, Martin. 2005. "Groundwork for a Metaphysic of Buddhist Morals: A New Analysis of *puñña* and *kusala*, in Light of *sukka*." *Journal of Buddhist Ethics* 12: 62–85.

———. 2010. "No Self, No Free Will, No Problem." *Journal of the International Association of Buddhist Studies* 33.1–2: 239–65.

Bilgrami, Akeel. 2006. *Self-Knowledge and Resentment*. Cambridge, MA: Harvard University Press.

———. 2010. "Précis of *Self-Knowledge and Resentment*." *Philosophy and Phenomenological Research* 81.3: 749–65.

———. 2012. "The Unique Status of Self-Knowledge." In *The Self and Self-Knowledge*, edited by Annalisa Coliva, 263–78. Oxford: Oxford University Press.

Bodhi, Bhikkhu, trans. 2000. *Connected Discourses of the Buddha: A Translation of the Saṃyutta Nikāya*. Boston: Wisdom Publications.

Buddhaghosa. 1987–91. *The Dispeller of Delusion (Sammohavinodanī)*. 2 vols. Translated by Bhikkhu Ñāṇamoli. Revised for publication by L. S. Cousins, Nyanaponika Mahāthera, and C. M. M. Shaw. Oxford: Pali Text Society.

———. 1991. *The Path of Purification: Visuddhimagga*, 5th ed. Translated by Bhikkhu Ñāṇamoli. Kandy: Buddhist Publication Society.

Candrakīrti. *Prasannapadā*. See Vaidya 1987.

Dreyfus, Georges, and Evan Thompson. 2007. "Asian Perspectives: Indian Theories of Mind." In *The Cambridge Handbook of Consciousness*, edited by Morris Moscovitch, Evan Thompson, and Philip David Zelazo, 89–116. Cambridge: Cambridge University Press.

Ekstrom, Laura. 2005. "Alienation, Autonomy, and the Self." *Midwest Studies in Philosophy* 29: 45–67.

Frankfurt, Harry. 1971. "Freedom of the Will and the Concept of a Person." *The Journal of Philosophy* 68.1: 5–20.

———. 1998. *The Importance of What We Care About: Philosophical Essays*. Cambridge: Cambridge University Press.

Hahn, Michael, ed. 1982. *Nāgārjuna's Ratnāvalī, Volume 1: The Basic Texts (Sanskrit, Tibetan, Chinese)*. Bonn: Indica et Tibetica Verlag.

Harvey, Peter. 2017. "Psychological Versus Metaphysical Agents: A Theravāda Buddhist View of Free Will and Moral Responsibility." In *Buddhist Perspectives on Free Will: Agentless Agency?*, edited by Rick Repetti, 158–69. London: Routledge.

Karunadasa, Yakupitiyage. 2010. *The Theravāda Abhidhamma: Its Inquiry into the Nature of Conditioned Reality*. Hong Kong: Centre of Buddhist Studies, The University of Hong Kong.

Meyers, Karin. 2014. "Free Persons, Empty Selves." In *Free Will, Agency, and Selfhood in Indian Philosophy*, edited by Matthew R. Dasti and Edwin F. Bryant, 41–67. New York: Oxford University Press.

Moran, Richard. 2002. "Frankfurt on Identification: Ambiguities of Activity in Mental Life." In *Contours of Agency: Essays on Themes from Harry Frankfurt*, edited by Sarah Buss and Lee Overton, 189–217. Cambridge, MA: MIT Press.

Nāgārjuna. *Mūlamadhyamakakārikā*. See Vaidya 1987.

Nāgārjuna. *Ratnāvalī*. See Hahn 1982.

Nyanaponika Thera. 1977. *The Worn-Out Skin: Reflections on the Uraga Sutta*. Kandy: Buddhist Publication Society.

Peacocke, Christopher. 2014. *The Mirror of the World: Subjects, Consciousness, and Self-Consciousness*. Oxford: Oxford University Press.

Seyfort Ruegg, David. 1981. *The Literature of the Madhyamaka School of Philosophy in India*. Wiesbaden: Otto Harrassowitz.

Strawson, P. F. 1959. *Individuals: An Essay in Descriptive Metaphysics*. London: Methuen.

Tillemans, Tom J. F. 2016. *How Do Mādhyamikas Think? And Other Essays on the Buddhist Philosophy of the Middle*. Studies in Indian and Tibetan Buddhism. Somerville, MA: Wisdom Publications.

———. 2022. *Views from Tibet: Studies on Tibetan Buddhist Logic, the Philosophy of the Middle, and the Indigenous Grammatic-Linguistic Tradition*. Vienna: Austrian Academy of Sciences.

Vaidya, P. L., ed. 1987. *Madhyamakaśāstra of Nāgārjuna, with the Prasannapadā by Candrakīrti*. Darbhanga: The Mithila Institute.

Watson, Alex. 2014. "The Self as a Dynamic Constant: Bhaṭṭa Rāmakaṇṭha's Middle Ground Between a Naiyāyika Eternal Self-Substance and a Buddhist Stream of Consciousness-Moments." *Journal of Indian Philosophy* 42: 173–93.

Bhāviveka's Proof Formulation
in Light of Dignāga's Logic*

Shōryū Katsura

I MET TOM in August 1982 at the fifth conference of the International
Association of Buddhist Studies held at Oxford University. He presented
a paper, "Identity and Referential Opacity in Tibetan Buddhist *Apoha*
Theory," in the special session on Buddhist logic and epistemology organized
by B. K. Matilal. I was much impressed by his presentation, and by his
kindness in helping a Japanese scholar reconstruct a paper that was lost with
his luggage on the way to England. I invited him to come to Hiroshima
to read Dharmakīrti with me. He came and we read the fourth chapter of
the *Pramāṇavārttika* together; he later published an annotated translation
of the first 148 verses of that chapter (Tillemans 2000). Toward the end of
his stay in Hiroshima, I offered to read with him the Chinese translation of
Dharmapāla's commentary on Āryadeva's *Catuḥśataka*, which was one of the
main research targets of his doctoral thesis at the University of Lausanne.
On the first meeting I discovered that he could read and understand that
classical Chinese text much better than I could, and I immediately canceled
my proposal. That was the beginning of our long and fruitful friendship.

Bhāviveka, the sixth-century Buddhist philosopher of the Madhyamaka
school of Indian Buddhism, is well known for his enthusiasm to present logical proofs of Nāgārjuna's philosophy of emptiness. In this paper, I examine
how far his proof formulations (*prayoga*) can be justified in light of the fifth-
to-sixth century Buddhist logician and epistemologist Dignāga's system of
logic.

* I would like to thank Mark Siderits and Sara McClintock for correcting my English and giving me good suggestions, and Ryo Nishiyama and Toshikazu Watanabe for providing me with
valuable information.

According to Bhāviveka there is only one ultimate (*paramārtha*), which he also calls *reality* (*tattva*), understood as defined by Nāgārjuna in *Mūlamadhyamakakārikā* 18.9.[1] Following Yogācāra analysis of the compound *paramārtha* in *Madhyāntavibhāgabhāṣya* 3.10, Bhāviveka analyzes it in three ways. The term *paramārtha* can be analyzed (1) as a *karmadhāraya* compound, meaning the ultimate goal, *nirvāṇa*; (2) as a *tatpuruṣa* compound, meaning the object of the ultimate nonconceptual cognition (*nirvikalpa-jñāna*), *tattva*; and (3) as a *bahuvrīhi* compound, meaning the nonconceptual cognition that possesses the ultimate reality as its object and that is conducive to the ultimate goal. This ultimate nonconceptual cognition is obtained by the practice of learning (*śruta*), contemplation (*cintā*), and meditation (*bhāvanā*) on the nonorigination (*anutpāda*) of *dharma*s and so on. In short, there is only one reality (*tattva/paramārtha*), which is beyond our verbalization and conceptualization. Yet to attain that reality, one needs to rely on multiple verbal expressions and conceptual proliferations such as *emptiness* (*śūnyatā*), *nonorigination*, and so on. Bhāviveka explains this by means of the simile of a staircase to an upper chamber; conceptual cognition of conventional reality is the staircase to ultimate reality.[2]

Before analyzing Bhāviveka's proof formulations, I will give a typical example of Dignāga's influential proof formula.[3] It consists of three members—namely, an assertion (*pakṣa*; henceforth *p*), a reason (*hetu*; henceforth *h*), and an example (*dṛṣṭānta*; henceforth *d*), where the example consists of two statements: a similar example (*sādharmya-dṛṣṭānta*; henceforth *sd*) and a dissimilar example (*vaidharmya-dṛṣṭānta*; henceforth *vd*). Although the assertion is presented, it is not regarded as a positive probative element on its own because

---

1. *aparapratyayaṃ śāntaṃ prapañcair aprapañcitam / nirvikalpam anānārtham etat tattvasya lakṣaṇam //* "Not to be attained by means of another, free [from intrinsic nature], not populated by hypostatization, devoid of falsifying conceptualization, not having many separate meanings—this is the nature of reality." Translation in Siderits and Katsura 2013, 202.

2. MHK 3.12–13: *tattvaprāsādaśikharārohaṇaṃ na hi yujyate / tathyasaṃvṛtisopānam antareṇa yatas tataḥ // pūrvaṃ saṃvṛtisatyena praviviktamatir bhavet / tato dharmasvasāmānyalakṣaṇe suviniścitaḥ //* "Indeed it is impossible to climb to the top of an upper chamber of ultimate reality without a staircase of correct conventional [reality]; therefore one should first have one's cognition clarified by the conventional reality; then one will be well determined regarding the particular and universal characteristics of dharmas."

According to Saitō 2020, 522–23, based on TJ ad MHK 3.26, Bhāviveka, taking *paramārtha* as a *bahuvrīhi* compound, applies the modifier "ultimately" to both Nāgārjuna's and his own propositions in the sense of "with intellect consistent with, or leading to, the ultimate object/purpose."

3. For a brief history of the proof formulation in Indian logic and Dignāga's proof formulation in particular, see Katsura 2025.

it simply presents the assertion of some target property (*sādhyadharma*) in the subject of assertation (*pakṣadharmin*). A valid reason or proving property (*sādhanadharma*) is necessary to prove the assertion, and such a reason must possess three characteristics (*trirūpa*): (1) it must be a property (*dharma*) of the subject of the assertion; (2) it must exist only in the similar domain (*sapakṣa*)—that is, the domain where the target property exists—and (3) it must not exist in the dissimilar domain (*vipakṣa*)—the domain where the target property does not exist. The second and third characteristics, respectively, are called the affirmative concomitance (*anvaya*) and the negative concomitance (*vyatireka*). The two statements of example express the foundation of the proof—that is, the pervasion (*vyāpti*) of the domain of the reason or proving property by that of the target property in the forms of affirmative pervasion (*anvayavyāpti*) and negative pervasion (*vyatirekavyāpti*), respectively. Dignāga insists that in principle, both similar and dissimilar examples should be presented in a single proof, though one of them may be dropped if the other is well known. Here is a typical proof formulation of Dignāga:

> *Proof Formulation 1*
> [*p*] Sound is noneternal.
> [*h*] Because it arises immediately after a human effort [to produce it].
> [*sd*] Whatever arises immediately after a human effort is observed to be noneternal, like, for example, a pot.
> [*vd*] Whatever is eternal is observed not to arise immediately after a human effort, like, for example, space.[4]

In what follows, we will see to what degree Bhāviveka's proof formulations for emptiness correspond to this model proposed by Dignāga.

Previous Studies

Two Japanese scholars have contributed greatly to our understanding of Bhāviveka's logic. Yūichi Kajiyama (1952–53) analyzed Bhāviveka's independent inferences (*svatantrānumāna*) found in his *Prajñāpradīpa* and examined

---

4. [*p*] *anityaḥ śabdaḥ* /
[*h*] *prayatnānantarīyakatvāt* /
[*sd*] *yat prayatnānantarīyakaṃ tad anityaṃ dṛṣṭam, yathā ghaṭaḥ* /
[*vd*] *yan nityaṃ tad aprayatnānantarīyakaṃ dṛṣṭam, yathākāśam* //
This is reconstructed from the information given in NMukh and PSV chap. 3.

them from the perspectives of Dignāga's and Dharmakīrti's logic as well as in light of Candrakīrti's critique of Bhāviveka's logic. Regarding the structure of Bhāviveka's proof, Kajiyama makes the following four points:

1. Bhāviveka rejects the reduction to absurdity (*prasaṅga*) style of reasoning.
2. His reason lacks the third characteristic of a valid reason—its absence in the dissimilar domain.
3. His assertion is always a negative proposition, and the negation involved is a nonimplicative negation (*prasajyapratiṣedha*), not an implicative negation (*paryudāsa*).
4. His assertion is often endowed with the modifier "ultimately" (*paramārthataḥ*).

Let's take a look at one of Bhāviveka's proof formulations that Kajiyama studied.

> *Proof Formulation 2*
> [*p*] Ultimately, the internal supports of cognition (*āyatana*) certainly do not arise from themselves.
> [*h*] Because they are existent.
> [*d*] Like consciousness (*caitanya*), which is existent.[5]

When we compare the formulations 1 and 2, Bhāviveka's assertion contains two elements not found in Dignāga's assertion—the modifier *ultimately* and the negative particle ("not"). Also, Bhāviveka's proof formulation simply gives a similar example; it presents no dissimilar example and no statement of the pervasion, such as "Whatever is existent does not arise from itself, like existent consciousness." These differences correspond to Kajiyama's findings.

Kajiyama points out that Bhāviveka's logical formulation is fundamentally different from that of Dignāga and that by introducing the modifier *ultimately*, Bhāviveka attempts to present the ultimate reality (*paramārthasatya*) through a bit of logical reasoning (*yukti*). From recent studies of the Madhyamaka theory of two realities (*satyadvaya*), we know that Bhāviveka developed his theory under the influence of the Yogācāra school, especially their subdi-

---

5. PrPr 49a: [*p*] *don dam par nang gi skye mched rnams bdag las skye ba med par nges te* [*h*] *yod pa'i phyir* [*d*] *dper na shes pa yod pa nyid bzhin no* //. Candrakīrti quotes this proof formulation as follows: [*p*] *na paramārthata ādhyātmikāny āyatanāni svata utpannāni* [*h*] *vidyamānatvāt* [*d*] *caitanyavat* //. See MacDonald 2015, 167–68.

vision of the two realities, and that he wanted to establish continuity between conventional reality and ultimate reality—namely, that the true convention (*tathyasaṃvṛti*) or the pure worldly cognition (*śuddhalaukikajñāna*) leads to reality at the ultimate level.[6] Kajiyama's interpretation of the modifier *ultimately* in Bhāviveka's assertion seems to be in line with our knowledge of Bhāviveka's theory of two realities.

Also, regarding the negation in the assertion, we should note that Dignāga appears not to have presented negative propositions; his assertion was always affirmative. When Dignāga wished to reject the doctrinal position of an opponent, it seems he relied on a *prasaṅga* style of reasoning, although he never presented it in any formal fashion. It was only the seventh-century philosopher Dharmakīrti who formally introduced *prasaṅga* as a legitimate proof formulation, and who introduced "non-cognition" (*anupalabdhi*) as a valid reason in (certain) negative propositions.

In a later article, Kajiyama (1963) points out that Bhāviveka did not acknowledge the so-called "unique and indecisive reason" (*asādhāraṇānaikāntikahetu*) as an invalid reason, and consequently he paved the way for the later development of *antarvyāptivāda*, according to which the pervasion is established not in the similar and dissimilar domains (*sapakṣa-vipakṣa*) but within the subject of assertion (*pakṣa*) itself. Furthermore, he argues that Bhāviveka's proof formulations contain several logical errors in the eyes of his contemporary Indian logicians. Kajiyama concludes that Bhāviveka's independent inferences may look categorical, but in fact they are better understood to be hypothetical by nature just like Buddhapālita's *prasaṅga*-style argument, which cannot be regarded as a proper proof in the Indian tradition of logic. Kajiyama is of the opinion that it is impossible to systematize Madhyamaka philosophy by means of formal logic, for the Mādhyamikas wanted to establish a contradiction between logic and reality.

Yasunori Ejima (1939–99) is another Japanese scholar who systematically studied Bhāviveka's logic. Ejima (1980) minutely analyzes Bhāviveka's logic on the basis of the final portion of *Prajñāpradīpa* chapter 27 and *Tarkajvālā* ad *Madhyamakahṛdayakārikā* 3.26. Having examined Bhāviveka's various statements on logical issues, Ejima concludes that while Bhāviveka's logic was not exactly the same as that of Dignāga, it was definitely based upon it. Like Kajiyama, Ejima presents some discrepancies between the logic of the two philosophers. Ejima's list of the characteristics of Bhāviveka's proof formulation is similar to the list provided by Kajiyama:

---

6. See Hayashima 2011 and Nishiyama 2019.

1. Its assertion is restricted by the modifier *ultimately*.
2. Negative propositions in his proof always have a nonimplicative negation.
3. There is no dissimilar domain for his proof.

Ejima explains Bhāviveka's inference as an inference that makes clear the Mādhyamika's own view (*svatantra*)—ultimate emptiness—by means of non-empty verbal convention. He considers that Bhāviveka's logic operates in a domain different from the domain of general logic and distinguishes the former as logic inclining toward the ultimate reality in contrast with general conventional logic, which is concerned with mundane matters. According to Ejima, the presence of the modifier *ultimately* in Bhāviveka's assertion symbolically shows such a characteristic of his logic. Ejima seems to hold the idea that Bhāviveka's logical reasoning is a kind of bridge between conventional reality and ultimate reality.[7]

Let me quote one example of Bhāviveka's proof formulation from the *Madhyamakahṛdayakārikā*.

> *Proof Formulation 3*
> [*p*] Ultimately, earth and other things do not have the intrinsic
> nature of the material elements.
> [*h*] Because they are products.
> [*d*] Like cognition.[8]

The logical structure is exactly the same as formulation 2 above. Following Dignāga, we may assume Bhāviveka understands there to be a pervasion between the proving property and the target property, such as "Whatever is a product does not have the intrinsic nature of a material element, like cognition." Or, put in other words, "Whatever is a product is not a material element, like cognition." According to common Buddhist doctrine, cognition *is* a product but *is not* a material element; the earth and other things, however, *are both* products *and* material elements; hence, the above pervasion does not hold, and Bhāviveka's assertion that "the earth and other things are not mate-

---

7. According to Ejima (1980, 143n72), Kajiyama's evaluation that Bhāviveka regarded the unique and indecisive reason as a valid reason is not correct, because the example given by Kajiyama is not really a case of the unique and indecisive reason. As a result Ejima could deny the possible influence of Bhāviveka upon the later development of *antarvyāptivāda*.

8. MHK 3.26: [*p*] *paramārthata ūrvyādi na bhūtasvabhāvam* [*h*] *kṛtakatvāt* [*d*] *yathā jñānam* (Ejima 1980, 275).

rial elements" is wrong. Consequently, Dignāga would not regard proof formulation 3 as a valid proof because the pervasion is not acceptable.

In this connection, the presence of the modifier *ultimately* in the assertion is highly significant. Bhāviveka presents his assertion not at the conventional level but at the ultimate level of reality and tries to prove, by way of an example, that the earth and other things do not have the intrinsic nature of being material elements, with the aim to lead his audience to Nāgārjuna's ultimate position that everything is empty of intrinsic nature. From Bhāviveka's point of view, ultimately everything is empty of its intrinsic nature; therefore, even though at the conventional level, the earth and other things may be regarded as material elements, at the ultimate level, they are not material elements at all; in fact, they are without any intrinsic nature whatsoever. In other words, by denying the common or conventional understanding of the earth and other elements, he leads the audience to the ultimate understanding of reality—that everything is empty of its intrinsic nature. This seems to be a kind of educational process for those who have not realized the emptiness of all dharmas.[9]

The Members of a Proof Formulation: Prajñāpradīpa ad MMK 13.1

The most common pattern of Indian proof formulations consists of five members: assertion, reason, example, application (*upanaya*; henceforth *u*), and conclusion (*nigamana*; henceforth *n*). But as I noted above, Dignāga's proof formulation consists of only three members—assertion, reason, and example. Upon checking all the occurrences of proof formulations in the *Prajñāpradīpa*, we discover that when Bhāviveka presents his own arguments, he generally gives a three-membered proof just like Dignāga (though not exactly in the same way as Dignāga, and with some cases of five-membered proofs), while

9. In this connection, a question may be raised: How did Bhāviveka educate his audience by means of the invalid pervasion with an improper example such as cognition? TJ does not give any clue to answer this question, and the following is a mere conjecture of mine. The aim of Bhāviveka in MHK and TJ is to logically prove "emptiness of all *dharmas*" and the assertion that ultimately, earth and other things do not have the intrinsic nature of the material elements is just the first step toward that final aim. First, he probably states that a product such as cognition does not have the intrinsic nature of the material elements, which can be accepted by his audience; then he states that even though earth and other things are commonly regarded as having the intrinsic nature of the material elements, ultimately they do not have the intrinsic nature of the material elements because they are products like cognition. At the conventional level, the pervasion "whatever is a product does not have the intrinsic nature of the material elements" does not hold, but Bhāviveka seems to ignore it and claims that at the ultimate level, such a pervasion holds because ultimately everything is devoid of its intrinsic nature. Logically Bhāviveka's argument is a kind of circular argument.

when he presents his opponents' arguments, he gives both three-membered and five-membered proofs.

Bhāviveka discusses the number of members of a proof formulation[10] in *Prajñāpradīpa* ad *Mūlamadhyamakakārikā* 13.1, where Nāgārjuna says, "The Blessed One said that whatever is deceptive in nature is vain, and that all composite things, being deceptive in nature, are vain."[11] This can be put into a Barbara-type syllogism of Aristotelian logic:

> *Proof Formulation 4*
> [Major Premise] Whatever is deceptive in nature is vain.
> [Minor Premise] All composite things are deceptive in nature.
> [Conclusion] All composite things are vain.

Of course, Bhāviveka was not aware of the possible correspondence between Nāgārjuna's argument and the above syllogism 4, but he was aware that the last part of Nāgārjuna's argument, "all composite things are vain," can be treated as the conclusion of a proof.

After discussing the number of members of a proof formulation, Bhāviveka then presents the following three-membered formulation:

> *Proof Formulation 5*
> [*p*] Ultimately, internal things are empty of intrinsic natures.
> [*h*] Because they are deceptive in nature.
> [*d*] As, for example, the body of a woman miraculously created
>   by a magician.[12]

In this connection Bhāviveka makes some opponents, most likely the Naiyāyikas, raise a point that Buddhists who hold the position of the three-

---

10. See Ejima 1968 for pioneering work on this topic.

11. MMK 13.1: *tan mṛṣā moṣadharmaṃ ya bhagavān ity abhāṣita / sarve ca moṣadharmānaḥ saṃskārās tena te mṛṣā //.* Translation in Siderits and Katsura 2013, 138.

12. PrPr 148a1–2: [*p*] *don dam par nang gi dngos po rnams ni ngo bo nyid stong pa nyid yin te /* [*h*] *slu ba'i chos yin pa'i phyir /* [*d*] *dper na sgyu ma mkhan gyis sprul pa'i bud med kyi lus bzhin no //.* In order to support Bhāviveka's proof, Avalokitavrata adds the following formulation that looks like a combination of example, application, and conclusion formulae in PrPrT zha 278b6–7: "As, for example, the body of a woman miraculously created by a magician, being deceptive in nature, is empty of its intrinsic nature, so also internal things, being deceptive in nature, are empty of their natures." *dper na sgyu ma mkhan gyis sprul pa'i bud med kyi lus ni slu ba'i chos yin pa'i phyir ngo bo nyid stong pa de bzhin du nang gi dngos po rnams kyang slu ba'i chos yin pa'i phyir ngo bo nyid stong pa yin no //.*

membered proof formulation are not supposed to formulate the other two members, application and conclusion. To this Bhāviveka answers: "That is not right, for while application and conclusion are not admitted as separate members, it is not the case that they *must not* be formulated."[13] Then he gives the following pair of the five-membered formulations, one with a similar example and another with a dissimilar example.

> *Proof Formulation 6*
> [*p*] Sound is noneternal.
> [*h*] Because it is produced.
> [*sd*] The produced is observed to be noneternal as, for example, a pot.
> [*u*] Sound, too, is produced like that [i.e., like a pot].
> [*n*] Hence, being produced like that [i.e., like a pot], it is noneternal.[14]

> *Proof Formulation 7*
> [*p*] Sound is noneternal.
> [*h*] Because it is produced.
> [*vd*] Not-produced is observed to be eternal, as, for example, space.
> [*u*] It is not the case that sound is not produced like that [i.e., like space]; rather, it *is* produced.
> [*n*] Hence, being produced unlike that [i.e., unlike space], it is noneternal.[15]

It is to be noted that the example members of proofs 6 and 7 do not contain the statement of pervasion as we find in Dignāga's proof 1 because they are not formulated using a relative construction (such as *yad/gang . . . tad/de . . .*). If we follow Dignāga's rule for the formulation of the example that requires that the dissimilar example be formulated in contraposition with the similar example,

13. PrPr 148a2–3: *'dir kha cig gis smras pa / 'di ltar sangs rgyas pa dag ni yan lag gsum smra ba yin pas de'i phyir nye bar sbyar ba dang/ mjug bsdu ba'i tshig dag mi rigs so//de ni bzang po ma yin te / 'di ltar nye bar sbyar ba dang/ mjug bsdu ba dag yan lag gzhan nyid du mi 'dod mod kyi de dag sbyar bar mi bya ba ni ma yin no //.*

14. PrPr 148a3: *[p] sgra ni mi rtag ste / [h] byas pa'i phyir ro // [sd] byas pa ni mi rtag par mthong ste/ dper na bum pa bzhin no // [u] sgra yang de bzhin pas [n] de ltar byas pa'i phyir mi rtag go //.*

15. PrPr 148a4: *[p] sgra ni mi rtag ste [h] byas pa'i phyir ro // [vd] ma byas pa ni rtag par mthong ste/ dper na nam mkha' bzhin no // [u] sgra ni de ltar ma byas pa ma yin te byas pa yin pas / [n] de ltar byas pa'i phyir mi rtag go //.*

Bhāviveka should have formulated the dissimilar example of proof 7 as "The eternal is observed to be not produced, as, for example, space."[16] It is interesting that Bhāviveka inserts the expression "observed" in the above similar and dissimilar examples as Dignāga does in proof 1 because it suggests that Dignāga's and Bhāviveka's logical proofs are based on observation of the world and that they are inductive in nature.

In this connection, Bhāviveka has the opponents who hold that a proof should consist of all five members criticize Bhāviveka's own three-membered proof formulation. He has them say that if the reason (such as the property of being produced) is stated only with reference to the subject of the assertion (such as sound), then the implication is that the reason does not exist in examples (such as a pot); in that case, the reason must be reckoned as an erroneous "unique and indecisive reason."[17] Furthermore, if the reason is stated only with reference to examples, then it does not exist in the subject of the assertion, and it is the erroneous reason called *unestablished* (*asiddha*).[18] To this argument, Bhāviveka replies that the reason (such as the property of being produced) is not restricted to the subject of the assertion (such as sound) or to the examples (such as a pot), but it is the property generally known; hence the reason is connected with both the subject (*pakṣa*) of the assertion and the similar domain (*sapakṣa*) that includes similar examples (*sādharmyadṛṣṭānta*).[19]

Bhāviveka has the opponents go on to argue that if the reason is stated with reference to the general property, then there is no need to present the affirmative concomitance with the examples because the proving property of the

16. Bhāviveka might have formulated the pair of proofs 6 and 7 in the way Pakṣilasvāmin formulated a similar pair of proofs in NBh ad NS 1.1.39: [p] *anityaḥ śabdaḥ* / [h] *utpattidharmakatvāt* / [sd] *utpattidharmakaṃ sthālyādi dravyam anityam* / [u] *tathā cotpattidharmakaḥ śabadaḥ* / [n] *tasmād utpattidharmakatvād anityaḥ śabdaḥ* // [p] *anityaḥ śabdaḥ* / [h] *utpattidharmakatvāt* / [vd] *anutpattidharmakam ātmādi dravyaṃ nityaṃ dṛṣṭam* / [u] *na ca tathānutpattidharmakaḥ śabdaḥ* / *kiṃ tarhi* / *utpattidharmakaḥ* / [n] *tasmād utpattidharmakatvād anityaḥ śabdaḥ* //.

Commenting on this passage, Avalokitavrata suggests that Bhāviveka presented the five-membered proofs 6 and 7, respectively, to reveal the missing reasons of the following two proofs: [p] Sound is noneternal, [sd] like a pot, and [p] Sound is noneternal, [vd] not like the eternal space. Avalokitavrata insists that, as long as the first three members are presented, it is not necessary to present the last two members of a proof. See PrPrT zha 279a4–b6.

17. PrPr 148a5–6: *bsgrub par bya ba chos 'ba' zhig la gtan tshigs brjod na ni dpe la de med pa'i phyir thun mong ma yin pa nyid do* //.

18. PrPr 148a6: *dpe'i chos 'ba' zhig la gtan tshigs brjod na ni gtan tshigs kyi don ma grub pa nyid do* //.

19. PrPr 148b3: *gtan tshigs spyir grags pa nyid brjod pas gtan tshigs nyid phyogs dang mthun pa'i phyogs gnyi ga dang 'brel par 'grub bo* //.

examples is included by the general property of reason.[20] To this, Bhāviveka replies that the example ("As, for example, a pot") is formulated with reference to the specific similar domain, and the assertion ("Sound is noneternal") is formulated with reference to the specific subject of assertion (i.e., sound); thus the reason is stated to bring together (*upasaṃhāra) the subject of the assertion and the examples.[21] Therefore, even if the reason is stated in a general way, it is not useless—and indeed it is necessary—to present its affirmative concomitance with the example.[22]

Finally, to illustrate their point, Bhāviveka has the opponents put the Buddhist position into the following three-membered proof:

Proof Formulation 8

[*p*] Application and conclusion are not members of a proof different [from the reason].

[*h*] Because they have no distinction in content [from the reason].

[*d*] Like the reason itself.

Bhāviveka then has the opponents criticize this proof formulation by saying that the reason ("having no distinction in content") is unestablished (*asiddha*) in the subject of the assertion ("application and conclusion"). This is because they understand the application to have a distinct role in putting together the

20. PrPr 148a6: *spyi'i chos la gtan tshigs brjod na ni rjes su 'gro ba bstan pa don med de / dpe'i chos la yang spyir bstan pa'i phyir ro //*.

21. PrPr 148b3–4: *dpe bstan pa ni / mthun pa'i phyogs bye brag tu rtogs par bya ba'i phyir te / phyogs bye brag tu rtogs par bya ba'i phyir dam bcas pa bstan pa bzhin pas / de'i phyir gtan tshigs kyi don nyid nye bar sbyar bas brjod do //*.

22. PrPrT zha 282b6: *gtan tshigs spyir brjod kyang rjes su 'gro ba bstan pa don med pa ma yin no //*.
Furthermore, the opponents argue that although Buddhists think it is enough to present the reason's connection (i.e., affirmative concomitance) with the examples, not with the subject of the assertion, it is necessary to state another proposition (i.e., application) that presents the reason's connection with the subject to be proven. If Buddhists think that the reason's connection with the subject is established because the reason is stated immediately after the assertion, then even an erroneous argument such as "Sound is noneternal, because it is grasped by the eyes" would be established. And if Buddhists understand that the reason's connection with the subject of the assertion is established depending on common sense—in other words, it is commonly accepted that sound is produced but it is not commonly accepted that sound is grasped by the eyes—then the same is true with Buddhists' formulation of the example, because a pot and other things are commonly understood to be produced but sound is not commonly understood to be produced. Strangely enough, Bhāviveka does not give any counterargument in response to the above criticism. See PrPr 148a6–b1.

target property that is to be proven and the proving reason, even if these are not explicitly mentioned, and the conclusion repeats the reason, even if the latter is already known.[23] To this Bhāviveka replies that the reason under consideration ("because they have no distinction in content [from the reason]") is not unestablished because the conclusion that, as the opponents say, repeats the reason has no content distinct from the reason, and the application also states the same content as the reason.[24]

Bhāviveka concludes that when what is to be proven is proven by the three-membered proof formulation, then it is purposeless to formulate the fourth and fifth members of a proof. Therefore it is safe to say that the standard version of Bhāviveka's proof consists of the three members: assertion, reason, and example.

We should further note that toward the very end of the *Prajñāpradīpa* ad *Mūlamadhyamakakārikā* 13.1, he refers to the three characteristics (*trirūpa*) of a valid reason (i.e., *pakṣadharmatā*, *sapakṣe 'nvayaḥ*, and *vipakṣe 'sattvaḥ*) proposed by Dignāga, which indicates that Bhāviveka knew the core of Dignāga's logic.[25]

The Proof Formulations in the Prajñāpradīpa ad Mūlamadhyamakakārikā Chapters 1–12

Now let me examine Bhāviveka's proof formulations in the *Prajñāpradīpa*. Thanks to William L. Ames's translation of the first twelve chapters of this work, we can easily identify Bhāviveka's proofs. I have counted 308 proofs, of which 223 are given by Bhāviveka himself, and 85 are attributed to his various opponents. All but one of Bhāviveka's own proofs consist of three members—assertion, reason, and example. Among them there are twelve cases that present more than one reason. These would have been criticized by Dignāga, who insisted that only one reason should be mentioned in a single proof. As dis-

23. PrPr 148b1–2: [*p*] *nye bar sbyar ba dang / mjug bsdu bdag yan lag gzhan ma yin te / [h] don la khyad par med pa'i phyir [d] dper na gtan tshigs nyid bzhin no zhe na / de la gtan tshigs kyi don ma grub pa nyid de / nye bar sbyar bas bsgrub par bya ba dang / sgrub pa gtan tshigs ma brjod kyang gcig tu byed pa'i phyir dang / gtan tshigs grub na yang smos pas mjug bsdu ba brjod pa'i phyir ro zhes zer ro //*.

24. PrPr 148b4: *gtan tshigs smos na yang dam bcas pa'i yan lag gi don tha ma dad pa'i phyir don de nyid mjug sdud pas byed pa'i phyir gtan tshigs kyi don ma grub pa nyid ma yin no //*.

25. PrPr 148b5–6: *'di na bstan bcos byed pa'i tshig dag ni phal cher chos mthun pa'i mtshan nyid dang / chos mi mthun pa'i mtshan nyid dang / gtan tshigs kyi mtshan nyid gsum gyis tha snyad byed de phyogs kyi chos nyid dang mthun pa'i phyogs la rjes su 'gro ba dang / mi mthun pa'i phyogs la med pas te /*.

cussed above, Bhāviveka generally sticks to the three-membered proof formulation, but sporadically he presents five-membered proofs of his own. In the present portion of the *Prajñāpradīpa* we come across the following case:

> *Proof Formulation 9*
> [*p*] Ultimately, color-form (**rūpa*) is not substantially real
> (**dravyasat*).
> [*h*] Because, its cause being not grasped, there is no cognition
> of it.
> [*sd*] Here in this world whatever it may be, if, its cause not
> being grasped, there is no cognition of it, it is not substantially real, as, for example, an army and other things.
> [*u*] Similarly, regarding color-form too, its cause not being
> grasped, there is no cognition of color-form.
> [*n*] Therefore it is not substantially real.[26]

Bhāviveka formulates the above assertion with the modifier *ultimately*,[27] and the assertion itself is a negative proposition—the two characteristics of his formulation of assertion that were pointed out by Kajiyama and that we noted above. The reason is a little complicated, but it can be rewritten as "Because it is not cognized due to the lack of its cause"; hence it does not violate Dignāga's principle of one reason in a single proof. The example formula is most interesting because it contains not only a mere example but also a statement of the pervasion of the proving property by the target property, as Dignāga does in his proof formulation, which is yet another indication of Bhāviveka's knowledge of Dignāga's logic.[28] The expression "here in this world" is not found in Dignāga's formulation of an example, and it may suggest that for Bhāviveka

26. PrPr 84a3–4: [*p*] *don dam par gzugs rdzas su yod pa ma yin te* / [*h*] *rang gi rgyu ma bzung na de'i blo med pa'i phyir ro* // [*sd*] *'di na* **gang** *rang gi rgyu ma bzung na de'i blo med pa ni rdzas su yod pa ma yin te* / *dper na dmag la sogs pa bzhin no* // [*u*] *de bzhin du gzugs kyang rang gi rgyus la sogs pa dag ma bzung na* / *gzugs kyi blo med pas* [*n*] *rdzas su yod pa ma yin no* //.

27. Not all of Bhāviveka's proof formulations possess the modifier *ultimately*. See, for example, his proof formulation that reads: [*p*] Birth would not have the intrinsic nature of the old age and death either. [*h*] Because it is born even without old age and death. [*sd*] Whatever is born even without X does not have the intrinsic nature of X, as, e.g., a cow that is born without a horse does not have the intrinsic nature of that horse. PrPr 140b5–6: [*p*] *skye ba la rga shi'i ngo bo nyid med par yang 'gyur te* / [*h*] *rga shi med par yang skyes pa'i phyir ro* // [*sd*] *gang zhig gang med par yang skyes pa de la de'i ngo bo nyid med de*/ *dper na ba lang rta med par skyes pa de la de'i ngo bo nyid med pa bzhin no* //.

28. In the three-membered proofs, Bhāviveka does not formulate pervasion but simply presents an example by saying "Like so and so."

the pervasion relation holds only at the worldly conventional level, unlike the assertion that is given at the ultimate level. Indian logicians traditionally insisted that the example of a logical proof should be accepted by both ordinary people and learned scholars, and Bhāviveka might have followed them by inserting the expression "here in this world." The modifier *ultimately* in the assertion, on the other hand, seems to indicate that the assertion is made not from the ordinary view of the world but from the proponent's own philosophical view or from their understanding of what the world really is.

Of eighty-five proof formulations attributed to opponents, sixty-two are the three-membered proofs and thirty-three are five-membered proofs. Of the sixty-two cases of three-membered proofs, eleven have extra reasons and/or examples, and two lack an example. Of the thirty-three cases of five-membered proofs, two lack a conclusion. The impression one gets is that Bhāviveka tends to present his opponents' arguments in five-membered proofs. I would like to quote one example of a five-membered proof that is a counterargument against proof 9 above.

> *Proof Formulation 10*
> [*p*] Color-form is ultimately real (**paramārthasat*).
> [*h*] Because even if it ceases, its cognition does not cease.
> [*vd*] Here in this world, whatever it may be, if when it ceases its
> cognition ceases, then it is conventionally real (**saṃvṛtisat*),
> as, for example, a pot.
> [*u*] With color-form such as blue, even if it ceases, its cognition
> does not similarly cease.
> [*n*] Therefore color-form is substantially real (**dravyasat*).[29]

In this proof formulation, "ultimately real" (*paramārthasat*) is equivalent to the "substantially real" (*dravyasat*) in the conclusion, both here and in proof 9, where it also carries the sense of *paramārthataḥ*. Hence the above assertion can be rephrased as "Ultimately, color-form is substantially real," which is the reverse of the assertion of proof 9. Unlike Bhāviveka's own proofs, the assertions of the proofs that Bhāviveka attributes to his opponents are normally affirmative propositions. The above reason and example remind us of the well-known definition of *saṃvṛtisat* and *paramārthasat* in the *Abhidharmakośa*

---

29. PrPr 84a6–7: [*p*] *gzugs ni don dam par yod pa yin te* / [*h*] *de zhig kyang de'i blo mi 'jig pa'i phyir ro* // [*vd*] *'di na gang zhig na de'i blo 'jig pa de ni kun rdzob tu yod pa yin te* / *dper na bum pa bzhin no* // [*u*] *gzugs sngon po la sogs pa dag ni zhig kyang de'i blo de ltar mi 'jig pas* [*n*] *de'i phyir gzugs ni rdzas su yod pa yin no* //.

6.4.[30] The formulation of the dissimilar example is not correct from Dignāga's point of view. It should be formulated as "Whatever it may be, if it is conventionally real (i.e., not ultimately real), then, when it ceases, its cognition ceases, as, for example, a pot." However, Bhāviveka's formulation may be justified because he is simply quoting Vasubandhu's definition of *saṃvṛtisat* from the *Abhidharmakośa*. In any case, Bhāviveka is not especially rigorous in his formulation of examples.

Now the opponents' example can be either a similar or a dissimilar example, but Bhāviveka only formulates the similar example and never mentions the dissimilar example. That is because there is no dissimilar domain for the target property to be proven in his proofs. In this connection Kajiyama had stated that Bhāviveka's reason lacks the third characteristic of a valid reason— namely, its absence in the dissimilar domain. However, Bhāviveka often argues that since there exists no dissimilar domain, it is impossible for the reason to be present in the dissimilar domain, which implies that he thinks the third condition of a proper reason is fulfilled in such a case.[31] As a matter of fact, both Dignāga and Dharmakīrti admit that the third characteristic is automatically obtained if there is no dissimilar domain; in other words, a reason cannot be present in vacuum.[32]

Concluding Remarks

Generally speaking, it is evident that Bhāviveka was well acquainted with Dignāga's system of logic.[33]

30. AK 6.4: *yatra bhinne na tadbuddhir anyāpohe dhiyā ca tat /*
ghaṭāmbuvat saṃvṛtisat paramārthasad anyathā //. See Katsura 1976.

31. As an example, see PrPr 71b3–5: *'dir sbyor ba'i tshig ni don dam par 'gro ba po las 'gro ba gzhan pa nyid ma yin par shes par bya ste / brjod pa khyad par can 'jug pa'i ltos pa dang bcas pa'i phyir dper na / 'gro ba rang gi bdag nyid bzhin no // de bzhin du don dam par 'gro ba las kyang 'gro ba po gzhan pa nyid ma yin par nges par gzung bar bya ste / brjod pa khyad par can 'jug pa'i ltos pa dang bcas pa'i phyir dper na 'gro ba po'i rang gi bdag nyid bzhin no // mi mthun pa'i phyogs las ldog pa ma bstan pa ni de med pa'i phyir / de las ldog pa 'grub pai phyir ro //*. For translation, see Ames 2019, 92.

32. See NMukh 2a17–19: 若無常宗全無異品対不立有虚空等論、云何得説彼処此無。若彼無有、於彼不転、全無有疑、故無此過。(Katsura 1978, 128–30). Reconstructed PSV ad PS 3.20d: *yadā tarhy asapakṣasyābhāva eva syād anityatve pakṣe saty ākāśāder anabhyupagamāt / tadā kathaṃ tatra nāstīty ucyate // tadā sandeha eva nāsti / tadabhāvāt tatrāvṛtter ity ayam adoṣaḥ //*. Cf. PVSV 17.13–18.14 and PVin 2, 100.8–15.

33. In MHR (translated by Xuanzang) (269b16–17) Bhāviveka quotes and corrects a wrong proof (*nityaḥ śabdaḥ, sarvasyānityatvāt*) in exactly the same way as Dignāga in NMukh

1. He knew the theory of the three characteristics of a valid reason that is the core of Dignāga's theory of inference and proof.

2. From the passages of *Prajñāpradīpa* quoted above, we can assume that he followed Dignāga's formula for constructing the members of a proof.

3. Like Dignāga, he generally formulated three-membered proofs; most of his five-membered proofs are attributed to his opponents.

4. The assertion of his own proof is a negative proposition. It is characterized by the modifier *ultimately*, which is alien to Dignāga's formulation of an assertion.

5. The example of his own proof presents just a similar example, without the statement of pervasion (*vyāpti*) as in Dignāga's example formulation, but when he formulates the five-membered proofs of his opponents (and rarely of his own), he includes the statement of pervasion, which indicates his knowledge of Dignāga's theory of pervasion. When he formulates the statement of pervasion, he usually begins it with the phrase "here in this world," which must be contrasted with the modifier *ultimately* in the assertion. We may conjecture that Bhāviveka accepted Dignāga's theory of pervasion only at the worldly conventional level, not at the ultimate level.[34]

6. The presence of the modifier *ultimately* is the most distinctive characteristic of Bhāviveka's proof formulation. It is followed by Xuanzang, Śāntarakṣita, Haribhadra, and others.[35] It probably has a kind of educational purpose to lead people from the worldly conventional level to the ultimate level of enlightenment.

Finally, however, toward the end of *Prajñāpradīpa* chapter 27, Bhāviveka rejects the whole system of Dignāga's epistemology and logic from the ultimate point of view. He rejects the two means of a valid cognition (*pramāṇa*), perception and inference, as well as the three members of a proof—assertion,

(1a24–29) and the corresponding PSV 3, which shows that Bhāviveka had a good knowledge of Dignāga's works.

34. It is to be noted that Candrakīrti also refers to the proof formulation of the opponents in which the example begins with the term "here in this world" (*iha*) at the very beginning of *Prasannapadā* chapter 15.

35.   MHR   268b21–22:   眞性有爲空。如幻緣生故。無爲無有實。不起似空華。Xuanzang's proof of *vijñaptimātratā*: 真故極成色不離於眼識。自許初三摄、眼所不摄故。猶如眼識。See Moro 2015, 4; MAl 5.1: *bdag dang gzhan smra'i dngos 'di dag // **yang dag tu** na gcig pa dang // du ma'i rang bzhin bral ba'i phyir // rang bzhin med de gzugs bnyan bzhin //.* AAA 624,5–6: *ya ekānekasvabhāvā na bhavanti / na teṣāṃ **paramārthataḥ** svabhāvo 'sti / yathā māyādirūpasya / na bhavanti caikānekasvabhāvāḥ svaparoditā bhāvāḥ //.*

reason, and example.[36] For him epistemology and logic constitute the staircase to the ultimate reality (*tattva*) that is beyond verbalization and conceptualization. According to him, "Since emptiness is devoid of the intrinsic nature of emptiness and so on, the wise do not see even emptiness as 'emptiness.'"[37]

I conjecture that Bhāviveka's rejection of the *pramāṇa* system from the ultimate point of view might have led to Dharmakīrti's idea of the two kinds of *pramāṇa*, the conventional and the ultimate *pramāṇa*s. I deal with this topic in Katsura, forthcoming.

Abbreviations

AAA	*Abhisamayālaṃkārālokā* of Haribhadra. See Wogihara [1932–37] 1973.
AK	*Abhidharmakośa* of Vasubandhu. See Pradhan 1967.
d	*dṛṣṭānta*
h	*hetu*
MAl	*Madhyamakālaṃkāra* of Śāntarakṣita. See Ichigō 1985.
MHK	*Madhyamakahṛdayakārikā* of Bhāviveka. See Ejima 1980.
MHR	**Mahāyānahastaratna* of Bhāviveka. Taishō 1578.
MMK	*Mūlamadhyamakakārikā* of Nāgārjuna. See Ye 2011.
n	*nigamana*
NBh	*Nyāyabhāṣya* of Vātsyāyana/Pakṣilasvāmin. In Thakur 1997.
NMukh	*Nyāyamukha* of Dignāga. Taishō 1628.
NS	*Nyāyasūtra* of Gautama. See Thakur 1997.
p	*pakṣa/pratijñā*
PrPr	*Prajñāpradīpa* of Bhāviveka. Dergé 3853.
PrPrT	*Prajñāpradīpaṭīkā* of Avalokitavrata. Dergé 3859.
PS	*Pramāṇasamuccaya* of Dignāga. See PSV below.
PSV	*Pramāṇasamuccayavṛtti* of Dignāga. Reconstruction prepared by T. Watanabe.
PVin	*Pramāṇaviniścaya* of Dharmakīrti. See Steinkellner 2007.
PVSV	*Pramāṇavārttikasvavṛtti* of Dharmakīrti. See Gnoli 1960.
sd	*sādharmya-dṛṣṭānta*
Taishō	Taishō Tripiṭaka. See Takakusu and Watanabe 1924–35.
TJ	*Tarkajvālā* attributed to Bhāviveka. Dergé 3856.
u	*upanaya*
vd	*vaidharmya-dṛṣṭānta*

36. See Lindtner 1986.

37. MHK 3.263: *śūnyatādisvabhāvena yataḥ śūnyā hi śūnyatā / na paśyati tato vidvāñ śūnyatety api śūnyatām //*.

Bibliography

Ames, William L. 2019. *The Lamp of Discernment: A Translation of Chapters 1–12 of Bhāviveka's Prajñāpradīpa*. Honolulu: University of Hawai'i Press.

Ejima, Yasunori. 1968. "Bhāviveka's Formation of Anumāna in the *Prajñāpradīpa*" (in Japanese). *Journal of Indian and Buddhist Studies* 16.2: 656–61.

———. 1980. *Development of Mādhyamika Philosophy in India: Studies on Bhāviveka* (in Japanese). Tokyo: Shunjūsha.

Gnoli, Raniero, ed. 1960. *The Pramāṇavārttikam of Dharmakīrti: The First Chapter with the Autocommentary*. Serie Orientale Roma 23. Rome: Istituto Italiano per il Medio ed Estremo Oriente.

Hayashima, Satoshi. 2011. "The Interpretation of paramārtha in the *Prajñāpradīpa* and *Madhyāntavibhāga-bhāṣya*" (in Japanese). *Memoirs of the Graduate School of Letters, Ryūkoku University* 33: 1–16.

Ichigō, Masamichi, ed. and trans. 1985. *Madhyamakālaṃkāra of Śāntarakṣita with His Own Commentary or Vṛtti and with the Subcommentary or Pañjikā of Kamalaśīla*. Kyoto: Bunseido.

Kajiyama, Yūichi. 1952–53. "Logic of Mādhyamika Philosophy" (in Japanese). *Tetsugaku Kenkyū* 402, 415: 18–43, 20–60.

———. 1963. "Logic of Non-Self in the *Madhyamaka-śāstra*" (in Japanese). In *Self and Non-Self*, edited by Hajime Nakamura, 479–514. Kyoto: Heirakuji Shoten.

Katsura, Shōryū. 1976. "On *Abhidharmakośa* VI.4." *Indological Review* 2: 28.

———. 1978. "A Study of the *Nyāyamukha* (2)" (in Japanese). *Bulletin of Hiroshima University Faculty of Letters* 38: 110–30.

———. 2025. "A Brief History of Proof Formulation (*prayoga*) in Indian Logic up to Dharmakīrti." In *Remodeling Indian Thoughts: Homage to Bimal Krishna Matilal*, edited by Madhumita Chattopadhyaya and Gargi Goswami, 155–92. New Delhi: Motilal Banarsidass.

———. Forthcoming. "Why Dharmakīrti Introduced the Concepts of Conventional and Ultimate *Pramāṇas*." In the Proceedings of the 6th International Dharmakīrti Conference.

Lindtner, Christian. 1986. "Bhavya the Logician." *The Adyar Library Bulletin* 50: 58–84.

MacDonald, Anne. 2015. *In Clear Words: The Prasannapadā, Chapter One*. 2 vols. Beiträge zur Kultur- und Geistesgeschichte Asiens 86. Vienna: Verlag der Österreichischen Akademie der Wissenschaften.

Moro, Shigeki. 2015. *Logic and History, Formation and Development of Buddhist Logic in East Asia* (in Japanese). Kyoto: Nakanishiya Shuppan.

Nishiyama, Ryō. 2019. "Bhāviveka on Non-conceptual Cognitions: A Study of the *Madhyamakahṛdaya* Chapter 3, Verses 7 to 13 and 265." *Journal of Indian and Buddhist Studies* 67.3: 1112–17.

Pradhan, Prahlad, ed. 1967. *Abhidharmakośabhāṣyam of Vasubandhu*. Tibetan Sanskrit Works Series 8. Patna: Kashi Prasad Jayaswal Research Institute (Rev. ed., 1975).

Saitō, Akira. 2020. "Bhāviveka on Prajñā." In *Archaeologies of the Written: Indian, Tibetan, and Buddhist Studies in Honour of Cristina Scherrer-Schaub*, edited by Vincent Tournier, Vincent Eltschinger, and Marta Sernesi, 517–25. Naples: UniorPress.

Siderits, Mark, and Shōryū Katsura. 2013. *Nāgārjuna's Middle Way: Mūlamadhyamaka-kārikā.* Classics of Indian Buddhism. Boston: Wisdom Publications.

Steinkellner, Ernst, ed. 2007. *Dharmakīrti's Pramāṇaviniścaya: Chapters 1 and 2,* Sanskrit Texts from the Tibetan Autonomous Region 2. Vienna: Österreichische Akademie der Wissenschaften.

Takakusu Junjirō and Watanabe Kaikyoku, eds. 1924–35. *Taishō shinshū daizōkyō* 大正新脩大藏經 (*The Buddhist Canon in Chinese, Newly Edited in the Taishō Era*). 100 vols. Tokyo: Taishō issaikyō kankōkai.

Thakur, Anantalal, ed. 1997. *Gautamīyanyāyadarśana with Bhāṣya of Vātsyāyana.* New Delhi: Indian Council of Philosophical Research.

Tillemans, Tom J. F. 2000. *Dharmakīrti's Pramāṇavārttika: An Annotated Translation of the Fourth Chapter (Parārthānumāna). Volume 1 (k. 1–148).* Philosophisch-historishe Klasse Sitzungberichte 675. Vienna: Verlag der Österreichischen Akademie der Wissenschaften.

Wogihara, Unrai, ed. (1932–37) 1973. *Abhisamayālaṃkārāloka Prajñāpāramitāvyākhyā.* Tokyo: Toyo Bunkyo.

Ye Shaoyong. 2011. *Zhunglunsong: Fanzanghan Hejiao, Daodu, Yizhu* (《中论颂》: 梵藏汉合校 • 导读 • 译注) [*Mūlamadhyamakakārikā: New Editions of the Sanskrit, Tibetan, and Chinese Versions, with Commentary and a Modern Chinese Translation*]. Shanghai: Zhongxi Book Company (中西書局).

Stairway to the Ultimate Truth: Gyamarwa's Reinterpretation of the *Satyadvayavibhaṅga*

Chizuko Yoshimizu

Tom Tillemans has devoted much of his scholarly work to logical-epistemological issues concerning valid cognitions (*pramāṇa, tshad ma*), particularly in terms of their value for Mādhyamikas. In honor of and as an expression of deep gratitude for the great benefits his contributions have brought us, this paper explores how the early Tibetan Madhyamaka interpreter Gyamarwa Jangchup Drak (Rgya dmar ba byang chub grags, fl. 1095–1135)[1] defends the value of valid cognitions as a stairway to the ultimate truth, which he understands as the utter extinguishment of all proliferation. The exploration proceeds with a focus on Gyamarwa's reinterpretation of Jñānagarbha's (early eighth century) *Satyadvayavibhaṅga* ("Analysis of the Two Truths") from a perspective close to that of Śāntarakṣita (ca. 725–88) and Kamalaśīla (ca. 740–95).

How to Realize the Ultimate Truth

In the seventy-fifth verse of his *Madhyamakālaṃkāra*, Śāntarakṣita answers the question "Who realizes emptiness (*śūnyatā, stong pa nyid*) in all phenomena?":

> Skilled yogis who eliminate superimpositions (*samāropa*) on that
> which [is considered to be existent] and who know inferential

---

1. As for Gyamarwa and his works, see the project site of Pascale Hugon and Kevin Vose: https://www.oeaw.ac.at/ikga/forschung/tibetologie/materialien/the-dbu-ma-de-kho-na -nyid-of-rgya-dmar-ba-byang-chub-grags-12th-c. My special thanks to Pascale for her valuable suggestions on how to interpret Gyamarwa's text and thought.

proofs with logical reasons that demonstrate [emptiness] realize it
vividly [by] direct perception.[2]

The author clarifies that those who accumulate discriminative knowledge
born of rational reflection ascertain the emptiness that is free from discursive
proliferation (*spros bral*, **niṣprapañca*), which skilled yogins realize through
direct perception (*mngon sum*, *pratyakṣa*). According to the commentator
Kamalaśīla, one ascertains this emptiness free from discursive proliferation
through the arguments of being neither one nor many (*ekānekaviyogahetu*)
and so forth. This is because, by eliminating superimpositions, insight into
truth arises from the sequence of listening, rational reflection based on arguments, and contemplative cultivation (*nyan pa dang bsams pa dang bsgoms pa
las byung ba'i shes rab*; i.e., *śrutamayī, cintāmayī*, and *bhāvanāmayī prajñā*).[3]

This idea echoes Dharmakīrti's thought that at the completion of a contemplative cultivation, a practitioner gains a nonconceptual cognition in which its
objects—namely, the four truths for noble ones (*caturāryasatya*, i.e., *duḥkha,
samudaya, nirodha*, and *mārga*)—vividly appear, having previously grasped
the objects through an insight born of listening and ascertained them through
an insight born of rational reflection.[4] Through a nonconceptual yogic perception born of repeated meditative cultivation, a yogin directly and vividly
realizes the very truth through the valid cognition (*pramāṇa*) of perception
(*pratyakṣa*) that he had earlier ascertained by means of the valid cognition of
inference (*anumāna*).[5] Śāntarakṣita's verse presupposes this procedure.

In the Madhyamaka context, however, the object of yogic perception is not
specified as something definite like the four truths. It is merely emptiness or
absence—the absence of intrinsic nature, self, arising, cessation, and so on.
However, the absence or negation of these superimposed natures is regarded
by Jñānagarbha and Śāntarakṣita[6] as something conventional (*saṃvṛti*),

---

2. MAl verse 75 (D 74b2–3, Ichigō 1985, 248): *de la sgro btags gcod byed pa // shes par byed pa'i
gtan tshigs kyis // rjes su dpog pa rnam shes byed // rnal 'byor dbang rnams mngon sum gsal //.*
The interpretation of this verse is diverse. Cf. Ichigō 1985, CXLIII; Keira 2004, 97n147; and
Blumenthal 2004, 243.

3. See MAlV D 74b3–4 and MAlP D 122b1–3 (Ichigō 1985, 248–49).

4. PVin 1, 27.7–8: *yoginām api śrutamayena jñānenārthān gṛhītvā yukticintāmayena
vyavasthāpya bhāvayatāṃ tanniṣpattau yat spaṣṭāvabhāsi bhayādāv iva, tad avikalpakam
avitathaviṣayaṃ pramāṇaṃ pratyakṣam.*

5. See Eltschinger 2009 and 2014.

6. See SDVV ad SDV verse 9cd (Eckel 1987, 76 and 161; Akahane 2020, 10): *de yang rigs pas
dpyad na kun rdzob kho na ste / ci'i phyir zhe na / **dgag bya yod pa ma yin pas // yang dag tu na
bkag med gsal //** dgag bya med na bkag pa mi 'byung ba'i phyir te / yul med pa'i bkag pa mi rigs pa'i*

because it is the negation of nonexistent things. As it is a Madhyamaka princi-ple that ultimate truth comprises the extinguishment of all the nets of discur-sive proliferation (*prapañca*),[7] Mādhyamikas generally classify dichotomous conceptions such as existence and nonexistence, arising and nonarising, and emptiness and nonemptiness as conventional. Śāntarakṣita characterizes the teaching of nonarising, emptiness, and so on as the "correct conventional" (*tathyasaṃvṛti*) concordant with the ultimate,[8] and he quotes Bhāviveka (ca. 500–570) that such teachings are a stairway (*sopāna*) to ascend to the sum-mit of ultimate truth.[9] In his *Madhyamakahṛdayakārikā*, Bhāviveka defines the insight (*prajñā*) that cuts off the nets of conceptualization as ultimate (*pāramārthikī*).[10] And in his *Prajñāpradīpa*, he considers this insight to be a nonconceptual cognition, which he then contrasts with the insight born of lis-tening, rational reflection, and cultivation. While it is true that Bhāviveka also calls the latter insight *ultimate* along with the teachings of nonarising and so forth, because they are nonerroneous and the means of knowing the ultimate, the commentary *Tarkajvālā* specifies that they are ultimate only in the sense of being *concordant* with the ultimate.[11]

phyir ro //; MAlV ad MAl verse 71 (D 73a5, Ichigō 1985, CXLII and 234; Blumenthal 2004, 243): *ci'i phyir dngos su don dam pa ma yin pa bstan pa / skye ba la sogs med pa'i phyir // skye ba med la sogs mi srid // de yi ngo bo bkag pa'i phyir // de'i tshig gi sgra mi srid //*. SDV 9cd is quoted by Haribhadra in the *Abhisamayālaṃkārāloka* (Eckel 1987, 125n45): *niṣedhyābhāvataḥ spaṣṭam na niṣedho 'sti tattvataḥ*.

7. See, e.g., Nāgārjuna's MMK 18.9: *aparapratyayaṃ śāntaṃ prapañcair aprapañcitam / nirvikalpam anānārtham etat tattvasya lakṣaṇam //*.

8. MAlV ad MAl verse 70 (D 73a3–4, Ichigō 1985, 230; cf. Blumenthal 2004, 149): *skye ba med pa la sogs pa yang yang dag pa'i kun rdzob tu gtogs pa yin du zin kyang / dam pa'i don dang 'thun pa'i phyir // 'di ni dam pa'i don zhes bya ba // yang dag tu na srpos pa yi // tshogs rnams kun las de grol yin // don dam pa ni dngos po dang dngos po med pa dang / skye ba dang mi skye ba dang / stong pa dang mi stong pa la sogs pa spros pa'i dra ba mtha' dag spangs pa'o //*.

9. MHK 3.12 (Ejima 1980, 270 and 412; cf. Eckel 1992, 12; Eckel 2020, 141; Saitō 2020, 519): *tattvaprāsādaśikharārohaṇaṃ na hi yujyate // tathyasaṃvṛtisopānam antareṇa yatas tataḥ //* "Without the stairs of the correct conventional, it is not feasible to ascend to the summit of the upper story of thusness."

10. MHK 3.10–11 (Ejima 1980, 270 and 412; cf. Nishiyama 2019, 1112; Eckel 2020, 157; Saitō 2020, 519): *aśeṣakalpanājālapratiśedhavidhāyinī // śāntapratyātmasamvedyanirvikalpanir-akṣare // vigataikatvanānātve tattve gagananirmale / apracārapracārā ca prajñā syāt paramārthikī //*.

11. PrPr ad MMK 24.8 (D 228a3–6, P 286a5–b3; Akahane, Hayashima, Nishiyama 2013, 67–68; Eckel 2020, 153; Saitō 2020, 522), where Bhāviveka analyzes the compound *paramārtha* in three ways as *karmadhāraya* (*paramo arthaḥ*), *tatpuruṣa* (*paramasya arthaḥ*), and *bahuvrīhi* (*paramārthavat*) (see Matsumoto 1978, 114–15; Ejima 1980, 24, 102–3; Keira 2004, 28n61); TJ ad MHK 3.26 (D 59a7–b2, P 63a1–4): *yang na don dam pa dang mthun pa ste don dam pa*

Thus considered, one may portray Madhyamaka practitioners' realization of the ultimate truth as follows: First, they gain an insight into the truth born of listening and rational reflection and they ascertain the truth of non-arising and so forth; then, according to Śāntarakṣita and Kamalaśīla, they ascertain the emptiness that is free from all discursive proliferation by eliminating superimpositions through rational analysis based on valid inferential cognitions; finally, they engage in contemplative cultivation of the emptiness they have ascertained and, at the completion of this cultivation, they realize that emptiness, objectifying neither the negation nor emptiness itself. Relying on a statement in the *Dharmasaṅgītisūtra*, Bhāviveka, Jñānagarbha, and Kamalaśīla all explain that a yogin or ārya sees the ineffable ultimate truth by way of "nonseeing" (*adarśana*).[12] Although a doubt might arise about the similarity between the conceptual object of the rational ascertainment and the content of the final realization, Kamalaśīla assures the continuity between them in his *Bhāvanākrama* by his assertion that "nonseeing" arises for a yogin from the observation of all phenomena by correct cognition (*samyagjñāna*). Kamalaśīla's concern is to distinguish between this "nonseeing" and the "non-mentation" (*amanasikāra*) idea attributed to the Chinese Chan monk Heshang Moheyan.[13] As Tillemans (2016, 191) rightly points out, for Kamalaśīla as well as Dharmakīrti, yogic perception is nothing more than a vivid presentation of conclusions reached by a prior correct rational analysis.[14]

rtogs pa dang rjes su mthun pa'i shes rab la don dam pa de yod pas don dam pa dang mthun pa'o //. Kamalaśīla provides a similar analysis (MĀ D 233b2–4; see also Keira 2004, 28n61).

12. A quotation from the *Dharmasaṅgītisūtra* in the *Śikṣāsamuccaya*, which in Sanskrit reads *adarśanaṃ bhagavan sarvadharmāṇām, darśanaṃ samyagdarśanam iti*, is cited by Bhāviveka, Jñānagarbha, and Kamalaśīla, the Tibetan translations of which appear variously. See Eckel 1987, 115n15, and Keira 2004, 69–71 and 99.

13. BhK I (Tucci 1958, 211–12, cited in Tillemans 2016, 196n20). Cf. also Ichigō et al. 2025, 93.

14. In Eltschinger's words (2009, 196) based on Dharmakīrti: "The condition of a yogic cognition's reliability lies in its bearing on an object that has proved to stand critical analysis by means of *pramāṇas*." Tillemans (2016, 189) formulates this thesis as a "continuity thesis" in contrast with the "independence thesis"—meditative states of mind are independent of philosophy—that is represented by Heshang Moheyan. Kamalaśīla argues that although a yogin's nonconceptual cognition, being established solely conventionally, is devoid of content and nothing appears to it, it is proper to confer it the state of yogic perception, because a reflexive aspect of his cognition (*svasaṃvedana*) takes on the role of *anyopalabdhi* and has this nonseeing cognition as its object (see Keira 2004, 68–85, trans. 98–101). Candrakīrti (seventh century) in his *Yuktiṣaṣṭikāvṛtti* censures epistemologists such as Dignāga by indicating an inconsistency between a conceptual understanding of reality, which has general characteristics (*sāmānyalakṣaṇa*) such as "impermanence" as its object, and a yogic perception, whose object is the particular (*svalakṣaṇa*) (see MacDonald 2009, 152–57). For Candrakīrti, ultimate truth obtains its own nature by virtue of being the object of a particular gnosis of those who correctly

Among early Tibetan Madhyamaka interpreters of the intellectual lineage originated from Ngok Loden Sherab (Rngog Blo ldan shes rab, 1059–1109),[15] Gyamarwa and his disciple Chapa Chökyi Sengé (Phya pa Chos kyi seng ge, 1109–69) supported the position of Śāntarakṣita and Kamalaśīla that inference and yogic perception are valid cognitions for ascertaining and seeing reality as the ultimate truth, agreeing with Śāntarakṣita's *Madhyamakālaṃkāra* verse 75 cited above,[16] a position contrary to that of Ngok Loden Sherab, who rejects the ascertainment of the ultimate by any valid cognitions at all.[17] Ngok's student Drolungpa Lodrö Jungné (Gro lung pa Blo gros 'byung gnas, ca. 1040–1120) also defined the ultimate as surpassing all appearances (*snang ba thams cad las 'das pa*), free from all characteristics (*mtshan nyid thams cad dang bral ba*), and devoid of the characteristic of being known (*shes bya'i mtshan ma dang bral ba*).[18] This view invited an objection from Gyamarwa and Chapa.

The debate greatly concerns the interpretation of Jñānagarbha's verses in his *Satyadvayavibhaṅga* (hereafter, *Vibhaṅga*). Gyamarwa and Chapa each wrote a commentary on the *Vibhaṅga*,[19] based on which they each constructed their theory of the two truths. Gyamarwa addresses the question of whether Jñānagarbha defines reasoning (*rigs pa*, *nyāya*) and its object as ultimate or conventional, challenging the Indian commentary, the *Satyadvayavibhaṅgapañjikā*

see (*yang dag par gzigs pa rnams kyi ye shes kyi khyad par gyi yul nyid*), which is the sphere of only awakened or āryas' realization (MABh 102,16 ad MA 6.23). Aligning with Candrakīrti, Śāntideva (ca. 650–700) states in his BCA 9.2c: "[Ultimate] truth is not the object of cognition" (*buddher agocaras tattvam*) (see Vose 2009, 21–22; cf. also Sweet 1979).

15. See Hugon 2020, 140, table 3.

16. See note 48 below.

17. *Spring yig bdud rtsi'i thigs pa*, verse 12 (Kanō 2007, 153; Kanō 2020, 165).

18. *Bstan rim chen mo*, 614–16 (Cabezón 2010, 41–50; Nishizawa 2019, 49 and 58–59, ed. 160 and 163). The same view is attributed by the annotator of Gyamarwa's *Dbu ma de kho na nyid rnam par dpyod pa* (8b7–8) to "Jo btsun pa," whom Hugon (2020, 133–38) identifies with Khyung Rinchen Drak (Khyung Rin chen grags), one of the disciples of Ngok as well as Gyamarwa's teacher. The tenet that ultimate truth is not the object of valid cognitions seems to have been rather dominant even before Candrakīrti's works disseminated through Patsab Nyima Drak's (Pa tshab Nyi ma grags, ca. 1055–1145) translation. Although it is unlikely that Gyamarwa saw Candrakīrti's works, Candrakīrti's thought in all probability had been transmitted to Ngok's students (see Vose 2020, 166). Chapa cited Candrakīrti's *Madhyamakāvatāra* in its earlier Tibetan version (Tauscher 1983; Tauscher 2003, 245n22). See also Hugon's discussion in the present volume, where she considers whether Khyung's view on the division of the conventional reflects the influence of Jñānagarbha or Candrakīrti.

19. Both commentaries are titled *Bden gnyis rnam bshad*. For Gyamarwa's commentary, Akahane (2010, 78–80) proposes this title. The colophon presents: *Bden gnyis rnam bshad ti ka dag dang bcas pa* (45b4).

(hereafter, *Pañjikā*).[20] Whereas the *Pañjikā* reads Jñānagarbha as taking them as conventional, albeit concordant with the ultimate, Gyamarwa and Chapa read Jñānagarbha as unambiguously defining them as ultimate. Focusing on Gyamarwa's reinterpretation of Jñānagarbha's verses on the ultimate truth, the present paper will argue that Gyamarwa's defense of the ultimate truth's accessibility by reasoning agrees with the position of Śāntarakṣita and Kamalaśīla introduced above—that the ultimate truth, which is the emptiness free from proliferation, is ascertained by inferential cognitions.

Are Reasoning and Its Object Nonfigurative Ultimate or Figurative Ultimate?

From the second half of the third verse to the fifth verse (3cd–5) of the *Vibhaṅga*, Jñānagarbha presents the ultimate truth:

> Only what corresponds to appearances (*yathādarśana*) is conventional (*saṃvṛti*) [truth]. Only something different (*gzhan, anya*) is the opposite [i.e., ultimate truth]. (3cd)

> As it does not belie (*mi slu ba, avisaṃvāda*), reasoning (*rigs pa, nyāya*) is ultimate, not conventional, because [the conventional] is not nonbelying. Whatever corresponds to appearances is, to this [extent—namely, corresponding to appearances—only conventionally] true. (4)

> [The ultimate truth] is not appropriate to be classified as that which corresponds to appearances [because] it does not even appear at all to any occurring cognition. (5)[21]

20. The SDVP is extant only in the Tibetan translation by Prajñāvarman, Jñānagarbha (presumably a different Jñānagarbha from the author of the SDV; see Matsumoto 1978, 109–10), and Ye shes sde. Although the colophon to Tibetan canonical versions attributes the work to Śāntarakṣita, some Tibetans maintain this to be a different Śāntarakṣita from the author of the MAl. See Matsumoto 1978, 112; Seyfort Ruegg 1981, 69n224; Eckel 1987, 27–31; Blumenthal 2004, 29. Neither Gyamarwa nor Chapa mentions the author's name. In this paper, I keep the authorship of the SDVP open.

21. SDV 3cd–5 (Eckel 1987, 72 and 156–57; Akahane 2020, 4–5): *ji ltar snang ba 'di kho na // kun rdzob gzhan ni cig shos yin // slu ba med pas rigs pa ni // don dam yin te kun rdzob min // de ltar mi slu min phyir te // ji ltar snang ba de nyid bden // ji ltar snang ba'i dngos por ni // rnam par gnas par mi rung ste // shes pa'i dngos po thams cad la // ji lta bur yang snang mi 'gyur //.* The Tibetan translation *rigs pa* corresponds to the Sanskrit *nyāya*, and *ji ltar snang ba* to

In his own commentary on the *Vibhaṅga*, the *Satyadvayavibhaṅgavṛtti* (here-after, *Vṛtti*), Jñānagarbha identifies "reasoning" as that which is based on a log-ical reason with threefold characteristics (*trairūpya*), ascertainment by means of which is not belying.[22] Thus, rational analysis by means of inferential cog-nitions reveals the truth as it is. But objects' appearing as if they truly existed cannot bear such analysis. To this extent, Jñānagarbha seems to accept that the ultimate truth is the object of our inferential cognitions. However, the next verse (v. 5) and its autocommentary state that the ultimate truth does not appear to *any* cognition because it does not appear even to the cognition of an omniscient one (*thams cad mkhyen pa*, *sarvajña*), as the scripture states, "Not seeing anything is to see reality" (cf. *Dharmasaṅgītisūtra* quoted in note 12 above).[23] That is, the ultimate truth *corresponds* to reasoning, which is itself ultimate, but the ultimate truth does not *appear* to any cognition at all.

To solve this apparent contradiction, the *Pañjikā* proposes to interpret the statement in verses 3–4 as referring to that which is concordant with the ulti-mate (*don dam pa dang mthun pa*)—in other words, a "figurative ultimate" (*rnam grangs kyi don dam*, **paryāyaparamārtha*), in contrast to the statement in verse 5,[24] which is understood as referring to the "nonfigurative ultimate" (*rnam grangs ma yin pa'i don dam*, **aparyāyaparamārtha*).[25] This is a plausible

yathādarśana according to the citation of SDV 17cd in Haribhadra's *Abhisamayālaṃkārāloka* (see note 27 below). Akahane translates *rigs pa* as "logic" and Eckel as "reason."

22. SDVV ad SDV 4 (Eckel 1987, 71 and 156; Akahane 2020, 4–5): *de ni rigs pa'i rjes su 'gro ba can gyi bden pa nyid ces bya ba'i tha tshig go // . . . rigs pa'i stobs kyis don la nges pa ni slu bar mi 'gyur te / de'i phyir tshul gsum pa'i rtags kyis bskyed pa'i rtogs pa gang yin pa de ni dam pa yang yin la / don yang yin pas don dam pa'o // des gtan la phab pa'i don kyang don dam ste / mngon sum la sogs pa bzhin du brjod do //.*

23. SDVV ad SDV 5 (Eckel 1987, 72 and 157; Akahane 2020, 5): *don dam pa ni ji ltar snang ba bzhin du rnam par gnas pa med de // thams cad mkhyen pa'i mkhyen pa nyid la yang mi snang ba'i phyir ro // de nyid kyi phyir mdo sde las 'ga' yang mthong ba med pa ni de kho na mthong ba zhes gsungs so //.*

24. While the fifth verse states that the ultimate does not appear to any cognition, the third only denies the ultimate's correspondence to appearances. Jñānagarbha affirms its correspondence to reasoning in the fourth verse. Hence, Nishizawa's readings (2018, 40; 2019, 104 and 108) that the third verse defines ultimate truth as that which does not appear to any cognition and that the third and fourth verses contradict each other are not correct. A contradiction rather stands between the third and fourth verses taken together, on the one hand, and the fifth verse on the other hand.

25. SDVP ad SDV 5 (D 18b3–4, Akahane 2020, 70–71): *tshig de dag gis don dam pa dang mthun pa'i don dam pa gang yin pa de ni / de'i sa bon tsam zhig smos pa byas nas / zhib tu ni 'og nas rnam par byed par byed do // da ni rnam grangs ma yin pa'i don dam gang yin pa de / ji ltar snang ba'i dngos por ni // rnam par gnas par mi rung ste // shes pa'i dngos po thams cad la // ji lta bur yang snang mi 'gyur // zhes bya ba smos pa la sogs pa mdo tsam zhig byed do //.* The

interpretation conforming to Bhāviveka's notion that reasoning concordant with the ultimate is the stairway to reach the ultimate.[26] Jñānagarbha himself is explicit in saying in his *Vṛtti* on lines 17cd, in accordance with his own division of the two truths based on whether they correspond to appearance (*ji ltar snang ba, yathādarśana*) or not (v. 3), that reasoning is nothing other than something conventional because it also corresponds to appearances.[27]

As Eckel (1987, 27) suggests, because Jñānagarbha's text is elliptical rather than lucid, the *Pañjikā* helps modern scholars. Eckel follows the *Pañjikā*'s interpretation and construes the fourth verse as defining "the expressible ultimate" (i.e., *paryāyaparamārtha*) and the fifth verse as defining "the inexpressible ultimate" (i.e., *aparyāyaparamārtha*).[28] In his commentary, Gyamarwa mentions this division[29] by referring to its source under the appellation *ti ka*, which we may identify in this case as indicating the *Pañjikā*.[30] However, he expresses his disagreement when exploring the meaning of *Vibhaṅga* verses 3–5.

modern translation of the word *paryāya* is diverse: "expedient" or "approximative" (Tillemans 2016, 193); "non-concordant" (Hugon and Vose 2024). The expressions are known to appear in the *Madhyamakārthasaṃgraha* ascribed to Bhāviveka, a text thought to have been composed after Jñānagarbha (Ejima 1980, 18–33).

26. See notes 9–11 above.

27. SDVV ad SDV 17cd (Eckel 1987, 87, 173; Akahane 2020, 23): *rigs de yang // ji ltar snang ba bzhin du gnas // rigs pa yang ji ltar snang ba'i ngo bo yin pa'i phyir kun rdzob kho na yin te / rigs pa ni gzhan du mi 'jug go //*. Lines 17cd are cited in Haribhadra's *Abhisamayālaṃkārāloka* (Eckel 1987, 136n98): *abhedāt so 'pi hi nyāyo yathādarśanam āsthitaḥ*.

28. Akahane (2020, 4–5) describes the fourth verse as teaching "ultimate truth as logic," which he also terms "secondary ultimate" (Akahane 2012, 128), and the fifth verse as teaching "ultimate truth as non-proliferation."

29. Rgya dmar ba, *Bden gnyis rnam bshad*, 6b8: *rigs pa ji ltar ba bzhin nyid ni* (SDVV ad 3d) *zhes pa lasogs pas rnam grangs kyi don dam dang / ji ltar snang pa'i dngos po ni* (SDV 5a) *zhes pa lasogs pa rnam grangs ma yin pa'i don dam mdor bstan pa'o zhes 'grel par 'chad do //*. The subject of this sentence, or who interprets and explains (*'grel bar 'chad*) Jñānagarbha's SDVV ad 3d and SDV 5a as teaching figurative and nonfigurative ultimates, respectively, is the author of the *Pañjikā*. Nishizawa is not correct when he identifies the subject with Jñānagarbha and states that Gyamarwa accepts this interpretation (2019, 107).

30. According to Akahane (2010, 79–80), the appellation *ti ka* appears forty-five times in Gyamarwa's commentary in reference to diverse passages, not all of which have correspondences in the *Pañjikā*. The canonical version of the *Pañjikā* has the title *Bden pa gnyis rnam par 'byed pa'i dka' 'grel*.

Gyamarwa on Vibhaṅga 3–5

Gyamarwa reads *Vibhaṅga* verses 3–5 as consistently teaching a nonfigurative ultimate. The third verse presents the definition of the ultimate in the last quarter, "Only something different is the opposite [of the conventional]" (*gzhan ni cig shos yin*, 3d). Jñānagarbha himself explains, "It is the ultimate truth"—that is, "what corresponds to reasoning (*rigs pa ji lta ba bzhin nyid ni don dam pa'i bden pa'o*)."[31] The *Pañjikā* reads "different" (*gzhan*) as meaning "different from that which corresponds to appearances" (*ji ltar snang ba las gzhan pa*).[32] Gyamarwa likewise explains that it is indicating "objects that are [different] from the objects of the cognitions that operate on mere appearances without examination" (*ma dpyad par snang pa tsam du 'jug pa'i blo'i yul las g[zhan pa]'i*[33] *gnas pa'i don*).[34] But he also offers a second interpretation in which he understands the word "different" as meaning "different from discursive proliferation" (*spros pa las gzhan*). Gyamarwa counts this as one of the three properties of ultimate truth embedded in its definition alongside the properties of being "the opposite to the conventional" and being "true as the object of cognition (*blo'i yul du bden pa*)."[35] Linking these three properties to reasoning and its object, respectively, Gyamarwa identifies nine theses (*dam bca'*, *pratijñā*) and six arguments (*'thad pa*, *upapatti*), which he derives in the text from the autocommentary's statement, connected to the fifth verse, that "Truth in the ultimate sense is ultimate truth" (*don dam par bden pa ni don dam pa'i bden pa*, SDVV ad SVV 4).[36]

31. SDVV ad SVV 3d (Eckel 1987, 71 and 156; Akahane 2020, 4).

32. SDVP (D 17b4, Akahane 2020, 68).

33. The manuscript is illegible here. I assume the missing words are *g[zhan pa]'i*.

34. Rgya dmar ba, *Bden gnyis rnam bshad*, 10b1–2 (Nishizawa 2019, 103 and 185).

35. Rgya dmar ba, *Bden gnyis rnam bshad*, 11b3–4, where he refers to the *Pañjikā's* position that this verse summarizes a figurative ultimate: *'dir sngar bstan pa ltar rnam grangs kyi don dam mdor bstan pa zhes bya bar byas pa'i skabs 'dir dam bca' rgu* [= *dgu*] *'thad pa dang bcas pa ston to // gzhan ni gcig shos yin* (3d) *don dam pa'i bden pa* (SDVV) *zhes bya bas dam bca' rgu rzod de / 'di' ltar gzhan zhes pa dang / gcig shos zhes pa dang / bden pa zhes pa gsum po ni / spros pa las gzhan spros bral dang / kun rdzob las gcig shos don dam pa dang / blo'i yul du bden pas na bden pa zhes bya ba'i chos gsum yin pa na /*.

36. The first five theses demonstrate that reasoning and its object are the ultimate that is free from proliferation and the latter four theses demonstrate that the conventional is not free from proliferation and belying but true on the side of conventional knowledge (Rgya dmar ba, *Bden gnyis rnam bshad*, 11b4–6). Six arguments are identified in the text as follows (Rgya dmar ba, *Bden gnyis rnam bshad*, 11b7–8): *don dam par bden pa ni* (SDVV) *zhes pa dang / gang gi phyir*

190 TRUTH AND KNOWLEDGE IN AN EMPTY WORLD

Here Gyamarwa's interpretation of "different" (*gzhan*)—that is, "different from discursive proliferation"—draws our attention.[37] Although Jñānagarbha does not mention "proliferation" in this context, Gyamarwa seems to rely on *Vibhaṅga* verse 11b, which states that reality (*yang dag pa'i don*) is free from discursive proliferation (*spros pa med pa*) in the same manner as Śāntarakṣita's *Madhyamakālaṃkāra* 70cd (see note 8 above).

Notably, Gyamarwa advances several reasons for dismissing the *Pañjikā's* attribution of the figurative ultimate to *Vibhaṅga* verses 3–4. I summarize his points: [1] Verses 3–5 are the occasion for advancing the truth free from proliferation. [2] The figurative is not that which is established by reasoning (*rnam grangs pa ni rigs pas gtan la phab pa nyid kyang ma yin pa*). [3] The figurative ultimate is a specific conventional (*kun rdzob nyid kyi khyad par*). [4] [Truth] is taught in the expression "truth that follows reasoning" (SDVV, *rigs pa'i rjes su 'gro ba can gyi bden pa nyid*). [5] It is negated in line 4b that ultimate truth is something conventional (*kun rdzob min*). [6] Something conventional is explained as belying in line 4c (*de ltar mi slu min phyir te*).[38] His main contention is that what Jñānagarbha propounds at the very beginning of his treatise, whose subject is the two truths, must be the definition of the nonfigurative ultimate, not the figurative ultimate. Moreover, in his view, what Jñānagarbha opposes to the conventional in verses 3–4 must also be the nonfigurative ultimate.[39] Gyamarwa claims, "Furthermore, because it is tenable that reasoning cognition (*rigs pa'i shes pa*) is a primary ultimate (*rtso bo'i don dam*) here, and that its object is the nonfigurative ultimate truth, it is wrong to interpret [as the *Pañjikā* does] that nonfigurative ultimate is only explained later [in the fifth verse]."[40]

If it is granted that his claims are correct, two questions may arise. How does Gyamarwa interpret the second half of the fifth verse and its autocom-

(SDVV) *zhes pa dang* / *des gtan la phab pa'i* (SDVV) *zhes pa dang* / *kun rdzob min* (4c) *zhes pa dang* / *de ltar mi slu min phyir* (4d) *zhes pa dang* / *ji ltar snang pa'i dngos po ni* (5a) *zhes pa yin la* /.

37. Chapa modifies Gyamarwa's interpretation as follows (Phya pa, *Bden gnyis rnam bshad*, 7a6–7b1): "Different" in the definition means "different from the [conventional] truth as the object of nonanalytic cognition" (*ma dpyad pa'i blo'i yul du bden pa las gzhan mthar thug dpyod pa'i rigs pa'i yul du bden pa*)—that is, the truth as the object of analytic reasoning.

38. Rgya dmar ba, *Bden gnyis rnam bshad*, 12b1–2.

39. Chapa also refutes the view, attributing it to someone (*kha cig*) with similar arguments in Phya pa, *Bden gnyis rnam bshad*, 9a5–8.

40. Rgya dmar ba, *Bden gnyis rnam bshad*, 12b4–5: *gzhan yang rigs pa'i shes pa ni 'dir rtso bo'i don dam pa yin la de'i yul rnam grangs ma yin pa'i don dam pa'i bden pa nyid du 'thad pas na* / *rnam grangs ma yin pa phyi nas 'chad pa kho nar byed pa yang* / *nor ba yin no* //.

mentary, which states, "The ultimate truth does not appear to any occurring cognition because it does not appear even to the cognition of an omniscient one"? The statement in the seventeenth verse that reasoning is nothing other than something conventional because it corresponds to appearances (see note 27 above) also seems to contradict his position. Regarding the fifth verse and the cognition of an omniscient one, establishing Gyamarwa's solution in his *Bden gnyis rnam bshad* is difficult because folios 13b–16b of the manuscript, where this verse should be discussed, are missing.[41] In this respect, Chapa may be able to help us; he construes the verse as follows: The ultimate, *which is the object of reasoning*, cannot occur in cognitions *endowed with the appearances of conventional things* because an omniscient one does not see *that it occurs in them*.[42] According to Chapa, the statement of the *Dharmasaṅgītisūtra* (see note 12) means that not seeing the appearances of conventional things as the object of reasoning is the seeing of truth in the sense that conventional things are not established if examined by reasoning.[43] Thus Chapa interprets the fifth verse as differentiating the object of reasoning, which is ultimate, from the appearances of conventional objects. It is possible that Gyamarwa held a similar view.

Gyamarwa's interpretation of the seventeenth verse is unclear, partially due to illegible letters in the manuscript, but he identifies the reasoning consciousness (*rigs shes*) as something conventional by replacing the word *rigs pa* in the *Vibhaṅga* and *Vṛtti* with *rigs shes*.[44] Consciousness exists only conventionally, though it appears as if existing in reality. However, as reasoning is also consciousness, differentiating it from reasoning consciousness is difficult. What Gyamarwa intends might be that the reasoning consciousness itself does not ultimately exist if analyzed by reasoning.[45]

41. His *Dbu ma de kho na nyid rnam par dpyod pa* (Hugon and Vose 2024) contains many parallel discussions, but there is no direct mention of SDV 5.

42. This is my paraphrase of his inference based on the logical reason of nonperception of the pervader (*khyab byed mi dmyigs pa, vyāpakānupalabdhi*). See Phya pa, *Bden gnyis rnam bshad*, 9b6–8.

43. Chapa demonstrates the logical reason's being the property of the subject (*phyogs chos, pakṣadharmatā*) resorting to a reasoning and scriptural statement—that is, from the *Dharmasaṅgītisūtra*. See Phya pa, *Bden gnyis rnam bshad*, 9b8–10a1.

44. Rgya dmar ba, *Bden gnyis rnam bshad*, 36a1–2: *rigs shes don dam nyid chos kyi de ltar shes pa snang bas 'khrul pa ku[n] rdzob dang gcig pa ni **rigs de yang** (SDVV ad 17c) zhes pa lasogs pa'o //*; 36b3–4: *de ltar **de nyid kyi phyir** zhes pas / rigs shes don dam de'i ngor med pa don dam par med pa de nyid kyi phyir te /.*

45. Regarding this, his statement that reasoning consciousness (*rigs pa'i shes pa*) is a primary ultimate (*rtso bo'i don dam*) (see note 40 above) is puzzling, but this suggests that *rigs pa* and

Gyamarwa also reveals another distinction between figurative and nonfigurative ultimates: whereas the complete extinguishment of proliferation is a nonfigurative ultimate, the negation of a specific portion of proliferation, such as arising, is a figurative ultimate,[46] as *Madhyamakālaṃkāra* verse 70 states (see note 8 above). In this respect, Gyamarwa seeks to compromise with the *Pañjikā* as follows: "Although it is correct here that what is established by reasoning is nothing other than the nonfigurative, it cannot discredit the *ti ka* [i.e., the *Pañjikā*] by stating that [what is established by reasoning] is not something figurative, because [the *ti ka*] does not explain the elimination of all discursive proliferation as figurative, but it explains about the figurative ultimate by depending on the positive determination of nonarising subsequent to the negation of arising."[47]

Concluding Remarks

For Gyamarwa, the concepts that describe truths such as nonarising and emptiness are figurative ultimates or correct conventional truths. Reasoning (*rigs pa*) eliminates superimposition and proliferation, including these correct conceptions, through analytical examinations via inferences. Thus reasoning ascertains emptiness in terms of the absence of all proliferation— that is, the nonfigurative ultimate. As Gyamarwa and Chapa defined yogic perception and inferential proof as the valid cognitions that ascertain the ultimate truth and see it by way of not seeing,[48] a practitioner is expected to realize in meditation exactly what he has rationally ascertained: the extinguishment of all discursive proliferation. Gyamarwa's interpretation that the stairway of reasoning is not the figurative ultimate does not seem to

rigs shes are not different. In his *Dbu ma de kho na nyid rnam par dpyod pa* 5b2 (Hugon and Vose 2024), *rigs pa'i shes pa* is identified as *don dam*, although one should note that *don dam* is not *don dam bden pa*.

46. Rgya dmar ba, *Bden gnyis rnam bshad*, 12b5: *mthun pa'i don dam ni rigs pas spros pa'i phyogs 'ga' bcad pa yin no //.*

47. Rgya dmar ba, *Bden gnyis rnam bshad*, 12b6–7: *'dir rigs pas rnam par gtan la phab pa ni rnam grangs ma yin pa kho na 'thad kyi / rnam grangs pa ni ma yin no zhes zer bas ni ti ka la mi gnod de / skye ba bkag nas skye med yongs gcod du bzung pa la ltos nas rnam grangs kyi don dam du bshad kyi / spros pa mtha' dag rnam par bcad pa la ni rnam grangs par ma bshad pas so //.*

48. Rgya dmar ba, *Bden gnyis rnam bshad*, 10b4 (Nishizawa 2019, 103 and 185): *nges par byed pa'i tshad ma ni don dam kyi spyi mtshan nyid spros bral la gnas par / snang pa med pa'i yes shes mngon sum gi tshad ma'am / gcig dang du bral lasogs pa'i rtags kyis nges pa'i rjes dpag go //; Bden gnyis rnam bshad* (Phya) 7a8: *mtshan gzhi spros pa dang bral ba ni spros pa gcod pa'i rjes dpag dang rnal 'byor gyi mngon sum gyis nges la /.*

agree with Bhāviveka, who accepts this stairway of insight into truth only as the correct conventional concordant with the ultimate. On this point, Jñānagarbha appears to follow Bhāviveka. According to these Indian scholars, the insight (*prajñā*) born of listening, rational reflection, and cultivation reveals each of the specified truths—such as the absences of intrinsic nature, self, arising, and so on, which are not free from proliferation—and the nonfigurative ultimate truth is only accessible by nonconceptual cognition. In contrast, Gyamarwa maintains that the insight endowed with reasoning reveals the nonfigurative ultimate truth free from proliferation by eliminating all dichotomous conceptions. He defends a rational stairway to the ultimate truth based on valid cognitions.

His position is close to that of Śāntarakṣita and Kamalaśīla to the extent that they acknowledge the realization of the ultimate truth to be reached through inference and yogic perception. It is not improper to say that for these scholars, the stairway to the realization of ultimate truth is exactly the "stages of cultivation" (*bhāvanākrama*), where reasoning plays a central role in analytic discrimination (*vipaśyanā*).

Endorsing the influence of the introducers of Buddhism into Tibet, Śāntarakṣita and Kamalaśīla, on Gyamarwa, one may assume that the academic circumstances in which Gyamarwa engaged[49] also urged him to reinterpret the *Vibhaṅga* in order to show his disapproval of the positions inspired by Candrakīrti that leaned toward denying reasoning's ability to attain the ultimate truth. The split between Svātantrika and Prāsaṅgika pertaining to the logical method of *svatantrānumāna* or *prasaṅga* was brought by Patsab Nyima Drak;[50] however, the theoretical split regarding valid cognitions had already been born among Tibetan Madhyamaka thinkers, which Gyamarwa revealed and, from the Svātantrika side against Candrakīrti's followers, Chapa crystallized.[51]

Abbreviations

BCA   Śāntideva, *Bodhisattvacaryāvatāra*. See La Vallée Poussin 1901–14.

BhK   Kamalaśīla, *Bhāvanākrama*. See Tucci 1958 and Ichigō et al. 2025.

MA   Candrakīrti, *Madhyamakāvatāra*. See La Vallée Poussin 1907–12.

MĀ   Kamalaśīla, *Madhyamakāloka*. D 3887, P 5287.

49. See note 18 above.

50. See, e.g., Vose 2009, Vose 2020, and Yoshimizu 2020.

51. See also Hugon's article in the present volume.

MABh   Candrakīrti, *Madhyamakāvatārabhāṣya*. See La Vallée Poussin 1907–12.

MAl   Śāntarakṣita, *Madhyamakālaṃkāra*. D 3884, P 5284. See Ichigō 1985.

MAlP   Kamalaśīla, *Madhyamakālaṃkārapañjikā*. D 3886, P 5285. See Ichigō 1985.

MAlV   Śāntarakṣita, *Madhyamakālaṃkāravṛtti*. D 3885, P 5285. See Ichigō 1985.

MHK   Bhāviveka, *Madhyamakahṛdayakārikā*. See Ejima 1980.

MMK   Nāgārjuna, *Mūlamadhyamakakārikā*. See Ye Shaoyong 2011.

PrPr   Bhāviveka, *Prajñāpradīpa*. D 3853, P 5253.

PVin   Dharmakīrti, *Pramāṇaviniścaya*. See Steinkellner 2007.

SDV   Jñānagarbha, *Satyadvayavibhaṅga*. D 3881. See Eckel 1987, Akahane 2020.

SDVP   *Satyadvayavibhaṅgapañjikā*. D 3883, P 5283. See Akahane 2020.

SDVV   Jñānagarbha, *Satyadvayavibhaṅgavṛtti*. D 3882. See Eckel 1987, Akahane 2020.

TJ   Bhāviveka, *Tarkajvālā*. D 3856, P 5256.

Bibliography

Akahane Ritsu. 2010. "Chibetto ni okeru 'Nitai funbetsu ron' ni taisuru sanpen no chūshakusho" (Three Tibetan Commentaries on *Dbu ma bden gnyis*). *Nihon chibetto gakkai kaihō* (*Report of the Japanese Association for Tibetan Studies*) 56: 77–85.

———. 2012. "Jñānagarbha no chūgan shisō" (Jñānagarbha's Madhyamaka Theory). In *Kū to chūgan* (Śūnyatā and Madhyamaka), edited by Katsura Shōryū, 113–35. Tokyo: Shunjūsha.

———. 2013. "The Influence of rGya dmar ba Byang chub grags on Early Tibetan Buddhism in the Period of the Second Diffusion." *Nihon chibetto gakkai kaihō* (*Report of the Japanese Association for Tibetan Studies*) 59: 89–104.

———. 2020. *A New Critical Edition of Jñānagarbha's Satyadvayavibhaṅga with Śāntarakṣita's Commentary*. Edited by Nishiyama Ryō, Yamanaka Yukio, and Muroya Yasutaka. Wiener Studien zur Tibetologie und Buddhismuskunde 98. Vienna: Arbeitskreis für Tibetische und Buddhistische Studien Universität Wien.

Akahane Ritsu, Hayashima Satoshi, and Nishiyama Ryō. 2013. "*Prajñāpradīpaṭīka* XXIVshō tekisuto to wayaku (2)—uttarapakṣa 1—" (Chapter 24 of the *Prajñapradipaṭīkā*, Tibetan Text and Japanese Translation (2)—uttarapakṣa 1—). *Indogaku chibettogaku kenkyū* (*Journal of Indian and Tibetan Studies*) 17: 63–86.

Blumenthal, James. 2004. *The Ornament of the Middle Way: A Study of the Madhyamaka Thought of Śāntarakṣita*. Ithaca, NY: Snow Lion Publications.

Cabezón, José Ignacio. 2010. "The Madhyamaka in Gro lung pa's *Bstan rim chen mo*." In *Studies in the Philosophy and History of Tibet: Proceedings of the Eleventh Seminar of the International Association of Tibetan Studies, Königswinter 2006*, edited by Maret Kark and Horst Lasic, 11–58. Beiträge zur Zentralasienforschung 22. Andiast: International Institute for Tibetan and Buddhist Studies.

Eckel, Malcolm David. 1987. *Jñānagarbha's Commentary on the Distinction between the Two Truths: An Eighth-Century Handbook of Madhyamaka Philosophy*. Albany: State University of New York Press.

———. 1992. *To See the Buddha: A Philosopher's Quest for the Meaning of Emptiness*. New York: HarperSanFrancisco.

———. 2020. "The Two Truths and the Structure of the Bodhisattva Path in 'The Introduction to the Nectar of Reality.'" *Indogaku chibettogaku kenkyū (Journal of Indian and Tibetan Studies)* 20: 140–65.

Ejima Yasunori. 1980. *Chūgan shisō no tenkai: Bhāvaviveka kenkyū* (Development of Mādhyamika Philosophy in India: Studies of Bhāvaviveka). Tokyo: Shunjūsha.

Eltschinger, Vincent. 2009. "On the Career and the Cognition of *Yogins*." In *Yogic Perception, Meditation and Altered States of Consciousness*, edited by Eli Franco and Dagmar Eigner, 169–213. Vienna: Österreichische Akademie der Wissenschaften.

———. 2014. "The Four Nobles' Truths and Their 16 Aspects: On the Dogmatic and Soteriological Presuppositions of the Buddhist Epistemologists' Views on *Niścaya*." *Journal of Indian Philosophy* 42: 249–73.

Hugon, Pascale. 2020. "Wonders *in margine*: Mapping the Madhyamaka Network of Gyamarwa Jangchupdrak." *Journal of South Asian Intellectual History* 3.1: 123–47.

Hugon, Pascale, and Kevin Vose. 2024. *rGya dmar ba—dBu ma'i de kho na nyid*, edition and translation. Available at https://www.oeaw.ac.at/ikga/forschung/tibetologie /materialien/the-dbu-ma-de-kho-na-nyid-of-rgya-dmar-ba-byang-chub-grags-12th-c.

Ichigō Masamichi. 1985. *Madhyamakālaṃkāra of Śāntarakṣita with His Own Commentary or Vṛtti and with the Subcommentary or Pañjikā of Kamalaśīla*. Kyoto: Buneido.

Ichigō Masamichi, Ozawa Chiaki, and Ōta Fukiko. 2025. *Zenyaku Kamalaśīla: Shujū shidai-shohen, chūhen, kōhen-* (Complete Japanese Translation of the *Bhāvanākrama*). Kanagawa: Kishinshobō.

Kanō Kazuo. 2007. "Gok loden sherab cho 'Shokan Kanro no shizuku,' kōtei tekusuto to naiyō gaikan" (Rngog Blo ldan shes rab's *Spring yig bdud rtsi'i thig le*, edition and survey). *Kōyasan Daigaku mikkyō bunka kenkyūsho kiyō (Bulletin of the Institute of Esoteric Buddhism and Buddhist Culture)* 20: 105–162.

———. 2020. "Gok loden sherab cho 'Shokan Kanro no shizuku' no shinshutsu hanpon" (A xylograph version of Rngog Blo ldan shes rab's *Spring yig bdud rtsi'i thig le*). *Komazawa Daigaku Bukkyōgakubu kenkyū kiyō (Journal of the Faculty of Buddhism of the Komazawa University)* 78: 145–72.

Keira Ryūsei. 2004. *Mādhyamika and Epistemology. A Study of Kamalaśīla's Method for Proving the Voidness of All Dharmas*. Wiener Studien zur Tibetologie und Buddhismuskunde 59. Vienna: Arbeitskreis für Tibetische und Buddhistische Studien Universität Wien.

La Vallée Poussin, Louis de, ed. 1907–12. *Madhyamakāvatāra per Candrakīrti*. Bibliotheca Buddhica 9. St. Petersburg: Imprimerie de l'Académie Imperiale des Sciences.

———, ed. 1901–14. *Prajñākaramati's Commentary to the Bodhicaryāvatāra of Çāntideva*. Bibliotheca Indica. Calcutta: Asiatic Society of Bengal.

MacDonald, Anne. 2009. "Knowing Nothing: Candrakīrti and Yogic Perception." In *Yogic Perception, Meditation and Altered States of Consciousness*, edited by Eli Franco and Dagmar Eigner, 133–68. Vienna: Österreichische Akademie der Wissenschaften.

Matsumoto Shirō. 1978. "Jñānagarbha no nitai setsu." *Bukkyō gaku (Journal of Buddhist Studies)* 5: 109–37.

Nishiyama Ryō. 2019. "Bhāviveka on Non-Conceptual Cognitions: A Study of the

Madhyamakahṛdaya Chapter 3, Verses 7 to 13, and 265." *Indogaku bukkyōgaku kenkyū* (*Journal of Indian and Buddhist Studies*) 67.3: 1112–17.

Nishizawa Fumihito. 2018. "Chibetto shoki chūgan shisō ni okeru kūshō rikai: gok honyakushi, torunpa, gyamaruwa, chapa" (On the Interpretation of Emptiness in Early Tibetan Madhyamaka Thought: Rngog lo tsā ba, Gro lung pa, Rgya dmar ba, and Phya pa). *Nihon chibetto gakkai kaihō* (*Report of the Japanese Association for Tibetan Studies*) 64: 35–51.

———. 2019. "Chibetto shoki chūgan shisō ni okeru nitai setsu: Torunpa to Gyamarba no nitai wo meguru ronsō" (The Theory of Two Truths in Early Tibetan Madhyamaka). *Otani daigaku shinshū sōgō kenkyūsho kenkyū kiyō* (*Annual Memoirs of the Otani University Shin Buddhist Comprehensive Research Institute*) 36: 1–204.

Phya pa Chos kyi seng ge. *Bden gnyis rnam bshad* (*Dbu ma bden pa gnyis kyi rnam par bshad pa*). In *Bka' gdams gsung 'bum*, 6:185–250 (1–33b3).

Rgya dmar ba Byang chub grags. *Bden gnyis rnam bshad* (*Dbu ma bden gnyis kyi rnam bshad ti ka dang bcas pa*). In *Bka' gdams gsung 'bum*, 19:247–316 (4a1–45b3).

———. *Dbu ma de kho na nyid rnam par dpyod pa* (*Dbu ma'i de kho na nyid gtan la dbab pa*). In *Bka' gdams gsung 'bum*, 31:7–67 (1–31a4). See Hugon and Vose 2024.

Rngog Blo ldan shes rab. *Spring yig bdud rtsi'i thigs pa*. See Kanō 2007.

Saitō, Akira. 2020. "Bhāviveka on Prajñā." *Archaeologies of the Written: Indian, Tibetan, and Buddhist Studies in Honour of Cristina Scherrer-Schaub*, edited by Vincent Tournier, Vincent Eltschinger, and Marta Sernesi, 517–25. Series Minor 89. Naples: UniorPress.

Seyfort Ruegg, David. 1981. *The Literature of the Madhyamaka School of Philosophy in India*. Wiesbaden: Otto Harrassowitz.

Steinkellner, Ernst, ed. 2007. *Dharmakīrti's Pramāṇaviniścaya: Chapters 1 and 2*. Beijing and Vienna: China Tibetology Publishing House / Austrian Academy of Sciences Press.

Sweet, Michael J. 1979. "*Bodhicaryāvatāra* 9:2 as a Focus for Tibetan Interpretations of the Two Truths in the Prāsaṅgikā Mādhyamika." *Journal of International Association of Buddhist Studies* 2.2: 79–89.

Tauscher, Helmut. 1983. "Some Problems of Textual History in Connection with the Tibetan Translation of the *Madhyamakāvatāra* and Its Commentary." In *Contributions on Tibetan and Buddhist Religion and Philosophy, Proceedings of the Csoma de Körös Symposium held at Velm-Vienna, Austria, 13–19 September 1981*, edited by Ernst Steinkellner and Helmut Tauscher, 293–303. Wiener Studien zur Tibetologie und Buddhismuskunde 11. Vienna: Arbeitskreis für Tibetische und Buddhistische Studien Universität Wien.

———. 2003. "Phya pa Chos kyi seng ge as a Svātantrika." In *The Svātantrika-Prāsaṅgika Distinction: What Difference Does a Difference Make?* edited by Georges B. J. Dreyfus and Sara L. McClintock, 207–55. Studies in Indian and Tibetan Buddhism. Boston: Wisdom Publications.

Tillemans, Tom J. F. 2016. *How Do Mādhyamikas Think? And Other Essays on the Buddhist Philosophy of the Middle*. Studies in Indian and Tibetan Buddhism. Somerville, MA: Wisdom Publications.

Tucci, Giuseppe. 1958. *Minor Buddhist Texts, Part II: First* Bhāvanākrama *of Kamalaśīla, Sanskrit and Tibetan Texts with Introduction and English Summary*. Rome: Istituto Italiano per il Medio ed Estremo Oriente.

Vose, Kevin. 2009. *Resurrecting Candrakīrti: Disputes in the Tibetan Creation of Prāsaṅgika.* Studies in Indian and Tibetan Buddhism. Boston: Wisdom Publications.

———. 2020. "Absence and Elimination: Madhyamaka Interpretation in the Formation of Scholastic Traditions in Tibet." *Journal of South Asian Intellectual History* 3.1: 148–84.

Ye Shaoyong. 2011. *Zhonglunsong: Fanzanghan Hejiao, Daodu, Yizhu* [*Mūlamadhya-makakārikā: New Editions of the Sanskrit, Tibetan, and Chinese Versions, with Commentary and a Modern Chinese Translation*]. Shanghai: Zhongxi Book Company (中西書局).

Yoshimizu Chizuko. 2020. "Updating Prāsaṅgika and *prasaṅga.*" *Indogaku bukkyōgaku kenkyū* (*Journal of Indian and Buddhist Studies*) 68.3: 1193–99.

On Levels in Madhyamaka

John D. Dunne

Introduction

The modern academy promotes specialization. Not only do neuroscientists, for example, focus on the brain in a way that often treats the body as the "periphery," but many specialize in particular brain functions or networks. While the academic study of Buddhism sometimes falls prey to this same urge, Tom Tillemans clearly stands out as a scholar who nimbly moves across boundaries: Western philosophy and Buddhist thought; Sanskrit, Tibetan, and Chinese languages; grammatical theory and the translation of texts; intellectual history and philosophical analysis; and Madhyamaka thought and *pramāṇa* theory, to name a few areas of divergent specialization. As a dissertation advisor, Tom did not wear his broad and deep erudition as a mantle to impress his students, but his brilliance served as an inspiration that, in my own humble career, continues to be a guiding light. In this essay, I aim to make a small contribution toward a puzzle discussed at length by Tom that has caught the attention of several contributors to this volume: namely, the way that Dharmakīrtian attempts at refining our understanding of perception and reason run up against what Tom has called the potentially "dismal" reluctance that some Mādhyamikas exhibit when invited to move beyond our unrefined account of the world (Tillemans 2016, 47).

One way to introduce this tension between Madhyamaka and *pramāṇa* theory is to recall that, for most Buddhist philosophers, much that seems intuitively and obviously true to ordinary beings is actually distorted or deluded (*bhrānta*) in ways that perpetuate suffering. For Mahāyāna Buddhist philosophers who adopt the analytical tools developed by Dharmakīrti, this finally applies even to the mundane cognitions that are counted as fully reliable or *pramāṇa* in that they enable us to accomplish goals within our lifeworld such as slaking our thirst.[1] We are not speaking of ordinary delusions. To mistake a mirage for water is easily understandable, but here even the perception of the "water" that experientially slakes our thirst is called into question, no matter how obvious and intuitive it may seem. So why does the world, ultimately delusional and distorted, appear so intuitively real to us? Dharmakīrti thinks that our "stable imprints" (*dṛḍhavāsanā*) play a role, such that all our ordinary perceptions and inferences, even when they seem completely reliable within our shared lifeworld, are merely conventional *pramāṇa*s (*saṃvyavahārika-pramāṇa*). Following the standard Buddhist model, Dharmakīrti agrees that this delusion can be uprooted by a cognition of the way things actually are, which he counts as an ultimate *pramāṇa* (*pāramārthikapramāṇa*).[2] Dharmakīrti never specified what this ultimate way of knowing might be, but his commentator Śākyabuddhi did:

> The bodhisattva who is knowing things as essenceless is knowing
> only mere reflexive awareness that is devoid of duality.[3]

This model suggests, first, that within the various conventional lifeworlds constituted by shared and stable imprints or cognitive propensities, the beings within those shared lifeworlds experience distinct conventional realities. Here, what comes to mind is the famed example of *preta*s, humans, and *deva*s gazing upon a river that they perceive, respectively, as pus, water, and the immortal nectar of the gods. When a *preta* sees pus, that experience is not restricted to the mind of just that *preta*; the other *preta*s also see pus.[4] In short, their perceptions of pus are indeed perceptual *pramāṇa*s, albeit conventional ones whose reliability is tied to their shared lifeworld.

Since this is a Buddhist model, it must posit some way to emerge out of this delusion such that, by experiencing reality as it truly is, one recognizes that one's seemingly indubitable perceptions of a coherent lifeworld—shared

---

1. The translation of *pramāṇa* remains a challenge. The Dharmakīrtian account holds that a moment of awareness (*jñāna*) is a *pramāṇa* not only because it guides efficacious action in a trustworthy (*avisaṃvāda*) way but also because it motivates one to act (*pravartaka*) toward some goal. There is apparently no English translation that captures both the epistemic reliability and the psychologically motivating function of a *pramāṇa*, and with that in mind, I will leave the term untranslated. For an overview of the Dharmakīrtian account, see Dunne 2004, 252–314.

2. Steinkellner 2007, 43–44.

3. Śākyabuddhi, *Tshad ma rnam 'grel kyi 'grel bshad* [=*Pramāṇavārttikaṭīkā*], 99:508: *byang chub sems dpa' chos rnams bdag med par mkhyen pas ni gnyis kyis dben pa rang rig tsam mkhyen to.* For a translation of the whole passage, see Dunne 2004, 396–411.

4. Vasubandhu famously deploys this metaphor in his *Viṃśikāvṛtti* on verses 3–4.

by others and replete with an efficacy for realizing our mundane goals—is actually like a nightmare from which one must awake. Śākyabuddhi takes a Yogācāra perspective, whereby reflexively aware consciousness itself, devoid of subject-object duality, remains at the ultimate level. As we will see below, other Buddhist thinkers hold that Dharmakīrti's final view is the Madhyamaka. In any case, whatever one's account of the ultimate might be, an obvious question arises: How is this possible? How can one awaken when one's very perceptions and the confirmations provided by others seems so indubitable, as if one were living in a massive, shared delusion, a conspiracy theory of the "real"?[5]

After Dharmakīrti, and perhaps before, some Mahāyāna thinkers held that to liberate beings from their delusions, one must initially shift them not to an ultimate perspective but to a better conventional one that, while still deluded, brings them closer to the liberative experience of the ultimate. This introduces the notion of different accounts of conventional reality that are progressively more useful, at least for the purpose of liberating beings. In academic discourse, we refer to this notion as "levels of analysis," echoing the metaphor of a "stairway" (*sopana*) or "ladder of views that lead to the ultimate."[6] A historical endpoint that valorizes Dharmakīrti's role in the emergence of this theory is found in the commentary by Sahajavajra (writing in the eleventh century) on the *Tattvadaśaka* by his teacher Advayavajra, an avowedly Mādhyamika philosopher.[7] Advayavajra's second verse says:

> For the one who wishes to know suchness, the middle [way] is not the Sākāra or Nirākāra [Yogācāra], and the Middle [i.e., Madhyamaka] that is not ornamented with the guru's instructions is only middling.[8]

5. Kellner (2020, 40) discusses this in terms of what she describes as the "entry rules" that explain how a bodhisattva can move from ordinary conventional awareness to the nonconceptual awareness of the ultimate.

6. In Madhyamaka contexts, the metaphor of a *sopana* ("stairway" or "ladder") formed by the conventional leading to the ultimate is coined by Bhāviveka (see Eckel 1992). See Apple 2008, 15n17, for the use of ladder-like metaphors in a parallel context. As a potential resolution to the "dismal" approach to Madhyamaka epistemology, Tom Tillemans also muses about the notion of a ladder of truths (2016, 57).

7. For a discussion of Advayavajra's life, see Mathes 2015 and Isaacson and Sferra 2014, which also briefly discusses Advayavajra's students, including Sahajavajra.

8. Advayavajra, *Tattvadaśaka*, verse 2: *na sākāranirākāre tathatāṃ jñātum icchataḥ / madhyamā madhyamā caiva guruvāganalaṃkṛtā //*. Note the pun here, where Madhyamaka as the "middle" philosophy is only "middling" or mediocre when it is not accompanied by direct instructions from the guru.

Earlier in his commentary, Sahajavajra has already raised the role of reason, and now he returns to it:[9]

> Here, someone might think, "Madhyamaka does not engage *pramāṇa*s and their objects (*prameyas*) because [those two] do not withstand the analysis that begins 'not from self nor other.'"
>
> This is not tenable. Since there would be no *pramāṇa*s, it would be difficult to establish the relation of probandum and evidence. In other words, *pramāṇa*s are just conventional; how would they be ultimate?
>
> The objector responds, "If [ultimately] nonexistent *pramāṇa*s and their objects just exist conventionally, how does one perform the analysis that begins, 'not from self, nor other'?"
>
> We accept it just as it is.[10] For the most part, this path here follows Dharmakīrti, the crown jewel of *pramāṇa*. By relying on him and following his path, we are employing the presentation of all those [*pramāṇa*s and their objects]—it is not that we negate them through our own understanding.

9. Sahajavajra, *Tattvadaśakaṭīkā*, 487–88. My translation differs slightly from Brunnhölzl's (2007, 148–49). With him, I read *mtshan ma dang gzhal bya* (488,1) as *tshad ma dang gzhal bya*; that portion of the passage is underlined below. This passage includes noncanonical translations of material from the *Pramāṇavārttika*, and my translation of those materials is based on the Sanskrit (see note 11 below). The passage reads: *'dir dbu mas ni tshad ma dang gzhal bya 'jug pa ma yin te/ rang dang gzhan zhes bya ba la sogs pa'i rnam par dpyad pa mi bzod pa'i phyir ro zhes snyam du sems so/ de ni 'thad pa ma yin te/ tshad ma med pa'i phyir bsgrub par bya ba dang sgrub par byed pa'i dngos po gnas pa dka'o/ de rnams kun rdzob nyid yin gyi don dam par ni ji ltar 'gyur zhes bya ba'i tshig gis so/ <u>tshad ma dang gzhal bya</u> med pa rnams kyang kun rdzob du yod pa nyid yin na/ de ji ltar rang dang gzhan las zhes bya ba la sogs pa brtag ce na/ ji ltar 'gyur ba de ltar khas len pa yin te/ phal cher lam 'di 'dir tshad ma rnams kyi gtsug gi nor bu chos kyi grags pa'i rjes su 'brangs te/ de la brten nas de'i lam gyi rjes su 'brangs nas 'di thams cad kyi rnam par bzhag pa sbyar ba yin te/ rang gi yid kyis de dag 'gegs pa ni ma yin no/ de'i lam gyi rjes su 'brangs pas yang rang bzhin grub par 'gyur ro zhe na/ ma yin te/ ji lta bu zhe na/ re zhig phyi rol gyi don rgyas pa rnam par bzhag dgos pa'i dbang gis byas kyang gong ma gong ma'i rigs pas rtsad nas phyung ba yin no/ de nyid kyi skabs dbye bar bya ste/ gang gis dngos por dpyad bya ste/ de nyid la ni dngos po med/ gang phyir gcig dang du ma dag/ rang bzhin de la yod ma yin/* [*Pramāṇavārttika* 3.359] *'di dag de nges las 'ongs pa/ gang yang mkhas rnams kyis smras pa/ ji lta ji ltar don bsams pa/ de lta de ltar rnam par nyams/* [3.310] *des na mtshan nyid stong pa'i phyir/ rang bzhin med par bstan pa yin/* [3.215cd] *zhes bya ba la sogs pa shin tu gsal bar brjod do zhes shin tu spros pas chog go //.*

10. This may be an allusion to Dharmakīrti's statement *astu yathā tathā* (*Pramāṇavārttika* 3.4d).

The objector says, "But by following his path, an essence [of things] would be established." That is not the case. How so? Temporarily, for a purpose, [Dharmakīrti] gives an extensive presentation of external objects, but through progressively superior reasoning, he completely eradicates [the notion of truly existing objects]. The contexts for these [different levels of reasoning] should be distinguished as follows:

> The nature that things are perceived to have does not ultimately exist because they have neither a singular nor a nonsingular nature. [*Pramāṇavārttika* 3.359]

> Those who analyze reality make a statement that is entailed by things themselves—namely, that the way in which they reflect on objects is the way in which those objects disappear. [*Pramāṇavārttika* 3.310]

> Hence, since things are empty of any character (*lakṣaṇa*), it is explained that they are essenceless. [*Pramāṇavārttika* 3.215cd][11]

Dharmakīrti states this very clearly, so enough with this long excursus!

Clearly, whatever contemporary scholarship might say about Dharmakīrti's use of progressive levels,[12] for Sahajavajra Dharmakīrti provides the tools to "level up" one's perspective to eventually reach a realization of the ultimate in Madhyamaka terms. And that progression begins from a stance that asserts the existence of real external objects and moves through a Yogācāra account to finally reach the Madhyamaka perspective.

For the endorsement of Dharmakīrtian levels as an analytical tool, Sahajavajra provides a clear historical endpoint within the Sanskritic world, but how does this reflect earlier Madhyamaka? As we will see, we can point to precedents even in the work of Nāgārjuna, the founder of Madhyamaka, but can we

11. The verses from the third chapter of Dharmakīrti's *Pramāṇavārttika* are: 3.359: *bhāvā yena nirūpyante tad rūpaṃ nāsti tattvataḥ / yasmād ekam anekaṃ vā rūpam teṣām na vidyate //*; 3.209: *idaṃ vastubalāyātaṃ yad vadanti vipaścitaḥ / yathā yathārthāś cintyante viśīryante tathā tathā //*; and 3.215cd: *ato lakṣaṇaśūnyatvān niḥsvabhāvāḥ prakāśitāḥ //*.

12. Dharmakīrti's use of levels of analysis has been a topic of some debate in academic scholarship. The latest foray is McCrea 2020, who rejects the notion that Dharmakīrti employs a hierarchy of progressive views, although Sahajavajra would not agree. Brunnhölzl 2007, 524n529, notes that Sahajavajra anticipates this academic discussion by many years.

find a clear philosophical justification for the need to use this method, or an explanation of how it functions, in some earlier text that might have inspired Sahajavajra? Or is Sahajavajra idiosyncratically refusing to maintain the epistemologically dismal perspective proper to a Mādhyamika?

To explore these issues, I will first examine some basic principles and precedents for the notion of ranking and deploying conceptual systems. I will then turn to an apparently promising precedent for Sahajavajra's approach—namely, some key verses in the work of the Mādhyamika Śāntideva along with passages from his commentator Prajñākaramati. There, we will find that the notion of levels raises "dismal" problems that undermine Prajñākaramati's attempts to make sense of the verses, and we will see how his difficulties suggest that the notion of levels itself might be best understood in a contemplative context rather than in a strictly philosophical one.

On Ranking Conceptual Systems: Some Principles and Precedents

The notion of progressive levels relates to an overall framework within Mahāyāna Buddhism that uses various tools, especially reasoning and scripture (*yuktyāgama*), to enable individuals to advance along the path toward nirvāṇa. At least some Mādhyamika thinkers before Sahajavajra seem to endorse a "ladder" of progressive levels for leading beings out of suffering and to nirvāṇa. Fundamentally, Mādhyamika thinkers conceptualize the path's final endpoint as requiring direct insight into emptiness (*śūnyatā*) as a meditative experience that uproots the ignorance that prevents one from achieving that final goal. This realization itself is understood to be utterly beyond the words and concepts that play a central role in the conventional. Nāgārjuna himself, the first Mādhyamika author, clearly states that conceptualizations (*vikalpa*) are inherently part of the problem in the eighteenth chapter of his *Mūlamadhyamakārikā*:

> Liberation (*mokṣa*) comes from the extinction of karma and afflictive states (*kleśa*). Karma and afflictive states come from conceptualizations (*vikalpa*). They come from fabrication (*prapañca*), and fabrication ceases in emptiness.[13]

But later in the text, Nāgārjuna also famously states:

---

13. Nāgārjuna, *Mūlamadhyamakakārikā* 18.5: *karmakleśakṣayān mokṣaḥ karmakleśā vikalpataḥ / te prapañcāt prapañcas tu śūnyatāyāṃ nirudhyate //*.

Without relying on the conventional, the ultimate is not pointed out, and without understanding the ultimate, nirvāṇa is not attained.[14]

Nāgārjuna here suggests that our ordinary, conventional experience—structured by words and concepts—must somehow be harnessed to the task of realizing the ultimate, even though our ordinary conventional reality is distorted by the ignorance that the realization of emptiness is meant to uproot. Except by modeling this process in his own texts, Nāgārjuna does not explicitly state how a Mādhyamika should make use of the conventional, but in the eighteenth chapter, just after the verse about liberation cited above, he says:[15]

The buddhas have pointed out "self"; they have also taught "no-self"; and they have also taught "There is neither self nor no-self at all."

Already some notion of levels seems operative here, but one might claim that Nāgārjuna simply articulates the range of the Buddha's teaching, without implying that these different kinds of teaching are progressively leading to some conclusion. In his *Ratnāvalī*, however, Nāgārjuna implies a progression:

A grammarian will make some students
recite even the alphabet.
Likewise, the Buddha taught the Dharma
in accord with disciples' abilities.

To some he taught the Dharma aimed at
stopping negativity. To some,
one aimed at the practice of virtue. To some,
he taught one based upon duality.

He taught to some a Dharma not based on duality.
And to some, he taught a profound Dharma that terrifies
the timid; its source is emptiness and compassion,
and it is the means to attain awakening.[16]

14. Nāgārjuna, *Mūlamadhyamakakārikā* 24.10: *vyavahāram anāśritya paramārtho na deśyate / paramārtham anāgamya nirvāṇaṃ nādhigamyate //*.

15. Nāgārjuna, *Mūlamadhyamakārikā* 18.6: *ātmety api prajñapitam anātmety api deśitam / buddhair nātmā na cānātmā kaścid ity api deśitam //*.

16. Nāgārjuna, *Ratnāvalī* 4.94–96: *yathaiva vaiyākaraṇo mātṛkām api pāṭhayet / buddho 'vadat*

Presumably, grammarians do not teach certain students only the alphabet, and their education ends there. Instead, some students must begin with the alphabet, but they are eventually taught to read sentences. Otherwise, why bother studying? Likewise, Nāgārjuna implies a progression along different levels of understanding, where at least some disciples begin at a lower level and then advance.

Nāgārjuna's metaphor of the grammarian resonates with the notion of "skill in means" (*upāyakauśalya*), a key feature of the Mahāyāna.[17] In short, one must offer teachings that accord with the abilities and propensities of one's target audience in ways that address not only their level of understanding but also the specific types of errors that prevent them from reaching a Mahāyāna (and, in this case, a Madhyamaka) perspective. This approach motivates the development of typologies for conceptual systems, and in the history of Mahāyāna philosophy, that project emerges with particular clarity in the work of Bhāviveka,[18] with doxographical work continuing to this day among traditional Tibetan scholars.[19] But, despite Nāgārjuna's metaphor of the grammarian, one might still maintain that the ranking of conceptual systems does not necessarily mean that they should be deployed as a ladder for reaching the Madhyamaka pinnacle. What, then, is at stake for Mādhyamikas if they choose to build such a ladder?

Building a Ladder (or Not)

For Mādhyamikas, the problem with the conventional is that it rests on cognitions distorted by ignorance, which manifests in the attribution of essences (*svabhāva*) to entities that actually lack them. As Nāgārjuna indicated in the verse cited above (*Mūlamadhyamakārikā* 18.5), conceptualizations—perhaps especially philosophical ones—play a central role in that process, and they are therefore dangerous. Like a venomous snake, conceptualizations might be properly held such that their venom can be harvested for medicinal purposes. But wrongly grasped, concepts will bite, infecting us with the venom of ignorance.[20]

---

tathā dharmaṃ vineyānāṃ yathākṣamam // keṣāṃcid avadad dharmaṃ pāpebhyo vinivṛttaye / keṣāṃcit puṇyasiddhyarthaṃ keṣāṃcid dvayaniśritam // dvayāniśritam ekeṣāṃ gāmbhīraṃ bhīrubhīṣaṇam / śūnyatākaruṇāgarbham ekeṣāṃ bodhisādhanam //.

17. See Federman 2009.

18. See Eckel 1992.

19. For example, see Jinpa 2022.

20. Nāgārjuna, *Mūlamadhyamakakārikā*, 24.11.

Mādhyamikas thus remain suspicious of conceptual systems, and if one is acutely suspicious, even reason itself looks poisonous, especially since it might tempt one to "prove" the truth of Madhyamaka in a way that essentializes the ultimate. One would thereby be "incurable" (*asādhya*), according to Nāgārjuna.[21] One who adopts this deep pessimism about the conventional—including rationality itself—must avoid positive arguments for the Madhyamaka perspective and instead employ methods that defuse others' positions without affirming any stance for oneself. On most academic interpretations, Candrakīrti (writing in the seventh century) took this approach, and this is what Tom Tillemans has called a "dismal" attitude toward the conventional. What follows from it? Tillemans says (2016, 47):

> It might well seem to imply an extreme conservatism that nothing the world ever endorsed could be criticized or rejected and that, on the customary level at least, a Mādhyamika's principal epistemic task is just to passively acquiesce and duplicate.

In contrast to this "dismal" approach, the most optimistic view would maintain that one can completely defang the conventional serpent such that Mādhyamikas can now blithely engage with the conventional, with all its words and concepts, in ways that have somehow removed venomous ignorance through the exercise of reason. Words, concepts, and inferential reasoning can now be freely used because ignorance is not in any way intrinsic to them. It is not clear that any Indian Mādhyamika would endorse this position, but in Tibet, Tsongkhapa and his followers could be characterized in this way. As Tillemans puts it, "they believe and prove truths in a minimalist fashion not involving a metaphysics of intrinsic natures" (2016, 5). Between these options one might locate another kind of Mādhyamika, namely, one who is less optimistic than Tsongkhapa and less pessimistic than Candrakīrti. On this approach, the tools of language, concepts, and reason may be confidently but carefully used to arrive at progressively more liberative conceptualizations that eventually culminate in the Mādhyamika insight into the ultimate. On this view, words and concepts are necessarily poisoned by ignorance, but one can carefully use them in a way that gradually reduces the poison so that the transition to the nonconceptual wisdom of the ultimate becomes far easier than making a leap from ordinary, naïve cognition. Again, Sahajavajra clearly endorses this approach, but can we find an equally clear endorsement from an

---

21. Nāgārjuna, *Mūlamadhyamakakārikā*, 13.8.

earlier Mādhyamika, perhaps along with some justification or explanation of the process itself? Let us now examine what seems to be a likely source.

Śāntideva and Prajñākaramati

As noted above, Nāgārjuna's own words leave room for a Mādhyamika to teach different content to different audiences. Bhāviveka, who coins the metaphor of a staircase or ladder, moves beyond the dismal approach of Candrakīrti, but scholarship on his work thus far suggests that his ladder is rather short— between the naïve intuitions of ordinary persons and the Mādhyamika, he apparently proposes just one level.[22] A far more promising source is the work of Śāntideva (writing in the eighth century), especially the ninth chapter of his *Bodhicaryāvatāra* (*Entering the Bodhisattva Way*), where he explicitly articulates a model that involves progressive levels. Since Śāntideva's verses are terse, one might hope that the commentary by Prajñākaramati (writing in the ninth or tenth century) would provide a detailed justification or explanation of a Mādhyamika approach to progressive levels of analysis. As we will see, however, Prajñākaramati finds this task befuddling, but his difficulties raise some productive questions.

The ninth chapter of Śāntideva's *Bodhicaryāvatāra* concerns the perfection of wisdom (*prajñāpāramitā*), presented as the culmination of the bodhisattva's practice of the perfections (*Bodhicaryāvatāra* 9.1). Śāntideva next lays out (in 9.2) the standard motif of the two truths: the ultimate and conventional. He distinguishes them in relation to what he calls *buddhi*: the ultimate is not the object of *buddhi*, and *buddhi* itself constitutes the conventional. Śāntideva does not clarify what he means by *buddhi*, but Prajñākaramati provides a gloss: "All instances of *buddhi*, by virtue of having or not having objects (*ālambananirālambanatayā*), are by nature conceptualization. And all conceptualization has the nature of ignorance because conceptualizations apprehend an unreal thing."[23] For Prajñākaramati, then, *buddhi* means "conceptual cognition," and this raises the problem of teaching the ultimate. As Prajñākaramati puts it:

> The suchness that is the ultimate reality is by nature devoid of all fabrication (*prapañca*); hence, since it is devoid of all delimitations (*upādhi*), how could one see it by means of any conceptualization?

22. See Eckel 2008.

23. Prajñākaramati, *Bodhicaryāvatārapañjikā*, 177: *sarvā hi buddhiḥ ālambananirālambanatayā vikalpasvabhāvā vikalpaś ca sarva eva avidyāsvabhāvaḥ avastugrāhitvāt /.*

And that whose nature is beyond concepts is not the object of language, since all words, which arise from concepts, would not be able to refer to that which is not an object of conceptual cognition. Therefore, since it is devoid of all conceptualization and linguistic expression, the ultimate reality is unimputed, unobscured, and inexpressible—in what way could it be pointed out?[24]

To illustrate what can be done, Prajñākaramati turns to a well-worn Madhyamaka example: an encounter between someone afflicted by ocular floaters (*taimirika*) and someone who is unafflicted by them. The unafflicted person sees the afflicted one looking around anxiously, and when she approaches him, he tells her that he sees hairs in the space all around him. But she does not see anything of the kind, and so she says to him, "There are no hairs here" (*nātra keśāḥ santi*). But she says this in a particular way:

> The unafflicted person makes this statement focused just on negation in conformity with the perception of the person with ocular floaters. And neither a negation nor an affirmation of anything has been performed by that unafflicted person who is pointing this out.[25]

On this account, Mādhyamikas must speak carefully to ordinary persons who experience things as having essential identities. In negating essences, the Mādhyamika must speak just from the mistaken standpoint of the ordinary person without affirming some ultimately real locus or subject of which the negation of essence is predicated. In short, their words must be "just focused on negation" (*pratiṣedhaparam eva*). And here lies the worry about introducing a level of conventional analysis that "upgrades" the perspective of ordinary persons: namely, that the refined account will be construed as pointing to some essentialized ultimate precisely because that account is not "just focused on negation." This is what apparently leads Candrakīrti (whom

24. Prajñākaramati, *Bodhicaryāvatārapañjikā*, 175–76: *tathā hi sarvaprapañcavinirmuktasvabhāvaṃ paramārthasatyatattvam ataḥ sarvopādhiśūnyatvāt kathaṃ kayācit kalpanayā paśyet? kalpanāsamatikrāntasvarūpaṃ ca śabdānām aviṣayaḥ / vikalpajanmāno hi śabdā vikalpadhiyām aviṣaye na pravartitum utsahante / tasmāt sakalavikalpābhilāpavikalatvād anāropitam asāṃvṛtam anābhilāpyaṃ paramārthatattvaṃ katham iva pratipādayituṃ śakyate?*

25. Prajñākaramati, *Bodhicaryāvatārapañjikā*, 176: *nātra keśāḥ santīti / taimirikopalabdhānurodhena pratiṣedhaparam eva vacanam āha / na ca tena tathā pratipādayatāpi kasyacit pratiṣedhaḥ kṛto bhavati vidhānaṃ vā //.*

Prajñākaramati cites in this context) to a dismal reluctance to pass judgments about conventional accounts, other than to point out that they are confused.

Prajñākaramati uses the metaphor of floaters to introduce Śāntideva's solution to this problem, which explicitly endorses progressive levels. Prajñākaramati's choice of metaphors, however, is odd because it does not involve—or even implicitly rejects—progressive levels. There are just those who see reality correctly and those who do not, with no gradations in between. But that is not what Śāntideva says in the next two verses (*Bodhicaryāvatāra* 9.3–4):

> In regard to the two truths, it is observed that there are two kinds of people: the yogi[26] and the ordinary one. The ordinary person is refuted[27] by the yogi.
>
> And due to a distinctive quality of awareness, yogis are also refuted by progressively higher ones through examples that are accepted by both, without analysis, for the sake of an effect.[28]

The first verse (9.3) is compatible with the metaphor of ocular floaters: just as the cognition of those afflicted by floaters is refuted by those without floaters, so too, those with the affliction of ignorance are refuted by those without it. But in the next verse (9.4), Śāntideva adds a twist to this account that renders the metaphor inapplicable: yogis at lower levels are also refuted by yogis at higher levels "by a distinctive quality of awareness" (*dhīviśeṣeṇa*). The floater metaphor fails here because the person without floaters just does not see anything, but what would be distinctive about the vision of a person with "higher" vision such that it would somehow overrule that non-seeing by the person without floaters? How can there be something more to be said than just "There are no hairs here" (*nātra keśāḥ santi*)?

The metaphor of floaters no longer applies because Śāntideva has made a clear appeal to progressive levels of "awareness" (*dhī*). When an ordinary person reports what they believe to be real, a yogi can provide an account that refutes the ordinary person's naïve ontology, but that yogi's account, while superior

---

26. In Sanskrit, contemplative practitioners are frequently called *yogi* (*yogin*).

27. The term "refuted" (*bādhyate*) here translates a verb that, in philosophical discourse, is typically used when one claim or position is negated by another.

28. Śāntideva, *Bodhicaryāvatāra* 9.3–4: *tatra loko dvidhā dṛṣṭo yogī prākṛtakas tathā / tatra prākṛtako loko yogilokena bādhyate // bādhyante dhīviśeṣeṇa yogino 'py uttarottaraiḥ / dṛṣṭāntenobhayeṣṭena kāryārtham avicārataḥ //.*

to the ordinary one, can itself prove to be inadequate for higher yogis. And this process continues until finally one presumably reaches the best account—namely, Madhyamaka. This progressive method, moreover, proceeds by employing "examples that are accepted by both" (*dṛṣṭāntenobhayeṣṭena*), such that some commonality in the experience at two different levels can be used to "level one up" to a higher understanding by engaging with a conceptual system that is a rung on the ladder to the Madhyamaka perspective. Importantly, Śāntideva assumes a dialogical context, presumably involving not just examples but also inferential reasoning, even if only *reductio ad absurdum*. The proviso here is that, to engage effectively in that dialogue, the yogi at a higher level suspends analysis (*vicāra*), which suggests a "provisional acceptance" (*abhyupagama*) of the lower-level ontology—perhaps through a form of "fictionalism"—in order to communicate effectively with the person at a lower level.[29] This suspension of analysis is performed not willy-nilly but strategically "for the sake of an effect" (*kāryārtham*)—namely, to move the lower-level person closer to the Madhyamaka.

The reading I have suggested for these verses (*Bodhicaryāvatāra* 9.3–4), while straightforward, leaves much to be explained. For example, exactly how does the process of adducing examples function to change perspectives, and what kind of examples are they? In the next verse (9.5), Śāntideva notes that the dispute between the Mādhyamika and ordinary persons is that the latter see and conceptualize things as ultimately real while the Mādhyamika yogi sees them as like illusions and such (*māyādivad*). Engaging in dialogue with an ordinary person, Mādhyamikas can use the example of an illusion such as a mirage to point out that, just as a mirage appears to be truly water, so too, things appear to be truly real. Upon closer inspection, however, one finds that things are not truly real, just as a mirage, when examined, no longer seems to be water. But how does this method apply to the progressive levels of yogic awareness? Are the Yogācāra, for example, considered lower-level "yogis" that higher level Mādhyamikas will "upgrade" by "examples that are accepted by both, without analysis"?

With such questions in mind, one might turn to Prajñākaramati's commentary for clarification, but unfortunately, his comments add little clarity.[30] Commenting first on the phrase "due to a distinctive quality of awareness," Prajñākaramati cites cases of higher yogis refuting lower yogis that downplay the dialogical argumentation implied by Śāntideva's model. Specifically,

---

29. Tillemans 2016, 52–53, discusses fictionalism as a way to conceptualize related issues in Madhyamaka.

30. The section in question is *Bodhicaryāvatārapañjikā*, 178–79.

Prajñākaramati only cites progression along the bodhisattva stages (*bhūmi*) from the first stage onward and progression in levels of meditative attainment from the first stage of meditative concentration upward (*prathamadhyānādi*). The latter case—progression to higher meditative states—is not a matter of argumentation but rather the refinement of contemplative technique. Likewise, progression through the bodhisattva stages can also be seen as primarily concerned with deepening the nonconceptual insight into the ultimate that is achieved at the first bodhisattva stage rather than a matter of further conceptual analysis through dialogic argumentation.[31] This is reinforced by Prajñākaramati's gloss of the term *yogi*, since it assumes that the practitioner has had the meditative experience of the "nonperception" of all things, a motif that characterizes the Madhyamaka view.[32]

As we read further in Prajñākaramati's comments on these verses, he seems to become more befuddled about how to make sense of progressive yogic levels that require "examples that are accepted by both, without analysis, for the sake of an effect" (*Bodhicaryāvatāra* 9.4cd). Commenting on this phrase specifically, Prajñākaramati never explains how this applies to yogic levels, even though this part of the verse clearly concerns the progressive refutation of lower yogis by higher ones. Interpreting the phrase "accepted by both," he construes it as referring to "both the yogi and the ordinary person" (*yogiprākṛtaka*) from the previous verse, rather than lower and higher yogis in the present verse. Continuing in this vein, his comments focus on examples for a dialogue with ordinary persons. When he finally turns to two cases that might be considered "yogis," he excludes them from Śāntideva's progressive model. The first case is the Mīmāṃsakas, and perhaps we can grant that Śāntideva's progressive model does not apply to interactions with them. They are not ordinary persons because their specialized training replaced the ordinary perspective with a highly detailed conceptual system, but they do not count as yogis, since Śāntideva holds that a yogi's perspective supersedes the ordinary one

---

31. We are wading into the crosscurrents of the complex theories about progression along the bodhisattva path that are articulated most prominently in the *Abhisamayalaṃkāra* literature. Apple 2011 provides a helpful overview, and Apple's work on the so-called twenty sanghas (2008) demonstrates the tremendous complexity of this domain. One of the main issues here is just how well defined one's conceptual understanding of the Madhyamaka version of emptiness must be for it to reach the first bodhisattva stage, and likewise, the role (if any) of additional philosophical analysis on the path of meditation (*bhāvanāmārga*) traversed by the remaining bodhisattva stages. See Lopez 1988 for a related issue about the realization of emptiness by non-Mahāyāna practitioners.

32. Prajñākaramati, *Bodhicaryāvatārapañjikā*, 178: *yogaḥ samādhiḥ sarvadharmānupalambha-lakṣaṇaḥ so 'syāstīti yogī . . .*

by refuting its errors. And for Mādhyamikas, the Mīmāṃsaka perspective is just as wrong (or even more so) than the ordinary one. But after dispensing with the Mīmāṃsaka, Prajñākaramati then excludes the Yogācāra from Śāntideva's progressive model as well. Instead, they are "refuted later through the refutation of reflexive awareness (*svasaṃvitti*)."[33] Why do the Yogācāra not count as yogis who could be "leveled up" through examples and the suspension of analysis? Referring to the discussion between the Yogācāra and the Madhyamaka, Prajñākaramati briefly notes that "what is proven by reason is also proven for both."[34] But this comment just reinforces how that interaction is focused on correcting the Yogācāra's conceptual understanding of the ultimate, which would presumably need to occur before they could reach the first bodhisattva stage. In short, it seems that by locating progressive levels within the framework of the bodhisattva stages, Prajñākaramati is excluding the Yogācāra by assuming that one cannot achieve the first bodhisattva stage—involving direct, nonconceptual insight into the ultimate—through a Yogācāra conceptual system.

Prajñākaramati's comments on Śāntideva's model for progressive levels thus offer very little in the way of clarification. He certainly does not provide any clear rationale for the kind of progression that Sahajavajra assumes, where Yogācāra plays a key role. Indeed, Prajñākaramati seems perplexed by how Śāntideva's dialogic and conceptual model could apply to yogis at all. What causes his befuddlement? Perhaps Śāntideva's comments in the next verse provide a clue. After noting (in *Bodhicaryāvatāra* 9.5) that the disagreement between the yogi and ordinary persons concerns the perception and conceptualization of things as real, Śāntideva moves to the question of perception itself. Prajñākaramati introduces the verse with a concern and then cites the verse's first line:

> Or there might be this concern: "The nature of form and such is to be capable of telic function (*arthakriyā*); it is perceived by a perceptual *pramāṇa* and shared by everyone. How could it be denied?" Concerned about this worry, Śāntideva said:

> > Although form and such are perceptible, that is due to what is commonly accepted and not by virtue of *pramāṇa*. (*Bodhicaryāvatāra* 9.5ab)[35]

33. Prajñākaramati, *Bodhicaryāvatārapañjikā*, 179: *svasaṃvedananirākaraṇān nirākariṣyante*.

34. Prajñākaramati, *Bodhicaryāvatārapañjikā*, 179: *yuktisiddham apy ubhayasiddham eva*.

35. Prajñākaramati, *Bodhicaryāvatārapañjikā*, 180: *athāpi syāt yad etat samastajanasādhāraṇam*

Śāntideva's response to the seeming indubitability of our perceptions is that, although they appear to be fully trustworthy cognitions, what seems so indubitable to us is just a matter of "what is commonly accepted" (*prasiddhi*). Here, we seem to have arrived at the "dismal" epistemological attitude discussed by Tom Tillemans, for if even our most reliable cognitions—efficacious perceptions themselves—are simply a matter of mutual agreement and commonly shared conventions, how can we claim that one conventional account is better than another? In particular, how would one yogi convince another yogi to "level up" to a superior level of awareness if the perceptual worlds given at all levels of awareness before the ultimate are simply a matter of what is commonly accepted? To put it another way, on this dismal account, perceptual experience becomes a language game, and this sets aside the notion that the errors in my distorted perceptual content are phenomenally presented prior to conceptual judgments.[36]

Responding to Śāntideva's move toward the dismal, Prajñākaramati interprets "perception" in another way:

> Because perception and so on are conventional *pramāṇas* (*saṃvyavahārikapramāṇa*), the form and so on cognized by them are just conventional. The ultimate nature (*tāttvikaṃ rūpam*) is not realizable by worldly *pramāṇas* because it would otherwise absurdly follow that everyone would know the ultimate.[37]

Although Śāntideva clearly denies that perception is *pramāṇa*, Prajñākaramati blithely says that it is, albeit a conventional one. This is a straightforward reference to Dharmakīrti's approach, mentioned at the outset of this essay. In other words, our perceptions do provide reliable, efficacious knowledge: when I drink what I perceive as "water," my thirst will be experientially slaked in a nonconceptual perception, and that experience is not merely a matter of conceptual convention. But that experience only occurs from the standpoint of a deluded lifeworld.

---

arthakriyākṣamaṃ pratyakṣapramāṇapratītaṃ vasturūpam tat katham apahnotuṃ śakyata iti parasya hṛdayam āśaṅkyāha pratyakṣam apītyādi—pratyakṣam api rupādi prasiddhyā na pramāṇataḥ /.

36. What I am suggesting here is that the Dharmakīrtian notion of nonconceptual error (see Dunne 2020) is rejected by dismal accounts.

37. Prajñākaramati, *Bodhicaryāvatārapañjikā*, 180: *sāṃvyavahārikapramāṇatvāt pratyakṣādīnām tadadhigatam sāṃvṛtam eva rupādi / na ca laukikapramāṇasamadhigamyaṃ tāttvikaṃ rūpam sarvajanānāṃ tattvaveditvaprasaṅgāt /.*

Why does Prajñākaramati choose to introduce this idea, even though it seems contrary to Śāntideva's words? Perhaps he is still grappling with some way to understand the progressive model for "leveling up." After all, the notion of conventional *pramāṇa* can justify a model of progressive levels, since each level can be constituted by the shared lifeworld secured by "stable imprints" (*dṛḍhavāsanā*), even for yogis. Progression would then effectively mean eliminating some degree of confusion and emerging into a less confused conventional reality that is closer to the Madhyamaka perspective. But on Dharmakīrti's view, talk about conventional *pramāṇa* also leads to the notion of ultimate *pramāṇa* (*pāramārthikapramāṇa*). Despite Śāntideva's eschewal of *pramāṇa*, will Prajñākaramati go this far? Well, yes. He does so earlier in his commentary, when discussing the ultimate truth:

> The Blessed One, inwardly illuminated by the light of wisdom that pervades the vastness of endless things, stated that the ultimate truth is devoid of all distinctions of conventional things and free of all delimitations. As such, since by nature it is reflexively known (*svasaṃvidita*), it is to be personally known (*pratyātmavedyam*) just by *ārya*s. And in this context, that alone is *pramāṇa*.[38]

Not only does Prajñākaramati accept conventional *pramāṇa*, he does so at the ultimate level as well, even to the point of apparently endorsing some role for reflexive awareness (*svasaṃvedana*) in a way that echoes Śākyabuddhi, a Yogācāra thinker. Since Śāntideva sets aside *pramāṇa* and refutes reflexive awareness, one wonders what has driven Prajñākaramati to be such a disobedient commentator. Perhaps it is precisely the question we have been considering: How can one move beyond one's seemingly real experiences, and can one do so by building a Madhyamaka ladder?

Conclusion: A Productive Befuddlement?

Prajñākaramati's comments on Śāntideva's model do not provide a clear justification or explanation that could undergird Sahajavajra's enthusiastic endorsement of a Dharmakīrtian approach to progressive levels of analysis

---

38. Prajñākaramati, *Bodhicaryāvatārapañjikā*, 177: *pratyastamitasamastasāṃvṛtavastuviśeṣam aśeṣopādhiviviktam uktam anantavastuvistaravyāpijñānālokāvabhāsitāntarātmanā bhagavatā paramārthasatyam iti / tad etad āryāṇām eva svasaṃviditasvabhāvatayā pratyātmavedyam / atas tad evātra pramāṇam /*. Note that this passage occurs directly after Prajñākaramati's citation of a passage from the *Pitāputrasamāgamasūtra* that describes the ultimate in highly cataphatic terms.

for Mādhyamikas, especially one that employs Yogācāra as a rung on the ladder. Nevertheless, a closer look at Prajñākaramati's befuddlement may prove instructive. We first see that, despite the clearly dialogic and conceptual model for progressive yogic levels, Prajñākaramati construes progression in contemplative contexts where the emphasis is no longer on conceptual models and argumentation. But when Śāntideva rejects *pramāṇa*, Prajñākaramati disobediently uses the Dharmakīrtian notion of ultimate and conventional *pramāṇa* to address the problem of the apparent indubitability of our perceptual world. Can we draw any lessons from this muddle? For example, when one builds a Madhyamaka ladder, does the experiential aspect of contemplative contexts motivate the use of the Dharmakīrtian account of conventional *pramāṇa*? And are progressive levels not so much a philosophical tool for ascending to the most defensible view of reality but rather a contemplative method for inducing certain kinds of experiences?

Such questions might help guide future research on progressive levels as a Madhyamaka method. Here, a good place to look would be the works of Śāntarakṣita and Kamalaśīla (both writing in the eighth century), who deploy the tools of Dharmakīrtian *pramāṇa* theory and Yogācāra discourse. So far, I have yet to find in their works any explicit philosophical justification or mechanistic explanation that warrants the use of levels, but something like progressive levels certainly seems to be present. In his first *Bhāvanākrama* (*Stages of Meditation*), for example, Kamalaśīla, citing a verse from the *Laṅkāvatārasūtra*, advises the Mādhyamika to begin by recognizing that external objects are just consciousness itself; then one reaches a point where subject-object duality no longer appears within a state of nondual awareness. One then abandons any clinging to the reality of that nondual awareness itself, and having thus reached the Mādhyamika perspective, one realizes the ultimate.[39] Here, one might claim that Kamalaśīla is urging Mādhyamikas to progressively refine their rational analysis to arrive at the most defensible philosophical account, but this interpretation seems incomplete. That is, Kamalaśīla articulates this progressive approach when he is offering guidance for obtaining the wisdom (*prajñā*) that arises from meditation (*bhāvanāmayī*), where he articulates a progression of meditative experiences. And that section itself draws on a similar sequencing in the preceding section on the wisdom that arises from reflection (*cintāmayī*).[40] While all this allegedly occurs in the context of debate, perhaps this progressive approach

---

39. Kamalaśīla, *Bhāvanākrama I*, 210–12. See Kellner 2020 for textual emendations, translation, and analysis.

40. Kamalaśīla, *Bhāvanākrama I*, 198–204.

enables Kamalaśīla to persuade his audience not just through philosophical analysis but also through the promise of contemplative outcomes.

This brings to mind, in closing, one of the clearest endorsements—indeed, an injunction—for the use of progressive levels. It comes in the *Hevajratantra*:

> Then the goddess, pleased with what she heard,
> uttered this question:
> "How can unruly, unworthy beings
> become capable of being tamed?"
>
> The Blessed One replied:
> "First, they should be given fasting vows,
> and then the ten points of ethical training.
> Next, they should be taught Vaibhāṣika
> and then, likewise, Sautrāntika.
>
> "Thereafter, one should teach them Yogācāra,
> and after that, Madhyamaka.
> After understanding the entire tantric approach,
> they should then begin Hevajra.
> When disciples take this up with devotion,
> without a doubt they will gain accomplishment."[41]

As Isaacson (2013, 1038), notes, "It is clear that this passage presents a hierarchy or upward progression," and within the context of the *Hevajratantra*, that progression concerns not simply philosophical prowess but also contemplative accomplishment. As research advances on the role that progressive levels play in late Indian Madhyamaka, perhaps further attention to the integration of philosophy with contemplation will prove fruitful. Perhaps we will find that some Mādhyamikas might even remain dismal in philosophical analysis but still feel free to build a ladder for contemplative practice.

---

41. *Hevajratantra* 2.8.8 (Snellgrove 1959, 90): *tatra tuṣṭā tu sā devī idaṃ vacanam abravīt / durdāntā dundurāḥ sattvā vineyaṃ yānti kena hi //*; 2.8.9–10 (Isaacson 2013, 1038): *poṣadham dīyate prathamaṃ tad anu śikṣāpadaṃ daśa // vaibhāṣyaṃ tatra deśyeta sūtrāntaṃ punas tathā // yogācāraṃ tataḥ paścāt tad anu mādhyamakam diśet / sarvatantranayaṃ jñātvā tad anu hevajram ārabhet / gṛhṇīyād ādaraṃ śiṣyaḥ sidhyate nātra saṃśayaḥ //.* Isaacson notes that Ratnākaraśānti resists aspects of this obvious hierarchy, which shows that not all late Indian Mahāyāna thinkers fully endorsed progressive levels. Thanks to Thomas Doctor and Ryan Conlon for their assistance with locating this passage.

Bibliography

Primary texts

Advayavajra, *Tattvadaśaka*. In Mathes 2015, 485–88.
Dharmakīrti, *Pramāṇavārttika: Pratyakṣapariccheda*. In Tosaki 1979/1985.
Dharmakīrti, *Pramāṇaviniścaya I*. In Steinkellner 2007.
Kamalaśīla, *Bhāvanākrama I*. In Tucci 1958.
Nāgārjuna, *Mūlamadhyamakakārikā*. In La Vallée Poussin 1903–13.
Nāgārjuna, *Ratnāvalī*. In McClintock and Dunne 2024.
Prajñākaramati, *Bodhicaryāvatārapañjikā*. In Vaidya 1960.
Sahajavajra, *Tattadaśakaṭīkā*. See Sahajavajra 1998.
Śākyabuddhi, *Pramāṇavārttikaṭīkā*. See Śākyabuddhi 2002.
Śāntideva, *Bodhicaryāvatāra*. In Vaidya 1960.
Vasubandhu, *Viṃśikāvṛtti*. In Lévi 1925.

Editions, translations, and secondary sources

Apple, James B. 2008. *Stairway to Nirvāṇa: A Study of the Twenty Saṃghas Based on the Works of Tsong Kha Pa*. Albany: State University of New York Press.
———. 2011. "The Mahāyāna Path of the Bodhisattva in the *Ornament for Clear Realization*." *Religion Compass* 5.5: 166–79.
Brunnhölzl, Karl. 2007. *Straight from the Heart: Buddhist Pith Instructions*. Ithaca, NY: Snow Lion Publications.
Dunne, John D. 2004. *Foundations of Dharmakīrti's Philosophy*. Studies in Indian and Tibetan Buddhism. Boston: Wisdom Publications.
———. 2020. "Pac-Man to the Rescue? Conceptuality and Non-Conceptuality in the Dharmakīrtian Theory of Pseudo-Perception." *Philosophy East and West* 70.3: 571–93.
Eckel, Malcolm David. 1992. *To See the Buddha: A Philosopher's Quest for the Meaning of Emptiness*. Princeton, NJ: Princeton University Press.
———. 2008. *Bhāviveka and His Buddhist Opponents: Chapters 4 and 5 of the Verses on the Heart of the Middle Way (Madhyamakahṛdayakārikā) with the Commentary Entitled the Flame of Reason (Tarkajvāla)*. Harvard Oriental Series 70. Cambridge, MA: Harvard University Press.
Federman, Asaf. 2009. "Literal Means and Hidden Meanings: A New Analysis of Skillful Means." *Philosophy East and West* 59.2: 125–41.
Isaacson, Harunaga. 2013. "Yogācāra and Vajrayāna According to Ratnākaraśānti." In *The Foundation for Yoga Practitioners: The Buddhist Yogācārabhūmi Treatise and Its Adaptation in India, East Asia, and Tibet*, edited by Ulrich Timme Kragh, 1036–53. Harvard Oriental Series 75. Cambridge, MA: Harvard University Press.
Isaacson, Harunaga, and Francesco Sferra. 2014. *The* Sekanirdeśa *of Maitreyanātha (Advayavajra) with the* Sekanirdeśapañjikā *of Rāmapāla: Critical Edition of the Sanskrit and Tibetan Texts with English Translation and Reproductions of the MSS*. Serie Orientale Roma 107. Naples: Università degli Studi di Napoli L'Orientale.
Jinpa, Thupten, ed. 2022. *Science and Philosophy in the Indian Buddhist Classics, Volume 3: Philosophical Schools*. Conceived and introduced by His Holiness the Dalai Lama.

Developed by the Compendium Compilation Committee. Translated by Donald S. Lopez Jr. and Hyoung Seok Ham. Somerville, MA: Wisdom Publications.

Kellner, Birgit. 2020. "Using Concepts to Eliminate Conceptualization: Kamalaśīla on Non-Conceptual Gnosis (*Nirvikalpajñāna*)." *Journal of the International Association of Buddhist Studies* 43: 39–80.

La Vallée Poussin, Louis de, ed. 1903–13. *Mūlamadhyamakakārikās (Mādhyamikasūtras) de Nāgārjuna avec la Prasannapadā commentaire de Candrakīrti.* Bibliotheca Buddhica 4. St. Petersburg: Commissionnaires de l'Académie Impériale des Sciences.

Lévi, Sylvain, ed. 1925. *Vijñaptimātratāsiddhi: Deux traités de Vasubandhu.* Bibliothèque de l'École des Hautes Études. Paris: Librairie Ancienne Honoré Champion.

Lopez Jr., Donald S. 1988. "Do Śrāvakas Understand Emptiness?" *Journal of Indian Philosophy* 16.1: 65–105.

Mathes, Klaus-Dieter. 2015. *A Fine Blend of Mahāmudrā and Madhyamaka: Maitrīpa's Collection of Texts on Non-Conceptual Realization (Amanasikāra).* Beiträge zur Kultur- und Geistesgeschichte Asiens 90. Vienna: Austrian Academy of Sciences Press.

McClintock, Sara, and John Dunne. 2024. *Nāgārjuna's Precious Garland: Ratnāvalī.* Classics of Indian Buddhism. New York: Wisdom Publications.

McCrea, Lawrence J. 2020. "Balancing the Scales: Dharmakīrti Inside and Out." In *Reverberations of Dharmakīrti's Philosophy: Proceedings of the Fifth International Dharmakīrti Conference*, edited by Birgit Kellner, Patrick McAllister, Horst Lasic, and Sara L. McClintock, 251–64. Beiträge Zur Kultur- und Geistesgeschichte Asiens 104. Vienna: Austrian Academy of Sciences Press.

Sahajavajra. 1998. *"De kho na nyid bcu pa'i rgya cher 'grel pa"* [=*Tattadaśakaṭīkā*]. Translated by Kalyāṇavarman and Jñānākara. In *Bstan 'gyur (Dpe bsdur ma)*, 26:481–530. Beijing: Krung go'i bod kyi shes rig dpe skrun khang.

Śākyabuddhi. 2002. *Tshad ma rnam 'grel kyi 'grel bshad* [=*Pramāṇavārttikaṭīkā*]. Translated by Subhutiśrī and Dge ba'i blo gros. In *Bstan 'gyur (Dpe bsdur ma)*, 98:955–1802 and 99:1–714. Beijing: Krung go'i bod kyi shes rig dpe skrun khang.

Snellgrove, David L. 1959. *The Hevajra Tantra: A Critical Study, Part 2: Sanskrit and Tibetan Texts.* London Oriental Series 6. London: Oxford University Press.

Steinkellner, Ernst, ed. 2007. *Dharmakīrti's Pramāṇaviniścaya: Chapters 1 and 2.* Sanskrit Texts from the Tibetan Autonomous Region 2. Beijing and Vienna: China Tibetology Publishing House / Austrian Academy of Sciences Press.

Tillemans, Tom J. F. 2016. "How Far Can a Mādhyamika Reform Customary Truth? Dismal Relativism, Fictionalism, Easy-Easy Truth, and the Alternatives." In *How Do Mādhyamikas Think? And Other Essays on the Buddhist Philosophy of the Middle*, 47–61. Studies in Indian and Tibetan Buddhism. Somerville, MA: Wisdom.

Tosaki, Hiromasa. 1979/85. *Bukkyō ninshikiron no kenkyū.* 2 vols. Tōkyō: Daitō Shuppansha.

Tucci, Giuseppe. 1958. *Minor Buddhist Texts, Part II: First Bhāvanākrama of Kamalaśīla: Sanskrit and Tibetan Texts with Introduction and English Summary.* Rome: Istituto Italiano per il Medio ed Estremo Oriente.

Vaidya, P. L., ed. 1960. *Bodhicaryāvatāra of Śāntideva with the Commentary Pañjikā of Prajñākaramati.* Buddhist Sanskrit Texts 12. Darbhanga, India: The Mithilā Institute.

One, Many, or Neither? Neither-One-Nor-Many Arguments in Dharmakīrti's Philosophy of Mind

Birgit Kellner[1]

IN THE EARLY 1980s, Tom Tillemans published two articles on a type of argument widely used in Buddhist philosophical literature, commonly dubbed the "neither-one-nor-many argument."[2] He has now followed up with a third paper in his recent collection *Views from Tibet*.[3] Versions of the neither-one-nor-many argument, to which I will refer with the acronym NONMA, feature in refutations of selves that are declared to be neither identical with nor different from the five psychophysical aggregates. Such an argument appears, for instance, in Candrakīrti's *Madhyamakāvatāra* 6.124–33. NONMAs also occur in analyses of part-whole relationships, as, for example, in Candrakīrti's deconstruction of different types of possible relationships between a cart and its parts in *Madhyamakāvatāra* 6.150–57. And such arguments also feature in Vasubandhu's refutation of the partless atom in his *Viṃśikā Vijñaptimātratāsiddhiḥ* verses 12–13.

The particular argument that stood in the focus of Tillemans's attention was a historically influential Madhyamaka proof that derives the absence of intrinsic nature (*niḥsvabhāvatā*) in all putatively existing entities from the fact that they ultimately exist neither as unitary, indivisible simples nor as pluralities that consist of such simples. This proof is found in Śrīgupta's *Tattvāvatāra* (seventh century),[4] but it is in the formulation in the first verse of Śāntarakṣita's

---

1. I thank Pascale Hugon and Jonathan Samuels for illuminating some obscure Tibetan passages, the participants of the Madison workshop for their constructive criticism, and Sara McClintock for their incisive and careful editing.

2. Tillemans 1982 and Tillemans 1983.

3. Tillemans 2022.

4. Ejima 1980, 223–26; see also Aitken 2021. Cf. Śrīgupta's TA k.1 (TAV D 39b5–6 = P 44b4): *phyi rol nang na gnas 'di kun // yang dag tu ni rang bzhin med // gcig dang du ma'i rang bzhin*

(ca. 725–88) *Madhyamakālaṅkāra* that it exerted its influence on later Indian as well as Tibetan Madhyamaka thought:

> Entities asserted by ourselves and others are without intrinsic nature because, in reality, they have neither the nature of oneness nor that of manyness, like a reflection.[5]

In this paper I want to expand the scope of investigation of this type of argument by exploring whether Dharmakīrti uses it, as has on occasion been suggested. I hope that this will be seen as a fitting tribute to Tillemans, whose philosophical and textual studies of the Madhyamaka NONMA serve as a model for a critical philosophical engagement with Buddhist philosophy that pays due attention to the historical contexts and conceptual frameworks within which Indian and Tibetan thinkers elaborated their theories and to the highly specific ways in which they articulated, developed, and deployed their logical tools.

Does Dharmakīrti Use Neither-One-Nor-Many Arguments?

There is undoubtedly a discernible argument pattern in Buddhist philosophical literature that operates with a conjoined denial of singularity and plurality. Within this literature, one occasionally finds labels that refer to such reasons or investigations, but these appear to remain limited in their scope to particular instances of NONMAs and are not coined to define a general type of argument. Thus the term *ekānekaviyogahetu* is used specifically for the Śrīgupta/Śāntarakṣita NONMA. Perhaps beginning with Kamalaśīla's *Madhyamakāloka*, this term features in standardized lists of reasons—numbering either four or five—that Mādhyamikas use to prove emptiness.[6] The term *ekānekavicāra* is used in Śākyabuddhi's (ca. 660–720) commentary on the *Pramāṇavārttika* in connection with one of the Dharmakīrtian arguments that will be discussed here, referring to an investigation in terms of

---

nyid // bral ba'i phyir na gzugs brnyan bzhin //. In the Tibetan tradition, Śrīgupta is considered the teacher of Jñānagarbha, who in turn is regarded as Śāntarakṣita's teacher; this is the basis for his dating.

5. *Niḥsvabhāvā amī bhāvās tattvataḥ svaparoditāḥ / ekānekasvabhāvena viyogāt pratibimbavat //.* The Sanskrit text comes from Prajñākaramati's BCAP 358,1–2 on BCA 9.2.

6. For such sets, see the detailed discussion in Keira 2004, 10–14n32, as well as Tillemans 2022, 141–44.

"one" or "many" that establishes something not to exist ultimately.[7] I have not been able to find a term like *ekānekavicāra* in earlier philosophical literature,[8] and it remains to be seen whether (and, if so, when) it ever became used as a generic term. At present, it appears that the NONMA did not become a fixed category in the metalanguage of Buddhist logical theory.

The various examples that were referred to as NONMAs so far appear to have in common that a class of entities is proclaimed not to exist in an ultimate sense or, sometimes more specifically, that entities do not exist as having an inherent nature (*svabhāva*), which is understood as tantamount to their being empty (*śūnya*). The subject matter of NONMAs varies, as they are used for, among other things, selves, wholes, atoms, and even all entities; hence there is some variation in their philosophical function. Dharmakīrti, for his part, has also been claimed to have formulated NONMAs, in particular in his discussion of perceptual awareness (*pratyakṣa*) and its relationship to its object. The first to have drawn attention to Dharmakīrtian NONMAs appears to have been Yasunori Ejima, who specifically pointed to an argument in *Pramāṇavārttika* 3.359 that indeed at first sight looks like a prototypical NONMA.[9] In Ernst Steinkellner's translation, the verse reads:

> That form in which entities are [normally] perceived does not exist
> in reality, for these (things) have neither a unitary nor a multiple
> form.[10]

More recently, and in more general terms, John Dunne has argued that a mereological strategy made up of NONMAs is the backbone of Dharmakīrti's philosophical framework, which is constructed through hierarchically arranged levels of analysis.[11] For Dunne, these levels differ in their ontologies. One ascends through them in a gradual process of reductive analysis, in the course of which a successively higher number of entities are reduced to

---

7. Cf. the expression *gcig dang du mas dpyad mi bzod pa nyid*, occurring three times in Śākyabuddhi's commentary on PV 3.211 (Ś$_t$ D 203a2 = P 250a6, D 203a6 = P 250b3, D 204a4–5 = P 251b6). This can be determined as a translation of Sanskrit *ekānekavicārākṣamatā*, a term used by Karṇakagomin—who incorporates much material from Śākyabuddhi's commentary on the PV into his own—in a related context in K$_1$ 210,19. See also note 32 below.

8. Anne MacDonald informs me that she is unaware of its use in pre-Dharmakīrti Madhyamaka literature (personal communication).

9. Ejima 1980, 223–26.

10. Steinkellner 1990, 78. For the Sanskrit text, see note 44 below.

11. Dunne 2004, 53–64.

infinitesimal particles: a spatio-temporally extended macroscopic object, supposedly existing over and above its parts (like the Vaiśeṣika's whole, the *avaya-
vin*), is reduced to its parts on the ground that it is neither identical with nor
different from them. The "factors" (*dharma*) that Abhidharma postulates as
constituents of reality, which retain conceptual, spatial, and temporal extension, are also reduced to indivisible parts, on the grounds that entities with
any of these forms of extension are neither identical with nor different from
such parts. Dunne also believes that a NONMA is involved in Dharmakīrti's
move from a realist to an idealist analysis of perception or, in his terminology, from "external realism" to "epistemic idealism,"[12] the two analyses of perception that are respectively associated with the philosophical frameworks of
Sautrāntika and Yogācāra. Indeed, at *Pramāṇavārttika* 3.211, we find an argument that, again, looks at first sight like a NONMA. In Dunne's translation:

> Therefore, neither the objects nor the awareness has a spatially
> extended appearance because, since that kind of property-*svabhāva*
> [—namely, spatial extension—] has already been disproved in the
> case of a singular entity, it is also not possible in the case of what
> is many.[13]

Both these supposed NONMAs have been cited within the later Indian
and Tibetan tradition as evidence for Dharmakīrti's ultimately Madhyamaka intention. Steinkellner convincingly demonstrated that this attribution
is ahistorical because Dharmakīrti on closer analysis does not deny the ultimate reality of consciousness.[14] Still, the question of whether Dharmakīrti
employs NONMAs of some kind in his analysis of perception merits further
attention, as does the broader issue of how he avails himself of mereological analysis in this connection. In the following, I will discuss the two verses
Pramāṇavārttika 3.211 and 3.359 in their immediate textual context and offer
an interpretive hypothesis for each of them. This will also motivate some
reflections on the category of the NONMA in general and how we should
approach such arguments.

12. Dunne 2004, 58–59; on the qualifier "epistemic," see 59n14. For a critique of Dunne's
account of Yogācāra as epistemic idealism, see Arnold 2008.

13. Dunne 2004, 404.

14. Steinkellner 1990.

The Śrīgupta/Śāntarakṣita Argument for Emptiness: Basic Features for Comparison

To have a more solid basis for assessing Dharmakīrti's arguments, it will be helpful to carve out some features of the Śrīgupta/Śāntarakṣita NONMA for emptiness and in the process also recall basic premises of Dharmakīrti's analysis of consciousness and perception. First, this Madhyamaka NONMA is universal in its scope, applying to all putatively existing entities—not surprisingly, as it serves to prove universal emptiness. This feature will not be relevant to the discussion of the two supposed Dharmakīrtian NONMAs, as Dharmakīrti is not arguing from a Madhyamaka vantage point. Rather, these two arguments are premised on the ultimate reality of consciousness. Dharmakīrti's ultimate position is that an awareness event is unitary and undivided, while any division, especially into apprehending subject (*grāhaka*) and apprehended object (*grāhya*), is erroneous and ultimately the product of ignorance (*avidyā*); in what follows, I will refer to this position as the principle of unitary awareness.[15] Although this position is characteristic for the Yogācāra system, it is worth noting that Dharmakīrti on occasion appeals to the singularity of awareness events also when arguing on the level of a realist, Sautrāntika analysis.[16]

Three further features of the Śrīgupta/Śāntarakṣita NONMA will be useful to track in the discussion of Dharmakīrti's arguments. First, it works with a destructive dilemma between contradictory opposites: if anything has intrinsic nature, it is either one or many. Since nothing can satisfy the conditions for being either one or many, nothing can have intrinsic nature. The predicates *eka*, "one," and *aneka*, "many"—in the sense of "not-one," i.e., more than one—exhibit the logical structure F and not-F. Being neither one nor many thus logically amounts to an exclusive disjunction, which is subject to the law of the excluded middle. "One" and "many," in other words, are contradictory opposites. Second, Allison Aitken has highlighted that in this NONMA, "one" and "many" have a peculiar relationship that affects the structure of the argument. The word *aneka* for "many" conceptually presupposes *eka*, and there is also a metaphysical priority relation involved: the existence of something that is not-one presupposes the existence of some things that are one. A plurality presupposes singular things as its members or building blocks. This effectively means that the main work of this NONMA is done in the

---

15. This principle is expressed at PV 3.212 and 3.353; for the erroneous nature of division see also PV 3 verses 214, 217, 330–32, 361, and 431. Cf. also Kellner 2017a, 107.

16. Cf. PV 3.207 and the premise in the objection in PV 3.208.

demonstration that there are no simples, as the nonexistence of pluralities logically follows from the nonexistence of simples of which these pluralities consist. Both Śrīgupta and Śāntarakṣita expressly recognize this peculiarity of
their NONMA.[17] Third, and last, in his discussion of Tibetan interpretations
of NONMAs, Tillemans distinguishes versions that use monadic predicates
from those that use dyadic predicates.[18] The Śrīgupta/Śāntarakṣita NONMA
uses one-place, or monadic, predicates of the type Fx and not-Fx, "one" and
"not-one." Relational, or dyadic, predicates feature, for example, in the argument that the self is neither the same as nor different from the aggregates. The
neither-one-nor-many arguments that Dunne considers to be constitutive for
Dharmakīrti's mereological method are all dyadic—when, for example, it is
denied that the supposedly extended Abhidharmic factors are identical with
or different from their parts. This in itself is not a critical issue, as presenta-
tions of NONMAs in Indian or Tibetan texts in general frequently switch
between monadic and dyadic predicates, and between the concepts of one-
ness/identity and manyness/difference. Tillemans notes that Indian and
Tibetan authors found the switch from "manyness" to "difference" (and also
the one from "oneness" to "identity") perfectly natural.[19] Still, for understanding such composite arguments and their structure it is vital to see where and
how such switches occur. In the Śrīgupta/Śāntarakṣita case, this switch seems
to occur because an overarching NONMA is supplemented by a neither-identical-nor-different argument (henceforth NINDA)[20] that helps support its
core claim that entities cannot exist as indivisible simples. When Tsongkhapa
summarizes Śāntarakṣita's NONMA in his *Drang nges legs bshad snying po*, he
argues that oneness is impossible because all material and mental entities must
have parts, but these parts can be neither identical with their part-possessors
nor different from them.[21] In other words, the parts are eliminated through a
NINDA, which in combination with the premise that entities must have parts
supports the overarching claim that there can be no simples. But the NINDA
in and of itself characteristically takes a certain type of entity—here, the part-
possessor—for granted and investigates another type of entity in its relationship to it. Moreover, the logical nature of a NINDA critically depends on the

17. TAV ad TA 2b, MA 61; see Aitken 2021, 7, as well as Tillemans 1983, 317. The conceptual
dependence of plurality on unity is also raised in Nāgārjuna's *Ratnāvalī* 1.71abc (Hahn 1982,
30) as well as by Āryadeva in *Catuḥśataka* 14.19 (Lang 1986, 132).

18. Tillemans 1983, 305.

19. Tillemans 1983, 306.

20. I think this term was first used in Moriyama 2014, with respect to Ratnākaraśānti.

21. Tillemans 1983, 308–12.

notions of identity and difference that are involved in it, which makes it formally different from a NONMA in and of itself. Buddhist philosophers may regard it as natural to switch between these argument types, but these nevertheless exhibit certain differences that merit being explored.

A Mereological Argument about Spatially Extended Appearances (sthūlābhāsa) from Pramāṇavārttika 3.211

With these preliminaries in mind, we can now approach the first putative NONMA in Dharmakīrti's analysis of perception. In *Pramāṇavārttika* 3.211, Dharmakīrti proclaims a neither-one-nor-many analysis to support a thesis about a "coarse appearance" (*sthūla*)—that is, a perceptual appearance that presents a phenomenal object like blue color with spatial extension. Following Dignāga, Dharmakīrti regards perceptual appearances generally to be "coarse,"[22] so that this analysis concerns sense perception as such and pertains to its very nature:

> There is consequently no extended appearance either when it comes to external objects or when it comes to cognition, since such a[n extended] nature (*tadātmanaḥ*)[23] was denied with respect to what is one (*ekatra*); it is also not possible for many.[24]

This argument serves as a conclusion to a section that began with *Pramāṇavārttika* 3.194. Dharmakīrti first defended the (realist) proposal that a plurality of external atoms, when aggregated (*sañcita*), cause a perception that bears an extended appearance and exists as a unitary mental event (3.195–96). This does not mean, as an objector had argued in verse 194, that perception must be conceptualizing because it has something common, a *sāmānya*, for its object. Indeed, Dignāga's fundamental understanding of perception as nonconceptual (*kalpanāpoḍha*) and applying only to particulars (*svalakṣaṇa*), not to universals (*sāmānyalakṣaṇa*), is not violated. Dharmakīrti thus at first assents to a view of perception that assumes mental unitariness in conjunction with external plurality. This view turns out to be problematic, however, given that there is an underlying expectation of what Tillemans once called

---

22. ĀP(V) verses 1–2.

23. Dunne translates *ātman* as "property-*svabhāva*" (2004, 404); Prueitt (2017, 29) and Yiannopoulos (2020, 280) translate simply "nature."

24. PV 3.211: *tasmān nārtheṣu na jñāne sthūlābhāsas tadātmanaḥ / ekatra pratiṣiddhatvād bahuṣv api na sambhavaḥ //*.

"congruence," an isomorphic correspondence between perceptual appearances and external reality.[25] Dharmakīrti next discusses the perception of
multicolored (*citra*) objects such as butterflies (3.200), which accentuates the
problem of congruence. Here the perceptual appearance obviously contains a
multiplicity of different color-regions, while it is also unitary, displaying the
different regions in a manner that is distinct—for example, from one's seeing blue and yellow pieces of cloth next to each other. Dharmakīrti refutes
the postulation of a singular extended external object such as the Vaiśeṣika's
"multicolor" (*citra*) (3.201–6) and reaffirms the idea that perception is one
and has multiple external objects (*nānārthā*)—that is, the atoms—without
thereby being conceptualizing (3.207). The objector pushes the point and
argues that just as external objects that appear in a multicolored perception
cannot be one, so perception, too, when it appears variegated, cannot be singular (3.208). Dharmakīrti responds with the proverbially enigmatic statement
"the more [external] objects (*artha*)[26] are examined, the more they dissolve."[27]
After verse 211 with the neither-one-nor-many analysis, Dharmakīrti takes on
a Yogācāra-Vijñānavāda perspective. He affirms the undivided and unitary
nature of awareness and proclaims that the appearance of a division of subject and object is merely a distortion (*upaplava*, 3.212); he also appeals to the
Yogācāra-Vijñānavāda notion of the "emptiness of duality" (*dvayaśūnyatā*,
3.213). From this flow of argument we can surmise, first, that whatever stance
Dharmakīrti takes in the enigmatic verse 210, he considered the incongruence between external objects and perceptual appearances irresolvable within
the confines of the version of the realist Sautrāntika analysis that he had ini-

25. Tillemans 1999, 9; cf. also Dunne 2004, 100.

26. The interpretation of *artha* in the more limited meaning of "external objects" is in accordance
with Śākyabuddhi; for Prajñākaragupta's Madhyamaka interpretation of PV 3.208–10, see
Steinkellner 1990, 77.

27. PV 3.209cd: *yathā yathārthāś cintyante vivicyante tathā tathā //*. Tosaki's edition adopts
viśīryante instead of *vivicante*. The reading *viśīryante* is attested in glosses in Prajñākaragupta's
and Manorathanandin's commentaries (Pr$_2$ 186,25 = Pr$_B$ 144a5, M$_1$ 181,11 = M$_A$ 35b1).
However, for the text of the PV that is embedded in Prajñākaragupta, the sole extant manuscript
for this part actually reads *vivicyante* (Pr$_B$ 144a2). Sāṅkṛtyāyana's edition Pr$_2$ has *viśīryante*,
while his earlier edition of the PV on its own, PV$_1$, had *vivicyante*. The verse text contained
in his edition of Manorathanandin, M$_1$, was supplied by Sāṅkṛtyāyana; the sole manuscript of
Manorathanandin does not contain the text of the PV. The reading *vivicyante* is on the whole
much better attested. It is found in the sole independent manuscript of the PV (PV$_H$ 31a6), and
attested through all three Tibetan translations *rnam par bral* De$_t$ D 193a4 = P 225a8–b1, *rnam
bral* PV$_t$ P 224b1 (*bral* against *'brel* D 126b1), and *dben par* R$_t$ D 88b7 = P 107a1. Śālikanātha's
Prakaraṇapañcikā also quotes the verse with *vivicyante* (Kyuma 2010, 253n23). The reading
viśīryante might well have crept into the transmission of the PV from Prajñākaragupta's gloss.

tially defended. And we can further surmise that at the same time he maintained the unitary nature of awareness.[28] A nondualist stance is closer to the true nature of reality and allows one to perhaps not resolve but to bypass the problem of congruence, for it removes the premise of duality upon which the realist analysis is based.[29]

Devendrabuddhi summarizes the main thesis of *Pramāṇavārttika* 3.211 as "what appears [in perception] as extended exists neither externally nor internally."[30] The reason is that this kind of nature (*tadātmanaḥ*)—being spatially extended—has been refuted for one and is therefore also not possible for many. Devendrabuddhi and Manorathanandin offer different interpretations of the two denials that are subsumed under the options "one" and "many":

	One	Many
Devendrabuddhi [De_t D 193b2–5 = P 225a8–b4]	Extension does not belong to a unitary whole.	Extension does not belong to many atoms individually, and it also does not belong to atoms in aggregation.
Manorathanandin [M_1 182,3–8]	Extension does not belong to a single atom or a single part (*avayava*). Extension as "multicolor" (*citra*) does not belong to a single color-form (*ākāra*) such as blue.	Extension does not belong to many atoms or parts. Extension as multicolor does not belong to blue and other colors together.

Manorathanandin's interpretation pursues a dependence relation between *eka* and *aneka*, which he takes to refer, respectively, to individual and many atoms or parts. He argues that when extension does not belong to a single

28. Cf. also Steinkellner 1990, 76.

29. In this respect I disagree with McCrea, who reads this section as presenting separate but equally viable alternatives and takes Dharmakīrti *not* to express a clear preference for a Yogācāra analysis (McCrea 2020). Dharmakīrti's claim, in PV 3.219, that the Buddhas taught external objects just in conformity with worldly understanding, setting aside the true nature of reality (*tattvārtha*), is a clear enough statement of the superiority of a Yogācāra analysis.

30. De_t D 193b2–3 = P 226a1: *gang 'dir rags pa'i rnam par snang ba de phyi 'am nang na yod pa ma yin no //*.

entity, it also cannot belong to many.[31] Śākyabuddhi refers to Vasubandhu's *Viṃśikā* verse 12 for an argument to support this point.[32] Vasubandhu there argues that if an atom were linked with six other atoms on either side, it would have to have (spatial) parts because none of the surrounding atoms can be in the same place as the central one. However, atoms by definition do not have parts. If all six atoms were linked with the same place, then a "lump" (*piṇḍa*), a macroscopic object with spatial extension, would only have the dimension of one single atom. The claim that extension cannot belong to many atoms if it cannot belong to one requires, in any case, a separate argument; the dependence relation here is not the kind of metaphysical priority relation that characterizes the Śrīgupta/Śāntarakṣita NONMA. In contrast to Manorathanandin, Devendrabuddhi reads no straightforward dependence relation in *Pramāṇavārttika* 3.211, as he takes "one" to refer to the whole, while "many" refers primarily to many atoms individually and, secondarily, to many atoms in aggregation. Interpreted in this way, Dharmakīrti can be taken to refer back to his own earlier refutation of the whole at *Pramāṇavārttika* 2.85–86. Despite its limitation to two commentators, this divergence shows that there was no fixed schema for interpreting this particular neither-one-nor-many argument within Dharmakīrti's tradition.

Can this argument be interpreted as a NONMA that denies the existence of a class of entities on the ground of their existing neither as simples nor as pluralities? Śākyabuddhi seems to present Dharmakīrti's argument in this manner when he says that "the extended form assumed to be perceptible is ultimately nonexistent because it does not withstand an analysis in terms of one or many (*ekānekavicārākṣamatayā*)."[33] But the analysis performed in

---

31. M₁ 182,5–6: *te* (i.e., *paramāṇavaḥ/avayavāḥ*) *ca pratyekaṃ sthaulyavikalā iti samuditā api tathaiva syuḥ.*

32. Ś_t D 202b2–4 = P 249b7–8, translated in Dunne 2004, 405. Cf. also AKBh 32,12–15. Vetter (1964, 70) also refers to Vś 11–15 in connection with Dharmakīrti's PV 3.211. Note that Śākyabuddhi summarizes Vś 12 as part of a position that he rejects, but my point here is simply that this argumentation was within the horizon of Dharmakīrti's commentators when they explained verse 211.

33. Ś_t D 203a2–3 = P 250a6: *mngon sum du 'dod pa'i rags pa'i rnam pa ni gcig dang du mas dpyad mi bzod pa'i phyir don dam par med pa nyid yin pa ni bla ste /*, translated also in Dunne 2004, 405n14, and Yiannopoulos 2020, 286. See also the slightly later passage Ś_t D 204a4–5 = P 251b6: *'on kyang de rnam par shes pa las phyi rol bzhin du sngon po la sogs par snang ba gang yin pa de gcig dang du mas dpyad mi bzod pa nyid kyi phyir de kho na nyid ma yin no /.* For the Sanskrit, cf. K₁ 210,19=K_A 78a6–7: *ekānekavicārākṣamatayā na paramārthasat.* Karṇakagomin applies this analysis to blue and so on that appears as separate (*vicchinna*) from awareness, at the same time as awareness, and is intended as what is apprehended by it (*grāhya*).

Dunne at one point claims that for Dharmakīrti, the "inability to specify whether the image

Pramāṇavārttika 3.211 is not concerned with whether the appearance itself is singular or multiple. Rather, it investigates whether extension, a feature of all perceptual appearances, can belong to entities that exist as simples or as pluralities, since these are supposedly the only two ways in which entities can exist at all. The term *ekānekavicāra* is thus here used as a shorthand for a more complex investigation that relates appearances to reality and ultimately concerns congruence. This complexity also distinguishes Dharmakīrti's argument from a NINDA, as the reason does not turn on the identity of extension with simples or pluralities but on whether simples or pluralities can be extended.[34]

In terms of its function to refute realism, we can classify the argument from *Pramāṇavārttika* 3.211 together with a type of argument that I have elsewhere dubbed "arguments from incongruence," as they essentially raise as a problem that "there is a fundamental incongruence between what might serve as an external object of perception and what appears as its content."[35] In terms of the elements of Sautrāntika realism, these arguments target specifically the resemblance relationship (*sārūpya*) between perceptual appearance and external reality, and they take their inspiration from Dignāga's *Ālambanaparīkṣā* and *-vṛtti* (verses 1–2). More precisely, the argument in *Pramāṇavārttika* 3.211 demonstrates that whatever appears in perception as extended does not exist externally, since extension is not a feature of anything existing externally. In the discussion of the instrument of trustworthy awareness and its result (*pramāṇa* and *pramāṇaphala*) later in the same chapter, Dharmakīrti picks up this part of the argument again at *Pramāṇavārttika* 3.321cd: "How can the atoms make that [perception], which has an extended appearance, resemble them?"[36] He finally offers a comprehensive and systematic presentation of a very similar argument in the *Pramāṇaviniścaya*: (1) The extended form in perception does not exist in each of the individual atoms that supposedly cause it. (2) The extended form enters perception as one (but it is supposedly caused by many atoms, which is a contradiction). (3) Many atoms do not cause perception when aggregated (*sañcita*); they cannot appear in one

in perception is singular or multiple" serves as a primary argument against the existence of extra-mental objects (Dunne 2004, 63). This might be based on Śākyabuddhi, who, however, at least in this passage, concludes the nonexistence of extended appearances, not of external objects. Cf. also Kellner 2011, 292, as well as my remarks further below.

34. Dreyfus 1997, 102, expands the argument differently, through a NINDA that denies external objects to be identical with their parts or different from them. This may be based on Mkhas 'grub rje's interpretation (Dreyfus 1997, 489n67).

35. Kellner 2011, 296.

36. PV 3.321cd: *sarūpayanti tat kena sthūlābhāsaṃ ca te 'navaḥ //*. For *sthūlābhāsaṃ*, the manuscript Pr_B 176b7 reads *sthūlākāraṃ*.

singular form because what has one form in perception cannot in external reality be many. (4) The option that there might be a single extended object of perception that would correspond to this appearance, such as the Vaiśeṣika's whole, is untenable.[37]

The argument from *Pramāṇavārttika* 3.211, as interpreted here, differs in one respect from these arguments from incongruence: The reason denies that *extension* does not belong to external entities, while the arguments from incongruence deny that the *extended object-form* in perception belongs to them. That said, the impossibility of real extension—which can be supported with arguments from Vasubandhu—is still used to support a thesis about perceptual appearances. The focus of the argument is ultimately on denying congruence. In fact, the argument in *Pramāṇavārttika* 3.211 could be made fully identical with the other arguments from incongruence if the compound *tadātmanaḥ* in the reason were taken as a *bahuvrīhi* compound rather than a *karmadhāraya*: "because [an appearance] with such a[n extended] nature has been denied [in the *Ālambanaparīkṣā*] for one..." rather than "because such a[n extended] nature..." While there remains a certain range of interpretative options, both construals support a classification of the argument as belonging to the larger complex of arguments from incongruence. As I have argued elsewhere,[38] among Dharmakīrti's various and scattered arguments against realism, this complex belongs to a weaker group of arguments that point out defects in a particular version of realism—Sautrāntika representationalism, which Dharmakīrti considers to be the best possible realist theory. His stronger arguments—such as the *sahopalambhaniyama* inference when interpreted as directed against realism—derive the impossibility for perception to apprehend anything outside itself from the very nature of perception itself; they are stronger because they are independent of any particular version of realism.[39] None of the arguments outside the section *Pramāṇavārttika* 3.194–224,

37. PVin 1 34,5–35,6, discussed at Kellner 2011, 295–96. For some problems in the interpretation of the entire PVin passage, see Kellner 2011, 295n13.

38. Kellner 2017b discusses Dharmakīrti's refutation of realism compared with Vasubandhu's and Dignāga's, while Kellner 2017a concentrates on Dharmakīrti. Both papers expand on Kellner 2011, where I examined a more limited range of arguments specifically in light of Dunne's ontological construal of the sliding scale of analysis and concluded that an ontological construal of the transition from realism to idealism was not well supported. My present analysis of PV 3.211 further confirms this point.

39. Taber 2020 offers a philosophical reconstruction of this inference as an original argument to prove idealism without an analogue in Western philosophy. Dharmakīrti admits of stronger and weaker interpretations of the inference, the latter being consistent with Sautrāntika realism. On this point, cf. also the pertinent remarks in McCrea 2020.

on which Dunne based his ontological version of Dharmakīrti's sliding scale of analysis, are straightforwardly "ontological" insofar as they would deny the very existence of external objects. Within this section, *Pramāṇavārttika* 3.211 most straightforwardly presents a mereological argument, but this too does not accomplish a denial of the very existence of extramental matter. The Yogācāra principle that duality is erroneous, at one point presented by Dunne as an argument against the existence of extramental matter,[40] appears in Dharmakīrti rather as a background idea that is invoked on various occasions, in connection with the principle of unitary awareness. But it does not seem to be used in an *argument* that would support the nonexistence of physical objects. Moreover, even if our impression that our perceptions are of something other that exists independently of them may be erroneous, this does not logically entail the unreality of the external world; it simply entails the more limited phenomenalist claim that perception is not of anything outside consciousness.[41]

Mereological considerations thus form a part of Dharmakīrti's rejection of realism, and more precisely of his claim that perception cannot be congruent with reality, but not in the form of a straightforward NONMA. On the whole his broader array of pertinent arguments stops short at proving the imperceptibility of external objects and does not go as far as to establish their nonexistence.[42] There are reasons to believe that Dharmakīrti simply regarded it as unnecessary to produce stronger arguments than he did—according to Manorathanandin, Vasubandhu's mereological arguments, which demonstrate the necessity as well as impossibility of atoms, merit consideration only if a realist were to stubbornly insist after Dharmakīrti's proofs of the imperceptibility of external reality had been pointed out to them.[43]

40. Dunne 2004, 61.

41. This applies equally to Prueitt's attempt to defend Dunne's account against my earlier criticism (Prueitt 2017, 24–30), which expands the sphere of consideration from PV 3.194–224 to PV 3.301–66, but as far as I can tell does not affect this critical issue. I am grateful to Prueitt for pushing me to offer an interpretation of relevant arguments from PV 3.194–224 and explain how they fit my own understanding.

42. On this point as well as its significance cf. Kellner 2017a, 116–18.

43. M₁ 220,16–20 (text-critical discussion in Kellner 2017a, 123n67), translated and discussed in Kellner 2017a, 117–18, based on an earlier translation in Ratié 2014, 359n22; cf. also Arnold 2008, 16.

The Relationship Between Unitary Perception and the Many "Forms" (ākāra): Pramāṇavārttika 3.359 in Its Context

The second main verse that has been claimed as a NONMA in Dharmakīrti's philosophy of mind is *Pramāṇavārttika* 3.359. In Steinkellner's already cited translation, the verse reads:[44]

> That form in which entities are [normally] perceived (*nirūpyante*) does not exist in reality, for these (things) have neither a unitary nor a multiple form.[45]

At first sight this seems to structurally conform to the Śrīgupta/Śāntarakṣita NONMA: a thesis that claims something does not exist in reality (*nāsti tattvataḥ*) is supported by the reasoning that that thing is neither one nor many. The first thing to note about this argument in formal terms, however, is that its thesis is more complex. It is not a simple denial that a class of entities does not exist; rather it is a qualified denial that entities (*bhāvāḥ*) exist in a certain way—namely, in the form in which they are perceived (*nirūpyante*) or, as the verb can also be rendered in accordance with Devendrabuddhi's commentary and Tibetan translations, "examined."[46] Steinkellner's "perceived" follows the lead of Manorathanandin's commentary, where *nirūpyante* is glossed with *anubhūyante*.[47]

Like the first putative NONMA in *Pramāṇavārttika* 3.211, this one also comes as the conclusion of a preceding discussion, one that began with *Pramāṇavārttika* 3.353; the section was taken over without modifications into the *Pramāṇaviniścaya*, where it starts with *Pramāṇaviniścaya* 1.44.[48] Dharmakīrti here argues as a Yogācāra, explaining the instrument of trustworthy awareness and its result (*pramāṇa* and *pramāṇaphala*) solely on the basis of consciousness, without reference to any external reality. The argument

44. *Bhāvā yena nirūpyante tad rūpaṃ nāsti tattvataḥ / yasmād ekam anekaṃ vā rūpaṃ teṣāṃ na vidyate //.* For variant readings in the verses PV 3.353–62 discussed in the following, see Kellner forthcoming.

45. Kellner 2026 1990, 78.

46. Cf. the paraphrase in De_t D 224a4 = P 266b5 with *dpyod par 'gyur*; all three main Tibetan translations of the verse (PV_t D 132a4 = P 230b6, R_t D 131a7 = P<?>157b8, and the translation embedded in De_t D 224a3 = P 266b3) translate "examine" (*rnam dpyad*).

47. M₁ 227,10–12.

48. A detailed analysis of the entire section PV 3.353–62, including Sanskrit text and translation, is given in Kellner 2026.

in *Pramāṇavārttika* 3.359 concludes a multipart argument that supports the principle of unitary awareness and the erroneous nature of any division, be it that into apprehending subject and apprehended object or that between key elements of epistemological analysis such as the instrument, its result, and the object (*prameya*). According to Dignāga's and Dharmakīrti's Yogācāra analysis, these are just concepts projected onto different aspects of unitary awareness.[49] The erroneous nature of dualistic experience is defended in basically two different ways. On the one hand, Dharmakīrti makes the error plausible with the help of examples for perceptual error, as when a lump of clay appears as an elephant or gold to persons whose sense of vision is impaired by a sorcerer's spells, or when a small object is seen as big from afar in the desert by someone who lacks context to interpret its size correctly.[50] Moreover, while in such cases the error is due to mistaking one thing for another, the error of duality is purely internal, produced by ignorance.[51] On the other hand, Dharmakīrti argues for the erroneous nature of dualistic experience by essentially claiming that it is baseless: it is impossible that the different forms in which awareness appears, and which supposedly belong to it, are ultimately real. In *Pramāṇavārttika* 3.357–58, two reasons are given for their unreality. These consist in two *prasaṅga*s that point out hypothetical and unwanted consequences that issue from their reality, as well as a subsidiary argument in 358b–d:

> Otherwise [i.e., if the different elements of epistemological analysis ultimately existed as distinct parts of awareness] how could [many] forms truly exist for one singular entity (*bhāvasya*) [i.e., awareness] that appears in various forms? [They could not because then] the oneness of that [awareness would] be destroyed (*tadekatvasya hānitaḥ*), and [if that oneness were insisted upon,] the [mutual] otherness of the other [i.e., the forms] would be destroyed (*anyasyānyatvahāneḥ*).[52] [Subsidiary argument:] There is [on the other hand] no non-difference [between the many forms] because

49. PS 1.10 and PV 3.356.

50. The examples are given in PV 3.354–55; see again Kellner 2026 for detailed discussion.

51. PV 3.360–63 (Kellner 2026).

52. The rhetorical question receives either an implicit negative answer, as reflected in my translation, or the particle *na* in 358d is construed twice, both as an answer to this question and with the following argument. The latter option where one word is construed with two sentences is indicated by Manorathanandin in M₁ 227,1–2, as an application of the interpretative rule of a "crow's eyeball" (*kākāṣi(golaka)nyāya*), which, supposedly single, moves from one side of the eye cavity to the other. Both possibilities yield the same argument.

no such nature is perceived [by ordinary beings], for awareness [conceptually] determines a non-difference of forms [only] when it sees it.[53]

The thesis of Dharmakīrti's argument can be extrapolated from the introductory rhetorical question that expects a negative answer:

Thesis
The many forms of a unitary awareness that appears as manifold are not ultimately real (as distinct parts).

If the forms were ultimately real, they would have their own distinct natures and exist as distinct parts within awareness. If they were ultimately real, the first unwanted consequence that awareness could not be unitary—that is, simple—follows. The indivisible nature of awareness, supported by the principle of unitary awareness stated only a few verses earlier in *Pramāṇavārttika* 3.353, would have to be abandoned. A further tacit premise of this first unwanted consequence is that there is a strong relationship between the forms and awareness, perhaps even a relationship of identity in the sense that the forms would be of the nature of awareness. For it is only when such a strong relationship is presupposed that the unitary nature of awareness is endangered by the plurality of forms.

Following this line of reasoning, we can extrapolate the first *prasaṅga* as follows:

Prasaṅga 1: tadekatvasya hānitaḥ
If the many forms in unitary awareness were ultimately real and identical with awareness, awareness could not be unitary.

As there is no indication that the second unwanted consequence issues from a different set of premises, we may surmise that the premises of this first *prasaṅga*—namely, that the forms are ultimately real and that they are identical with awareness—continue to inform the second *prasaṅga*, which concludes that the "otherness" (*anyatva*) of the "other" (*anya*) would be abandoned. Dharmottara interprets this as meaning that the plurality and variety of the forms would become lost; it would become meaningless to speak of

53. PV 3.357–58: *anyathaikasya bhāvasya nānārūpāvabhāsinaḥ / satyaṃ kathaṃ syur ākārās tadekatvasya hānitaḥ // anyasyānyatvahāneś ca nābhedo 'rūpadarśanāt / rūpābhedaṃ hi paśyantī dhīr abhedaṃ vyavasyati //.*

"many" appearances within awareness.[54] This, however, only results if the oneness of awareness is presupposed—in other words, if the (tacit) response to the
first *prasaṅga* is to insist on the unitary nature of awareness.

> *Prasaṅga 2: anyasyānyatvahāneḥ*
> If the many forms in unitary awareness were ultimately real, and
> each is identical with *unitary* awareness, they could not be differ-
> ent from each other.

From here, Dharmakīrti goes on to offer a subsidiary argument, which can
be understood as responding to an unstated assent to the second *prasaṅga*:
let's bite the bullet and say that the different forms are in fact "non-different."

> *Subsidiary Argument*
> There is no non-difference [among the many forms] because no
> such nature is perceived, for awareness [conceptually] determines a
> non-difference of forms [only] when it sees it.

By this subsidiary argument, Dharmakīrti rules out the possibility that different forms are "non-different" on the ground that they are not experienced as
non-different—by ordinary beings—which is why there is no basis for determining them to be one.

The neither-one-nor-many argument in *Pramāṇavārttika* 3.359 can now be
read on the backdrop of these two *prasaṅgas*. When read in this way, it essentially summarizes their conclusion; the "entities" (*bhāvāḥ*) in this context then
refer to the many forms in awareness.[55] To paraphrase:

> The nature (*rūpa*) in terms of which the forms (*bhāvāḥ*) are exam-
> ined [or experienced] (*nirūpyante*) does [therefore] not truly exist
> [for them] because neither a nature (*rūpa*) as one nor a nature as
> many exists for them.

---

54. PVinṬ₁ D 155b7–a1 = P 181a8–b1: *de lta na 'o na ni // rnam pa gsum po rnams gcig nyid
yin pas gcig las tha dad pa med par 'gyur ro zhe na / bshad pa / gzhan gyi* [= *anyasya*] *ste du ma
rnams kyi du ma nyid ldog par thal ba'i phyir ro // du ma nyid kyi tha snyad yul med par 'gyur ro
zhes bya ba'i don to /.* Manorathanandin takes *anyatva* to refer to the mutual difference between
individual forms such as pleasure, pain, etc., or blue, yellow, etc. (M₁ 226,24–25). This seems
to assume not the scenario of plurality *within* unitary awareness but variation across different
instances of awareness.

55. Cf. also M₁ 227,10–12: *bhāvāḥ grāhyādayaḥ . . . na ca grāhyādyābhāsa* (*-sa* marginal
correction in manuscript M_A 44a7) *eko 'neko vā yuktaḥ.*

Later interpreters in the tradition who regard Dharmakīrti to ultimately pursue a Madhyamaka intention, like Jitāri and Mokṣākaragupta, interpret *bhāvāḥ* with universal scope, as referring to both external objects and instances of awareness.[56] Read in its immediate textual environment, on the other hand, the verse states that if one examines (*nirūpyante*) the various forms in terms of whether they are the apprehended, the apprehender, and so forth, one realizes that such natures (*rūpa*) do not truly exist for them because the forms are neither one nor many.[57] The forms are not one—which would ultimately mean that they would be identical with unitary awareness—because, as was argued with the second *prasaṅga*, they would then not be different from each other, and they could not be many. The forms are also not many because, as the first *prasaṅga* argues, if they are still identical with awareness (to which they belong), awareness would then not be one. If we take the verb *nirūpyante* in the meaning of "experienced," the verse states that in terms of whatever nature persons *experience* forms in cognition—apprehender, apprehended, and so on—that nature does not exist for them. Both possibilities for interpreting *nirūpyante* yield meaning; their difference does not affect the structure of the argument.

Understood in this manner, the whole argument from *Pramāṇavārttika* 3.357–59 denies the reality of the multiple forms under the premise of the unitary nature of awareness; one can draw a line to Dharmakīrti's earlier claim from *Pramāṇavārttika* 3.217 that for those under the sway of ignorance, awareness arises with false forms (*vitathākārā*). The argument in *Pramāṇavārttika* 3.357–59 is consequently of use to those later Yogācāras who advocate a "False-Form" (*alīkākāravāda*) position. One finds it— as far as I can tell without acknowledgment of Dharmakīrti as a source or model—used as a critique of a "True-Form" (*satyākāravāda*) position in Kamalaśīla's *Madhyamakālaṅkārapañjikā* and in Haribhadra's *Abhisamayālaṅkārāloka*[58] and used in support of an *alīkākāravāda* position in the *Madhyamakālaṅkāropadeśa* by Ratnākaraśānti.[59]

In logical terms, this kind of argument is quite different from the monadic NONMA in Śrīgupta and Śāntarakṣita; it is a dyadic NINDA. For the forms to be either "one" or "many" means that they would be identical with unitary

<hr>

56. Steinkellner 1990, 79.

57. Steinkellner instead considers Dharmakīrti in PV 3.359 to refer back to the earlier discussion in PV 3.208ff. because he does not explain the argument from PV 3.359 in detail. This, however, can also be accounted for by considering it a summarizing conclusion relating to the immediately preceding arguments.

58. MAP 128,14–17 on MA verse 46, parallel in AAA 626,15–20.

59. MAU D 227b4–7 = P 262a5–b1, summarized in Moriyama 2014, 346.

awareness or different from each other. If they are different from each other, they are also different *from* unitary awareness. A restatement of the argument from *Pramāṇavārttika* 3.359 with identity and difference yields:

> The forms in unitary awareness are not ultimately real because they are neither identical with awareness nor different from each other (and awareness).

The logical relationship between the predicates depends on the precise understanding of "identity" and "difference"; this is one of the major difficulties (and problems) of this argument, as one can also see from Ratnākaraśānti's much later elaboration, as recently discussed by Davey Tomlinson.[60] If, for instance, one were to argue that the forms are neither *fully* identical nor *fully* different from awareness, one can always construe a third option of partial identity and partial difference, or use this as an argument in support of an ultimately indeterminate nature. The predicates are then not contradictory opposites, and the argument does then not present, like the Śrīgupta/Śāntarakṣita NONMA, a destructive dilemma. This is more generally true of NINDA-type arguments; it is not coincidental that Candrakīrti's refutation of the self begins with a NINDA but supplements it with considerations of additional types of whole-part relationships (*Madhyamakāvatāra* 6.150–57). The differences between Dharmakīrti's NINDA and the Madhyamaka NONMA can be explained through the overarching purpose and background of the argument. Informed by a Yogācāra-Vijñānavāda position, it takes one type of unitary entity—awareness—to be ultimately real and evaluates whether a seeming plurality that belongs to this unitary entity can be real or not.

Conclusions: Mereological Considerations in Dharmakīrti's Philosophy of Perception

In Dharmakīrti's philosophy of mind, mereological considerations are at work in at least two contexts in his discussion of perceptual awareness: first, in the rejection of Sautrāntika representational realism, where the idea that there is a congruence between extended perceptual appearances and external objects is denied; second, in the defense of the merely erroneous nature of a division of awareness, where the ultimate reality of multiple forms within unitary awareness is negated. Two putative neither-one-nor-many arguments at *Pramāṇavārttika* 3.211 and 3.359, each belonging to one of these contexts, turn

60. Tomlinson 2023.

out to be significantly different from a NONMA if we take a NONMA to deny the ultimate existence of something on the ground that that something neither exists as an indivisible simple nor as a plurality of such simples. Based on the analysis given here, the first argument denies simply that extended perceptual appearances can belong to any existing entity, external or internal, because (on the reading offered by Devendrabuddhi and Manorathanandin) extension cannot be a property of either simples or pluralities. I have argued that this argument can be classified together with a larger complex of arguments that Dharmakīrti uses against realism. These arguments from incongruence target the very possibility of congruence. The second argument can be analyzed as a neither-identical-nor-different argument, or NINDA, one that is offered independently and is not subservient to an overarching NONMA—as is the case with at least some NINDAs that are used to support the overarching Śrīgupta/Śāntarakṣita NONMA. Dharmakīrti's NINDA, as I understand it, supports the position that multiple forms within awareness, which is ultimately unitary, cannot be truly real. There is certainly much more to be said about putative NONMAs in Dharmakīrti, but these two case studies should suffice to show that it is worthwhile looking at specific instances of neither-one-nor-many analysis in Buddhist philosophy more closely and to attempt to delineate their variation.

As a final point, it is worth noting that both Dharmakīrtian arguments occur in conclusions to preceding argumentations. In addition, the absence of a clear-cut schematic interpretation of the argument at *Pramāṇavārttika* 3.211 in the commentarial tradition suggests that within the Dharmakīrtian tradition, these patterns were seen to allow space for interpretation: one can link them with different kinds of mereological arguments from the body of knowledge constituted by preceding tradition. Besides analyzing the logical function and philosophical import of NONMAs, we might in the end also be well advised to look at such patterns as hermeneutic and rhetorical devices that allowed Buddhist philosophers to form, record, and transmit structured clusters of arguments in support of their main philosophical positions.

Abbreviations

AAA	Haribhadra's *Abhisamayālaṅkārāloka*. In Wogihara 1935.
AKBh	Vasubandhu's *Abhidharmakośabhāṣya*. In Pradhan 1967.
ĀP(V)	Dignāga's *Ālambanaparīkṣā* and *-vṛtti*. In Frauwallner 1930.
BCA	Śāntideva's *Bodhicaryāvatāra*. In La Vallée Poussin 1904–12.
BCAP	Prajñākaramati's *Bodhicaryāvatārapañjikā*. In La Vallée Poussin 1904–12.

D	Takasaki, Yamaguchi, and Ejima 1977ff.
De$_t$	Devendrabuddhi's *Pramāṇavārttikapañjikā*. Tibetan translation: *Tshad ma rnam 'grel gyi dka' 'grel*. D 4217 che 1–326b4, P 5717b che 1–390a8.
K$_1$	Sāṅkṛtyāyana 1943.
K$_A$	Watanabe 1998a.
M$_1$	Sāṅkṛtyāyana 1938–40.
M$_A$	Watanabe 1998b.
MA	Śāntarakṣita's *Madhyamakālaṅkāra*. In Ichigō 1985.
Madhyama-kāvatāra	Candrakīrti's *Madhyamakāvatāra*. Tibetan translation edited in La Vallée Poussin 1907–12.
MAP	Kamalaśīla's *Madhyamakālaṅkārapañjikā*. Tibetan translation edited in: Ichigō 1985.
MAU	Ratnākaraśānti's *Madhyamālaṅkāropadeśa*. Tibetan translation: *Dbu ma rgyan gyi man ngag*. P 5586 ku 257b2–267a4, D 4085 hi 223b2–231a7.
P	Suzuki 1955–61.
Pr$_2$	Sāṅkṛtyāyana 1953.
Pr$_B$	Prajñākaragupta's *Pramāṇavārttikālaṅkārabhāṣya*. Complete Sanskrit manuscript from Sa skya Monastery written by Dānaśīla in Watanabe 1998c.
PS 1	Dignāga's *Pramāṇasamuccaya*, chapter 1. In Steinkellner 2005.
PV 3	Dharmakīrti's *Pramāṇavārttika*, third chapter on *pratyakṣa*. In Tosaki 1979–85.
PV$_1$	Sāṅkṛtyāyana 1938.
PV$_H$	Sanskrit manuscript of Dharmakīrti's *Pramāṇavārttika*, kept by Hemrāj Śarmā. Facsimile edition in Kellner and Sferra 2008.
PVin 1	Dharmakīrti's *Pramāṇaviniścaya*, chaps. 1 and 2. In Steinkellner 2007.
PVinṬ$_t$ 1	Dharmottara's *Pramāṇaviniścayaṭīkā*, chap. 1. Tibetan translation: *Tshad ma rnam par nges pa'i 'grel bshad*. P 5727 dze 1–we 209b8 (references in this paper point to volume dze), D 4229 dze 1–289a7.
PV$_t$	Dharmakīrti's *Pramāṇavārttika*. Tibetan translation: *Tshad ma rnam 'grel gyi tshig le'ur byas pa*. D 4210 ce 94b1–151a7, P 5709 ce 190a4–250b6.
R$_t$	Ravigupta's *Pramāṇavārttikavṛtti*, third chapter. Tibetan translation: *Tshad ma rnam 'grel gyi 'grel pa las le'u gsum pa*. D 4225 phe 1–174a7, P 5722 phe 1–208a7.
Ś$_t$	Śākyabuddhi's *Pramāṇavārttikavṛtti*. Tibetan translation: *Tshad ma rnam 'grel kyi 'grel bshad*. D 4220 je 1b1–ñe 282a7 (references in this paper point to volume ñe), P 5718 je 1–348a8.
TA	Śrīgupta's *Tattvāvatāra*. Embedded in his TAV.

TAV   Śrīgupta's *Tattvāvatāravṛtti*. Tibetan translation: *De kho na la 'jug pa'i 'grel pa*. D 3892 ha 39b45–43b5, P 5292 ha 44b2–49a5.

Vś   Vasubandhu's *Viṃśikā Vijñaptimātratāsiddhiḥ*. In Lévi 1925.

Bibliography

Aitken, Allison. 2021. "No Unity, No Problem: Madhyamaka Metaphysical Indefinitism." *Philosophers' Imprint* 21: 1–24.

Arnold, Dan. 2008. "Buddhist Idealism, Epistemic and Otherwise: Thoughts on the Alternating Perspectives of Dharmakīrti." *Sophia* 47: 3–28.

Dreyfus, Georges. 1997. *Recognizing Reality: Dharmakīrti's Philosophy and Its Tibetan Interpreters*. Albany: State University of New York Press.

Dunne, John. 2004. *Foundations of Dharmakīrti's Philosophy*. Studies in Indian and Tibetan Buddhism. Boston: Wisdom Publications.

Ejima, Yasunori. 1980. *Chūganshisō no tenkai—Bhāvaviveka-kenkyū* (*The Development of Madhyamaka Thought: Studies on Bhāvaviveka). Tokyo: Shunjūsha.

Frauwallner, Erich. 1930. "Dignāga's *Ālambanaparīkṣā*: Text, Übersetzung und Erläuterungen." *Wiener Zeitschrift für die Kunde des Morgenlandes* 37: 175–94.

Hahn, Michael. 1982. *Nāgārjuna's Ratnāvalī: The Basic Texts (Sanskrit, Tibetan, Chinese)*. Bonn: Indica et Tibetica.

Ichigō, Masamichi. 1985. *Madhyamakālaṃkāra of Śāntarakṣita with His Own Commentary or Vṛtti and with the Subcommentary or Pañjikā of Kamalaśīla*. Kyoto: Bun'eido.

Keira, Ryūsei. 2004. *Mādhyamika and Epistemology: A Study of Kamalaśīla's Method for Proving the Voidness of All Dharmas. Introduction, Annotated Translations and Tibetan Texts of Selected Sections of the Second Chapter of the Madhyamakāloka*. Vienna: Arbeitskreis für Tibetische und Buddhistische Studien, Universität Wien.

Kellner, Birgit. 2011. "Dharmakīrti's Criticism of External Realism and the Sliding Scale of Analysis." In *Religion and Logic in Buddhist Philosophical Analysis: Proceedings of the Fourth International Dharmakīrti Conference, Vienna, August 23–27, 2005*, edited by Helmut Krasser, Horst Lasic, Eli Franco, and Birgit Kellner, 291–98. Vienna: Verlag der Österreichischen Akademie der Wissenschaften.

———. 2017a. "Proofs of Idealism in Buddhist Epistemology: Dharmakīrti's Refutation of External Objects." In *Indian Epistemology and Metaphysics*, edited by Joerg Tuske, 103–28. London: Bloomsbury Academic Publishing.

———. 2017b. "Proving Idealism in Indian Buddhist Philosophy: Vasubandhu and Dharmakīrti." In *Oxford Handbook of Indian Philosophy*, edited by Jonardon Ganeri, 307–26. New York: Oxford University Press.

———. 2026. "Non-Duality in Dharmakīrti." In *Bloomsbury Research Handbook of Non-Duality in Indian Thought*, edited by Jonathan Duquette and James Madaio. London: Bloomsbury.

Kellner, Birgit, and Francesco Sferra. 2008. "A Palm-Leaf Manuscript of Dharmakīrti's *Pramāṇavārttika* from the Collection Kept by the Nepalese Rājaguru Hemarāja Śarman." In *Sanskrit Texts from Giuseppe Tucci's Collection. Part I*, edited by Francesco Sferra, 229–48. Rome: Istituto Italiano per l'Africa e l'Oriente.

Kyuma, Taiken. 2010. "Śālikanātha's Criticism of Dharmakīrti's *Svasaṃvedana* Theory." *Journal of Indian Philosophy* 38: 247–59.

La Vallée Poussin, Louis de. 1904–12. *Prajñākaramati's Commentary to the Bodhicaryā-vatāra of Çāntideva*. Bibliotheca Indica. Calcutta: Asiatic Society.

———. 1907–12. *Madhyamakāvatāra par Candrakīrti: Traduction tibétaine*. Bibliotheca Buddhica 9. St. Petersburg: Imprimerie de l'Académie Impériale des Sciences.

Lang, Karen. 1986. *Āryadeva's Catuḥśataka*. Copenhagen: Akademisk Forlag.

Lévi, Sylvain, ed. 1925. *Vijñaptimātratāsiddhi: Deux Traités de Vasubandhu: Viṃśatikā et Triṃśikā*. Paris: Librairie Ancienne Honoré Champion.

McCrea, Lawrence. 2020. "Balancing the Scales: Dharmakīrti Inside and Out." In *Reverberations of Dharmakīrti's Philosophy: Proceedings of the Fifth International Dharmakīrti Conference Heidelberg August 26 to 30, 2014*, edited by Birgit Kellner, Patrick McAllister, Horst Lasic, and Sara McClintock, 251–65. Vienna: Verlag der Österreichischen Akademie der Wissenschaften.

Moriyama, Shinya. 2014. "Ratnākaraśānti's Theory of Cognition with False Mental Images (*alīkākāravāda*) and the Neither-One-Nor-Many Argument." *Journal of Indian Philosophy* 42: 339–51.

Pradhan, Prahlad, ed. 1967. *Abhidharmakośabhāṣya of Vasubandhu*. Patna: K. P. Jayaswal Research Institute.

Prueitt, Catherine. 2017. "Shifting Concepts: The Realignment of Dharmakīrti on Concepts and the Error of Subject/Object Duality in Pratyabhijñā Śaiva Thought." *Journal of Indian Philosophy* 45: 21–47.

Ratié, Isabelle. 2014. *Une critique bouddhique du Soi selon la Mīmāṃsā: Présentation, édition critique et traduction de la Mīmāṃsakaparikalpitātmaparīkṣā de Śāntarakṣita; (Tattvasaṅgraha 222–284 et Pañjikā)*. Vienna: Verlag der Österreichischen Akademie der Wissenschaften.

Sāṅkṛtyāyana, Rāhula. 1938. *Pramāṇavārttikam by Ācārya Dharmakīrti*. Appendix to the *Journal of the Bihar and Orissa Research Society* 24.

———. 1938–40. *Dharmakīrti's Pramāṇavārttika with a Commentary by Manorathanandin*. Appendix to *Journal of the Bihar and Orissa Research Society* 24–26.

———. 1943. *Ācārya-Dharmakīrteḥ Pramāṇavārttikam (svārthānumānaparicchedaḥ) svopajñavṛttyā, Karṇakagomiviracitayā taṭṭīyakā ca sahi tam*. Ilāhābād: Kitāb Mahal.

———. 1953. *Pramāṇavārtikabhāshyam or Vārtikālaṅkāraḥ of Prajñākaragupta (Being a Commentary on Dharmakīrti's Pramāṇavārtikam)*. Patna: K. P. Jayaswal Research Institute.

Steinkellner, Ernst. 1990. "Is Dharmakīrti a Mādhyamika?" In *Earliest Buddhism and Madhyamaka*, edited by David Seyfort Ruegg and Lambert Schmithausen, 72–90. Leiden: Brill.

———. 2005. *Dignāga's Pramāṇasamuccaya, Chapter 1. A hypothetical reconstruction with the help of the two Tibetan translations on the basis of the hitherto known Sanskrit fragments and the linguistic materials gained from Jinendrabuddhi's Ṭīkā*. Available online https://www.oeaw.ac.at/fileadmin/Institute/IKGA/PDF/forschung/buddhismuskunde/dignaga_PS_1.pdf. Links to corrigenda can be found at https://www.oeaw.ac.at/ikga/digitales/steinkellner-repositorium (last accessed 19 October 2023).

———. 2007. *Dharmakīrti's Pramāṇaviniścaya: Chapters 1 and 2, Critically Edited*. Beijing/Vienna: China Tibetology Publishing House / Austrian Academy of Sciences Press. Links to corrigenda can be found at https://www.oeaw.ac.at/ikga/digitales/steinkellner-repositorium (last accessed 19 October 2023).

Suzuki, Daisetz Teitaro. 1955–61. *The Tibetan Tripiṭaka, Peking Edition*. Tokyo and Kyoto: Tibetan Tripitaka Research Institute.

Taber, John. 2020. "Philosophical Reflections on the *Sahopalambhaniyama* Argument." In *Reverberations of Dharmakīrti's Philosophy: Proceedings of the Fifth International Dharmakīrti Conference Heidelberg August 26 to 30, 2014*, edited by Birgit Kellner, Patrick McAllister, Horst Lasic, and Sara McClintock, 441–62. Vienna: Verlag der Österreichischen Akademie der Wissenschaften.

Takasaki, Jikidō, Zuihō Yamaguchi, and Yasunori Ejima. 1977ff. *Tibetan Tripiṭaka, Sde dge Edition, Bstan Ḥgyur, Preserved at the Faculty of Letters, University of Tokyo*. Tokyo: Sekai Seiten Kanko Kyokai Co. for the Faculty of Letters, University of Tokyo.

Tillemans, Tom J. F. 1982. "The 'Neither One nor Many' Argument for *śūnyatā*, and Its Tibetan Interpretations: Background Information and Source Materials." *Études de Lettres (Faculté des Lettres de l'Université de Lausanne)* 3: 103–28.

———. 1983. "The 'Neither One nor Many' Argument for *śūnyatā*, and Its Tibetan Interpretation." In *Contributions on Tibetan and Buddhist Religion and Philosophy: Proceedings of the Csoma de Körös Symposium Held at Velm-Vienna, Austria, 13–19 September 1981*, vol. 2, edited by Ernst Steinkellner and Helmut Tauscher, 305–20. Vienna: Arbeitskreis für Tibetische und Buddhistische Studien, Universität Wien.

———. 1999. *Scripture, Logic, Language: Essays on Dharmakīrti and his Tibetan Successors*. Studies in Indian and Tibetan Buddhism. Boston: Wisdom Publications.

———. 2022. "Two Tibetan Texts on the 'Neither One nor Many' Argument for *śūnyatā*." In *Views from Tibet: Studies on Tibetan Buddhist Logic, the Philosophy of the Middle, and the Indigenous Grammatico-Linguistic Tradition*, 141–73. Vienna: Austrian Academy of Sciences Press.

Tomlinson, Davey K. 2023. "Limiting the Scope of the Neither-One-Nor-Many Argument: The Nirākāravādin's Defense of Consciousness and Pleasure." *Philosophy East and West* 73.2: 392–419.

Tosaki, Hiromasa. 1979–85. *Bukkyō-ninshikiron no kenkyū* (*Studies in Buddhist Epistemology). 2 vols. Tokyo: Daitōshuppansha.

Vetter, Tilmann. 1964. *Erkenntnisprobleme bei Dharmakīrti*. Vienna: Hermann Böhlaus Nachf. Kommissionsverlag der Österreichischen Akademie der Wissenschaften.

Watanabe, Shigeaki. 1998a. *Sanskrit Manuscripts of Karṇakagomin's Pramāṇavārttika(Sva)Vṛttitīkā. Facsimile Edition*. Patna/Narita: Bihar and Orissa Research Society / Naritasan Institute for Buddhist Studies.

———. 1998b. *A Sanskrit Manuscript of Manorathanandin's Pramāṇavārttikavṛtti. Facsimile Edition*. Patna/Narita: Bihar and Orissa Research Society / Naritasan Institute for Buddhist Studies.

———. 1998c. *Sanskrit Manuscripts of Prajñākaragupta's Pramāṇavārttikabhāṣyam. Facsimile Edition*. Patna/Narita: Bihar and Orissa Research Society / Naritasan Institute for Buddhist Studies.

Wogihara, Unrai. 1935. *Abhisamayālaṅkārāloka Prajñāpāramitāvyākhyā: The Work of Haribhadra*, vol. 2. Tokyo: The Toyo Bunko.

Yiannopoulos, Alexander. 2020. "The Structure of Dharmakīrti's Philosophy: A Study of Object-Cognition in the Perception Chapter (*pratyakṣapariccheda*) of the *Pramāṇasamuccaya*, the *Pramāṇavārttika*, and Their Earliest Commentaries." PhD dissertation, Emory University.

Negative Dialectics in Madhyamaka Buddhist Practice

Kenneth Liberman

DECADES AGO, the then director of the American Institute of Indian Studies Joe Elder, a fellow sociologist from the University of Wisconsin, asked me the following question: "Tibetan philosophy places great emphasis upon overcoming egocentrism, so can you tell me why it is that Tibetological scholars are so frequently embroiled in ego-competitive struggles with their academic colleagues?" It was a good question. But I didn't have a good answer. Many years later we now have the career of Tibetologist Tom Tillemans to offer as a counter-illustration. In the twenty-plus years I have known him, Tom has not once displayed a shred of ego-competitiveness or anger. For Tom, it is always about the academic inquiries. And it is for that reason that the contributors to this volume are eager to laud him, as well as hope that one day we can supply the same sort of professional generosity. Tom's ecumenical spirit has affected the organizers of this volume to the extent that they have invited this sociologist to contribute some social scientific reflections to this volume of Tibetological scholarship.

The Context

What are the best practices and contexts for formal analytic thinking? While this is an august topic in philosophical anthropology, it can and should be investigated not only theoretically but also via case studies. My book on Tibetan debating is one such empirical endeavor, and my study of professional coffee tasters and sensory science is another. The thinking set into motion by the complex social organization of early *Homo sapiens* society (*sapiens* refers to thinking, *sapere*) led our line of hominids to prevail over the more physically powerful *Homo neanderthalensis* of Europe and *Homo erectus* of Asia. In our time, computers and cell phone usage have so supercharged our mentations—

"

in quantity if not in quality—that a species of *Homo* subsequent to *Homo sapiens* may be emerging at the present moment.

What we consider modernity began with a critique of alienation, including the ways our thinking can entrap and alienate us from ourselves, depositing us into prisons of our own making. Just how is it that humans perpetually become trapped inside the very social forms that they devise for improving the human condition? Georg Simmel (2009 and throughout his corpus) described with precision the increasing objectification in modern society and recognized that the alienation imposed by our objectifications is not simply modernity or capitalism but something more deeply embedded in social organization and human experience.

The better part of social scientific scholarship on alienation focuses on scourges of social organization like inequality and capitalist avarice, with the idea that reforms might remedy problems; however, a pre-Marxist Hegelian analysis survives that is less sanguine and considers alienation inherent to thinking, language, and society. My question here is, what can we learn from Madhyamaka interrogations of this human situation? That is, to what extent does alienation ensue from reifications that naturally occur as consequences of everyday practices of thinking? How can we reduce the frequency with which we knot ourselves up through the ways we structure our knowing?

Dreyfus (Cowherds 2011, 106) commends the twelfth-century Tibetan thinker Patsab Nyima Drak for his attentiveness to practices that eliminate our tendency to reify knowledge, suggesting that the principal concern of late Madhyamaka thinkers is "the elimination of the reification of knowledge" and the development of ways "to counteract this tendency toward reification." The moment I noticed the seriousness with which Tibetan Buddhists tackle the problem of reification in thinking, I commenced an examination of their efforts on behalf of the sociology of knowledge tradition to which I belong. In short, I am asking what is the proper place for our *rtog pa*, or more particularly, cognition by means of formulating aspects (*rnam par rtog pa*) and, when its reference is to analytic reason, what Tsongkhapa (2002, 40) sometimes calls *rigs shes*.

Everywhere in human society there exists a compulsion to settle the unity of knowledge, to organize what we know into concise forms conducive to retention and communication and to seek to unify these forms under a single overarching structure or idea. One of my early professors Herbert Marcuse (1964, 128–29) writes, "Thinking, in its quest for the truth behind the facts, seeks a stable base for orientation, a universal and necessary law amid the endless flux and diversity of things. Such a universal, if it is really to be the beginning and the basis for all subsequent determinations, must not itself be determinate." Marcuse (1964, 130–31) commends Hegel's insight that logic as we know it "ceases to be the source of rules and forms for correct thinking. In fact, it takes rules, forms, and all categories of traditional logic to be false because they disregard the negative and contradictory nature of reality… Formal logic accepts the world-form as it is and gives some general rules for theoretical orientation to it. Dialectical logic, on the other hand, rejects any claim of sanctity for the given." Or more simply, as Hegel (1969, 831) concluded, "Dialectics is necessary to reason."

Negative Dialectics

Theodor Adorno devoted his life to clarifying the role that negative dialectics plays in European philosophy. Adorno (1973, 12) cautions against "the compulsive identification which the concept brings" and insists that thought resist the very unities of identification with which it must work. He writes, "If thinking is to be true, it must also be a thinking against itself" (Adorno 1973, 365). The task of negative dialectics is to expose the delusions of consciousness (148) by using reason against reason to promote "a disintegration of the objectified form of the concept" (145), turning our identifications toward nonidentity since "our objects do not go into their concepts" (5). Giving an object "a turn toward nonidentity is the hinge of negative dialectics" (12). I suggest that Tillemans's (2016, 58) proposition that "The Mādhyamika could cheerfully accept the truth of '*p*' and also 'not REALLY *p*'" has kinship with the perspective of negative dialectics.

The turn to negative dialectics is a strategy for remediating the excesses of reason's endless capacity to restrict us inside of how it has organized knowledge. Negative dialectics can inhibit some of the excesses that result from our compulsion to ground knowledge and fetishize certainties, which impresses me as being the acme of philosophical wisdom, and more specifically *jñāna*, European or Buddhist. That rigorous formal analytic practices themselves routinely carry scholars to a perspective where philosophizing ceases is an irony that haunts philosophical efforts everywhere and is one that Tibetan Mādhyamikas vigorously investigate.

It is the strategy of thinkers to fix identities and make meanings determinate. The Tibetans call these determinations "sign fixations" (*mtshan ma 'dzin pa*), which they accept as a path to entrenched self-delusion. One of the attractions of Tibetan epistemology is that whereas in the Western academies, the truth habits of logical positivism—what Tibetans call the *dngos po smra ba*, which Tillemans (2016, 56) has translated as "metaphysical realism"—have controlled most of the funds and positions, in the Tibetan academy it is just the reverse: the negative dialectics of Madhyamaka inquiry holds a dominant position. It is important to appreciate that the reference to *dngos po smra ba* is not simply to tenets or ideas but to *practices*. A phenomenologist like myself could not have hoped for a more congenial research environment.

Can the wisdom that realizes just-the-way-it-is (*de kho na nyid*)—that does not reify its thinking—avoid reliance upon an independent, positively grounded, and authoritative system? Can a negative dialectics lead either Europeans or Tibetans to a solution to the aporiae of analytic reasoning? According to Maurice Merleau-Ponty (1968, 39), this is far from certain, but it is the only alternative to dogmatism:

> We know neither what exactly is this order and this concordance of the world to which we thus entrust ourselves, nor therefore what the enterprise will result in, nor even if it is really possible. But the choice is between it and a dogmatism of reflection concerning which we know only too well where it goes, since with it philosophy concludes the moment it begins and, for this very reason, does not make us comprehend our own obscurity.

I suggest that this obscurity has affinity with what Tillemans and his colleagues have called *moonshadows*.

Analyzing the Ultimate

Like Tibetan Mādhyamikas, we subscribe to reason. We are sober thinkers who refuse to accept just anything. So how should we employ formal thinking for our practical benefit? According to Tsongkhapa (2002, 41), although an innate comprehension of entities as inherently existing is not produced intellectually, it can be removed by way of logical analysis and intellection. Geshé Rabten's account of his teacher Trijang Rinpoché is illustrative (Rabten 1983, 73): "Usually when he taught he would point out that no matter how difficult the view may be, it could still be proven by logic." So, in the absence of inherently existing entities, how do we ground knowledge? And what role should analytic reasoning play in establishing the view of reality?

In the *King of Meditative Stabilization Sūtra*, the Buddha himself commends formal analyses of selflessness (Hopkins 1987, 377) but cautions that one must couple the discoveries of formal analysis with meditation. Similarly, Nāgārjuna acknowledges the vital role that conventional reasoning needs to play, yet he admits that formal analytic reasoning is not the complete solution. Nāgārjuna writes (*Mūlamadhyamakakārikā* 24.10),

> Without depending upon what is conventional,
> one will be unable to teach the ultimate meaning;
> and without understanding the ultimate meaning,
> nirvāṇa will not be attained.

Conventional understanding is not to be forsaken; accordingly, logical reasoning must be sustained. However, it seems that by itself, it is insufficient for attaining the "ultimate" meaning. Logic tends to reify our thinking by searching for fixed truths and presuming real entities. One must wage a battle, continuously, against one's own philosophical tools. Yet it is those very tools with which we wage the battle.

We are also continuously constrained by social demands that accompany occasions of philosophizing for and with others, which is another component of the "conventional." Formalization, a necessary tool for any thinking that aims to communicate, was a central phenomenon examined in my ethnography of Tibetan debating (Liberman 2004, 84). These demands of communicability are always present and introduce contingencies with which every exercise of formal analytic reasoning must contend. As Newland and Tillemans (2011, 11) recognize, "we are dealing with some type of agreement between members of a community." While logic is commonly viewed as a means for ascertaining truth, my research into practices of reasoning (both among Tibetans and Europeans) reveals that from the start, logic has possessed an additional function, one that lies within the realm of what Tibetan scholars label "the conventional." Central to any employment of logic is a linguistic structure, which is the means by which collaborating thinkers are able to enhance the adequacy and clarity of their communication. That is, formalized reason provides ready analytic frameworks that enable philosophers to think together, to work on the same page. Every Tibetan debate on the monastic debate grounds includes some live production of shared bases that the debaters can use for thinking together.

The Israeli philosopher Yehoshua Bar-Hillel (1964) places the origins of logic in the civil jurisprudence that operated on the streets of ancient Greek municipalities, during which disputing parties would employ formal and objective arguments to win decisions in primitive outdoor courts. Simmel (2009, 103) says much the same about the origin of objectivity, suggesting that it was based in arbitration practices. Instead of fetishizing objectivity, Tibetan thinkers productively employ formalization as a tool, but they do so without elevating its status to ultimate truth. I suggest that Tibetan Mādhyamikas' recognition that their formal analytic reasoning is conventional, and the fact that they do not mistake it for what is ultimate, gives us further incentive for remaining attentive to what—and *how*—they undertake their investigations.

The turn of the last century Madhyamaka scholar Shamar Gendun Tenzin (Shamar 2012, 418) considers the relation between inferential reasoning and what is ultimate when he comments on Nāgārjuna's *Mūlamadhyamakakārikā* 24.10:

> By severing the proliferation of all dualistic thinking, the ultimate will manifest. While inferential thought derived from analytic reasoning can impede excessive conceptual elaborations about the true existence of an object, such reasoning can never sever the proliferation of dualistic thinking entirely.

Shamar reaffirms the status of ultimate reality, but he suggests that it is impossible to be utterly without conceptual elaborations while inferring an "ultimate truth." In the same passage, Shamar (2012, 420) cites Tsongkhapa from the *Ocean of Reasoning* (*Rtsa she tik chen*): "Reality and the fabrication of appearances are inextricable" (cf. Samten and Garfield 2006, 495). From the Gelukpa perspective, absence is not separable from presence, and so even a direct witnessing of just-the-way-it-is must include some reference to dualistic thinking.

Shamar (2012, 421) comments, "Some say that when formal analysis uses inferential reasoning (*rigs shes rjes dpag*) to comprehend (*rtogs*) the noematic correlate (the object universal; *don spyi*) of emptiness and negate objectifications, no implied traces of objectification remain, yet according to the *Ocean of Reasoning*, except for merely holding the notion 'Analytic reasoning has grasped that there are no inherent essences,' it seems doubtful that all explicit and implicit objectifications have actually been eliminated." Does not a reliance upon a noematic correlate entail a degree of objectification? At the same time, it is not quite a satisfactory solution to hold that an ultimate truth occurs when one perceives emptiness directly without any noematic correlate, for what this can consist of is uncertain. Even worse, making it certain will contaminate it. This is what it means to be condemned to reason.

Gendun Chöphel takes an even more radical position: "Ultimate analysis is necessarily a conventional consciousness" (cited in Lopez 2006, 105). Chöphel (Chopel 2009, 52, my translation) expands the problem this way:

> Inferential valid knowledge is derived from direct perception,
>   yet inference evaluates whether direct perception is true or
>   false:

the child is judging the father.

This formulation of conventional validation is unsettling.

Just what is "ultimate meaning," which is the telos of Madhyamaka practice? Do the Mādhyamikas not need something more than "merely an understanding of the ultimate through concepts" (Dreyfus and Garfield 2011, 119)? Can we somehow reach the nonrepresented ultimate via representations? Just what is it that the person who has completed the so-called path of seeing is seeing?

The Mādhyamikas' Toolbox

Mādhyamikas use a variety of practices for applying what Dreyfus and Garfield (2011, 122) call "the relentlessly skeptical negative dialectic" to their truth habits. Here we review some features of "the negative approach favored by Gelukpa versions of Prāsaṅgika Madhyamaka" (Jackson 2019, 372) and describe resources they bring to bear upon the reification of thinking.

Projection (*btags pa, kun btags*)

In the very earliest stages of Tibetan students' careers, young scholars are confronted with the discovery that their thinking is constructed by notions that they themselves project (*btags*) upon their experience. The notion of projection or imputation has played an important role in epistemology from the beginning. Graham Priest (2002, 41–44) has outlined the skepticism of Sextus Empiricus (second century), which involves a total suspension of one's commitment to any rationally formulated reasoning, a suspension that can lead one to an equipoise Sextus called *epoché*. Edmund Husserl picked up this notion of *epoché* and built his methodology for phenomenology around it, since suspending one's belief (any affirmation or denial) can expose naïve presuppositions we have adopted blindly and projected upon experience, as well as synthetic unities that consciousness has constructed for organizing those notions—that is, their "construction of them into a structure" (Matilal 1986, 24).

The basic curriculum of the Collected Topics (*bsdus grwa*) naturally leads students to a transcendental *epoché*, which remedies their inattentiveness to how their minds have always already infiltrated their world. Tillemans (forthcoming) observes that the Collected Topics has been undervalued by modern researchers. For the Tibetans, the task of removing intellectual obscurations has a lengthy itinerary, but it begins with Collected Topics. In an online interview, Thupten Jinpa described this task as follows: "Those who approach emptiness via an analytic method have the task to go ever deeper in removing the layers and layers of our superimpositions." The purpose of the *epoché* is to allow a person to take a step backward from their reflections and witness their antecedent syntheses that turned their perceptions and concepts into a unity.

Madhyamaka literature advocates reining in our projected elaborations (*spros pa*; *prapañca*). Nāgārjuna, in *Mūlamadhyamakakārikā* 18.5, deftly indicates that proliferating thoughts only generate more proliferating thoughts (*spros pas spros pa*). It is insufficient simply to complain that all thoughts are false; we must identify the specific way in which each thought usurps our world, even though these thoughts, taken together, are like a runaway train. And we must accomplish this while desisting from instituting further mechanisms of self-delusion. One thought takes off following another like a continuously branching tree. Observing how the projection of our thoughts actively contributes to the world we experience is an elementary epistemological step, and this "transcendental" dimension (Husserl 1969) comes as a happy revelation to most students. Observing the architecture of the reflexivity (cf. Garfinkel 2002, 203–4) of these meanings we project— that is, how what our understanding projects into a situation is used as a resource and an organizing pole for our further assembling the intelligibility of the situation—this is a vigilance we cannot set aside if we are to avoid deluding ourselves.

The reductio ad absurdum (*thal 'gyur*)

Drawing out one's thinking to its absurd consequences (*thal 'gyur*) can awaken original insight. Marcuse (1960, ix) observes, "The principle of dialectic drives thought beyond the limits of philosophy." We can avoid believing our own propaganda by undermining (*gnod*) how we have built up the world, and we use dialectics to reduce the force that our thoughts have over us. Tsongkhapa (1997, 758) explains the *reductio ad absurdum* this way: "Inferential knowledge can be gained based upon consequences that expose contradictions in our thinking, without employing a formal proposition (*sbyor ngag*) that proves a thesis directly." This is the famous deconstructive method of the consequential reasoning used by Nāgārjuna in *Mūlamadhyamakakārikā* 20.16:

> If a cause is empty of an effect,
> how can it produce an effect?
> If a cause is not empty of an effect,
> how can it produce an effect?

Rather than relying upon something like a formal syllogism, the notion of the independence of causes and effects is undermined by posing questions about the consequences that presuming that they bear an independent existence would have. When one's dialectical partner is placed in a quandary and left with no place to turn, the way is opened for more original thinking. Negative dialectics continuously decompose the proliferation of reifications (*mtshan ma*) by confounding our categories, exposing contradictions, and forcing us to abandon our truth habits. Nowhere is human knowledge able to progress in the absence of critical examination and negation.

Public debate forums (*chos ra*)

In the Tibetan academies, public debating exploits the beneficial role that negation can play in repairing, sharpening, and deconstructing knowledge. Debaters rely upon what Tillemans (2016, 29) calls "logical reasoning that pushes one's limits." The point is to confound our thinking to the point of disrupting our analytic practices that have become routine. It is the aim of negative dialectics to be constantly pulling the rug out from under our thinking, and in the Tibetan monastic universities, others are always nearby to help us do this work. This occurs daily in the debating courtyards, where fellow monks take turns laboring at transforming routine thinking into fudge. When the dialectics in the debating courtyard is working properly, not only does it furnish a cohort of dialectical thinkers who monitor the logic of our reasoning, it also provides practitioners who mutually and reciprocally monitor the scope of each other's *jñāna* and bring collective wisdom to bear upon misapplications or excesses of reason. *Jñāna* is reason that has retained some sense for when its employment is appropriate. It not only reasons clearly; it recognizes its limits.

Tibetan debaters are highly adept at exploiting the resources that irony can provide for immobilizing thinking. Here are two excerpts, taken from transcribed live debates that topicalized the aporia to which formal analytic reasoning regarding emptiness can lead. The challengers attempt to entangle a defender in his logical formulations that refute inherent existence only by outward relations but do not necessarily entail an actual realization of emptiness. The point of each challenger's dialectics is to loosen the threads of a tightly organized logical argument and lead the defender to experience a naturally occurring *epoché* that affords them a seminal moment for philosophical growth and insight. The rendition attempts to replicate the prosodic qualities of the debaters' speech and physical actions and not just rotely translate its literal content.

> Challenger: When the object of attachment produced by an
> imputed reification is refuted, it follows that one does not
> necessarily realize emptiness. [Handclap]
> Defender: I acce—But by what reason does it follow that one
> does not necessarily realize emptiness? There must be a real-
> ization of emptiness.

And in another debate from the same debate grounds, where the audience also chimes in,

> Challenger: A person who abides in the Middle Way view of
> this system must necessarily be a person who has realized the
> Middle Way view as explained by this system. [Handclap]
> Defender: It is necessary.
> Challenger: It does not follow that a person who abides in
> the view that all things do not exist according to their own
> inherent characteristics is necessarily a person who abides in
> the view as explained by this system. [Handclap]
> Defender: *CHEE-CHEER*! [*phyi phyir*, "I reject that
> assertion!"]
> Audience [many yell at once]: IT DOES PERVADE!
> Challenger: It does not follow that, this fine distinction, that a
> person who abides in the Middle Way view as it is explained
> in this system necessarily realizes "just-the-way-it-is" as it is
> explained by this system. [Handclap]
> Defender: There is not necessarily such a *realization*. It is only
> necessary that he *accept* it.
> Challenger: [Reverse hand-slap] *tsa*! [*tshar*, "You are being con-
> tradictory!"] [Reverse hand-slap] *tsa*!

The point of this debate is that one can subscribe to a course of logically ordered reasoning about emptiness without having gained genuine insight or developed real experience regarding emptiness. When made routine, rigorous formal analytic practices can carry scholars to a perspective where philosophizing ceases. This debating converts what is a docile philosophical notion into a *dynamic* and alert philosophical praxis. Its primary achievement lies not in the logical value of its ideation but in how actively it entraps the thinking of the defender inside the irony. The aims of such negative dialectics are practical, which can be more instructive than simply reading a philosophical text while sitting on one's sofa. Debating is an important instrument in the negative dialectic tool chest.

Cultivation (*goms*)

If one genuinely wishes to relinquish one's hold upon one's truth habits, the understanding one gains must be made operative at an instinctual level of behavior (*bag chags*). Tsongkhapa (1997, 791) tells us that merely making an assertion or formulating a thesis is insufficient; one must analyze matters carefully with reasoning and then *sustain* the perspective that results from those analyses. Genuine understanding is not sufficient: one must cultivate continual familiarization with this understanding, which is accomplished by a meditative stabilization that is centered upon the results of "an analytic wisdom" (*shes rab kyi dpyad pa*) that has investigated the aspects (*so sor rtog pa*) that are in play. Analysis alone is incapable of reaching deeply enough to transform our latent propensities (*bag chags*). One needs to meditate while sustaining an understanding that proceeds from analysis (Tsongkhapa 1997, 783). Similarly, Paṇchen Losang Chökyi Gyaltsen (2013, 54) emphasizes that even learned yogis with much experience engage in analytic reflection (*dpyad nas sgom pa*).

By itself, nonconceptual (*mi rtog pa*) meditative stabilization is insufficient; nevertheless, analytic wisdom can culminate in a nonconceptual state. Tillemans (2023, 238) notes that "The particularity of the Mādhyamikas, including Āryadeva, is that they emphasize philosophical analysis as a method leading to that quietening of thought." Tsongkhapa (1997, 798–99) explains in some detail, "Analytic meditation is capable, by its own power, of drawing out of one an experience of extreme pliancy . . . When it is able to draw out such pliancy, it also establishes single-pointed concentration, and that enables an analytic meditation's discriminative investigation of matters to enhance serenity (*zhi gnas*). For one who has established serenity well, analytic meditation is an ally, so do not entertain any notion that an analytic meditation's investigation of matters will reduce one's serenity." Further, the process of knowing itself can become the basis for the meditative stabilization, as the active flow of one's mindstream can become both the object and the subject. This is a moment, common in tantra, when being is identified with one's consciousness, which Timalsinha (2022, 314) suggests is a central aspect of meditative praxis.

A realization of the suchness of phenomena that proceeds from a wisdom that has pacified the generation of notions of inherent existence can naturally lead to a state of peace. In other words, negative dialectics can lead one to a bliss (*sukha*) of *jñāna*, and the capacity of reason to have transformative influences upon the body's energy should not be overlooked. Also, it can be noted that sometimes the poetics itself of Nāgārjuna's negative dialectics is able to carry us to a *sukha* of *jñāna*, and at times Nāgārjuna is not so much attempting to resolve contradictions as to embrace them, for their salubrious effects.

For Mādhyamikas the act of understanding emptiness is the *śunyatā jñāna*, the wisdom regarding the emptiness of inherent essences. A mantra dedicated to this aspiration is inserted several times into the important daily Guhyasamāja *sādhana*: *Oṃ śūnyatā jñāna vajra svabhāvā ātmako 'ham* ("I myself *am* the nature of indestructible wisdom regarding emptiness"). What is the status of this mantra? At one of the culminating points of this sixty-folio daily practice, the meditative stabilization centers upon a visualization that actively simulates or embodies this *śunyatā jñāna*. In the section of the Guhyasamāja *sādhana* known as "the three bodies" or "the three-tiered beings" (cf. Lobsang Jampa 2019, 612), much recommended by the Fourteenth Dalai Lama, one appears as a blue Vajradhara in whose heart, sitting on a moon seat, is a red wisdom being who is embracing a like-formed consort, and "through their union, the wisdom being and his consort cause my body to thrive" (Lobsang Jampa 2019, 611). The third "tier" involves another moon cushion at the red wisdom being's heart, on which a *vajra* stands, bearing in its center a blue *hūṃ* syllable, which is the concentration being. Gyumé Khensur Lobsang Jampa (2019, 340) explains, "This object is said to be 'ever-shining' because it represents the mental aspect of your most subtle combination of wind and mind, which never ceases to exist." The indestructible being aspect is due to our being interconnectedly related to everything that has previously existed.

It is at this climactic moment that a knowledge consort emerges from one's heart, stimulating one to recite the above mantra, after which the consort dissolves into emptiness. With this mantra, one is not engaged simply in striving to *know* the emptiness of inherent essences; one is rehearsing *being* that emptiness. Ultimate being, emptiness, sexuality, and one's subtle combination of wind and mind become identified with each other, with wisdom regarding emptiness playing a central role.

Paṇchen Losang Chökyi Gyaltsen (n.d., 75) explains a similar section of the *sādhana* where the *śunyatā* mantra is invoked: "The yogi who is an accomplished practitioner, invoking thirty-two deities in undividable union at thirty-two locations of the body, abides in a pacification of dualistic proliferations." After this is accomplished, one recites the *śunyatā* mantra, and the Paṇchen Lama advises practitioners to "consider deeply the mantra's meaning," specifying that the *śūnyatā* mantra is used as a vehicle for cultivating a highly stabilized indivisible union of wisdom and bliss. Negative dialectics is implicit in the pacification of dualistic proliferations and in the assertion (see subsequent section) that "No meditation is perceivable," which undercuts the foundation of the very activity of meditating, in which the practitioner has been engaged. The efficacy of negative dialectics in this practice depends upon the acumen of the practitioner, and we should be mindful that we are dealing not simply with tantric forms that work by themselves or by magic but with how the practitioner understands and institutes these forms.

Practices of steadfast nonabiding (*rab tu mi gnas pa*)

The fact that Buddhist philosophy takes for its topic the ways that philosophy betrays itself offers little protection against its betraying itself anyway. This is part of the aporia of philosophical praxis, or what Priest (2002, 33) calls "contradiction at the limit of thought." The Tibetans describe their remedy in several ways: *mi gnas pa* (nonabiding), *dmigs med* (abstinence from dualistic conceiving), and *rnam par dben pa* (without anything at all). A practice of nonabiding affords no room for exceptions: one must avoid an addictive relation with one's own thoughts, without fixating upon the results of one's thinking, analytic or otherwise. Emptiness is not a thing. It is an epistemic practice. Śāntideva (1998, 264) commends nonabiding that undermines becoming attached or addicted to reified signs (*mtshan ma*). Further, in a stunning repudiation of reificatory practice, Śāntideva cites the Buddha's instruction from the *Ugraparipṛcchā Sūtra*, "What is called 'living in a remote retreat' (*dgon pa*) is living without abiding in dependence upon any absolute basis whatsoever" (*chos thams cad la mi brten par gnas pa'o*).

Tibetan negative dialectics is a vigilant attack upon objectification and reification. The first stanza of Nāgārjuna's *Reason Sixty* (Loizzo 2007, 218) addresses the *mi gnas pa* (nonabiding), offering a way to avoid subscribing to one's own propaganda. The same stanza also commends "profound abstinence from conceiving" (*dmigs med*). Nothing that we think should become a truth habit, and this also applies to spiritual practices. Tsongkhapa (1988, 59) elaborates, "If one thinks, 'I have obtained the fruit of a stream-enterer,' it is a form of reifying experience." Unfortunately, negative dialectics itself can fall prey to what Siderits (2011, 172) has called "*svabhāva*-mongering."

Rnam par dben pa, remaining utterly unconfined by one's own thinking, also appears in Nāgārjuna's *Reason Sixty* (stanza 30), and similar advice reappears in various forms throughout Buddhist epistemological literature. Dialectics is always ready to pull the rug out from under one (even delighted to do so—think dancing *ḍākinīs*). In his *Middle-Length Lamrim*, Tsongkhapa (1999, 373) speaks of abandoning constructs (*mtshan 'dzin spong ba*). Negative dialectics is like carrying a pugnacious Jiminy Cricket on one's shoulder all the time. Importantly, again, practice is more important than theory.

Suchness (*chos nyid*) itself does not escape this praxis. Tsongkhapa (1997, 646) writes, "Suchness, the ultimate reality, does not possess even a shred of inherent nature." In verse 58 of *Reason Sixty*, Nāgārjuna (Loizzo 2007, 237) advises those who are devoted to detachment to evolve beyond the piety of being detached; and in verse 20, he brilliantly undermines the idea of there being anything corresponding to the label "termination" (*zad*) by arguing that what has no inherent being cannot possibly be "terminated."

There is a consummate example of deconstructing one's practice during a critical section of the Guhyasamāja sādhana. Just when one has become comfortable sustaining an intricate meditative visualization, the *sādhana* states, "There is no meditation upon a nonexistent. Nor is meditation, indeed, meditation" (cf. Engle in Lobsang Jampa 2019, 203). An abstinence from conceptualizing must prevail, and from this *sādhana*, "No meditation is perceivable" (*dmigs su med pa*). In a *coup de grâce*, the text (Lobsang Jampa 2019, 570) proclaims, "Since phenomena have no ultimate nature, the three aspects—meditation, an object meditated upon, and a meditator—are not perceived" (*sgoms pa dang bsgom par bya ba dang sgom pa po gsum mi dmigs pa*). Practitioners who are engaging in truth addictions regarding their meditative practice are left with no leg to stand on. Similarly, the *Heart Sūtra* says, "There is no attainment and also no nonattainment."

Negative dialectics doesn't only address the profound; it operates during every mundane course of thinking. Gendun Chöphel (Chopel 2009, 52) raises the everyday example of the true existence of a friend: "A friend's aspects are reified and then grasped as real." Self-delusion like this operates in most mundane interactions one has with one's friends or colleagues. As Lama Thubten Yeshe (1998, 41) summarizes, "Not only are we wide open to whatever intellectual garbage comes our way, we've got a big welcome sign out." Or as Nāgārjuna (Loizzo 2007, 227) describes it, "Our minds are an insufferable city of our delusions." Negative dialectics in the form of a variety of essential tools constitutes effective means for taming this city of our minds.

Conclusion

Practices of negative dialectics decompose the rigid edifice of our conceptual constructions and replace it with "an ascertaining consciousness that recognizes the way phenomena exist in just the way they exist" (Tsongkhapa 1997,

652). To illustrate this, we can travel around the landscape with the notion "river" in hand, naming rivers, but there are only molecules of water (themselves adventitious phenomena) being driven about by gravity and the shape of the landscape: there is no river identity, although there is something that can be conventionally designated as flowing. According to Madhyamaka thinking, it is not that we should avoid pragmatic uses of conventional notions like "river"; it is only that we must remain mindful of the actual state of things and recognize phenomena just the way they are. This latter is the interdependent arising of phenomena, with no intrinsic arising.

Logic and dialectics have developed together. Truth exceeds reason yet is founded upon it, an irony that may not be resolvable. Logic and dialectics need each other, which may be why Tibetans retain both *pramāṇa*—valid cognition—and negative dialectics. To say that logic cannot secure certainty is a facile observation—the point is how we best employ reason effectively. In skillful hands and with continuous supervision, analytic thinking assists us. As José Cabezón (1994, 51) has opined,

> The dGe lugs pas . . . believe themselves to be true to their intellectual predecessors in attempting to strike this very delicate balance . . . It is not unfair to characterize the entire dGe lugs pa philosophical enterprise as an attempt to maintain this balance between the necessity and the ultimate inadequacy of scripture as a necessary means but insufficient end.

Finally, it is probable that some initial philosophical impulses from India arrived in Persian courts during pre-Socratic times (McEvilley 2002, 9–11) and inspired Greek thinkers, who took the ideas home and radicalized them, developing both the syllogism and a robust negative dialectics. These returned to India with Alexander, whereupon Indian thinkers adapted them to their own uses. In any event, it certainly has always been a two-way street, and here the collection of us, a monomaniacal cohort of rationally committed dialecticians, are evidence that this global collaboration of philosophical cultures is not going to ebb any time soon, as the philosophical career of Tom Tillemans makes plain. We are all in agreement here—conceptual understanding is not to be forsaken, but one needs to wage a continual battle against the very philosophical tools we routinely use. The Tibetans offer up a splendid set of methods, but how—just how, and under what conditions—do they put them into practice and make them efficacious? In other words, how and when can *Homo sapiens* achieve genuine epistemic success?

Bibliography

Adorno, Theodor. 1973. *Negative Dialectics.* New York: Continuum.

Bar-Hillel, Yehoshua. 1964. "Bgidat Halogicanum" [Logician's Treason]. *Iyyun* 63: 359–79.

Cabezón, José. 1994. *Buddhism and Language: A Study of Indo-Tibetan Scholasticism.* Albany: State University of New York Press.

Chopel, Gendun. 2009. *In the Forest of Faded Wisdom: 104 Poems.* Translated by Donald S. Lopez Jr. Chicago: University of Chicago Press.

Cowherds, the. 2011. *Moonshadows: Conventional Truth in Buddhist Philosophy.* New York: Oxford University Press.

Dreyfus, Georges. 2011. "Can a *Mādhyamika* Be a Skeptic?" In Cowherds 2011, 89–113.

Dreyfus, Georges, and Jay L. Garfield, "Madhyamaka and Classical Greek Skepticism." In Cowherds 2011, 115–30.

Garfinkel, Harold. 2002. *Ethnomethodology's Program.* Lanham, MD: Rowman & Littlefield.

Hegel, G. W. F. 1969. *Science of Logic.* New York: George Allen & Unwin.

Hopkins, Geoffrey. 1987. *Emptiness Yoga.* Ithaca, NY: Snow Lion.

Husserl, Edmund. 1969. *Formal and Transcendental Logic.* The Hague: Martinus Nijhoff.

Jackson, Roger R. 2019. *Mind Seeing Mind: Mahāmudrā and the Geluk Tradition of Tibetan Buddhism.* Studies in Indian and Tibetan Buddhism. Somerville, MA: Wisdom Publications.

Liberman, Kenneth. 2004. *Dialectical Practice in Tibetan Philosophical Culture: An Ethnomethodological Inquiry into Formal Reasoning.* Lanham, MD: Rowman & Littlefield.

———. 2022. *Tasting Coffee: An Inquiry into Objectivity.* Albany: State University of New York Press.

Lobsang Jampa, Gyume Khensur. 2019. *Guhyasamāja Practice in the Ārya Nāgārjuna System.* Translated and annotated by Artemus Engle. Boulder: Snow Lion.

Loizzo, Joseph John. 2007. *Nāgārjuna's "Reason Sixty" with Chandrakīrti's "Reason Sixty Commentary."* New York: American Institute of Buddhist Studies.

Lopez Jr., Donald S. 2006. *The Madman's Middle Way.* Chicago: University of Chicago Press.

Marcuse, Herbert. 1960. *Reason and Revolution.* Boston: Beacon Press.

———. 1964. *Negations.* Boston: Beacon Press.

Matilal, Bimal. 1986. *Perception.* Oxford: Clarendon Press.

McEvilley, Thomas. 2002. *The Shape of Ancient Thought.* New York: Allworth Press.

Merleau-Ponty, Maurice. 1968. *The Visible and the Invisible.* Evanston, IL: Northwestern University Press.

Newland, Guy, and Tom J. F. Tillemans. 2011. "An Introduction to Conventional Truth." In Cowherds 2011, 3–22.

Panchen Losang Chökyi Gyaltsen [Paṇ chen Blo bzang chos kyi rgyal mtshan]. 2013. *Dge ldan bkha' rgyud rin po che'i phyag chen rtsa ba rgyal ba'i gzhung lam.* Bylakuppe, India: Tashi Lhunpo Library. Translated in Jackson 2019, 461–79.

———. n.d. *Bskyed rim dngos grub kyi rgyas mtsho'i rim nga gsal sgron* [*Commentary Clarifying the Generation Stage of the Ocean of Attainments*]. Lhasa: Ser gtsug nang bstan dpe rnying 'tshol bsdu phyogs sgrig kang. English translation by Yael Bentor and Penpa Dorjee, *The Essence of the Ocean of Attainments* (Somerville, MA: Wisdom Publications, 2019).

Priest, Graham. 2002. *Beyond the Limits of Thought.* Oxford: Clarendon Press.

Rabten, Geshe. 1983. *Echoes of Voidness.* Translated by Stephen Batchelor. London: Wisdom Publications.

Samten, Geshe Ngawang, and Jay L. Garfield, trans. 2006. *Ocean of Reasoning: A Great Commentary on Nāgārjuna's Mūlamadhyamakakārikā* by rJe Tsong khapa. New York: Oxford University Press.

Shamar Gendun Tenzin (Zhwa dmar Dge 'dun bstan 'dzin, 1852–1912). 2012. *Byang chub lam gyi rim pa'i khrid yig, vol. 4.* Manipal, India: Yongzin Lingtsang Labrang.

Siderits, Mark. 2011. "Is Everything Connected to Everything Else?" In Cowherds 2011, 167–80.

Simmel, Georg. 2009. *Sociology Inquiries into the Construction of Social Forms.* Leiden: Brill.

Śāntideva. 1998. *Bslab pa kun btus* [*Śikṣāsamuccaya*]. Kathmandu: Modern Printing Press.

Tillemans, Tom J. F. 2016. *How Do Mādhyamikas Think? And Other Essays on the Buddhist Philosophy of the Middle.* Studies in Indian and Tibetan Buddhism. Somerville, MA: Wisdom Publications.

———. 2023. "Āryadeva." In *The Routledge Handbook of Indian Buddhist Philosophy*, edited by William Edelglass, Pierre-Julien Harter, and Sara McClintock, 236–51. London: Routledge.

———. 2025. "Pramāṇa in Tibet: Debate Traditions (Bsdus grwa)." In *Brill's Encyclopedia of Buddhism Online*, edited by Jonathan A. Silk, Richard Bowring, and Vincent Eltschinger. Brill. https://doi.org/10.1163/2467-9666_enbo_COM_3128.

Timalsinha, Sthaneshwar. 2022. "The Phenomenology of Meditation: An Advaita Approach." In *The Routledge Handbook of the Philosophy of Meditation*, edited by Rick Repetti, 313–26. London: Routledge.

Tsongkhapa (Tsong kha pa Blo bzang grags pa). 1988. *Dbu ma dgongs pa rab gsal.* Sarnath: Gelukpa Students Welfare Committee. Translated in *Illuminating the Intent: A Commentary on Candrakīrti's Entering the Middle Way* (Somerville, MA: Wisdom Publications, 2021).

———. 1997. *Lam rim chen mo.* Amdo, China: The Blue Lake Publishing House. Translated in *The Great Treatise on the Stages of the Path to Enlightenment*, 3 vols. (Ithaca, NY: Snow Lion Publications, 2000–2004).

———. 1999. *Lam rim 'bring ba.* Bylakuppe, India: Sera Je Library Computer Project. Translated in *The Middle-Length Treatise on the Stages of the Path to Enlightenment* (Somerville, MA: Wisdom Publications, 2021).

———. 2002. *Rtsa shes tik chen.* Karwar, India: Drepung Gomang Monastery. Translated in Samten and Garfield 2006.

Yeshe, Lama Thubten. 1998. *Becoming Your Own Therapist.* Boston: Lama Yeshe Wisdom Archive.

Symmetric Existential Dependence Relations in Madhyamaka

Jan Westerhoff

THE WORK OF Tom Tillemans is characterized by detailed knowledge of the Indian and Tibetan Buddhist sources, combined with a focus on systematic questions these sources raise, often discussed against the background of key developments in contemporary Western analytic philosophy. In his discussions he has often shown how analysis of specific concepts (such as *sapakṣa*, *āśrayāsiddha*, or *samāropa*, to name but a few) can give us an insight into the tremendous complexity of the conceptual structures of which these form a part. In this paper I will investigate a single notion in a somewhat similar manner: that of symmetric dependence relations in Madhyamaka. Not only is this notion quite perplexing in itself, but it also, so I argue, provides a direct link to key Madhyamaka ideas.

Dependence relations play a large role in Madhyamaka thought. This is hardly surprising; given that the principal target of Madhyamaka refutations, the notion of *svabhāva*, is characterized as standing outside of the network of dependence relations,[1] to argue for the ubiquity of dependence relations is a central step in advancing Madhyamaka's theory of emptiness.

Often Madhyamaka characterizes dependence relations as symmetric.[2] For example, Nāgārjuna refers to the relation between long and short, nearer and further shore, agent and object, knower and object known, or epistemic instrument and epistemic object:[3]

---

1. Nāgārjuna, *Mūlamadhyamakakārikā*, 15.2b: "*svabhāva* is not adventitious, and not dependent on something else," *akṛtrimaḥ svabhāvo hi nirapekṣaḥ paratra ca* (Siderits and Katsura 2013, 155).

2. Symmetric dependence relations also play a key role in the Huayan school. See Odin 1982, 27–31.

3. There are also passages where Madhyamaka appears to reject symmetric dependence relations

But when, due to not being essentially so, there is no short, then there is no long. And when a lamp's flame is not produced, light also does not arise.[4]

When there is own-ness, there is other-ness; when other-ness, own-ness is accepted; the proof of these two is said to be mutual, like this shore and the other shore.[5]

The agent occurs in dependence on the object, and the object occurs in dependence on the agent; we see no other way to establish them.[6]

There is no object of knowledge unless it is being known. Consciousness does not exist without it. Therefore you have said that knowledge and its object do not exist substantially.[7]

The epistemic instrument is established from the epistemic object, and the epistemic object is also established from the epistemic instrument. Therefore the epistemic instrument becomes the epistemic object's epistemic object, and the epistemic object also becomes the epistemic instrument's epistemic instrument.[8]

These are examples of what we might call *conceptual dependence relations*: two concepts form a pair such that we cannot make sense of one without the other. We cannot understand what it means to be short without also understanding what it means to be long, what it means to be our own without understand-

(see, e.g., *Mūlamadhyamakakārikā* 10.10, 11.5, and 20.7). What is rejected in these cases, however, is the idea that one could simultaneously accept the symmetric dependence of two entities while also holding that one or both of them exist by *svabhāva*.

4. *Ratnāvalī* 1.49 (McClintock and Dunne 2024, 84); *hrasve 'sati punar dīrgham na bhavaty asvabhāvataḥ / pradīpasyāpy anutpādāt prabhāyā apy asaṃbhavaḥ //* (Hahn 1982, 20).

5. *Acintyastava* verse 1: *svatve sati paratve syāt paratve svatvam iṣyate / āpekṣikī tayoḥ siddhiḥ pārāvāram ivoditā //* (Lindtner 1982, 144).

6. *Mūlamadhyamakakārikā* 8.12: *pratītya kārakaḥ karma taṃ pratītya ca kārakam / karma pravartate nānyat paśyāmaḥ siddhikāraṇam //* (Siderits and Katsura 2013, 96–97). See also Aitken 2021, 15n50.

7. *Lokātītastava* verse 10: *ajñāyamānaṃ na jñeyaṃ vijñānaṃ tad vinā na ca / tasmāt svabhāvato na sto jñānajñeye tvam ūcivān* (Lindtner 1982, 132).

8. *Vaidalyaprakaraṇa* on *Vaidalyasūtra* 2: *gzhal bya las tshad ma grub pa dang / tshad ma las kyang gzhal bya grub par byas nas / tshad ma ni gzhal ba'i gzhal byar 'gyur la / gzhal bya yang tshad ma'i tshad mar 'gyur ba* (Tola and Dragonetti 1995, 22).

ing what it means to belong to another, what it means to be an agent without understanding what it means to be an object, what it means to know something without understanding what the object known is, or what it means to be an epistemic instrument without understanding what its object is. In each case the two concepts form a mutually implicative pair, where the presence of one requires the other. As such this dependence relation is also an *existential* dependence relation. One concept could not exist without the other existing; we could not conceive of a network of concepts containing only the concepts "long" or "our own" without also containing the concepts "short" or "another's" (at least as when the network includes the familiar logical relations). As a consequence, the concepts depend on one another for their existence.

Other instances of dependence relations described in Madhyamaka literature as symmetric are somewhat more puzzling, such as the relation between father and son and that between part and whole. Regarding the pair of father and son, Nāgārjuna notes that

> A father is not a son, a son is not a father. The two do not exist without mutual correlation. Nor are they simultaneous. The twelve members likewise.[9]

> If the son is to be produced by the father and if the father is to be produced by this very son, you have to say which produces which in this context.[10]

The same example is taken up later by Śāntideva:

> If you say the father is not without the son, from where is the
>   existence of the son?
> While the son does not exist, the father does not exist, the exis-
>   tence of these two is like that.[11]

---

9. *Śūnyatāsaptati* verse 13: *pha ni bu min bu pha min // de gnyis phan tshun med min la / de gnyis cig car yang min ltar // yan lang bcu gnyis de bzhin no /* (Lindtner 1982, 40–41).

10. *Vigrahavyāvartanī* 49: *pitra yady utpādyaḥ putro yadi tena caiva putreṇa / utpādyaḥ sa yadi pitā vada tatrotpādayati kaḥ kaṃ* (Yonezawa 2008, 294).

11. *Bodhicaryāvatāra* 9.114: *pitā cen na vinā putrāt kutaḥ putrasya sambhavaḥ / putrābhāve pitā nāsti tathā sattvaṃ tayor dvayoḥ* (Vaidya 1960, 257). Prajñākaramati comments on this passage: "If without the son, apart from the son, there is no father, no producer, since his designation presupposes the generation of a son, then through what will the son arise? From what, because of what, because of the nonexistence of the father, will the son, the one to be produced, arise, be born? If one asks why, the reason is stated as in the absence of the son there is no father.

Speaking about causes and effects more generally, Nāgārjuna notes:

> A cause has an effect when the effect exists; when that does not
> exist, it is like a non-cause.[12]

In relation to parts and wholes, Nāgārjuna points out that

> Because there is no whole, there are no parts.[13]

And Candrakīrti adds

> If the chariot were the mere collection, chariotness would abide
> precisely in the heap [of parts]. It is also not reasonable that the
> chariot is the mere shape since the parts do not exist without the
> whole.[14]

Because in the absence—given the nonexistence—of the son, there is no father, then the father does not exist, for the son is to be produced by the father. And to the extent that he does not produce the son, the father himself does not exist. And to the extent the father does not exist, the son does not arise from him. Hence, because they are based on each other, through the nonexistence of one, the other would be nonexistent. Therefore that both those two are nonexistent is the overall meaning." *pitā janakaḥ yadi putraṃ vinā putram antareṇa na syāt, putrajananasāpekṣatvād asya vyapadeśasya, tarhi kutaḥ putrasya saṃbhavaḥ, kutaḥ kasmāt pitur abhāvāt putrasya janyasya saṃbhavaḥ janma astu? kim iti cet, putrābhāve pitā nāsti / hetupadam etat / yataḥ putrasya abhāve asattve pitā nāsti na bhavati / pitrā hi putro janayitavyaḥ / sa ca na putraṃ yāvaj janayati, tāvat pitaiva na bhavati / yāvac ca pitā na bhavati, tāvat putrasya tasmāt saṃbhavo nāsti / ataḥ itaretarāśrayaṇād ekābhāvād anyatarābhāvaḥ syād iti dvayor apy anayor abhāva iti samudāyārthaḥ* (Vaidya 1960, 257).

12. *Śūnyatāsaptati* verse 6: *'bras yod 'bras dang ldan pa'i rgyu // de med na ni rgyu min mtshungs* (Lindtner 1982, 36–37). Compare also *Mūlamadhyamakakārikā* 4.3b: "There is no cause that is without an effect," *nāsty akāryaṃ ca kāraṇam* (Siderits and Katsura 2013, 53); *Prasannapadā* on *Mūlamadhyamakakārikā* 4.3: "The causeness of the cause has as a cause the coming about of the effect; the coming about of the effect cannot be established as separate from a cause that is independent of an effect. A cause without an effect, as it is not a cause, does not exist anymore than the horn of a man, a snake, or a horse." *kāraṇasya hi kāraṇatve kāryapravṛttir hetuḥ, kāryanirapekṣāc ca kāraṇāt pṛthak siddhā nāsti kāryapravṛttiḥ / yac cākāryakaṃ kāraṇaṃ tan nirhetukatvān naror agaturagaviṣāṇavan nāsti* (La Vallée Poussin 1992a, 124.9–10). See also May 1959, 89–90; Āryadeva, *Catuḥśataka*, 9.8: "A cause that lacks an effect does not have the property of being a cause," *'bras bu med par rgyu la ni / rgyu nyid yod pa ma yin te* (Lang 1986, 90).

13. *Vaidalyaprakaraṇa* verse 33: *yan lag can med pa'i phyir yan lag yod pa ma yin no* (Tola and Dragonetti 1995, 35).

14. *Madhyamakāvatāra* 6.152: *saṃhātamātraṃ hi ratho yadi syāt kūṭasthiteṣv eva bhaved rathatvam / saṃsthānamātraṃ ca ratho na yuktaḥ santy aṅginaṅgāni vinā na yasmād* (Li 2015, 23).

> If you say that the chariot does not exist, at that time, without
> a whole, its parts also do not exist. Just as when the chariot has
> been burned up, the parts do not exist, likewise when the whole is
> burned up by reason's fire, so are the parts.[15]

The first three quotations concern examples of a *causal dependence relation*, while the latter three are examples of *mereological dependence*. Causal and mereological dependence relations are also existential dependence relations, as the existence of the effect depends on the existence of the cause, and the existence of the whole depends on the existence of the parts. Yet the characterization of these relations as symmetric is much harder to make sense of than in the case of conceptual dependence relations. While not all conceptual dependence relations are symmetrical (logical implication being an obvious counterexample), some of them are, and the examples Nāgārjuna gives provide plausible examples.

Causal and mereological dependence relations, on the other hand, are generally conceived of as asymmetric; that is, if a causal or mereological dependence relation holds in one direction, it does not hold in the other direction.[16] This is why the son existentially depends on the father as a cause, though the father could go on existing had he never fathered a son, and why the whole existentially depends on the parts, while the parts would have still been there even if they had never been assembled into a whole. The acorn does not appear to depend on the oak tree it might one day produce (the acorn is still sitting here, even if it will never give rise to any tree), and LEGO bricks do not depend

Candrakīrti comments in his *Bhāṣya*, "Since there can be no parts when there is no owner of the parts, the parts do not exist," *gang gi phyir yan lag can med na yan lag dag yod pa ma yin pa de'i phyir yan lag dag med pa nyid do* (La Vallée Poussin 1992b, 272.14–15).

15. *Madhyamakāvatāra* 6.161: *sattvaṃ rathasyāsti na cet tadānīṃ vināngināngāny api santi nāsya / dagdhe rathe 'ngāni yathā na santi dhīvahnidagdhe 'ngini tadvad angam* (Li 2015, 24).

16. The puzzling feature of symmetric causal relations is also noted by Oetke (1991, 320): "There are at least some passages which suggest that Nāgārjuna took relationships which we could describe as relationships of semantical entailments or of logical requirements as identical or at least similar to causal dependencies. We must only assume that the author of the MMK regarded the fact that e.g. the existence of a cause or that of a bearer of attributes can be said to require the existence of an effect or respectively of an attribute and similar ones as instantiations of the *pratītyasamutpāda*-principle. As this supposition quite directly leads to the result that relationships of *pratītyasamutpāda* must be mutual, while on the other hand the idea of a mutual dependence contradicts the asymmetrical character of causal relationships and the paradigmatic instances of the *pratītyasamutpāda* in Buddhist tradition, this assimilation inevitably leads to paradoxes."

on the structure one might assemble from them (even if no structure is ever built from them, the individual bricks still exist).

How are we then to explain Madhyamaka's apparent reference to *symmetric* causal and mereological dependence relations?

A first possibility would be to assume that the Mādhyamikas accept that there are at least some instances of causal relations and of the part-whole relation that are indeed symmetric. But it is difficult to make this argument. Apart from the fact that Madhyamaka authors reject the existence of causal symmetric relations at the level of conventional reality,[17] such a causal symmetry would entail that cause and effect are simultaneous, while Madhyamaka rejects the idea of simultaneous causation.[18] When it comes to mereology, there likewise appears to be no textual evidence that the Mādhyamikas defended a general view of parthood according to which things, like the Borgesian *Aleph*, can be their own proper parts.[19]

An alternative and at least *prima facie* more plausible response resorts to parameterization. Here the idea is that when the Mādhyamika says that the son causally depends on the father and the father on the son, or that the whole mereologically depends on the parts and the parts on the whole, *different forms of dependence* are intended in each case, so that the situation is not really symmetrical. The son depends *for its existence* on the father, but the father only depends *for its description* on the son;[20] without the son, he would still exist but could no longer be described as a father. Without the father, the son would not exist at all. Analogous considerations would apply in the mereological case, where the whole would depend *for its existence* on its parts, but the parts would only depend *for their description* on the whole.

17. Candrakīrti refers to the "absence of the mutual relationship of what is to be brought and what brings about," *paraspara-nirvartya-nirvartakatva-abhāva*; *Prasannapadā* on *Mūlamadhyamakakārikā* 7.6 (La Vallée Poussin 1992a, 150.11).

18. *Madhyamakāvatāra* 6.17ab: "The sprout does not exist at the same time as the seed. How then is the seed to be other without otherness?" *asty aṅkuraś ca na hi bījasamānakālo bījaṃ kutaḥ paratayāstu vinā paratvam* (Li 2015, 6). See also Westerhoff 2009, 120–21.

19. A position that might, for example, be plausibly attributed to sections of the *Chāndogya Upaniṣad* and the *Avataṃsakasūtra* and can be found in many other intellectual traditions (see Cotnoir and Varzi 2021, 65–67).

20. Tibetan scholastic philosophy distinguishes the notion being identical or different *in terms of its description* from various forms of substantial identity or difference. "Pāṇḍu" and "father of Arjuna," for example, are considered substantially identical (*ngo bo gcig*) but conceptually different (*ldog pa tha dad*). The different forms of identity distinguished in the Tibetan literature (*rdzas gcig, don gcig, rang bzhin gcig, bdag nyid gcig, ngo bo gcig,* and *ldog pa gcig*) still require a more thorough study. For some remarks, see Tillemans 1983, Tillemans 1986, Tillemans 2022, and Stoltz 2006.

While parameterization has the obvious theoretical advantage of providing an intelligible explanation of what it would mean for the effect to depend on the cause and for the part to depend on the whole, there seem to be some limitations when trying to employ it as general interpretative principle for cases of symmetric dependence. First, it is obviously not appropriate to apply it to all cases of symmetric dependence the Mādhyamika discusses. In the case of long and short, there is no need to parameterize, since each depends on the other in exactly the same way. Second, it is not clear whether it helps us even in the case of the more puzzling cases of symmetric dependence cited above. *Śūnyatāsaptati* verse 13, for example, claims that father and son are mutually correlative (*phan tshun*, **anyonya*), just like the twelve links of dependent origination. Assuming that the son depends existentially on the father while the father depends only nominally on the son would have the peculiar implication that, for example, *saṃskāra* depended existentially on *avidyā* while *avidyā* depended only nominally on *saṃskāra*—an interpretation that is both at odds with the way the twelve links of dependent origination are usually understood and with the fact that they form a circle, where the dependence of *b* on *a* will always imply the dependence of *a* on *b*, if we follow the cycle of dependence relations the other way round. Moreover, when Nāgārjuna refers to the father-son example in *Vigrahavyāvartanī* verse 49 to argue for the mutual dependence of epistemic instrument and epistemic object, he clearly is not setting out to show that one of the two depends on the other nominally but not existentially. Parameterization, it seems, does not get us much further in trying to understand what these passages mean.

The best way to resolve this difficulty, it appears, is to point out that father and son, and part and whole, are indeed symmetrically dependent on one another, but that this dependence is not causal or mereological but conceptual. This has the advantage of both avoiding the introduction of causal and mereological loops, together with all the problems they bring, and avoiding parameterization, which brings with it the implication that the text is not really saying what it seems to be saying. To see how this is supposed to work, we need to start with the idea that for Madhyamaka, cause and effect, part and whole, and in fact all phenomena are conceptual constructions (*kalpana*). This is stated quite explicitly by Nāgārjuna in the *Acintyastava*:

> You have said clearly that the entire world is a mere name. Nothing expressible is to be found apart from the expressed. Therefore you have said that all things are merely conceptual constructions.[21]

---

21. *Acintyastava* verses 35–36a: *nāmamātraṃ jagat sarvam ity uccair bhāṣitaṃ tvayā / abhidānāt*

The suggestion is then that the symmetric dependence of entities like father and son or part and whole is not an instance of causal or mereological dependence but of the conceptual dependence of each conceptual construct on each other. "The son," as a construct of a multitude of momentary property particulars, is a construct that depends on the memory of another multitude of momentary property particulars, "the father," which stands at the beginning of the constructed sequence of property particulars that is "the son." Similarly, "the father," as a construct of a multitude of momentary property particulars, consists of various conceptual pieces, one of which is the anticipation of another multitude of momentary property particulars, branching off from it at a future time, which is "the son." Take away the memory or the anticipation from these bundles, and the bundles are no longer what they are. It might be possible to reconceptualize what is left of these bundles to form new conceptual constructs,[22] but this does not affect the central point that the dependence between these two as dependence between conceptual constructs is wholly symmetric. Each requires the other to be what it is, and since each construct only exists as a specific conglomerate, each requires the other for its existence.

The same point applies to a structure built from LEGO bricks and the individual bricks. The structure, as a multitude of momentary property particulars, depends on other multitudes of momentary property particulars that constitute the bricks. These bricks, on the other hand, depend, as conceptual constructs, on the conceptual construct that is the whole. Again, if we subtract the conceptual construct that is the whole from the conceptual construct that is the part, we might end up with something that we can conceptually unify as an individual (as we frequently do when we speak of LEGO bricks in a disassembled state), but we are speaking about a different conceptual construct in this case. To support this point, consider that we take a single LEGO brick and transport it to a different possible world where there are no other LEGO bricks. The material constitution of the brick will not have changed (it is still the same shape, made of plastic, and so on), but it is a different conceptual construct and hence a different entity. In the present world, the brick forms part of a system and can combine with other LEGO bricks in interest-

---

pṛthagbhūtam abhidheyaṃ na vidyate // kalpanāmātraṃ ity asmāt sarvadharmāḥ prakāśitāḥ (Lindtner 1982, 152–53). The conception of the world as a linguistic-conceptual construct is widespread among Indian Madhyamaka thinkers. See Bronkhorst 1996, 117–19, for further references.

22. As we indeed do, when we conceive of the multitude of momentary property particulars without the anticipation of the son as "a person" rather than as "a father."

ing ways to form more complex entities, whereas in the other world it is a mere block of plastic without combinatory potential. As such the brick *qua* conceptual construct depends on the structures built from it as much as the structures depend on it.[23]

To use a different example, in a language where different syntactic categories, such as nouns and verbs, can be combined to form larger grammatical units, such as sentences, these larger units then depend on the categories that constitute them. But no sense can be made of the categories independent of the larger units they help to form:[24] there is nothing more to a specific syntactic category than its ability to combine with other syntactic categories in a specific way to form larger units. Both the parts (the syntactic categories) and the wholes (the larger units) existentially depend on one another.

It is evident that *Śūnyatāsaptati* verse 6 cited above is to be interpreted along the same lines. The cause depends on the effect not causally but conceptually. (Causation relates concrete objects, like seeds and sprouts, not abstractions like causes and effects.) In his commentary Candrakīrti notes that it is only in conceptual dependence on an effect that entities are differentiated into causes and non-causes, as when we conceive of milk but not of water as a cause relative to yogurt as an effect.[25] In the absence of the conceptual construct that constitutes a specific effect, there is no basis for the conceptual construction of any entity that would constitute its cause. Of course in this context, "being the cause of yogurt" is not a mere relational label, which disappears if the effect disappears, leaving the entity labeled behind. Rather, it is one constituent of a conceptual construct that, once disappeared, entails the disappearance of the entire construct.

While the symmetry of causal and mereological relations involves a variety of philosophical complications, symmetric conceptual dependence is unproblematic, as we saw in our initial examples of long and short, nearer and farther shore, and so on. Symmetric conceptual dependence is, indeed, precisely what we would expect in a structuralist system where the nature and existence of each entity depends on the nature and existence of various others, so that dependence relations between two entities can often be traced in both directions. The conceptual vision of Madhyamaka, with its denial of any entities

---

23. Compare Aitken 2021, 15: "According to the Mādhyamika, the dependence between a part and a composite is more similar to that between the north and south poles [of a magnet] than may be initially supposed."

24. For the notion of categorial grammar presupposed here, see Ajdukiewicz 1967 and Gardies 1985.

25. Erb 1997, 240.

that constitute the endpoints of chains of dependence can, I believe, be successfully spelled out in such structuralist terms,[26] explaining the prominence that symmetric dependence relations have in the Madhyamaka system. Such symmetric dependence relations cannot simply be conceived as dependence for description but must be regarded as full existential dependence relations. This is because a structuralist system does not consist of a set of individuals characterized or described by the various relations in which the individuals stand; it is rather the network of relations itself that creates the individuals or "nodes" in the network. As such the network of dependence relations makes the individual what it is rather than simply characterizing it in a specific way.

I hope that the brief discussion just presented can also shed some light on the complicated issue of the "principle of coexisting counterparts" associated with Madhyamaka by modern commentators.[27] The term is due to John Taber (1998, 216), who refers to Richard Hayes's earlier discussion of this principle.[28] Though Hayes does not use the term "principle of coexisting counterparts," this "principle" has, under different names, captured the interest of Western Madhyamaka scholars for nearly a century. Already in 1931 Stanisław Schayer (36n29) refers to it as "*das* pratidvandvin-*Gesetz der mahāyānistischen Metalogik*," understanding it as saying that "when *A* is an unreal entity, its opposite, *non-A*, must also be unreal." While the predicate "real" is rarely understood as a logical notion, so that the concept of a meta-logical law is not entirely clear in this context, the idea seems to be that we are dealing here with a general philosophical principle that is applicable across a variety of different argumentative contexts. This is very much Jacques May's understanding of the principle, which he calls "le principe de solidarité des contraires" (1959, 16, 66n68, and 118n299). He takes it to mean that "if A does not exist, its opposite will not exist either. Opposites are correlated in their existence or nonexistence, not opposed to each other as we usually believe." In 1967 Richard Robinson (147) characterized the principle as the "counter-twin rule," "axiom 4" in his "classical Indian axiomatic," taking it to say that "the existence of non-A implies the existence of A." It is taken up again in 1977 by David Seyfort Ruegg, who refers to it as "the well-known Madhyamaka principle of the complementarity of binary concepts and terms," which he takes to state that for specific concepts that form "a nexus of complementary terms which are conceptually, linguis-

---

26. Of course Madhyamaka would not, like many structuralists, regard structuralism as an ultimately true theory. For some discussion of this point, see Westerhoff 2020, chaps. 3 and 4.

27. For a potential predecessor see the idea of "reciprocal designation" (*anyonya prajñapti*) held by the Prajñaptivāda, a subsect of the Mahāsāṅgikas (Walser 2005, 234–44).

28. Hayes 1994.

tically, and logically, but not causally, interrelated," "the negation of one necessarily involves the negation of the other" (Seyfort Ruegg 2010, 110). Ruegg thus considers this to be a principle specifically applicable to intentional items, such as concepts and terms, rather than to the entities (such as properties and relations) these terms refer to.

More recent formulations, though arguably still referring to the same principle, emphasize other aspects. For Taber (1998, 216) the principle says "that a thing cannot be a certain type unless its counterpart exists simultaneously with it," while Mark Siderits (2016, 102) takes it to mean that "an entity whose nature is in essential relation to some other thing cannot exist apart from that thing." Giuseppe Ferraro (2019, 110) notes that "the idea of x arises and endures—for the whole span of its existence—due to the simultaneous existence of its logical counterpart, that is, non-x or y: this latter, in turn, owes its origin and existence to x. Hence x and y are two reciprocally dependent logical counterparts," while Dan Arnold (2021, 8) takes the principle to claim that "relations can obtain only between real relata."

Even looking at just these four authors, it is far from obvious whether all these formulations of the principle intend to say the same thing. While Taber and Ferraro refer to "counterparts"—that is, to a form of negation operating between the entities in question—Siderits and Arnold refer only to relations or essential relations, apparently making a more general point that includes, but is not restricted to, the "counterpart" relation.

What is more, Madhyamaka scholars are also divided on the question of whether or not the principle is fallacious,[29] on whether it is even a principle (in the sense of a background assumption) at all, or whether it is rather the grand conclusion of the Madhyamaka system that "expresses Nāgārjuna's key metaphysical insight,"[30] and even on whether Nāgārjuna endorses it at all or whether it is merely attributed to him by an opponent.[31]

---

29. Robinson (1967, 150) considers the use of the principle by classical Indian thinkers to be "fraught with difficulties . . . Obscurity and uncertainty persisted after all their best effort." Hayes (1994) regards the principle as fallacious, Siderits (2016, 103) takes it to be "of dubious legitimacy," while Taber (1998) argues that it "appears to embody a metaphysical mistake" (218) and "clearly seems erroneous, at least from the standpoint of common sense" (233), noting, however, toward the end of his discussion (237–38) that the philosophical defense of common sense can hardly be regarded as an objective of Nāgārjuna's project.

30. Taber 1998, 237.

31. See Taber 1998, 233, and Arnold 2021, 8 and 22. A prominent formulation of the principle, which we find in Candrakīrti's *Prasannapadā* on *Mūlamadhyamakakārikā* 2.14 (*yasya ca pratipakṣo 'sti, tadasti, ālokāndhakāravat pārāvāravat saṃśayaniścayavac ca*; La Vallée Poussin 1992a, 101.13–14), is presented in an objection by an opponent, though the subsequent

I believe that the nature and status of this principle can be clarified some-what if we note that (1) it is supposed to apply to conceptual constructs and (2) these constructs are to be conceived of in a structuralist manner. The principle refers to pairs of constructs, many of which are related to one another by means of negation (as in the case of "long" and "short," "my own" and "another's"), though its scope is considerably wider than this (the father is not the negation of the son, nor is the agent the negation of the object of action). In the case of constructs related in this way, it is impossible to remove one from the network of constructs while leaving the other in place, or to put it another way, if one of the constructs is introduced, the other is introduced as well.

How plausible is this principle? If we consider a set of concepts closed under negation, all negations of the original concepts will be included as well, and if we consider a set of concepts closed under implication, all concepts implied by the original concepts will be included too. This, of course, says nothing about whether all (or any) of these concepts are actually instantiated. In this set, the principle of coexisting counterparts or symmetric existential dependence relations holds for some pairs of concepts, though not for all. If the set contains the concept "round" and is closed under negation, it has to contain the concept "not round," and if it lacks one, it has to lack the other, though if it contains the concept "round," it does not have to contain the concept "green." As such, the fact that the principle of coexisting counterparts is instantiated, or the claim that there are symmetric existential dependence relations, is not controversial. What is controversial, and what the Mādhyamika's arguments must establish, is that the world is such that this principle and these relations apply to a large number of cases. For this to be true, it needs to be the case that the world does not consist of a collection of mutually independent bits, each of which can go out of existence without affecting any of the others. Furthermore, the entities in the world need to be such that they are closed under relations like complementarity (*pratidvandva*) and therefore need to be conceptual constructs (*kalpana*). No sense can be made of closing, for example, a set of material objects under complementarity in this sense.[32]

It is clear that this is not the commonsensical picture of the world, and

Madhyamaka response attacks not the principle itself but the conclusion the opponent draws from it.

32. The notion of complementarity (*pratidvandva*) is here understood as implying that we cannot remove one of a complementary pair without simultaneously removing the other. While there are senses in which material objects might be complementary (e.g., if the complement of a pot is taken to be the sum of everything else—that is, the object that has everything not identical with the pot as a part), the implication that we cannot remove one without the other does not hold for them.

Taber (1998, 233) is right to note that "In common experience a thing exists just by virtue of what it is, not by virtue of what it is related to. The nature of a thing in most cases is prior both logically and temporally to the things to which it gives rise, to the actions it carries out, to the things it is not, etc." However, this is precisely the picture of the world conceived in terms of *svabhāva* that Nāgārjuna sets out to refute in his theory of emptiness. If this refutation is successful, the existence of symmetric existential dependence relations for causes and effects and for parts and wholes, as well as the principle of coexisting counterparts, ceases to be philosophically problematic.

Bibliography

Aitken, Allison. 2021. "No Unity, No Problem: Madhyamaka Metaphysical Indefinitism." *Philosophers' Imprint* 21.31: 1–24.

Ajdukiewicz, Kazimierz. 1967. "Syntactic Connexion." In *Polish Logic 1920–1939*, edited by Storrs McCall, 207–31. Oxford: Clarendon Press.

Arnold, Dan. 2021. "Location, Location, Location! Thoughts on the Significance of a Grammatical Point for Some Mādhyamika Arguments." In *A Road Less Traveled: Felicitation Volume in Honor of John Taber*, edited by Vincent Eltschinger, Birgit Kellner, Ethan Mills, and Isabelle Ratié, 1–35. Vienna: Arbeitskreis für Tibetische und Buddhistische Studien, Universität Wien.

Bronkhorst, Johannes. 1996. "Sanskrit and Reality: The Buddhist Contribution." In *Ideology and Status of Sanskrit: Contributions to the History of the Sanskrit Language*, edited by Jan E. M. Houben, 109–35. Leiden: Brill.

Cotnoir, Aaron J., and Achille C. Varzi. 2021. *Mereology*. Oxford: Oxford University Press.

Erb, Felix. 1997. *Śūnyatāsaptativṛtti: Candrakīrtis Kommentar zu den "Siebzig Versen über die Leerheit" des Nāgārjuna (Kārikas 1–14): Einleitung, Übersetzung, textkritische Ausgabe des Tibetischen und Indizes*. Stuttgart: Franz Steiner.

Ferraro, Giuseppe. 2019. "Two Boats Fastened Together: Nāgārjuna's Solution to the Question of the Origin of Ideas." *Philosophy East and West* 69.1: 108–29.

Gardies, Jean-Louis. 1985. *Rational Grammar*. Munich and Vienna: Philosophia Verlag.

Hahn, Michael. 1982. *Nāgārjuna's Ratnāvalī: The Basic Texts (Sanskrit, Tibetan, Chinese)*. Bonn: Indica et Tibetica.

Hayes, Richard P. 1994. "Nāgārjuna's Appeal." *Journal of Indian Philosophy* 22.4: 299–378.

La Vallée Poussin, Louis de. 1992a. *Mūlamadhyamakakārikās (Mādhyamikasūtras) de Nāgārjuna avec la Prasannapadā Commentaire de Candrakīrti*. Delhi: Motilal Banarsidass.

———. 1992b. *Madhyamakāvatāra par Candrakīrti*. Delhi: Motilal Banarsidass.

Lindtner, Christian. 1982. *Nagarjuniana: Studies in the Writings and Philosophy of Nāgārjuna*. Copenhagen: Akademisk Forlag.

Lang, Karen. 1986. *Āryadeva's Catuḥśataka: On the Bodhisattva's Cultivation of Merit and Knowledge*. Copenhagen: Akademisk Forlag.

Li, Xuezhu. 2015. "*Madhyamakāvatāra-kārikā* Chapter 6." *Journal of Indian Philosophy* 43.1: 1–30.

May, Jacques. 1959. *Candrakīrti Prasannapadā Madhyamakavṛtti: Douze chapitres traduits du sanscrit et du tibétain.* Paris: Adrien Maisonneuve.

McClintock, Sara, and John Dunne. 2024. *Nāgārjuna's Precious Garland: Ratnāvalī.* Classics of Indian Buddhism. New York: Wisdom Publications.

Odin, Steve. 1982. *Process Metaphysics and Hua-yen Buddhism: A Critical Study of Cumulative Penetration vs. Interpenetration.* Albany: State University of New York Press.

Oetke, Claus. 1991. "Remarks on the Interpretation of Nāgārjuna's Philosophy." *Journal of Indian Philosophy* 19.3: 315–23.

Robinson, Richard H. 1967. "The Classical Indian Axiomatic." *Philosophy East and West* 17.1: 139–54.

Schayer, Stanisław. 1931. *Ausgewählte Kapitel aus der Prasannapadā:* (V, XII, XIII, XIV, XV, XVI). Krakow: Nakładem Polskiej Akademji Umiejętności.

Seyfort Ruegg, David. 2010. *The Buddhist Philosophy of the Middle: Essays on Indian and Tibetan Madhyamaka.* Studies in Indian and Tibetan Buddhism. Boston: Wisdom Publications.

Siderits, Mark. 2016. *Studies in Buddhist Philosophy.* Oxford: Oxford University Press.

Siderits, Mark, and Shōryū Katsura. 2013. *Nāgārjuna's Middle Way: Mūlamadhyamaka-kārikā.* Classics of Indian Buddhism. Boston: Wisdom Publications.

Stoltz, Jonathan. 2006. "Concepts, Intension, and Identity in Tibetan Philosophy of Language." *Journal of the International Association of Buddhist Studies* 29.2: 383–400.

Taber, John A. 1998. "On Nāgārjuna's So-Called Fallacies: A Comparative Approach." *Indo-Iranian Journal* 41: 213–44.

Tillemans, Tom J. F. 1983. "The 'Neither One nor Many' Argument for *śūnyatā* and Its Tibetan Interpretations." In *Contributions on Tibetan and Buddhist Religion and Philosophy,* edited by Ernst Steinkellner, Helmut Tauscher, 305–20. Vienna: Arbeitskreis für Tibetische und Buddhistische Studien Universität Wien.

———. 1986. "Identity and Referential Opacity in Tibetan Buddhist *apoha* Theory." In *Buddhist Logic and Epistemology: Studies in the Buddhist Analysis of Inference and Language,* edited by Bimal Krishna Matilal and Robert D. Evans, 207–27. Dordrecht: D. Reidel.

———. 2022. "Tibetan Developments in Buddhist Logic." In *Views from Tibet: Studies on Tibetan Buddhist Logic, the Philosophy of the Middle, and the Indigenous Grammatico-Linguistic Tradition,* by Tom J. F. Tillemans, 35–137. Vienna: Austrian Academy of Sciences.

Tola, Fernando, and Carmen Dragonetti. 1995. *Nāgārjuna's Refutation of Logic.* Delhi: Motilal Banarsidass.

Vaidya, P. L. 1960. *Bodhicaryāvatāra of Śāntideva with the Commentary Pañjikā of Prajñākaramati.* Buddhist Sanskrit Texts 12. Darbhanga, India: The Mithilā Institute.

Walser, Joseph. 2005. *Nāgārjuna in Context: Mahāyāna Buddhism and Early Indian Culture.* New York: Columbia University Press.

Westerhoff, Jan. 2009. *Nagarjuna's Madhyamaka: A Philosophical Introduction.* New York: Oxford University Press.

———. 2020. *The Non-Existence of the Real World.* Oxford: Oxford University Press.

Yonezawa, Yoshiyasu. 2008. "*Vigrahvavyāvartanī:* Sanskrit Transliteration and Tibetan Translation." *Journal of Naritasan Institute for Buddhist Studies* 31: 209–333.

PART 3
WORLD

Whose World Is This? Reflections on Customary Truth

Sara McClintock

To say I owe my professional life to Tom Tillemans would not be wrong, even if it would also be necessary to note that Tom has been something of a reluctant hero in this regard. If Tom's generosity in supporting me for two years as a visiting pre-doctoral research scholar at the University of Lausanne felt initially like a bit of magical realism, the high philosophical fantasy unfolding *au bord du lac* was in danger of plunging quickly into hard-boiled realism when I came to understand that Tom had very little appetite for the seemingly woo-woo topic I had chosen for my dissertation—the Buddha's omniscience. My first gleaning of this came soon after my arrival in Switzerland in the course of a conversation I had with Phyllis Granoff, who was visiting to attend a conference. Standing in a crowd of overly caffeinated scholars, Phyllis asked me about my dissertation. "Great topic!" she said when I told her about the project. "And who are you working with here?" she inquired. Cheerfully, I replied, "Tom Tillemans." But as soon as I had proclaimed this, Tom turned with alacrity from the conversation in which he had been engaged nearby and, with a bushy arched eyebrow and penetrating gaze worthy of the very best Bodhidharma, blurted out, "Not on that, you're not!" as he breezed on by.

I'm not sure if Tom began to feel sorry for me, or whether he reconsidered the merits of the topic, but not long after this episode he asked me to "delete" his comment—a turn of events at which my relief and gratitude were great. In the coming months, as I attended Tom's courses and read Sanskrit and Tibetan texts under his guidance, my eyes opened to a host of new ways of understanding philosophy, learning not only about such thinkers as Bhāviveka, Candrakīrti, Gorampa, and Tsongkhapa but also about Davidson, Murdoch, Nagel, and Quine. When my dissertation advisor in America, Masatoshi Nagatomi, passed away unexpectedly, Tom graciously agreed to step into the role of director, despite getting absolutely no compensation for doing so. There is not a trace of doubt in my mind that my dissertation and eventual book on omniscience would not have been even remotely possible without Tom's penetrating critiques, unflagging patience, extraordinary good humor, and relentless encouragement.

While Tom and I do not always see things in precisely the same ways—he still seems to worry that I may yet get sucked into a black hole of relativism—I know that my current research into truth, transactionalism, and worldmaking has its roots in the countless lively conversations we had over coffee in the university cafeteria on the shores of Lac Léman and over hearty meals of *filets de perche à la meunière* accompanied by *un bon fendant* at the Buffet de la Gare de Lausanne. In such settings, Tom, inevitably sporting a terrific grin and issuing a slightly maniacal laugh, always managed to put me into a difficult spot in such a way as to oblige me to clarify my thinking, reconsider my ideas, and come up with something new. Usually this involved me letting go of some cherished notion, just as Dazu Huike let go of his own cherished notions when Bodhidharma asked him to bring him his mind. In the end, Tom was and remains the kindly teacher in the Bildungsroman of my scholarly life, a source of joy and inspiration, a brilliant philosopher, and a trusted and true *kalyāṇamitra*. I offer what follows in the hope that he may find me, in some fashion at least, to be a worthy opponent.

Introduction

The genesis of this paper lies in the sense of discomfort I have felt around the idea of justification and ethics in relation to Madhyamaka thought. While justification is widely understood to be an important element of ethical reasoning insofar as a thoughtful and judicious person wants and needs to have good reasons for undertaking or refraining from particular actions, Madhyamaka thinkers, with their antifoundational and antimetaphysical leanings, also recognize problems in establishing the rational norms that such justification would seem to require. In his writings on Madhyamaka Buddhist ethics and epistemology, Tom Tillemans has extensively explored a Madhyamaka trope that stipulates that when it comes to norms, whether epistemic or ethical, a judicious Buddhist should not seek for foundations on which to ground them but rather should rely on "what is established for the world" (i.e., on what is *lokaprasiddha*). The notion that one can dispense with the need to provide robust justifications for actions or beliefs simply by turning to a populist view of things is deeply troubling to Tom, who has characterized this perspective as a dismal "trivialization of the idea of truth" (2016, 47). At the same time, Tom has worried about the consequences that could ensue for Madhyamaka thinkers like Kamalaśīla, who, in their attempt to maintain some nontrivial role for truth, adopt and adapt the bulk of the technical apparatus of Dignāga's and Dharmakīrti's epistemological theories. Like Tom, such thinkers seem to have been "duly horrified" (2016, 28) by the prospect that a judicious person would give up their analysis aimed at ascertaining whether what the world generally holds to be true is correct or not.

But while Tom shares Kamalaśīla's dismay at the prospect of relying on unexamined, popular beliefs, he also finds himself sympathetic to the qualms of another Madhyamaka thinker, Candrakīrti, whose thoroughgoing antifoundational and antimetaphysical outlook makes him rather cautious about the adoption of the tools of the professional epistemologists. Specifically, on Tom's reading, Candrakīrti worries that the Buddhist epistemological tools of perception and inference, the so-called instruments of reliable knowledge (*pramāṇa*), require a commitment to the existence of intrinsic natures or identities (*svabhāva*) to serve as the metaphysical grounds for the perceptual or inferential certainty (*niścaya*) that supposedly is reliably obtained through those exact instruments. Rescuing truth from trivialization should not be tainted by *this* kind of realism, even if it is relegated to a conventional level.

Tom is attracted to the antifoundational and antimetaphysical stance he finds in Candrakīrti's Madhyamaka, but at the same time he is not willing to simply endorse what the *hoi polloi* establish as true and false. Tom worries that if a Mādhyamika thinker too blithely relies on the world's customary truth, then a great deal of customary ignorance will proceed unchecked. As such, Tom has an interest in systematically pushing, through a process of rational reconstruction, to explore more fully what *kind* of worldly truth and what *kind* of worldly knowledge it would be possible, in theory, for a Mādhyamika to endorse. As he puts it, Madhyamaka's emptiness discourse (*śūnyavāda*) "should, if carried through, have significant implications for [Mādhyamikas'] conceptions of what worldly reality is and on the epistemology that governs knowledge claims and justification on the level of worldly truths" (2011, 361–62). Yet Tom finds that these implications are undertheorized in even the most antifoundational and antimetaphysical of the traditional texts. While questions about the justification of knowledge *are* taken up by Mādhyamikas like Kamalaśīla who avail themselves of the tools of the Buddhists epistemologists, those like Candrakīrti seem more inclined to adopt a Wittgensteinian-like silence on such matters, thereby ceding questions of rational justification to the ignorant world.[1] A driving question for Tom, then,

---

1. In my most recent conversations with Tom, he recognized that Candrakīrti does allow for the

is how an antifoundationalist, antimetaphysicalist like Candrakīrti could or should find methods to "reform customary truth" without resorting to any kind of language about what is "really going on" beneath the surface.

Tom does find examples of Mādhyamikas using what he takes to be everyday worldly reasoning to think through and even reform the pervasive misconceptions that ordinary people have about their lives. As an example, he looks at the discussion of the so-called four illusions as found in the *Catuḥśataka* of Āryadeva and in its commentary, the *Catuḥśatakaṭīkā* of Candrakīrti (2011, 365–66). According to these texts, ordinary people are confused about what is true, and this ignorance plays a central role in their ongoing suffering. In their confusion, people mistakenly take what is impermanent as permanent, what is painful as pleasant, what is impure as pure, and what is selfless as having a self. Correcting these misconceptions is important, but on Tom's reading, doing so does not involve stepping outside ordinary worldly reasoning. Rather, the corrections are made by recourse to what is already established for the world by pointing out how these mistaken perspectives stand in conflict with other "deep-seated," yet still ordinary, worldly intuitions (2011, 365). In other words, coming to see that there is no self where we previously had thought a self to exist is a process that can unfold entirely within the realm of what is established for the world, and this is done mainly through the urging of unwanted consequences (*prasaṅga*) on those who hold such mistaken views by those who no longer hold such views but have seen the truth of no self. Tom might still say that the theoretical underpinnings of such reasoning in terms of the impact of emptiness discourse remain underdeveloped, but the use of ordinary reasoning to reform customary truth at least is clear.

Moving the conversation into a more explicitly ethical domain, however, intensifies the urgency of the investigation. Now we are no longer asking only about what is true ("Is there a self or is there no self?") but also about what is right ("Should one tell a white lie or should one always stick strictly to the commitment to refrain from lying?"). Casting the problem in terms of justification, Tom points to what he takes to be the usual Buddhist approach to ethical argumentation, which he maintains crucially relies "on problematic facts, typically when actions are evaluated because of their total set of karmic consequences across several lives" (2011, 366). In such cases, Tom maintains, Buddhists turn to scriptures in which an omniscient Buddha informs the faithful about the good and bad karmic results they can expect in a future life as a result of the various good and bad actions they perform in this life. This

role of experts in adjudicating worldly truth, and he praised John Newman's most recent article (2024) on this topic. See my account of this conversation above, p. 21.

scripture-based inferential knowledge about epistemically extremely remote realities concerning karma and its results is then what serves as the justification for Buddhists to undertake or refrain from a host of actions of body, speech, and mind. Tom calls this a case of Mādhyamikas "having their cake and eating it, too" (2011, 367), since justification for knowledge relies on what is accepted for the world except in those cases where the world cannot know, in which case the justification shifts to the testimony of a supposedly omniscient authority. Indeed, Tom argues that challenging the problematic idea that what is established for the world should include "humanly inaccessible facts" (*atyantaparokṣa*) like karma theory and other religious dogmas is precisely "the type of discussion needed for Buddhism to figure rationally in future cross-cultural philosophy" (2018, 100).

Let us take a moment to reframe all this. Tom's project here is one of rational reconstruction. What is being rationally reconstructed is the Madhyamaka theory of the nature of what is established for the world (*lokaprasiddha*), known also as conventional or customary truth. The purpose of this rational reconstruction is to think through issues surrounding the justification of both ordinary truth claims and ethical norms in the context of Madhyamaka. Note that the question here is not just how *do* Mādhyamikas justify these things but how *can* or even how *should* they justify them. The project of rational reconstruction is thus not unlike the reasoning by consequences that we noted Candrakīrti using in debunking the four illusions: It starts with a position that someone takes to be true and then applies rational analysis to see how other beliefs hold up in light of that position. If there is a conflict, then one or more of the beliefs must be reformed. In the case of Tom, however, the tools of rational analysis that he marshals are derived mostly from modern analytic philosophy, and the questions he asks of Mādhyamikas therefore are cast in terms the ancient thinkers would not immediately recognize. This is not necessarily a problem, but it is important to understand that this is an integral component of rational reconstruction not found in the method of urging unwanted consequences. Tom wants to find out: Given a commitment to emptiness and to the idea of truth being not grounded in ultimate metaphysical realities, on what basis might one reform customary truth and on what basis might one justify ethical actions? We can take these questions one by one.

Reforming Customary Truth

We begin with the question of customary truth and whether and how it could ever be reformed by Mādhyamikas or others with antifoundational and antimetaphysical commitments. Tom has taken pains to show that there are a range of meanings for the Sanskrit term *saṃvṛtisatya*, a range reflected in the many modern translations for the term, which include conventional truth, obscurational truth, truth for a concealer, relative truth, *vérité d'enveloppement*, and the one Tom uses most often, customary truth. Drawing on Candrakīrti's presentation of three meanings for *saṃvṛti* in his *Prasannapadā* commentary on Nāgārjuna's *Mūlamadhyamakakārikā*, Tom sums up the situation:

> In short, one usage of *saṃvṛti* is to refer to *ignorance* whereby one takes as true what is not, thus concealing the actual way things are. Another usage is as dependent arising (*pratītyasamutpāda*), more exactly as "mutual dependence" (*parasparasaṃbhavana*), and hence means things that lack intrinsic nature (*svabhāva*). The third usage is to mean agreements governing the use of signs, i.e., *saṃketa*, as well as the various worldly practices, or more accurately, worldly *transactions* (*lokavyāvahāra*). Included here are both agreed-upon linguistic expressions (*abhidhāna*) and objects of expression (*abhidheya*), as well as cognitions (*jñāna*) and their objects (*jñeya*). (2019, 639)

Of Candrakīrti's three meanings for *saṃvṛtisatya*, the first presents the greatest problem for those who want to uphold a normative dimension to truth, even if only at the conventional level. Tom has worried about the tendency for some Mādhyamika thinkers to embrace a kind of panfictionalism or global error theory according to which "the world's customary truth is *wholly* erroneous (*bhrānta, 'khrul ba*) from the perspective of 'noble beings' (*ārya*), who see things properly" (2016, 51). On this view, while it is true that ordinary people do distinguish what is true from what is false, they nevertheless do so without realizing that *all* their judgments are in a certain respect erroneous, as they are *all* suffused with an innate, beginningless ignorance that attributes real natures or identities (*svabhāva*) to things that lack them. This kind of global error theory appears to be extremely common in Indian Madhyamaka texts, and Tom finds it to be especially prominent in the works of those (like Candrakīrti) whom later Tibetans have identified as Prāsaṅgikas (*thal 'gyur ba*)—those who rely on the urging of unwanted consequences (*prasaṅga*) to reform customary truth and who do not therefore invoke erroneous metaphysical commitments in the course of their use of reason. Tom dubs this approach to customary truth that of the "typical Prāsaṅgika" (2016, 51).

In contrast, Tom identifies what he calls the "atypical Prāsaṅgika" approach of the Tibetan thinker Tsongkhapa and his followers. Tom greatly prefers this approach to customary truth, which he sees as avoiding the problems of a global error theory or panfictionalism that accrue to the typical Prāsaṅgika. At the same time, this atypical approach seems to hew much closer to a strict antimetaphysical stance than what we find in the works of Kamalaśīla and others whom later Tibetans identify as Svātantrikas (*rang rgyud pa*)—those who seek to justify customary truths by means of independent (*svatantra*) proof statements that function owing to the force of real entities (*vastu*) with particular identities (*svabhāva*). Even if those identities are held by Kamalaśīla and others to be only conventionally real, they nonetheless function in such a way as to *conjure* a metaphysical grounding for truth, and that feels like a problem for both Tsongkhapa and Tom. In short, in the atypical Prāsaṅgika Madhyamaka of Tsongkhapa, Tom finds a kind of a middle way between two other forms of "middle way" (*madhyamaka*) philosophy: those exemplified by Candrakīrti on the one hand and Kamalaśīla on the other.

In drawing our attention to the important ways that Tsongkhapa's Madhyamaka differs from that of the Indian Prāsaṅgika tradition it claims to represent, Tom invokes language from contemporary philosophy. In particular, he wants first of all to argue that Madhyamaka thought at its most profound and interesting is best seen as a form of philosophical quietism, which he glosses as a kind of "reasoned disengagement from all philosophical theses, and hence debates (*vivāda*) about them" (2016, 3). Tom traces this quietism all the way back to Nāgārjuna's statements in the *Yuktiṣaṣṭikā* and elsewhere to the effect that "superior individuals have no theses (*pakṣa, phyogs*) and no philosophical debates" (2016, 3). For Tom, the quietism of Madhyamaka does not amount to a withdrawal from reason and argument. Rather, it is a philosophical position that holds that "one *cannot reasonably* have philosophical theses and take sides in debates on how things really are in themselves, or how they are in an ultimate fashion" (2016, 3). In other words, quietism is the position that metaphysics—which Tom equates with ontology, or "the attempt to find the widest ranging and most fundamental description of what exists and how it exists" (2016, 3)—is a bankrupt project that only leads persons into further misery by dint of reinforcing the problematic presumption that it is possible to discover what truly exists. If this is the core insight of Madhyamaka, then the atypical Prāsaṅgika is on a better track than is either the typical Prāsaṅgika or the Svātantrika because the atypical Prāsaṅgika can "believe and prove truths in a minimalist fashion not involving a metaphysics of intrinsic natures" (2016, 5). In other words, when metaphysics is left aside, ordinary reason and argumentation can proceed in an ordinary fashion, and Tom finds this a more sophisticated and promising way to take up Madhyamaka intuitions about emptiness.

The task of the Mādhyamika now is not to show people how everything they thought they knew was actually mistaken but rather to educate them about the "split between how things are confusedly grasped in the fashion of a metaphysical realist committed to intrinsic natures and how they are understood innocently and rightly without such commitments" (2016, 5). When people have understood this, then they might be in a position to "disentangle the innocent from the confused, and stay unengaged on positions that involve the latter" (2016, 5). This is the philosophical quietism of Madhyamaka that Tom favors. Importantly, he notes that Buddhist quietism extends beyond philosophy into meditation and practice, where a person might eventually reach a point where all views (*dṛṣṭi*) and even all conceptual thinking (*vikalpa, kalpanā*) disappear. But his interest remains in the strictly philosophical realm, where views and thinking still have a role, and he wants to investigate "how Mādhyamikas think" when they have renounced the intrinsic natures that other, more metaphysically inclined philosophers embrace. The atypical Prāsaṅgika approach strikes him as best because it does not fall into the dismal slough in which there can be no norms for truth, and yet it also does not aim to ground truth in metaphysical realities.

While Tsongkhapa's enthusiastic use of the technical apparatuses of the Buddhist epistemologists might remind us of Kamalaśīla, the difference, at least on Tom's reading, is that for Tsongkhapa there is nothing real (no *vastu*, no *svabhāva*) that serves as the warrant for whatever truth is ascertained through the instruments of reliable knowledge (*pramāṇa*). This stance is what Tom calls *deflationism*, the idea that there is nothing about truth statements that makes them true beyond the fact that they simply are so. A sentence such as "It is true that the earth revolves around the sun" adds nothing of any substance to the sentence "The earth revolves around the sun." Adding the phrase "it is true that" does not materially change anything, and it is also not necessary except for emphasis. Deflationists about truth thus see no use for truth theories since, as one encyclopedia puts it, all such theories share a common mistake in that they "assume that truth *has* a nature of the kind philosophers might find out about and develop theories of" (Armour-Garb et al. 2023, 1). The kind of nature that truth theorists attribute to truth is one that is metaphysically substantive or deeply explanatory. For those who hold that truth has such a nature, attributing truth to some statement or idea at the same time entails pointing to some deeper ontological reality that renders the statement true. But deflationists about truth think that truth is far less weighty.

The idea that truth has no substantive nature, it must be said, is a proposition Mādhyamikas should readily embrace.[2] Likewise, the notion that ordi-

2. See MacKenzie 2008.

nary truth claims are in fact just *ordinary* lines up well with Madhyamaka's thoroughgoing rejection of any ultimate truth or reality. Indeed, it is not difficult to perceive how Madhyamaka is deflationary, seeing as it systematically deflates such grand ideas as ultimate truth, ultimate reality, intrinsic nature, and even emptiness. With this in mind, the notion that a Mādhyamika would rely merely on what is established for the world makes perfect sense. But then the question becomes: What do we mean by "the world"? If a Mādhyamika claims that they have no quarrel with the world, does that necessarily mean that they are committed to accepting anything and everything that ordinary people claim? Tom suggests that Mādhyamikas may have been "playing with bad hands," in the sense that the scriptural passages that came down to them were truncated and left out important bits. He contrasts a passage from the Ratnakūṭa collection of Mahāyāna sūtras in which the Buddha states "What is agreed upon in the world to exist, I too agree that it exists" with a passage from the Pāli Saṃyutta Nikāya that reads "Of that which the wise in the world agree upon as existing, I too say that it exists" (2019, 366–67). Candrakīrti cites the first passage, and Tom sees in it an unfortunate source for the idea that "customary existence and truth are somehow copies or reflections of what the average worldlings in fact think across time and culture" (2019, 367). He notes, moreover, that Candrakīrti's scripture further glosses "the world" as meaning infantile, ordinary beings (*bāla* and *pṛthagjana*). The Pāli passage, in contrast, seems to allow "the wise" a special role in determining what is true from what is false. On Tom's reading, the Pāli passage is incompatible with a global error theory or panfictionalism, while the Mahāyāna passage quite easily lends itself to such an interpretation.

But need the Mahāyāna passage be taken in this way? Does the world not include distinctions such as ignorant and wise? Are these distinctions not part of what is established for the world? Does removing the heavy metaphysical claims associated with notions of truth necessarily require one to give up any and all discrimination about true and false? Deflationists about truth do not think so, and there does not seem to be any good reason to imagine that Mādhyamikas would think so either. Tom lauds Tsongkhapa for his recognition that there are parts of worldly knowledge that are indeed true, and that can be known by the ordinary (i.e., non-metaphysically grounded) instruments of reliable knowledge, while there are other parts that are false, and that can be disproved by those same instruments. And this does not seem to be all that far from what Kamalaśīla and his teacher Śāntarakṣita hold. In fact, they are explicit that ordinary perception and inferences, the basic tools of the Buddhist epistemologist, *are* in fact just how the world itself comes to distinguish true from false.[3] The appeal to identities (*svabhāva*) in the course of obtaining inferential or perceptual knowledge is not somehow an otherworldly activity, even if professional philosophers take their analysis to a more sophisticated (and sometimes weighty) level than do average persons. So long as the identities that serve as the warrants for reliable knowledge are themselves innocent and not metaphysically weighty, then appealing to them, even calling them "real things" (*vastu*), does not automatically conflict with being a deflationist about truth.[4] Even the passage from the Ratnakūṭa sūtras does not necessarily entail panfictionalism and can accommodate deflationism about truth if we understand that by infantile and ordinary beings the scripture simply means to remind us of the unawakened status of the vast majority of persons, whether wise people or fools.

Let us then charitably read *all* Mādhyamikas as deflationists about truth, where truth here is understood as something that can be predicated of truth-bearers like statements or beliefs. It seems to me that *no* Mādhyamika is seeking to ground these kinds of customary truths in some deep ontology. Indeed, the Madhyamaka project is to free us from the intuition that customary knowledge requires any ontological ground to be valid. But here there is a chance for a genuine confusion to arise, because, as is well known, when Mādhyamikas speak of truth (*satya*), they do not mean only or even primarily the kind of truth that can be predicated of truth-bearers. Rather, the term we translate as "truth," *satya*, can also signify, as Tom himself recognizes, "*states of affairs* or *sorts of things*—those generally taken to be real and those that are fully real" (2022, 237). In other words, the term *satya* can mean both propositionally true and existentially real, and for this reason, when Mādhyamikas speak of customary truth, they are not speaking only about truth-bearers. Because Tom is interested in truth as a property of statements and beliefs, he deliberately *chooses* not to engage with this other meaning of *satya*. Instead, he says he will "take the liberty to restrict our use of 'truths' to truth-bearers" (2022, 237) and that he will thereby "leave aside . . . the ambiguity between truth and reality inherent in the terms *satya* and [the Tibetan equivalent] *bden pa*" (2019, 638). What are the consequences of Tom making this move?

One important consequence is that discussions about truth are now reduced to questions about what it means for particular truth claims to be true with no room for conversations about how those claims came to be under

---

3. See McClintock 2019, 426–27.

4. In my recent conversations with Tom, it was clear that Tom is not an antirealist and he opposes an antirealist reading of Madhyamaka. Allowing for real things, so long as their reality is not being fixed by "ethereal rails," is not only innocent, it is necessary. See above, pp. 15–17.

consideration as truth claims in the first place. Let me stress that such conversations do not need to be metaphysical in nature. We can talk about how certain truth claims come to be regarded as legitimate topics of debate without invoking ontology. This, after all, is what the deflationist about truth maintains, as Tom himself asserts when he says, "deflationism does nonetheless retain the crucial minimal features of the concepts of truth, objectivity, and reality, namely that truth involves an all-important contrast between being right and just seeming to be right" (2016, 6). So an investigation into how particular truth claims come to be up for consideration is not at all off limits for the deflationist about truth. Tom gets closer to this kind of conversation in a recent article on metaphysics and metametaphysics, or the investigation of "the foundations of metaphysics as a whole" (2018, 95). Although he here calls Madhyamaka's quietism a "more promising metametaphysical stance" than the so-called *serious* metaphysics he finds in other Buddhist and non-Buddhist schools, he also states that Madhyamaka's "price to be paid for a cocktail of quietism and panfictionalism is potentially very high" (2018, 95). Once again, Tom worries that an emphasis in Madhyamaka on the deceptive nature of customary truth will result in the loss of *any* possibility for rational inquiry or for a genuine distinction between what is true and what is false beyond perhaps some weak form of pragmatism. Instead, Tom finds a better way via Tsongkhapa's "qualified argumentation," in which customary truth is understood to be entirely unproblematic except insofar as it includes the explicit or implicit modifier *really* (*bden par*), which Tom associates with the operator REALLY used in modern analytic philosophy. Getting free from the clutches of the kind of ignorance that causes suffering now becomes a matter of "recognizing what is to be rejected" (*dgag bya ngos 'dzin*), which turns out to be this extra operator REALLY that is "a very seductive but pernicious superimposition (*samāropa, sgro 'dogs*) on the other innocent truths *P, Q, R*" (2018, 95–96). With this qualification in place—that is, with the exclusion of the operator REALLY from argumentation—the Mādhyamika can now relax and allow what is established for the world to function free from either the encumbrance of a metaphysical ground or the perniciousness of a global error theory. So far so good.

Yet here again, the focus on truth at the expense of reality leaves out a critical concern: how that which is established for the world got to be that way in the first place. In speaking of one of the problems of pragmatism, Tom invokes the notion of a "vicious circularity":

> To determine usefulness in human enterprises, one already needs
> to have a world largely in place, with people and many macroscopic

> objects too. In short, usefulness of carts, tables, and the like to people *presupposes* a context in which there are people, their environments, and complex interactions with a lot of quite different sorts of objects. If strategies to further human ends were themselves responsible for the genesis of all these entities, their genesis would seem to become unintelligible. (2018, 95)

No doubt this is true, but neither Tsongkhapa's qualified argumentation nor any kind of panfictionalism can offer a way out of *this* conundrum. Instead, what is required is a strong dose of Madhyamaka analysis to remind us that an ultimate "genesis" for things cannot be located no matter *where* one begins the search. Instead, all realities, including all customary truths, arise within highly complex and interdependent causal nexuses that do indeed presuppose a context—one might even say a world.

What is established for the world thus depends, even for a deflationist, on *what was already established* for the world. The historical *a priori* of prior discoveries, ideas, concepts, and customary truths is part and parcel of the process of both making and judging truth claims. Here the Buddhist exclusion (*apoha*) theory of concept formation can be of use. While Tom sees the significance of this theory mainly in terms of its antimetaphysical and antifoundational emphasis on the ultimately fictional nature of universals, there is another way this theory can be helpful. That is, rather than stressing the truth or falsity of a universal, one can choose to focus on its truth as a social reality. When we take this tack, the questions of how particular objects and ideas have come to have standing in the world, and what has been excluded to get there, become extremely interesting and pertinent. We see that there *is* an important role for human ends, even if human ends are not the sole factor in determining what attains the status of customary truth. But insofar as human aims are one of the few areas where we seem to have some control in our worlds, it behooves us to inquire into the (perhaps hidden?) motivations that have gone into the construction of our truths. None of this impinges on the world's ability to adjudicate truth and falsity. But it does make it an ethical issue. What are the unintended consequences of producing the truths that we have produced to date? What has been elided, excluded, rendered invisible in the process? In short, of whose world do we speak when we speak about what is established for the world? Tom worries that the Mādhyamika imagines it to be a world of infantile or foolish beings, and he wants to make room for the wise to have a voice. My worry is that it is a world of those with privilege and power, and I want to make room for the excluded to have a voice.

Madhyamaka Buddhist Ethics

In an article dedicated to the question of Madhyamaka Buddhist ethics, Tom asks whether the antifoundational and antimetaphysical philosophical leanings of Madhyamaka thinkers impacts their ethics in any interesting way. For the most part, he maintains, it does not, stating that "Madhyamaka ethics is just general Mahāyāna Buddhist ethics, no more no less" (2011, 360). On his reading, the only real difference Madhyamaka philosophical intuitions make for Buddhist ethics is to shift canonical ethical norms (renunciation, compassion, generosity, and so on) from an ultimate to a conventional level of truth. Yet despite this apparent deflationism about Buddhist ethics, Tom nevertheless finds problems when Mādhyamikas rely on arguments that by their own account exceed the bounds of what is established for the world. Notwithstanding the presence of Buddhist ethical argumentation that appears to be directed at non-Buddhists and that relies only on ordinary reasons and facts—as, for example, in Candrakīrti's arguments concerning the four illusions discussed above—Tom maintains that much of Buddhist ethical argumentation crucially relies on "problematic facts," particularly, as we saw above, those "radically inaccessible" or "humanly inaccessible" (*atyantaparokṣa*) facts concerning the details of karmic cause and effect in past and future lives. In such cases, Mādhyamikas join other Buddhists in deferring to the extraordinary, omniscient knowledge of a Buddha to justify refraining from or engaging in unwholesome and wholesome activities, respectively. And Tillemans has written fairly extensively about the "scripturally based inference" (*āgamāśritānumāna*) that Dharmakīrti and other Buddhists have invoked as warrant for a judicious person (*prekṣāvant*) to use "when there is no other way."[5]

The problem with relying on scriptural teachings about karmic consequences as a justification for ethical actions is not so much the problem of a transfer of credibility according to which, on a reading favored by many Buddhists, because the Buddha can be shown through ordinary perception and inference to have been correct about such foundational things as the four noble truths, emptiness, and so on, he therefore is also to be trusted on such radically inaccessible topics as the details about karma. As Tom demonstrates, a transfer of credibility is fairly routine when it comes to matters of worldly expertise (e.g., it is not unreasonable to trust an expert in silver to counsel us about gold). But in this case, such a transfer is problematic since

---

5. See especially the articles collected in his *Scripture, Logic, Language*, particularly "How Much of a Proof Is Scripturally Based Inference?" (Tillemans 1999, 37–51).

there is no obvious relationship between knowledge of emptiness and so on and knowledge of karmic consequences. The authority of Buddhist scriptures when it comes to radically inaccessible matters is therefore *not* established for the world at large, even for those by whom the Buddha is recognized to be very wise, and a Mādhyamika who claims to operate only in terms of what is established for the world should presumably therefore not rely on the authority of scriptures to justify anything. Citing Owen Flanagan, Tom dismisses the Buddhist attempt to ground ethics in "humanly unfathomable facts" as found in Buddhist scriptures to be a form of "epistemological protectionism" (2011, 374). Instead of resorting to scriptures to justify their ethical positions, Tom advises contemporary Buddhists, including Mādhyamikas, to stick more closely to a secularized and humanized version of ethics. In doing so, he thinks, they will have a better chance of staying within the bounds of what is established for the world.

All this would be well and good were it not for the fact that Buddhist ethics does not actually require proof of past and future lives to function. Even ancient Indian Buddhists like Śāntarakṣita and Kamalaśīla recognize that not everyone is eager to jump on the Buddhist scriptural bandwagon, nor do they need to.[6] Justification for refraining from unwholesome actions and engaging in wholesome ones does not require proof of past and future lives, even if such proofs are not uncommon. An unwavering commitment to the reduction of suffering—which is one way to characterize the heart of the Buddhist ethical project—can rely solely on introspection and other forms of perception and inference to ascertain that unwholesome actions produce suffering while wholesome ones do not.[7] Recognizing that "this is suffering" is one of

---

6. See Śāntarakṣita's rejoinder (at *Tattvasaṃgraha* 2388–2391) to a Mīmāṃsaka claim that the intrinsic trustworthiness (*svataḥprāmāṇya*) of the Vedas ensures their scriptural statements will produce certainty (*niścaya*) in their hearers. Śāntarakṣita's initial response is to deny this is true. He grants that a certain "unshakability" (*niṣkampya*) of conviction may occur for believers due to their faith (*śraddhā*), and he admits that faithful Buddhists have a similar experience upon hearing scriptural statements from their own tradition. But such unshakability is not the same as the certainty that can be derived from the *pramāṇa*s of perception and inference, the only tools to produce true certainty for these thinkers. See McClintock 2010, 332–34, for translation and analysis.

7. In responding to an objection that a judicious person would not make any effort to undertake good or bad actions in the absence of an agent (*kartṛ*), Kamalaśīla responds in the *Tattvasaṃgrahapañjikā* ad *Tattvasaṃgraha* 540–541 that "skillful ordinary persons" (*pṛthagjanakalyāṇa*) are capable of recognizing the causal restrictions (*niyama*) that pertain between virtuous acts like generosity preceded by compassion and the beneficial effects of those acts for oneself and others. While the passage in question does mention understanding derived from scripture (*āgama*) as well as reasoning (*yukti*), the topics the skillful person is said

the goals of the teachings on dispelling the four illusions, and such recognition is enough to bring about a commitment to the reduction or even elimination of suffering through the actions of body, speech, and mind. Recognizing that "that is a cause of suffering" is one of the goals of the teachings on the four noble truths, and this recognition is sufficient to bring about the justification for refraining from unethical, unwholesome actions and engaging in ethical, wholesome ones. Scripturally based inference may be useful to inspire or increase enthusiasm for ethical action, but as a root justification it is pretty much irrelevant.

More interesting and relevant, though, is how a person comes to identify "this" and "that" in the course of seeking the reduction of suffering. Here the question of what is established for the world takes on a more compelling ethical dimension. To use Tom's own example, scripturally based arguments might be acceptable when used by committed Buddhists when debating, for example, the nature of the mind with other Buddhists, but such arguments will not carry weight for a "well meaning, but non-Buddhist, cognitive scientist working in a secular university."[8] This seems uncontroversial. What Tom overlooks here, however, is how the secular knowledge that the cognitive scientist produces, while it might be established for the world, is itself not at all ethically or epistemically neutral. A cognitive scientist comes to their discipline with a host of acquired ideas about all kinds of things, including bodies, brains, minds, health, illness, intelligence, gender, objectivity, evidence, and so on. These ideas are constructs that have arisen in dependence on a host of other historically and socially conditioned constructs and epistemological practices. While there is nothing inherently wrong with these constructs, they do exclude things. For example, the term "secular" here would seem designed to exclude the "religious," but these modern constructs are certainly far from

to need to understand are momentariness and selflessness (*kṣaṇikānatmatā*), both of which are said to be verifiable through ordinary inference (*anumāna*). See McClintock 2010, 334–36, for translation and analysis.

8. Tillemans 2011, 372. This calls to mind as well Śāntarakṣita's use of a scripturally based inference (*āgamāśritānumāna*) in the *Tattvasaṃgraha* in response to the Mīmāṃsaka reliance on scripture to deny the usual understanding of the Sanskrit term *pralaya*, often translated as "universal destruction." The Mīmāṃsaka wants to refute the charge that *pralaya* involves the utter annihilation of all things, as that would conflict with their commitment to the eternality of the meaning of the words of the Vedas. Under this circumstance, Śāntarakṣita deploys his own scripturally based inference based on Buddhist teachings in a kind of rhetorical tit for tat. His idea seems to be that while using such pseudo-inferences is not allowed normally, when arguing with non-judicious persons (e.g., persons who rely on scriptures to make public arguments), one may justifiably do so. See McClintock 2010, 337–39.

natural kinds.[9] If what is established for the world is restricted to what is secular, then does that mean that indigenous knowledge has nothing to offer? Likewise, the idea that a cognitive scientist would be an appropriate authority on the nature of the mind is fine, unless built into that claim is an assumption that the first-person knowledge of meditators is inherently suspect.[10] The problems proliferate when we realize that what is established for the world as a category only makes sense when we are able to specify what, or who, counts as the world. By overtly or inadvertently excluding certain people and ideas from the world, we risk overlooking not only valuable knowledge but also valuable persons (think women and cowherds) who possess that knowledge. Because the exclusions that produce what is established for the world tend to remain obscure due to our propensity to ignore differences in favor of superimposing essential identities, a Mādhyamika who understands that such identities are ultimately unreal should feel ethically compelled to seek out whether and how the particular exclusions in play further suffering or reduce it. As I see it then, what is established for the world is thus fine as a source of ethical justification for a Mādhyamika, provided that that Mādhyamika can make room in their understanding of the world for unfamiliar or divergent ways of knowing and provided that Mādhyamika can cultivate a high degree of epistemic humility regarding their own constructs and knowledge.

On Rational Reconstruction

Earlier, I said that Tom is engaged in a project of rational reconstruction regarding the Madhyamaka theory of customary truth, known also in this context as what is established for the world. Tom undertakes this rational reconstruction in order to think through issues surrounding how a Mādhyamika can justify both ordinary truth claims and ethical actions given Madhyamaka's antifoundational and antimetaphysical commitments. The tools Tom brings to this task are drawn mainly from analytic philosophy, including such methods as quietism about metaphysics and deflationism about truth. In undertaking this project in his work with the Cowherds and later, Tom echoes some of his earlier writings in which he draws inspiration from Imre Lakatos's method of rational reconstruction for the history of science and intellectual history. The goal of this method is to disentangle which aspects of scientific

9. On the construct of the secular and its political implications in modernity, see, for example, Asad 2003.

10. For an overview of the critique of first-person experience, as well as a defense of introspection as a valid source of scientific knowledge, see Petitmengin and Bitbol 2009.

progress are the result of the application of rational norms and which come from "residual non-rational factors" (Lakatos 1970, 105)—that is, empirical, historical, psychological factors and so on. Lakatos's method thus includes a distinction between internal and external history, with the former being, in Tom's words, "primarily logical deductions of what could have been said, given the key ideas of the philosopher in question," and the latter being "what was actually said, what actually took place" (1983, 312). Noting that the fifteenth-century Tibetan philosopher Tsongkhapa was himself engaged in a kind of rational reconstruction in his reading of the eighth-century Indian Buddhist thinker Śāntarakṣita, Tom makes a plea for the use of "fertile but foreign concepts" in our reading of ancient Buddhist texts. His idea seems to be that we can see what Mādhyamikas would have said—or would have been compelled to have said—had they had access to the rational thought of later times.

Of course, it is obvious to anyone who tries to write about ancient philosophy today that we cannot avoid using foreign concepts in our reading of the texts. We live and work in a different context, with a different set of languages, different reading practices, different technologies, and different concerns. And it is no less clear, to me at least, that such foreign concepts may indeed be fertile. But while this may be true, I am less certain about the value of rational reconstruction as a method for reading ancient philosophy. One impetus, it seems to me, for scholars of Buddhist philosophy to engage in rational reconstruction is that it allows us to play around within the structures of ancient texts so as to experiment with other ways to think about the ideas informing those structures. We see something like that in the distinction that Tom proposes between "a philosopher's 'thought,' viz his subjective states (henceforth 'thought$_1$'), or his philosophy taken as a set of propositions forming a system (henceforth 'thought$_2$')" (1990, 18). When examining a philosopher's thought$_2$ as a system, it then becomes "possible to attribute to him things which he never wrote, nor perhaps even thought$_1$ of" (1990, 18). Proceeding like this would appear to prioritize systems of thought$_2$ over the thought$_1$ of any particular thinker, and this process does indeed remind one of the hermeneutical moves that Tibetan scholars have made in their doxographical readings of Indian texts.[11] For a self-identified Prāsaṅgika Mādhyamika Buddhist like Tsongkhapa, it is perhaps unsurprising that he would treat Madhyamaka as a fully formed system (with its own well-defined subschools) and then place this system in conversation with other systems—for example, that of the Buddhist epistemologists—for the purpose of "imagining how the discussion

11. See McClintock 2018 for some reflections on the various uses of doxography in Indian Buddhist philosophy, including what I dub "doxographical hypostatization" (91–95).

could reasonably proceed" (1990, 18). Similarly, it is not surprising that modern interpreters as well would seek to bring Madhyamaka into dialogue with other kinds of philosophy, whether ancient or modern, to see what new ideas might emerge. But to attribute these new ideas to the earlier authors strikes me as unnecessary, misguided, even bizarre.

What tends to get lost when we do rational reconstruction is the historicity of rationality itself. The idea that there is a purely rational component to the historically embedded philosophical texts we encounter—and further, that we are in a position to recognize it—is only possible when we suppress the historically contingent and constructed (and thus exclusionary) dimensions of our own ideas. Lakatos himself claims that "rational reconstruction or internal history is primary, external history only secondary, since the most important problems of external history are defined by internal history" (1970, 105). He understands the history of philosophy as a battle between the normative-internal and the empirical-external, and in doing so he leaves rational norms as freestanding realities, seeing them independent of the persons, cultures, languages, contexts, and exclusions that give rise to them. From a Madhyamaka perspective, this makes no sense. *All* the norms of philosophy and of the rest of life are dependently arisen. None have independent autonomous identities. Philosophy cannot be disentangled from history, nor should we desire it to be so. Neither the normative-internal nor the empirical-external has precedence or independent existence, but both mutually condition one another and arise interdependently.

If the idea of rational reconstruction is invoked merely to create a bridge for us to engage in philosophical dialogue with persons whose embodied presence has become spectral for us, then we can rely on Richard Rorty's idea of the method according to which contemporary philosophers treat "great dead philosophers…as contemporaries, as colleagues with whom they can exchange views" (1984, 49). But this renders the method trivial. There is in that case no need for rational reconstruction. Philosophers today can read philosophy from the past and do with it what they will, including critiquing, augmenting, or adapting whatever it is that they find there. Ideally, they will attempt a respectful reading, and they will try to educate themselves in the historical factors (languages, cultural mores, idioms, genres, and so on) that condition the philosophical thinking that interests them. As Matthew Kapstein has eloquently demonstrated in relation to the study of Indian philosophy more generally, "it is not desirable to adopt here too restrictive a conception of philosophical research" (2017, 26). Urging us to "read around the edges of our sources," he points to the importance of taking into account a wide range of factors, including rhetorical strategies and literary constructions, that cannot be reduced to an ahistorical conception of what counts as rational.

Just as ancient philosophers have done, it is entirely valid for us modern people to use philosophical ideas derived from all manner of earlier sources whenever and wherever we find that they are "good to think."[12] Here, we need not claim to know what ancient Buddhists would have said, still less what they would have been *obliged* to say, were they here with us now. Rather, we need only claim that this is what *we* would say *to* those Buddhists, as we imagine them and as we encounter them in texts of diverse genres and degrees of canonicity, if we could meet them today. My qualms about what is established for the world are thus of this nature: I think that the Madhyamaka deflationist method of relying on what is established for the world, including for its experts, should be augmented through attending to the power dimensions that regulate whose world and whose knowledge attain credibility and how they do so. Further, I think this process has inevitable and serious ethical dimensions. It strikes me as very likely that the elite, conversative, male, monastic authors of the ancient Sanskrit texts with which I regularly engage would reject this way of thinking, just as they would reject me as any kind of authority. Very likely they would laugh at my plea for them to ask "whose world is this?" when considering the Madhyamaka criterion of what is established for the world. So be it. I do not care. I do not seek to rationally reconstruct their thought but to use it to think—accepting what is useful, rejecting what is not, and recognizing that my thinking, like theirs, is deeply and unquestionably historically conditioned and impermanent.

Bibliography

Armour-Garb, Bradley, Daniel Stoljar, and James Woodbridge. 2023. "Deflationism About Truth." In *The Stanford Encyclopedia of Philosophy* (Summer 2023 edition), edited by Edward N. Zalta and Uri Nodelman. https://plato.stanford.edu/archives/sum2023/entries/truth-deflationary/.

Asad, Talal. 2003. *Formations of the Secular: Christianity, Islam, and Modernity.* Stanford: Stanford University Press.

Kapstein, Matthew T. 2017. "Interpreting Indian Philosophy: Three Parables." In *The Oxford Handbook of Indian Philosophy*, edited by Jonardon Ganeri, 15–31. Oxford: Oxford University Press.

12. Kapstein 2017, 19–20, notes that Cannibhaṭṭa, the fourteenth-century logician and probable author of the *Compendium of All Viewpoints* (*Sarvadarśanasaṃgraha*), describes the Cārvākas by relying on a satirical passage from an eleventh-century drama, the *Rise of Wisdom Moon* (*Prabhodacandrodaya*). Cannibhaṭṭa does so, Kapstein maintains, because he finds the ideas attributed to the Cārvākas, even as derisively depicted in this literary work, "good to think."

Lakatos, Imre. 1970. "History of Science and Its Rational Reconstruction." *Proceedings of the Biennial Meeting of the Philosophy of Science Association* 1970: 91–136.

MacKenzie, Matthew. 2008. "Ontological Deflationism in Madhyamaka." *Contemporary Buddhism* 9.2: 197–207.

McClintock, Sara. 2010. *Omniscience and the Rhetoric of Reason: Śāntarakṣita and Kamalaśīla on Rationality, Argumentation, and Religious Authority.* Studies in Indian and Tibetan Buddhism. Boston: Wisdom Publications.

———. 2018. "Schools, Schools, Schools—Or, Must a Philosopher Be Like a Fish?" In *Buddhist Spiritual Practices: Thinking with Pierre Hadot on Buddhism, Philosophy, and the Path*, edited by David V. Fiordalis, 71–103. Berkeley: Mangalam Press.

———. 2019. "How to Do Things with Natures: A Madhyamaka Approach to Arguments and Appearances." *Journal of the International Association of Buddhist Studies* 42: 409–47.

Newman, John. 2024. "Candrakīrti on *lokaprasiddhi*: A Bad Hand, or an Ace in the Hole?" *Journal of Indian Philosophy* 52: 73–99.

Petitmengin, Claire, and Michel Bitbol. 2009. "The Validity of First-Person Descriptions as Authenticity and Coherence." *Journal of Consciousness Studies* 16.10–12: 363–404.

Rorty, Richard. 1984. "The Historiography of Philosophy: Four Genres." In *Philosophy in History*, edited by Richard Rorty, J. B. Schneewind, and Quentin Skinner, 49–75. Cambridge: Cambridge University Press.

Tillemans, Tom J. F. 1983. "The 'Neither One Nor Many' Argument for *śūnyatā* and Its Tibetan Interpretations." *Contributions on Tibetan and Buddhist Religion and Philosophy: Proceedings of the Csoma de Kőrös Symposium held at Velm-Vienna, Austria, 13–19 September 1981,* vol. 2, edited by Ernst Steinkellner and Helmut Tauscher, 305–20. Vienna: Arbeitskreis für Tibetsiche und Buddhistische Studien, Universität Wien.

———. 1990. *Materials for the Study of Āryadeva, Dharmapāla and Candrakīrti: Introduction, Translation, Sanskrit, Tibetan and Chinese Texts, Notes.* 2 vols. Wiener Studien zur Tibetologie und Buddhismuskunde 24. Vienna: Arbeitskreis für Tibetische und Buddhistische Studien Universität Wien.

———. 1999. *Scripture, Logic, Language: Essays on Dharmakīrti and His Tibetan Successors.* Studies in Indian and Tibetan Buddhism. Boston: Wisdom Publications.

———. 2011. "Madhyamaka Buddhist Ethics." *Journal of the International Association of Buddhist Studies* 33.1–2: 359–78.

———. 2016. *How Do Mādhyamikas Think? And Other Essays on the Buddhist Philosophy of the Middle.* Studies in Indian and Tibetan Buddhism. Boston: Wisdom Publications.

———. 2017. "Philosophical Quietism in Nāgārjuna and Early Madhyamaka." In *The Oxford Handbook of Indian Philosophy*, edited by Jonardon Ganeri, 110–32. Oxford: Oxford University Press.

———. 2018. "Metaphysics and Metametaphysics with Buddhism: The Lay of the Land." In *Buddhist Philosophy: A Comparative Approach*, edited by Steven M. Emmanuel, 87–107. Hoboken, NJ: Wiley Blackwell.

———. 2019. "Mādhyamikas Playing Bad Hands: The Case of Customary Truth." *Journal of Indian Philosophy* 47: 635–44.

———. 2022. "A Comparative Philosophy Excursus: Deflating the Two Images and the Two Truths." In *Views from Tibet: Studies on Tibetan Buddhist Logic, the Philosophy of the Middle, and the Indigenous Grammatico-Linguistic Tradition*, 235–57. Vienna: Austrian Academy of Sciences.

When the World Is Not Enough:
An Early Tibetan Discussion on
the Division of Customary Truth

Pascale Hugon

TWO DECADES AGO on a cold day of January, Tom Tillemans came into the assistants' office at the University of Lausanne and handed me an amazing belated Christmas present: a CD-ROM containing three works by Chapa Chökyi Sengé (Phya pa Chos kyi seng ge, 1109–69). The fortunate surfacing of these works was followed by the publication of rich additional material from that effervescent period, the exploration of which is already starting to shed a new light on the early developments of Tibetan Pramāṇa and Madhyamaka. Over the course of his career, Tom Tillemans has greatly contributed to our understanding of both these textual traditions. His inquiries into Madhyamaka have drawn forth the philosophical implications of Candrakīrti's antirealist and antifoundationalist stand, as well as the exegetical approaches within Indian and Tibetan intellectual history that address Candrakīrti's rejection of means of valid cognition advocated by Buddhist epistemologists in favor of reliance on "what is established for the world" (*lokaprasiddha*) on the level of customary truth. In honor of Tom's invaluable contribution to the field and as a token of gratitude for his admirable mentorship, I propose in this paper to add another layer of historical depth to the unfolding of this Madhyamaka debate by unveiling an early-stage Tibetan dispute on the option of "following the world."

The positions and arguments I discuss are those of late eleventh-to-twelfth-century scholars in the Madhyamaka lineage stemming from Ngok Loden Sherab (Rngog Blo ldan shes rab, 1059–1109), whose views are found in a work by Gyamarwa Jangchup Drak (Rgya dmar ba Byang chub grags) (fl. ca. 1095–1135), the *Dbu ma de kho na nyid rnam par dpyod pa* (hereafter *Dbu dpyod*).[1]

---

1. The *Dbu dpyod* is being edited and translated by Kevin Vose and myself (https://www.oeaw

The *Dbu dpyod* offers a fascinating panorama of ongoing debates predating the full bloom of Patsab Nyima Drak's (Pa tshab Nyi ma grags, b. 1055) influence and spread of Candrakīrti's thought in Tibet (on which see Vose 2009). Far from constituting a unified front, scholars in Ngok's lineage are seen throughout the work to have held diverging positions, prefiguring in some cases later debates that would become embedded in the Svātantrika/Prāsaṅgika divide. In the section dealing with the distinction between correct and mistaken conventionals (*yang dag pa'i / log pa'i kun rdzob*), on which the present paper is based,[2] in addition to the author himself, there are two other scholars involved in the conversation. We can identify them with a high degree of confidence as Khyung Rinchen Drak (Khyung Rin chen grags) and Gangpa Sheu Lodrö Jangchup (Gangs pa she'u Blo gros byang chub), both of whom were disciples of Ngok and teachers of Gyamarwa.[3]

Khyung's Position

I focus in this paper on Gangpa and Gyamarwa's criticism of Khyung's view that Mādhyamikas should just "follow the world" to establish the distinction between correct and mistaken conventionals.[4] Khyung's position contrasts with that of his peers (and, before them, of Ngok), who make this distinction in the framework of a specific tenet system (*grub mtha'*). The tenet sys-

.ac.at/ikga/forschung/tibetologie/materialien/the-dbu-ma-de-kho-na-nyid-of-rgya-dmar-ba -byang-chub-grags-12th-c/). See Hugon 2020a and 2020b for introductory remarks. Ma 2023 discusses a (reworked) Tangut version of that treatise as well as a Tangut summary of it.

2. This passage is located in the fourth section of the chapter on the definiens of the two truths (*Dbu dpyod*, 10a6–15a7). See Hugon 2020a, 347–49, for the structure of the passage and a preliminary survey of positions and arguments.

3. The author does not name the proponents of the views he reports, but they are often identified in interlinear and marginal annotations. These annotations are in great part included in the main text in the Tangut version (Ma 2023). I argued (Hugon 2020b) that the extent of the annotation and their precision lend support to the hypothesis that the annotator lived in relatively close temporal proximity to the author and can generally be trusted in his identifications. The annotations mentioning "gangs pa" or "she'u" obviously refer to Gangpa, and there is supporting evidence for identifying the scholar identified as "jo btsun" as Khyung, the latter being also identified a few times as "rin chen grags." To simplify the discussion in what follows, I assume the identifications to be accurate and take at face value the report of the respective positions. The reader should therefore be aware of the phrasing shortcuts applied— for instance, in writing "Khyung claims X" rather than "Gyamarwa ascribes claim X to an anonymous scholar whom the annotations identify as Jotsün, who can be argued to be Khyung."

4. This view is phrased *'jig rten gyis ji ltar rtogs dang mthun 'dod* (*Dbu dpyod*, 12a2), *'jig rten pas ji ltar bzhag pa de ltar khas blangs pa tsam* (12b2), and *'jig rten pa'i rjes 'brangs* (12b7).

tems presented as an option are labeled using Tibetan terms that translate the Sanskrit Yogācāra, Sautrāntika, and Vaibhāṣika(-like), but the classification boils down to two parameters: whether extra-mental objects are accepted to exist and, if they are, whether cognition is held to proceed via aspects (*rnam pa*).[5] Khyung's main argument to reject such tenet systems is that they cannot be supported by reasoning (*rigs pa*) on account of the lack of a distinguishing criterion between reasoning that refutes ultimate existence and reasoning that refutes conventional existence.[6] This "absence of distinction of reasoning" (*rigs pa'i rnam dbye med pa*) affects the Sautrāntika-Mādhyamikas who would like the argument refuting the existence of God to refute its conventional existence but the argument refuting the existence of external objects to refute their ultimate existence only. In the same way, it affects Yogācāra-Mādhyamikas who want to refute the conventional existence of extra-mental objects with a neither-one-nor-many argument but want that same argument, when applied to mind, only to refute its ultimate existence. Thus, in the absence of a criterion of differentiation, reasoning can support neither external realism nor idealism and generally speaking cannot be instrumental in establishing the distinction between correct and mistaken conventionals.

The gist of Gangpa and Gyamarwa's criticism of Khyung's position consists in exposing the incompatibility between following the world, rejecting tenet systems, and not relying on reasoning to establish what is correct/mistaken conventional.

Gangpa's Refutation of Khyung

Picking up primarily on Khyung's claim of "following the world," Gangpa points to two features of the world. The first is the absence of unanimity among people as to what is true and what is not. In other words, there is

5. The three options are referred to in the *Dbu dpyod* by the expressions *rnal 'byor spyod pa / rnam rig pa* (also, *sems tsam pa* in the annotations); *mdo sde spyod pa / mdo sde ba*; *bye brag du smra ba dang mthun par spyod pa / bye brag smra ba*. Yogācāra is opposed to *phyi rol gyi don yod pa* ("external realism") and *yul sems gnyis* ("mind-object dualism"). Sautrāntika is also referred to as *rnam bcas* ("representationalist") and Vaibhāṣika as *rnam med* and *rnam med don 'dzin* ("nonrepresentationalist"). Gyamarwa does not apply the *rnam bcas / rnam med* division to Yogācāra, but the annotations mention the subdivision *rnam bden / rnam rdzun* (*Dbu dpyod*, 2a7). See Hugon 2016, 54–59, on Chapa's doxographical division along similar parameters and the expressions he uses for the corresponding tenet systems.

6. Khyung adds that there is no proof of extra-mental reality and that an idealist position that does not refute extra-mental objects (which corresponds to the system adopted by Gangpa) is not proper (*Dbu dpyod*, 10b5–6 and 10b7).

no such thing as worldly *agreement*. There is also a diversity among people themselves—namely, a distinction between experts (*'jig rten mkhas pa*) and non-experts, which Gangpa connects with the difference between the opinions of the world: non-experts, for instance, assert mountains to be permanent, while experts assert this not to be true.[7] The expert here is not an enlightened being or a noble being (*ārya*), who knows appearances to be empty; they are just someone in the world who knows better than others about the conventional. That the example is about the impermanence of mountains and not, for instance, of sound, suggests that the expert is simply aware that mountains are not eternally existent although they appear to last, rather than their being more subtly aware of the momentariness of all things. Obviously, the expert is the one to be followed!

Tillemans (2016, chap. 2, and 2022, chap. 6) has pointed out the downsides of a "populist view" of customary truth upheld by Candrakīrti, noting that a possible impetus to this version could have been the disappearance of the mention of qualified experts—"the wise" (*paṇḍita*)—in the scriptural passage from the Ratnakūṭa sūtras Candrakīrti quotes in this connection.[8] Siderits (in the present volume) suggests that expertise might well offer a way out of what Tillemans (2011, 152) labeled the "dismal slough," while McClintock (also in the present volume) reflects on the potentially negative consequences of following experts in contrast to a more inclusive approach making room for the non-experts in adjudicating truth and falsity. Resorting to experts may indeed solve the problem of the absence of general consensus and bypass the often mistaken views of ordinary beings. However, an appeal to expertise raises several issues; for instance, expert opinion may be subject to revision, the privileged status of expert opinion itself is debatable (Tanaka 2015, 49), and experts themselves fail to agree. The problem that Gangpa points out is that of establishing who is the expert. If the distinction between experts and non-experts were to follow the world, lack of unanimity as to who are the experts would bring the need for experts capable of establishing who is an expert and who is not, a process leading to infinite regress. This option and its consequences are not explicit in Gangpa's argument, which directly moves to examining another option for establishing the expert/non-expert distinction—namely, relying on reasoning. Gangpa presents the following dilemma: Without reasoning of one's own, one cannot distinguish between experts and non-experts,

---

7. The example of the mountain is supplemented in the annotations to *Dbu dpyod*, 12b2.

8. Vose (2010, 577n84–85) cites passages of the *Madhyamakāvatāra* indicating that Candrakīrti would have acknowledged worldly expertise regarding particular subjects (e.g., recognizing precious gems) but denied expertise to the non-*ārya*s when it comes to deliberations on reality.

and therefore following the world is bound to fail on account of worldly disagreement. With reasoning of one's own, one can indeed identify the expert. But such reasoning can also apply to distinguish what is correct and incorrect.[9] The very process of resorting to experts thus becomes redundant, and Khyung's claim that such distinction is not achieved by reasoning but by following the world is contradicted.

Gyamarwa's Refutation of Khyung

While Gangpa's argument set forth from a world constituted of non-experts (who are deluded) and experts (who are not), the preeminent understanding of what "the world" is in Gyamarwa's analysis is the world of naïve people, of which cowherds are the epitome. Gyamarwa grants that among such people, unanimous agreement can be found regarding two key points: the existence of extra-mental objects and their being known themselves directly, rather than consciousness having only access to internal representations generated by extra-mental objects projecting their aspect to the perceiver's consciousness. Of course, it is not likely that cowherds (as caricatured in these discussions) would articulate their worldview in such terms, but it can be argued that if one asks a cowherd whether his cows are "in his head" or "out there in the field," and whether what he sees are cows or a mental image of cows, it is predictable what the cowherd's answer would be. Gyamarwa argues that what the world agrees upon—in short, the "apprehension of objects (distinct from the mind) without aspects" (*rnam med kyis don 'dzin*)—is no different from the Vaibhāṣika(-like) tenet system. Consequently, a Mādhyamika following the world would actually subscribe to Vaibhāṣika Madhyamaka.

In addition to this line of inquiry that considers what the world *thinks*, Gyamarwa considers worldly agreement in terms of what the world *sees*, bringing into play the notion of "worldly common appearance" (*'jig rten gyi mthun snang*). This could provide a degree of consensus but, Gyamarwa argues, leads

---

9. I see two ways of understanding Gangpa's argument here: One is that the identification of expertise *presupposes* knowing what the expert knows; that is, to "test" someone's expertise, one becomes oneself an expert by relying on one's own analytical faculty. Another interpretation is that the argument is about the applicability of the same analytical faculty to various objects: Someone who can distinguish *who* is right and *who* is wrong would also be able to distinguish *what* is true and *what* is false; the identification of expertise would *imply* the possibility of knowing oneself what the expert knows but not presuppose it. Because what is to be cognized here is potentially accessible to all, the case is different from the establishment of authority in order to gain knowledge pertaining to states of affairs that are completely inaccessible to ordinary beings, a question Gangpa and his peers must have been acquainted with via Dharmakīrti's treatment of the topic.

to the same conclusion: for naïve people, such common appearance—for example, the apprehension of "blue"—is understood as that of extra-mental objects without aspects, so that reliance on common appearance amounts to adopting the tenet system of Vaibhāṣika Madhyamaka. Further, if common appearance is understood in terms of "common understanding" (*rtogs pa mthun pa*), some analysis is involved that requires a decision about extramental reality and aspects, and hence the adoption of a tenet system.[10]

Thus the world is made of people who overtly follow tenet systems, people who do not but are led to adopt one when engaging in reflection about their epistemic practices, and naïve people. The first would not be candidates to be followed for Khyung, the second fall into one or the other pre-set tenet systems, and the worldview of the third turns out to match Vaibhāṣika. Thus "following the world," either in terms of "worldly agreement" or "common appearance," is incompatible with rejecting the adoption of a tenet system.

In Gyamarwa's analysis, the naïve who agree on external realism and non-representationalism are described as being "uninfluenced by tenet systems."[11] This notion of the world (and especially "common appearance") connotes a nonphilosophical approach rather than being tied with "ignorance" or "lack of understanding." In addition, let us note that, according to Gyamarwa, the naïve are actually the ones who "get it right"! The naïve are saved by their very lack of learning, as philosophical treatises might just have led them astray. Their intuitive worldview is confirmed when tenet systems are analyzed: Sautrāntika Madhyamaka and Yogācāra Madhyamaka are subject to refutation, whereas Vaibhāṣika Madhyamaka is demonstrated to be a suitable framework to distinguish correct and mistaken conventionals. This may be surprising to readers familiar with the "ascending scale of analysis" applied by scholars of the Great Vehicle, in which Vaibhāṣika is considered the lowest explanatory model.[12] To be clear, Gyamarwa does not subscribe to this tenet system by relying on the world. He does present a set of arguments proving

10. *Dbu dpyod*, 11b3–4 and 11b4–5. On the origin of the expression *mthun snang*, see note 25 below. Note that Patsab's commentary on Nāgārjuna's *Mūlamadhyamakakārikā* (Pa tshab, *Rtsa shes gsal byed*, 8b6, column 2) also delineates two understandings of *mthun snang*: common appearance to visual perception and common appearance of the subject for opponents in a debate. Gyamarwa's argument for "common understanding" implying the adoption of a tenet system is that *rtogs pa* itself must be determined to be extra-mental or not. This alternative would not make much sense if *rtogs pa* is "the understanding" (which is necessarily mental); the argument may thus be about "what is understood" or "the person who understands."

11. *Dbu dpyod*, 11a8: *grub mthas blo ma bcos*; 11b3: *grub mthas blo ma bsgyur*.

12. See McClintock 2010, 12 and 85–91, on the sliding scale of analysis in Śāntarakṣita and Kamalaśīla's works, and Dunne 2004, 53–79, and his contribution in the present volume.

the existence of extra-mental reality and refuting aspects and has answers for the classical arguments against Vaibhāṣika.[13]

Now, one may conceive that naïve people agree on external realism and nonrepresentationalism, but would their agreement extend to more specific issues? Do cowherds all agree on whether mountains are permanent or impermanent, or whether a permanent creator God exists? Gyamarwa does not address this question, because the point he wants to make in that context is that "following the world" amounts to adopting an external-realist nonrepresentationalist tenet system. Where does one go from there? It may be felt that the Vaibhāṣika tenet system is not elaborate enough and that the tenets of external realism and nonrepresentationalism would not fare better than just following the world when it comes to broadening our knowledge about conventional reality—for example, "technical subjects like logic, linguistics, and economics, not to mention physical science" (Tillemans 2011, 161). There is no indication that Gyamarwa's idea is that one should just adopt every Vaibhāṣika tenet in the book—the specification Vaibhāṣika-*like* (*bye brag du smra ba dang mthun par spyod pa*) could hint to the limited scope of the agreement.[14] Gyamarwa indicates that reasoning comes into play to decide on individual instances—for example, to refute the existence of God (and, one can expect, other instances of incorrect conventionals). Indeed Gyamarwa does offer a solution for distinguishing arguments that refute conventionally versus ultimately. He also holds that one can rely on valid cognition—perception and inference—to establish theses on the level of conventional reality. He thus has at his disposal a set of normative tools for distinguishing correct from incorrect conventionals, whose application can range to new domains of exploration, including those not directly relevant to the Buddhist path. What about Khyung?

Khyung on Valid Cognition

Khyung rejects the possibility that reasoning (*rigs pa*) could play a role in establishing what is correct or incorrect or in establishing a tenet system. Nevertheless, his position does not involve the rejection of reasoning as such, nor

---

13. A notable objection targets the object and the cognition of that object being distinct but simultaneous. See *Dbu dpyod*, 14a7–b1, for Gyamarwa's answer, and 10a8 for Ngok's. I discuss Gyamarwa's justification for his position in Hugon 2020a, 354–57.

14. Gyamarwa's agreement with Vaibhāṣika extends to the identification of the agent of cognition (Hugon 2020a, 356), whereas Chapa disagrees with the Vaibhāṣika on that point (Hugon 2016, 75).

that of valid cognition. On the contrary, Khyung is reported to claim, "Let us not get rid of valid cognition conventionally!"[15] What kind of valid cognition does he have in mind, and what should its scope be? Khyung wants to account for the inference of fire from smoke and the perception of pleasure or blue, but he surely also wants to account for more elaborate inferences such as the neither-one-nor-many argument, on which, as the *Dbu dpyod* section on this proof demonstrates, he has a lot to say.[16] There is no indication that Khyung means to follow the path Candrakīrti takes in disclaiming the twofold valid cognition model of the Buddhist epistemologists but conceding a fourfold set of perception, inference, scripture, and analogy that are means by which "the world knows things" (*lokasyārthādhigama*).[17] There is also no evidence that Khyung's appeal to preserve conventional valid cognition might be about allowing valid cognition based on what the world accepts but rejecting valid cognition relying on the force of facts, which would prefigure Maja Jangchup Tsöndrü (Rma bya Byang chub brtson 'grus, d. 1185?), who strove to integrate valid cognition in Candrakīrtian Madhyamaka by way of "valid cognition recognized in the world" (*'jig rten la grags pa'i tshad ma*) (Doctor 2009, 432–33). Rather, what transpires in Gyamarwa's arguments against Khyung is a model of valid cognition that is framed not in a specific tenet system but in worldly common appearance. In Gyamarwa's opinion, a nonspecific model of valid cognition—such that, for instance, fire can be inferred from smoke without determining whether this "fire" exists outside consciousness—is not acceptable, and even less so if a nonspecific model is adopted because the tenet systems supporting specific models of valid cognition have been refuted. Once again, the upshot of invoking the way the world conceives of valid cognition is that a specific tenet system is adopted.

Pramāṇa Context and Madhyamaka Context

There is an additional subtlety in Khyung's position regarding tenet systems, which has to do with his distinction of two "contexts" (*skabs*). Khyung claims

15. *Dbu dpyod*, 11b1: *tha snyad du yang tshad ma chad par ma gyur cig*; 11a5: *tha snyad chad par ma gyur cig*.

16. Gyamarwa reports Khyung's views pertaining to the subject, the negandum, the establishment of the qualification of the subject by the logical reason, and pervasion.

17. Vose 2021. See also Vose 2010, 556ff., which discusses Candrakīrti's avowal of these four in the *Prasannapadā* (see 556n11 for the reference) in relation to his critique of Dignāga's twofold valid cognition. Vose notes that even this fourfold valid cognition was discarded by exegetes such as Patsab (who simply does not mention it) and Jayānanda (who argues that they do not produce certainty).

that while tenets systems cannot be adopted in the Madhyamaka context (*dbu ma'i skabs*), they are acceptable in the Pramāṇa context (*tshad ma'i skabs*) or, less specifically, "in general" (*spyir*). Exemplifying the latter, he mentions the model of valid cognition matching Sautrāntika and the (Yogācāra) proof that external objects do not exist distinct from the mind—there is little doubt he is referring to Dharmakīrti's discussion.

Because the "Madhyamaka context" is also labeled the "context of endorsing Madhyamaka" (*dbu ma khas blangs pa'i skabs*), the distinction of context does not stand out as a mere hermeneutical device a commentator could resort to when explaining, respectively, an epistemological treatise or a Madhyamaka treatise. The two contexts are, rather, the perspectives of Mādhyamikas and of non-Mādhyamikas. Although there is no explicit statement of a hierarchy between the two contexts, the status of the Pramāṇa context is inferior in that views held in that context are, according to Khyung, refuted in the Madhyamaka context.

"This is something I do not subscribe to!" ripostes Gyamarwa to this distinction. Gyamarwa holds on to the notion that what is established by valid cognition cannot be invalidated. Thus what is established "in general" or in the Pramāṇa context by conventional valid cognition remains established even when one endorses Madhyamaka: "If smoke proves fire in another context, one should accept that it does so as well in the Madhyamaka context."[18] Simply, from a Madhyamaka perspective, this is established on the level of customary truth. What subscribing to Madhyamaka does undermine is the acceptance of *ultimate* entities, but this is not what is established by conventional valid cognitions. Thus Vaibhāṣika as a substantialist tenet system positing atoms and moments of consciousness to be ultimate entities *is* refuted in the Madhyamaka context on account of that view. On the other hand, external realism and nonrepresentationalism, once established by valid cognition, are not undermined by endorsing Madhyamaka. As such, the Pramāṇa context is embedded in the Madhyamaka context. This is the model that Chapa will adopt as well. In his works, the distinction of contexts is reflected in the use of a distinct terminology. Notably, the division of apprehended objects (*gzung yul*) into "real" (*dngos po*) or "unreal" (*dngos med*) in his epistemological works is transposed in his Madhyamaka works into a division between correct and mistaken conventionals (Hugon 2016). Both Gyamarwa and

---

18. *Dbu dpyod,* 11b7: <*tshad ma'i*> *skabs gzhan du du bas me sgrub* <*par 'dod*> *na ni dbu ma'i skabs su 'ang 'dod par bya ba nyid do //.* With the annotations in < > brackets, the sentence translates "If it is asserted that smoke proves fire in another context, that of Pramāṇa, one should accept that it does so as well in the Madhyamaka context."

Chapa are in favor of a blending of the two domains, whereas for Khyung the Madhyamaka context prevails. Their blending of Pramāṇa and Madhyamaka may be seen as an early manifestation of the combination that would come to be referred to with the term *dbu tshad* or, more poetically, "the yoked necks of the lions of the Middle Way and Epistemology" (*dbu tshad seng ge mjing snol gyi snyan ming*).[19]

Khyung was not only a Madhyamaka scholar. He was obviously very active in the field of epistemology; he is notably remembered for contributions to the theory of definition (van der Kuijp 1983, 59), and the *Tshad bsdus*, a twelfth-century epistemological summary that refers to him at least thirty-four times, reports his views on a variety of other topics as well (van der Kuijp 2003). Khyung was also an instrumental link in the transmission lineage of Dharmakīrti's *Pramāṇaviniścaya* (van der Kuijp 1983, 47). His division of contexts does not prevent his being an interpreter of Dharmakīrti—explaining Dharmakīrti's Pramāṇa works—but it would preclude his being a Pramāṇavādin. To follow Dharmakīrti, he would need to place a hold on his Madhyamaka endorsement. No epistemological work of Khyung is available that would enable us to see what his strategy would have been and how he would explain the relevance of "doing Pramāṇa" or of just studying Dharmakīrti's works. In contrast, Gyamarwa and Chapa have no problem wearing the two hats of Pramāṇavādin and Mādhyamika; simply, what they hold or establish via a valid cognition in the Pramāṇa context comes to be qualified with the adverb "conventionally" from the perspective of the second. On the other hand, because of their adoption of Vaibhāṣika Madhyamaka in the Madhyamaka context and therefore—and as attested for Chapa—of Vaibhāṣika(-like) in the Pramāṇa context, they face the accusation of "contradiction with scriptures" (*lung dang 'gal ba*), i.e., with the works of Dharmakīrti. Gyamarwa's answer is to argue that the discussion involving Sautrāntika and Yogācāra tenets in Dharmakīrti's works only represents Dharmakīrti's exposition of these tenet systems; they are not to be taken as Dharmakīrti's own position.[20]

19. The expression is used by Taktsang Sherab Rinchen (Stag tshang Shes rab rin chen, 1405–77) to criticize the approach of Tsongkhapa Losang Drakpa (Tsong kha pa Blo bzang grags pa, 1357–1419) (Hopkins 2003, 536).

20. The *Dbu dpyod* does not specify what Gyamarwa considers to be Dharmakīrti's own position—and whether he considers him a Mādhyamika. See Hugon 2016, 81–88, for a review of the scholarship dealing with Tibetan scholars' opinions on this topic and an assessment of the opinions of Chapa and some of his followers.

Conclusion

Khyung advocates "the world" as the norm for customary truth as an alternative to relying on specific tenet systems. Gangpa's and Gyamarwa's examination of Khyung's position introduced different notions of "the world" (non-experts/experts; cowherds/philosophers) and of "worldly agreement" (common appearance; common understanding), none of which was in itself found to support—without either presupposing or implying other normative factors—an acceptable model to account for distinctions within customary truth. The world alone is not enough. While keeping in phase with what the world (in its naïve understanding) accepts, Gyamarwa vouches for tenet systems, reasoning, and conventional valid cognition. Because Khyung preserves the third and does not reject reasoning as such (but because of the impossibility of specifying its range), a pertinent way of contrasting Gyamarwa and Khyung's positions is in terms of "following tenets" vs. "following the world." Such a distinction is described in the *Bden gnyis spyi bshad*, a work possibly dating to the late eleventh century that reports the teaching of Atiśa (982–1054) on the two truths.[21] It lists three methods to distinguish between correct and mistaken conventionals: relying on the world, relying on tenet systems, and relying on yogic awareness (Apple 2016, 641). The first is backed up by the citation of Candrakīrti's *Madhyamakāvatāra* 6.25.[22] Jñānagarbha is mentioned as an example for the second method, which can apply in any non-Buddhist or Buddhist system. The third method, connected to *Madhyamakāvatāra* 6.28,

21. See Apple 2016 for a study and translation of this work. The Drepung catalogue (item 19079) reports the author to be Gö Lotsāwa Shönu Pal ('Gos Lo tsā ba Gzhon nu dpal, 1392–1481), also given as author of the preceding five items in the catalogue, which share the same folio size. The manuscript however makes no mention of Gö. The text ends with the remark "taught by Atiśa" (*a ti sha'i gsungs yin no*, the "a" of Atiśa is not visible on the manuscript image). Based on the Madhyamaka lineage mentioned in the work, Apple identifies the author as a student or colleague of the eleventh-century Kadampa scholar Gya Chakri Gongkhawa Jangchup Pal (Rgya Lcags ri gong kha ba Byang chub dpal), possibly Gampopa Sönam Rinchen (Sgam po pa Bsod nam rin chen) (1079–1153) early in his career.

22. This method, termed *lo ka pa la ltos pa*, is explained by rephrasing MA 6.25 as follows: "Appearances of people from expert scholars to dumb cowherds established as the apprehended object of the six unimpaired sense faculties, which are posited to be true in common appearance, are all set forth as correct conventionals. What, like the eight similes of illusion, is not established as the apprehended object of the six sense faculties but is posited to be false in common appearance by the world, from expert scholars to dumb cowherds, are all set forth as mistaken conventionals." (Anon., *Bden gnyis spyi bshad*, 2b1–4. Translation mine. Apple's translation [2016, 641] omits the first part of the sentence.) Note that the expression *mthun snang* ("common appearance") does not appear in Atiśa's own works.

appears to correspond to that preferred by Atiśa.[23] This threefold division is echoed in a marginal annotation in the manuscript of Maja's *De snyid snang ba*. There, the division following the world (*'jig rten pa'i blo dang bstun pa*) is linked with Candrakīrti, that following tenets (*grub mtha' dang sgo btsun*) with Jñānagarbha.[24]

One question is whether Khyung's position was indeed influenced by Candrakīrti's works. As mentioned in the introduction, Khyung, Gangpa, and Gyamarwa were active before Candrakīrti's Madhyamaka interpretation rose to prominence through the teachings of Patsab and his students. Ngok and his successors are reported to have followed the Three Mādhyamikas from the East (*dbu ma shar gsum*) or Three Svātantrikas of the East (*rang rgyud shar gsum*)—Śāntarakṣita, Kamalaśīla, and Jñānagarbha (van der Kuijp 1983, 46; Seyfort Ruegg 2000, 27–36). Nevertheless, Candrakīrti's thought had already entered Tibet via Atiśa's oral Madhyamaka teachings (of which the above-mentioned *Bden gnyis spyi bshad* is an example) and the early circulation of the verses of the *Madhyamakāvatāra* (Apple 2016). Some discussions in the *Dbu dpyod* even suggest some familiarity with the *Prasannapadā* (Vose 2020). The *Dbu dpyod* however only mentions Candrakīrti's name once, along with that of Atiśa, and does not contain any direct citation. The expression "what is established for the world" (*'jig rten [la] grags pa, lokaprasiddha*) itself is never used in the *Dbu dpyod* and, should Khyung's appeal to "follow the world" be influenced by Candrakīrti, it is suspicious that it would not go hand in hand with the rejection of valid cognition in general and of autonomous inference in particular. An influence from Candrakīrti's thought on Khyung may not be excluded but would have remained shallow. It is conceivable that there is nothing Candrakīrtian in Khyung's appeal to rely on the world and that this represents, rather, a position grounded in his reading of Jñānagarbha's *Satyadvayavibhaṅga*, a frequent source for the debates chronicled in the *Dbu dpyod*. Indeed, several passages of the *Satyadvayavibhaṅga* on customary truth and on correct conventionals involve the notion of things as they appear to

23. On Atiśa's own position on what qualifies as correct and mistaken conventionals, see Apple 2016, 660.

24. See Rma bya, *De snyid snang ba*, 3b. The mention "taught by Atiśa" (*a ti sha'i gsungs*) at the end of this annotation presumably refers to the explanation of the third option. The annotation gives as its source "the instruction of the two lamas" (*bla ma rnam gnyis kyi man ngag*). Note that "two lamas" are also mentioned in the *Bden gnyis spyi bshad* in the lineage discussion. Apple 2016, 625, identifies them with Gönpawa Wangchuk Gyaltsen (Dgon pa ba Dbang phyug rgyal mtshan, 1016–83) and Langri Thangpa Dorjé Sengé (Glang ri thang pa Rdo rje seng ge, 1054–1123), but the text also mentions in this context the names Puṇyaratna and Lhatsun [Jangchup Ö] (Lha btsun [Byang chub 'od]) between two sentences mentioning the "two lamas."

anyone in the world and the idea of similarity of appearance as well as worldly consensus (how things are understood in the world).[25] Jñānagarbha's "world" ranges from cowherds, women, and the infantile to, on the other end—made explicit in Śāntarakṣita's commentary—experts (*mkhas pa*).[26]

In view of the discussion of Khyung's views in the *Dbu dpyod*, it seems justified to hold that this scholar qualifies as an early representative of "Madhyamaka following the world" (*'jig rten grags sde dbu ma*). As a doxographical category, it is attested at least from the late twelfth century onward[27] and is found to be associated with both Candrakīrti and, more seldomly, Jñānagarbha.[28] Jñānagarbha is otherwise mostly associated with Yogācāra Madhyamaka or with Sautrāntika Madhyamaka.[29] Gyamarwa (and before him Ngok) stands out in claiming that he was a Vaibhāṣika Mādhyamika.

The discussion in the *Dbu dpyod* on tenet systems as a framework for the division of customary truth finds a clear echo in Chapa's works. Chapa took

25. See SDVV ad SDV 3cd, SDV 8abc, and SDV 12. In the first passage, Jñānagarbha describes the customary as "things as they are seen (*ji ltar mthong*), including by cowherds, women, and so on," which denotes appearance characterized by a lack of analysis. In the second, he explains the correct conventional as what "similarly appears . . . (*mthun par . . . snang*) in the cognition of people, including the infantile," a passage that is likely the source of the expression *mthun snang* broadly used by Tibetan scholars from at least Patsab onward (see note 10), particularly with Chapa and his followers when discussing the subject of inference established for both debaters (see also Tillemans 1999, 275n20, and Tillemans 1990, 42n94). In the third passage, Jñānagarbha comments on the criterion of "causal efficacy" for distinguishing correct and incorrect conventionals, saying that "the world understands water and so on and mirage and so on to be [respectively] correct and incorrect, having determined their being delusive and nondelusive with regard to causal efficacy according to appearance (*ji ltar snang ba, yathādarśana*)" and that this being delusive/nondelusive is also "just a matter of what is accepted" (*ji ltar grags pa kho na bzhin*). Śāntarakṣita sums up, "It is attested according to worldly understanding" (SDVP 93,7: *'jig rten gyis ji ltar rtogs pa de bzhin du rnam par gnas so*).

26. See SDVP 69,2 ad SDV 3cd cum SDVV (*byis pa dang / mkhas pa dag bum pa la sogs pa gang la blo mthun pa . . .*), SDVP 83,24–25 ad SDV 8abc cum SDVV (*mkhas pa rnams nas bzung ste / byis pa'i bar du*). Śāntarakṣita also describes them as those "whose mind is informed by treatises" (SDVP 83,25–84,1: *bstan bcos kyis brtan* par byas pa'i blo dang ldan*. *I prefer the reading *brtan* to *bstan*).

27. The earliest attested occurrence being in the doxographical division by Drakpa Gyaltsen (Grags pa rgyal mtshan, 1147–1216). See Seyfort Ruegg 2000, 56 and 58n124; Hugon 2020a, 328.

28. Chomden Raldri (Bcom ldan ral gri, 1227–1305) and his disciple Üpa Losel (Dbus pa Blo gsal, 1270–1355) associate this position with both Candrakīrti and Jñānagarbha (Hugon 2020a, 330). The author of the *Tshad ma'i spyi skad*, a brief epistemological summary that I tentatively date to the thirteenth century, supports the notion of "common appearance as recognized in the world" (1b4: *lo ga grags sde'i 'thun snang*) by citing both MA 6.83cd and SDV 18ab.

29. See Seyfort Ruegg 2000, 56–59, and Hugon 2020a, 337.

over many of Gyamarwa's arguments against other tenet systems and adopts, like his teacher, external-realist nonrepresentationalism.[30] Surprisingly, however, there is no trace of "Mādhyamikas following the world" as a Madhyamaka subdivision in Chapa's discussion, either as a category to be rejected or adopted. Chapa probably knew however that such a position had been put forth by Khyung and was well aware that it was part of Candrakīrti's views, as can be observed in his discussion of the views of "Candrakīrti and others" (*zla ba grags pa la sogs pa*) in his *Snying po* (Hugon 2023). A possible reason for the absence of this doxographical category is that Chapa followed his teacher Gyamarwa in considering that this option boiled down to external-realist nonrepresentationalism (i.e., Vaibhāṣika Madhyamaka) and hence did not warrant an individual category.[31] Chapa acknowledges the match between this position and the naïve worldview, noting that apprehended objects "exist like they are recognized in the world" (*'jig rten la grags pa bzhin du gnas*) (Hugon 2016, 77–78), but does not concede that the world is enough when it comes to warrant epistemic practices.

Acknowledgments

This article was written as part of the project TibSchol—"The Dawn of Tibetan Buddhist Scholasticism (11th–13th c.)." This project has received funding from the European Research Council (ERC) under the European Union's Horizon 2020 research and innovation programme (grant agreement no. 101001002). I am grateful to Chizuko Yoshimizu and Kevin Vose for their insightful comments.

Abbreviations

D	*Sde dge Tibetan Tripiṭaka Bstan 'gyur.* See Takasaki et al. 1981–84.
Dbu dpyod	Rgya dmar ba Byang chub grags, *Dbu ma de kho na nyid rnam par dpyod pa*

---

30. Note that Chapa does not use the label Vaibhāṣika and also does not present a probative argument in favor of external realism and nonrepresentationalism. His position follows from the refutation of the other three options for tenet systems (Hugon 2016).

31. The blending of the two is attested in the epistemological summary by Jepa Shönu Jangchup ('Jad pa Gzhon nu byang chub, ca. 1150–1210), a student of Chapa's disciple Jangchup Kyab (Byang chub skyabs) (Stoltz 2020), in the use of the expression "like the Vaibhāṣika *śrāvakas*, who conform with what is recognized in the world" ('Jad, *Tshad bsdus*, 13: *lo ga grags sde dang bstun na nyan thos bye brag tu smra ba ltar*).

De nyid snang ba	Rma bya Byang chub brtson 'grus, *Dbu ma rig pa'i tshogs kyi rgyan de snyid snang ba*
MA	Candrakīrti, *Madhyamakāvatāra*
SDV	Jñānagarbha, *Satyadvayavibhaṅga*
SDVP	Śāntarakṣita, *Satyadvayavibhaṅgapañjikā*
SDVV	Jñānagarbha, *Satyadvayavibhaṅgavṛtti*
Snying po	Phya pa Chos kyi seng ge, *Dbu ma de kho na nyid kyi snying po*
Tshad bsdus	'Jad Gzhon nu byang chub, *Tshad ma'i de kho na nyid bsdus pa*

Bibliography

Indian and Tibetan sources

Anon. *Bden gnyis spyi bshad dang bden gnyis 'jog tshul.* In *Bka' gdams gsung 'bum,* 64:23–266.

Bka' gdams gsung 'bum. See under Karma bde legs et al.

Candrakīrti. *Madhyamakāvatāra* and *Madhyamakāvatārabhāṣya.* In La Vallée Poussin 1907–12.

Dpal brtsegs bod yig dpe rnying zhib 'jug khang, ed. 2004 *'Bras spungs dgon du bzhugs su gsol ba'i dpe rnying dkar chag (Drepung Catalogue).* 2 vols. Beijing: Mi rigs dpe skrun khang.

Gnyag. *Tshad ma'i spyi skad cung zad bsdus pa.* In *Bka' gdams gsung 'bum,* 44:199–214.

Jñānagarbha. *Satyadvayavibhaṅga* and *Satyadvayavibhaṅgavṛtti.* D 3881 and D 3882. See Eckel 1987 and Akahane 2020.

'Jad Gzhon nu byang chub (attributed to Klong chen pa Dri med 'od zer). *Tshad ma'i de kho na nyid bsdus pa* (= *Tshad bsdus*). Chengdu: Si khron mi rigs dpe skrun khang, 2000.

Karma bde legs et al., ed. *Bka' gdams gsung 'bum phyogs bsgrigs thengs dang po / gnyis pa / gsum pa / bzhi pa (Collected Works of the Kadampas, Collections 1–4).* 120 vols. Chengdu: Si khron mi rigs dpe skrun khang, 2006–15.

Pa tshab Nyi ma grags. *Dbu ma rtsa ba'i shes rab kyi ti ka bstan bcos sgron ma gsal bar byed pa* (= *Rtsa shes gsal byed*). In *Bka' gdams gsung 'bum,* 11:29–132.

Phya pa Chos kyi seng ge. *Dbu ma de kho na nyid kyi snying po* (= *Snying po*). In *Bka' gdams gsung 'bum,* 7:15–129.

Rgya dmar ba Byang chub grags. *Dbu ma de kho na nyid rnam par dpyod pa* (= *Dbu dpyod*). In *Bka' gdams gsung 'bum,* 31:7–67.

Rma bya Byang chub brtson 'grus. *Dbu ma rig pa'i tshogs kyi rgyan de snyid snang ba* (= *De nyid snang ba*). In *Bka' gdams gsung 'bum,* 13:753–820.

Śāntarakṣita. *Satyadvayavibhaṅgapañjikā.* D 3883. See Akahane 2020.

Takasaki et al., ed. 1981–84. *sDe dge Tibetan Tripiṭaka bsTan 'gyur: Preserved at the Faculty of Letters, University of Tokyo.*

Secondary literature

Akahane, Ritsu. 2020. *A New Critical Edition of Jñānagarbha's Satyadvayavibhaṅga with Śāntarakṣita's Commentary*, edited by R. Nishiyama, Y. Yamanaka, and Y. Muroya. Wiener Studien zur Tibetologie und Buddhismuskunde 98. Vienna: Arbeitskreis für Tibetische und Buddhistische Studien Universität Wien.

Apple, James B. 2016. "An Early Bka'-Gdams-Pa Madhyamaka Work Attributed to Atiśa Dīpaṃkaraśrījñāna." *Journal of Indian Philosophy* 44.4: 619–725.

Doctor, Thomas. 2009. "In Pursuit of Transparent Means of Knowledge: The Madhyamaka Project of Rma bya Byaṅ chub brtson 'grus." *Journal of the International Association of Buddhist Studies* 32.1–2: 419–41.

Dunne, John D. 2004. *Foundations of Dharmakīrti's Philosophy*. Studies in Indian and Tibetan Buddhism. Boston: Wisdom Publications.

Eckel, Malcolm David. 1987. *Jñānagarbha's Commentary on the Distinction between the Two Truths*. Albany: State University of New York Press.

Hopkins, Jeffrey. 2003. *Maps of the Profound: Jamyang Shayba's Great Exposition of Buddhist and Non-Buddhist Views on the Nature of Reality*. Ithaca, NY: Snow Lion Publications.

Hugon, Pascale. 2016. "Can One Be a Mādhyamika, a Crypto-Vaibhāṣika, and a Faithful Interpreter of Dharmakīrti? On Phya Pa Chos Kyi Seng Ge's Doxographical Divisions and His Own Philosophical Standpoint." *Journal of Tibetology / Zangxue Xuekan* 15: 51–153.

———. 2020a. "Vaibhāṣika-Madhyamaka: A Fleeting Episode in the History of Tibetan Philosophy." In *Archaeologies of the Written: Indian, Tibetan, and Buddhist Studies in Honour of Cristina Scherrer-Schaub*, edited by Vincent Tournier, Vincent Eltschinger, and Marta Sernesi, 323–72. Series Minor 89. Naples: Universita degli Studi di Napoli "L'Orientale."

———. 2020b. "Wonders *in margine*—Mapping the Madhyamaka Network of Gyamarwa Jangchupdrak." *Journal of South Asian Intellectual History* 3.2: 123–47.

———. 2023. "Who Is the Proponent of Candrakīrti Portrayed by Phya pa Chos kyi seng ge in the *Snying po*?" In *Burlesque of the Philosophers: Indian and Buddhist Studies in Memory of Helmut Krasser*, edited by Vincent Eltschinger, Jowita Kramer, and Chizuko Yoshimizu, 153–200. Hamburg Buddhist Studies Series 19. Bochum/Freiburg: projekt verlag.

La Vallée Poussin, Louis de, ed. 1907–12. *Madhyamakāvatāra par Candrakīrti*. St. Petersburg: Imprimerie de l'Académie Impériale des Sciences.

Ma, Zhouyang. 2023. "Unveiling Gsang Phu Madhyamaka Thought in Xixia: The Tangut Version of the Analysis of the Essence of Madhyamaka." *Acta Orientalia Academiae Scientiarum Hungaricae* 76.2: 239–71.

McClintock, Sara. 2010. *Omniscience and the Rhetoric of Reason: Śāntarakṣita and Kamalaśīla on Rationality, Argumentation, and Religious Authority*. Studies in Indian and Tibetan Buddhism. Boston: Wisdom Publications.

Seyfort Ruegg, David. 2000. *Three Studies in the History of Indian and Tibetan Madhyamaka Philosophy: Studies in Indian and Tibetan Madhyamaka Thought*. Wiener Studien zur Tibetologie und Buddhismuskunde 50. Vienna: Arbeitskreis für Tibetische und Buddhistische Studien, Universität Wien.

Stoltz, Jonathan. 2020. "On the Authorship of the *Tshad ma'i de kho na nyid bsdus pa*." *Revue d'Études Tibétaines* 56: 46–69.

Tanaka, Koji. 2015. "The Dismal Slough." In *Moonpaths: Ethics and Emptiness*, edited by the Cowherds, 43–53. New York: Oxford University Press.

Tillemans, Tom J. F. 1990. *Materials for the Study of Āryadeva, Dharmapāla and Candrakīrti: The Catuḥśataka of Āryadeva, Chapters XII and XIII, with the Commentaries of Dharmapāla and Candrakīrti. Introduction, Translation, Sanskrit, Tibetan and Chinese Texts, Notes.* 2 vols. Wiener Studien zur Tibetologie und Buddhismuskunde 24.1–2. Vienna: Arbeitskreis für Tibetische und Buddhistische Studien Universität Wien.

———. 1999. *Scripture, Logic, Language: Essays on Dharmakīrti and His Tibetan Successors.* Studies in Indian and Tibetan Buddhism. Boston: Wisdom Publications.

———. 2011. "How Far Can a Mādhyamika Buddhist Reform Conventional Truth? Dismal Relativism, Fictionalism, Easy-Easy Truth, and the Alternatives." In *Moonshadows: Conventional Truth in Buddhist Philosophy*, 151–65. Oxford; New York: Oxford University Press.

———. 2016. *How Do Mādhyamikas Think? And Other Essays on the Buddhist Philosophy of the Middle.* Studies in Indian and Tibetan Buddhism. Somerville, MA: Wisdom Publications.

———. 2022. *Views from Tibet: Studies on Tibetan Buddhist Logic, the Philosophy of the Middle, and the Indigenous Grammatico-Linguistic Tradition.* Österreichische Akademie der Wissenschaften, Philosophisch-Historische Klasse, 922. Band. Vienna: Austrian Academy of Sciences Press.

van der Kuijp, Leonard W. J. 1983. *Contributions to the Development of Tibetan Buddhist Epistemology: From Eleventh to the Thirteenth Century.* Wiesbaden: F. Steiner.

———. 2003. "A Treatise on Buddhist Epistemology and Logic Attributed to Klong Chen Rab 'byams Pa (1308–1364) and Its Place in Indo-Tibetan Intellectual History." *Journal of Indian Philosophy* 31.4: 381–437.

Vose, Kevin A. 2009. *Resurrecting Candrakīrti: Disputes in the Tibetan Creation of Prāsaṅgika.* Studies in Indian and Tibetan Buddhism. Boston: Wisdom Publications.

———. 2010. "Authority in Early Prāsaṅgika Madhyamaka." *Journal of Indian Philosophy* 38: 553–82.

———. 2020. "Absence and Elimination: Madhyamaka Interpretation in the Formation of Scholastic Traditions in Tibet." *Journal of South Asian Intellectual History* 3.2: 148–84.

———. 2021. "Candrakīrti's Middle Way Philosophy." *Oxford Research Encyclopedia of Religion.* Retrieved 9 July 2025, from https://oxfordre.com/religion/view/10.1093/acrefore/9780199340378.001.0001/acrefore-9780199340378-e-175.

Unity of the Two Truths:
Some Sources and Implications of a
Central Buddhist Tantric Doctrine

David Higgins

Query: Isn't the conventional mere appearance? *Reply*: This indeed
was taught to certain people who believe appearance to be conventional and who believe, in the back of their minds, that freedom
from conceptual elaborations regarding that is the ultimate. Still,
for a mind that does not believe in the reality of the two truths, to
ask whether they are one or two is like asking whether the son of a
barren woman is blue or white.

—Rongzom Chökyi Sangpo, *The Black Snake Discourse*

Iɴ concluding his landmark essay "How Far Can a Mādhyamika Buddhist
Reform Conventional Truth?" Tom Tillemans raises the question
of whether we can retain a Buddhist account of the two truths that
relinquishes both metaphysical realism and the "typical Prāsaṅgika" response
to it: the contention that "customary truth is wholly erroneous (*'khrul ba =
bhrānta*) for the profane and purely fictional for 'noble beings' (*ārya*)." He
suggests that a viable alternative to this Prāsaṅgika double whammy of error
theory and panfictionalism is to see the two truths as "a rung on a ladder that
we climb to finally know better a unitary world, one that was there all along
but veiled by conceptually created dichotomies and ignorance" (2016, 56–57).
With characteristic acuity and open-mindedness, Tillemans then proposes as a
radical but promising step in the right direction a return to truth "unqualified
as customary or ultimate" such as we find in the Tibetan Nyingma view of the
primordial unity of the two truths, a view he professes to "only rather dimly

understand" (62n23). This article investigates the substance and significance of the still little known and dimly understood unity-of-truth doctrine with the goal of shedding new light on its rich legacy and intriguing philosophical permutations. It is offered as a small token of gratitude for the many ways Tom has benefited and inspired me over the years as a mentor and a friend.

There is general agreement among scholars of the Tibetan Nyingma and Kagyü traditions that the doctrine known as the inseparability of the two truths (*bden gnyis dbyer med*) marks the culmination of Buddhist thinking about truth. The Nyingmapa polymath Longchenpa (Klong chen pa, 1308–64), for example, claims in the eighteenth chapter of his *Wish-Fulfilling Treasury* that this doctrine represents the definitive quintessence of all Buddhist attempts to capture the way things are (*gnas lugs*).[1] As a view first glimpsed via the inner tantras, it is said to transcend the various bivalent conceptions of truth advanced by the different schools of Buddhist philosophy, which are all, in one way or another, predicated on dubious realist attributions of truth and falsity to perceptions, propositions, and, most fatefully, the world itself. Tibetan proponents of the view framed it as the final cure for metaphysical realism (*dngos por smra ba : vastuvāda*), the view that the objects, properties, and relations the world contains exist independently of how and whether we perceive, experience, or think about them.

Some two and a half centuries before Longchenpa, the eleventh-century Nyingma thinker Rongzom Chökyi Sangpo (Rong zom Chos kyi bzang po, 1042–1136) had identified the inseparability of truth as the highest view of the equality (*mnyam nyid*) of all phenomena that is first recognized in the lower tantras but fully realized only in the Great Perfection or Dzogchen (*rdzogs chen*), the ninth and highest vehicle in the Nyingma doxography of views. Indeed, Rongzompa defines this Dzogchen approach in terms of the transcendence of bivalent truth constructs: "Finally, in the Great Perfection system, all phenomena are said to be in the state of great equality beyond acceptance or rejection, but this is not taught using the nomenclature of *two truths*, for it is said that all phenomena are indivisible."[2] While proposing a tantric provenance for this view, Rongzompa elsewhere refers to the "scriptural tradition that holds the two kinds of truth to be inseparable" (*bden pa rnam pa gnyis dbyer med par 'dod pa'i gzhung*) as "special Mahāyāna" (*theg pa chen po thun mong ma yin pa*). The sources and proponents of this special Mahāyāna are not specified in Rongzompa's extant works, though he does attribute its central claim that buddhahood is nothing but the pure—that is, empty—

1. Klong chen pa, *Yid bzhin mdzod*, 18.3–4.

2. Rong zom pa, *Lta ba'i brjed byang*, 12.16–18.

dharmadhātu to (1) those who follow sūtras and tantras of definitive meaning (*nītartha*) and (2) those who hold that all phenomena are without any
foundation (*sarvadharmāpratiṣṭhānavāda*),³ referring with this epithet to a
late (tenth- to eleventh-century) Madhyamaka-based strand of Indian tantric
Buddhism that included the indivisibility of truths among its core doctrines.

Roughly half a millennium after Rongzompa, the Eighth Karmapa Mikyö
Dorjé (Mi bskyod rdo rje, 1507–54) characterizes the "Middle Way based on
the unity of the two truths" as the view that, ultimately, all phenomena "are
not grounded in any speculative extremes such as existence or nonexistence,
and arising or cessation, and are also free from any foundation that could
be called a middle."⁴ In his final masterwork, a commentary on Karma Pak-
shi's *Direct Introduction to the Three Embodiments* (the commentary hereafter referred to as *Embodiments*), which contains his most extensive exposition
of the unity-of-truth doctrine, Mikyö Dorjé extols this "excellent Madhyamaka tradition of all who claim that the ultimate and conventional truths are
of the same nature" and names Rongzompa as a leading Tibetan proponent
of this tradition.⁵ However, he prefaces this remark with the cautionary note
that the idea that the two truths have a shared "single ground" (*gzhi gcig*) is
only a conceptual imputation, there being no substantially existent common
ground to be discovered.⁶

Mikyö Dorjé clarifies in his *Madhyamakāvatāra* commentary that the two
truths are neither the same nor different; more precisely, they are neither "different delimitations of a single essence" (*ngo bo gcig ldog pa tha dad*), a view he
ascribes to the Gelukpa, nor "a dichotomy based on negating identity" (*gcig
pa'i bkag pa'i tha dad*), a view he ascribes to the Jonangpa. The sameness and
identity accounts of the two truths are fallacious, he argues,⁷ because the former blurs the crucial distinction between conditions of bondage and freedom,
while the latter, in positing the conventional and ultimate as "two great king-
doms having nothing to do with one another,"⁸ situates the ultimate beyond

---

3. See Almogi 2009, 39.

4. *Dwags grub shing rta* (Rumtek edition), 66.4.

5. *Sku gsum ngo sprod rnam bshad* (*Mi bskyod rdo rje gsung 'bum* edition), 21:144.3–6.

6. *Sku gsum ngo sprod rnam bshad* (*Mi bskyod rdo rje gsung 'bum* edition), 21:141.3–4.

7. Mikyö Dorjé here takes his cue from the extended criticism of mutually exclusive identity
and difference accounts of the two truths advanced in the *Saṃdhinirmocana* (D 106: 7b2–4,
8a4–9b1, et passim).

8. See for example Dol po pa, *Ri chos nges don rgya mtsho*, 333. In the words of Padma
dkar po, *Phyag chen rgyal ba'i gan mdzod*, 176.4–5: "It is said by Jonangpas that there is an
immense dichotomy between the two truths, and between the pairs 'saṃsāra and nirvāṇa' and

space and time and dependent arising, and thus beyond the reach of any mind intent on liberation from error and confusion.[9] For Mikyö Dorjé, the reason that the two truths are, in the final analysis, inseparable lies precisely in the fact that there is no warrant for ontologically distinguishing appearance from reality. He could have been speaking for many of his coreligionists when he declares in his *Embodiments* that "so long as the mind has not let go of reifying the two truths in terms of true and false, and there persists conceptual reasoning that clings to and believes in them, it will never dwell in the lofty state of the equality of the two truths, inseparability of the two truths, single taste of the two truths, and unity of the two truths."[10]

Given the centrality of the unity-of-truth doctrine in Tibetan tantric Buddhist traditions and its far-reaching philosophical implications, it is rather surprising how little attention it has garnered in contemporary Buddhist scholarship on the two truths. My aim in this introduction to the doctrine is to offer a preliminary sketch of its provenance, scope, and philosophical significance. I will examine how the doctrine developed out of, and sometimes in reaction to, traditional bivalent truth conceptions, taking my cues from three of its most articulate Tibetan proponents: Rongzompa, Longchenpa, and Mikyö Dorjé. I will conclude by looking at how the unity doctrine came to be regarded as the final cure for metaphysical realism and tentatively explore some of the ramifications this has for contemporary reflections on truth, East and West.

Question of Provenance

The first evocations of the inseparability or nonduality of the two truths are found in the tantric songs and commentaries of a number of late (ca. eleventh century) Indian tantrikas, including Tilopa (Tillipa), Saraha, Indrabhūti, Sahajavajra, Vajrapāṇi, Alaṃkakalaśa, and Maitripāda (also known as Advayavajra).[11] The doctrine's genesis thus coincided with the Later Diffusion

'consciousness and wisdom,' together with their respective self-manifestations." For his critique of Jonang philosophy, see Higgins and Draszczyk 2016, 2:157–74.

9. Mi bskyod rdo rje, *Dwags grub shing rta* (Vajra Vidya edition), 1:278–86.

10. Mi bskyod rdo rje, *Sku gsum ngo sprod rnam bshad* (Vajra Vidya edition), 1:114.19–21. For this passage in context, see Higgins and Draszczyk 2019, 2:272–73.

11. Indian sources for the inseparability or nonduality of truth, or of the two truths, include *inter alia* the following: Indrabhūti's *Śrīcakrasaṃvaratantrarājaśambarasamuccaya*, D 1413: 13b4 and 15b5–6; Vajrapāṇi's *Mahāvajradharastotra* (which opens with an homage to the inseparability of the two truths), D 1126: 75b3; Sahajavajra's *Sthitisamuccaya*, D 2227: 96a4; Vṛddhakāyastha's *Suviśadasaṃputaṭīkā*, D 1190: 139b4–5; Indrabhūti's *Śrīsaṃputatilaka*, D

(*phyi dar*) of Buddhism in Tibet, which began in the eleventh century. During this time, the doctrine found fertile soil in scholasticism of the Ancient (*rnying ma*) and New (*gsar ma*) Tibetan Buddhist schools, which were actively engaged not only in assimilating Buddhist teachings from India, not least of all tantric ones, but also in developing new ways of interpreting and practicing them. In this fruitful climate of doctrinal formation and scholastic elaboration, a teaching that had only recently emerged on the tantric fringes of Indian society was taken up not only as a subject of avid intersectarian discussion and debate but also as an indispensable path toward a deeper understanding of the two truths.

From at least as early as the eleventh century, questions arose among Tibetan scholars as to the provenance of this doctrine, specifically, whether it is realized via Madhyamaka or Mantrayāna teachings. The two Nyingmapas mentioned above, Rongzompa and Longchenpa, maintain that the inseparability of truth is first recognized in Mantrayāna practice, but here too their observations differ. For Rongzompa, the practitioner gains a first glimpse of it via the outer tantras, when "the view of equality that realizes the inseparability of the ultimate and conventional is first attained, albeit to a small degree."[12] This insight is subsequently attained to a medium degree in the inner Mahāyoga and is fully realized in the Great Perfection. For Longchenpa, however, the inseparability of truth is first recognized via the inner tantras when one finally abandons ontological and meta-ontological concerns and glimpses the divine nature of conventional phenomena. Longchenpa explains in his *Wish-Fulfilling Treasury* autocommentary that, for "most Mantra[yāna] practitioners nowadays," the views of the three outer tantras (*kriyā, caryā, yoga*) are "similar to the Great Vehicle of Characteristics (*mtshan nyid theg pa chen po*) insofar as one ascertains that things are ultimately of the nature of being totally unestablished." He adds that it is through the three inner tantras (*māha, anu, ati*) that the conventional itself appears as divine in nature and truth is therefore known to be inseparable. "Abandoning the belief that truth is differentiated, all phenomena are ascertained as the quintessence (*snying po*) that alone is of definitive meaning. When one thus simply dispels what obscures the spontaneously present essential disposition, its nature is no longer held to be distinguishable

1197: 144a1–2; Abhayākara's *Śrīkālacakroddāna*, D 1380: 265b2; Bhavabhadra's *Śrīvajraḍāki-mahātantrarājasyavṛtti*, D 1415: 21a3; Alaṃkakalaśa's *Śrīvajramālāmahāyogatantraṭīkā*, D 1795: 14b7–15a1; Vitakarma's *Mudrācaturaṭīkāratnahṛdaya*, D 2259: 315a5; and Tilopa's **Vaidikāyopadeśa* (*Acintyamahāmudrā*), D 2310: 250b7–251a1.

12. *Sbrul nag po'i stong thun*, 67.15–16. For an annotated English translation of this text, see Higgins 2023.

in terms of cause and effect, and thus one recognizes it to be an unconditioned, self-manifesting maṇḍala."[13] The vision of the inseparability of truth gained via inner tantric practice is here regarded as a disclosive process occasioned by dispelling what obscures one's spontaneously present essential disposition (*lhun grub snying po'i khams*)—that is, innate buddha nature, rather than a developmental process of deducing via causes and conditions that things are ultimately unestablished.

Mikyö Dorjé, for his part, traces the inseparability-of-truth view to the Madhyamaka equation of emptiness and dependent arising but claims that its full realization is gained only through the Mantrayāna. In his *Embodiments*, he characterizes unity of truth as a doctrine discerned by "those who appeared in former generations like the glorious lord Saraha, the noble Nāgārjuna, the venerable Śavaripa, the teacher Buddhapālita, Candrakīrti, and the master Maitrīpa. Thus, in the same manner that the subject of the two truths was ascertained by the lord Maitrīpa and the exalted Atiśa,[14] so it appears to have also been explained by the Mahāpaṇḍita Rongzom Chösang."[15]

It is clear then that despite these thinkers' somewhat different opinions about the provenance of the doctrine, they commonly held that it was anticipated by Nāgārjuna's equation of emptiness and dependent arising but received its most lucid and thorough articulation in Mantrayāna. Here it is possible to identify two main transmission lineages of this doctrine in Tibet: an Ancient tantric line culminating in the Great Perfection (Dzogchen) tradition and a New tantric line culminating in the Great Seal (Mahāmudrā). Both were to some extent indebted to the antifoundationalist (*rab tu mi gnas pa'i smra ba : apratiṣṭhānavāda*) Madhyamaka system, as is certainly the case with Rongzompa and Mikyö Dorjé, who each integrated key elements of this tantric Middle Way philosophy into their Great Perfection and Great Seal interpretations of the unity doctrine.

Truth Beyond Bivalence

For Mikyö Dorjé and other advocates of this doctrine, what is fundamentally at stake in the distinction between conventional and ultimate truth is not an *ontological* distinction between different kinds or realms of being but a *phenomenological* distinction between more and less reifying (and thus distort-

13. Klong chen pa, *Yid bzhin mdzod 'grel*, 1390.5–1391.4.

14. For an overview of Atiśa's (982–1054) "unitary truth" thesis, see Higgins and Draszczyk 2019, 1:259n593.

15. See Higgins and Draszczyk 2019, 2:264.

ing) modes of cognition. In other words, in distinguishing how things are (*gnas tshul*) from how things appear (*snang tshul*), unity-of-truth theorists resisted the temptation to draw an *ontological* distinction in nature and kind between fraudulent appearances perceived by unenlightened ordinary beings and genuine reality perceived by noble beings (*ārya*) in favor of a firsthand account that begins with how we come to know perceptually and thoughtfully how things are through how they appear to us. This provided a framework for interrogating how conceptual judgments such as truth or falsity can become, perhaps mistakenly, ascribed to appearance and for charting a path beyond such reification of truth.

This is a crucial point, for in Indian philosophy, no less than in Western philosophy, there is a longstanding tradition of distinguishing reality from appearance and then fretting about whether and how we can peer behind the veil of appearances to gain access to what *really* is. It is instructive that the Buddhist division of truth or reality (*bden pa, satya*) into conventional and ultimate may have originally been used to distinguish Buddhist statements or discourses into those *held to be true* and those which *actually are true*, a role later relegated to the distinction between provisional meaning (*neyārtha*) and definitive meaning (*nītārtha*).[16] To this day, there are irreconcilable disagreements over whether the referents and grounds of justification of the two truths are semantic, ontological, or epistemic, as exemplified by intersectarian disputes over the correct basis for distinguishing the two truths, and particularly whether the distinction should be ontologically grounded (à la Tsongkhapa [Tsong kha pa]) or subjectively grounded (à la Gorampa [Go rams pa]).[17]

Against a large body of collective opinion, unity theorists considered this overwrought dichotomy between reality and appearance to be mistaken and misguided precisely to the extent that it conflates epistemic and ontological considerations and superimposes conceptual judgments of truth and falsity onto objects themselves. Most fatefully, it construes appearance itself as erroneous and deceptive *by nature*, thus erecting an impenetrable barrier between

---

16. See Tillemans and Newland 2011, 3–22.

17. See Thakchoe 2004, where he cites Jamyang Shepa's (1648–1721) useful codification of six bases for distinguishing the two truths (*bden gnyis dbye gzhi*) posited by non-Gelukpa Tibetan scholars: (1) mere appearance (*snang tsam*), (2) entities ranging from material form to omniscience (*gzugs nas rnam mkhyen bar gyi ngo bo*), (3) nonreified objects (*sgro ma btags pa'i yul*), (4) unanalyzed objects (*ma rtags ma dpyad pa'i yul*), (5) truth/reality (*bden pa*), and (6) unspecified basis. By contrast, the Gelukpa themselves ground the distinction in objects of knowledge (*shes bya*), while their Sakya rivals ground it in cognition (*blo tsam*). See Thakchoe 2004, 32–33.

us and reality.[18] Rongzompa rejects this paranoid view at the beginning of his *Black Snake Discourse*, when he contends that directly perceived appearance is indisputably there for everyone from beginners to tenth-level bodhisattvas[19] and that the Buddhist "debates concerning such appearance arise, instead, over the ways in which this appearance is characterized or reified."[20] This calls to mind the oft-repeated advice Tilopa is said to have imparted to his disciple: "You are fettered not by appearance but by your attachment to appearance. Let go of this attachment, Nāropa!"[21] Rongzompa devotes the remainder of this short text to showing how the aspirant's ascent up the ladder of Buddhist views and vehicles consists in the *progressive de-reification of phenomena*, culminating in the Great Perfection view of equality, the insight that all phenomena are equally without any foundation or properties and that reality or truth is thus indivisible.

Three important ramifications of this unity-of-truth viewpoint are worth noting at the outset before fleshing them out in some detail. The first is its antifoundationalist orientation: the goal is to arrive at the view of equality in which all phenomena are known to be without any ontic or epistemic grounding. The second ramification is that the distinction between ultimate and conventional truth is one *of degree*, not *of kind*. From this perspective, the point of the distinction is not to establish an unbreachable dichotomy between two discrete classes of phenomena (true/false) but rather to distinguish varying degrees of distortion vis-à-vis a single class of phenomena (*sarvadharma*). The third ramification of the epistemic unity thesis is that the operative contrast in distinguishing two truths is not between appearance *and* reality but between modes of appearance *in* reality. It is in this light that unity theorists typically regard conventional and ultimate truth as spheres of operation (*spyod yul, gocara*) of two discernable cognitive styles: dualistic mentation (*sems, rnam shes*) and nondual awareness (*sems nyid, rig pa, ye shes*). Let us now examine each of these three points in turn.

18. For recent parallel attempts, in Western philosophy, to abandon the appearance-reality dichotomy in favor of epistemological accounts that can be loosely grouped under the rubric of direct (or naïve) realism, see Putnam 1999, Rescher 2010, and Heil 2021.

19. The longstanding and vexing Buddhist debate over whether buddhas have any appearances, cognition, intention, or feelings at all is best left for another discussion!

20. Rong zom pa, *Sbrul nag po'i stong thun*, 66.4–6.

21. *Snang bas mi 'ching zhen pas 'ching // zhen pa chod cig nā ro pa //*. As quoted in Klong chen pa, *Chos dbyings mdzod 'grel*, 98b5.

Nonfoundational Unity

To appreciate how nonfoundationalist perspectives shaped our authors' interpretations of the unity-of-truth thesis, a good starting point is Rongzompa's cogent synopsis of this viewpoint in his *Memorandum of Views*:

> Nonfoundationalists maintain that all phenomena are described and established in terms of various characteristics via names, symbols, and conventions but that one cannot establish a foundation (*gnas pa*) for any such characteristics. Since phenomena are not founded on, and do not rely upon, a single foundation—not even an extremely subtle or extremely profound one, let alone a coarser one—they are said to be completely "nonfoundational." These thinkers also determine phenomena in this way when positively determining objects of knowledge and further claim that during the stage of buddhahood as well the purity [i.e., emptiness] of *dharmadhātu* is characterized by the quelling of conceptual elaborations.[22]

Rongzompa here draws attention to two related senses of the nonfoundationalist viewpoint—namely, that all phenomena are (1) without any determinate epistemic characteristics beyond or behind the linguistic conventions used to represent them and are (2) without any deeper ontic foundation, any shovel-stopping metaphysical bedrock that makes them what they are. In short, all phenomena are unfixed or indeterminate both in essence and origin. They have neither determinate essences that define what they are nor any ontological foundation on which they depend.

It is in this vein that Mikyö Dorjé identifies the philosophical stance of his Kagyü Mahāmudrā tradition as the Nonfoundational Middle Way of Unity (*Yuganaddha-Apratiṣṭhāna Madhyamaka). This nomenclature tells us much about the central philosophical orientation of the Karmapa and his Karma Kagyü school. As an exponent of *yuganaddha* (*zung 'jug*)—that is, unity (literally, "yoking together")—he espouses the tantric ground and goal of a unity beyond extremes: the unity of the two truths, of appearance and emptiness. This unity is only fully realized when one understands that the conventional has no independent existence apart from the ultimate (emptiness) and that the latter is a condition of possibility of the former. As an advocate of non-

---

22. See Almogi 2009, 228–29. Translation altered for consistency. See also Tauscher 2003, 209 and 244n10.

foundationalism, he maintains that all "inner and outer" phenomena, including deep features of reality disclosed through meditation, lack any epistemic and ontic grounding. Finally, as a proponent of Madhyamaka, the Buddhist Middle Way (specifically, its Prāsaṅgika strand), the author attempts to ply a middle course between the extremes of existence and nonexistence, eternalism and nihilism. In the context of two truths, this amounts to avoiding an eternalist view of the ultimate and nihilist view of the conventional (à la Jonangpas) or a nihilist view of the ultimate and eternalist view of the conventional (à la Gelukpas). These various doxographical strands are deftly interwoven in the Karmapa's view of the two truths, which accepts self-manifestation *simpliciter* (*snang tsam*) while denying it any ontological status.[23] Longchenpa, for his part, presents the Prāsaṅgika Madhyamaka antiessentialist viewpoint as the summit of the so-called Cause-Oriented Vehicle of Characteristics (*rgyu mtshan nyid kyi theg pa*) and defends it as the most effective preparation for a nondistortive understanding of the Goal-Oriented Mantrayāna and, in particular, its doctrine of the unity of truth.[24]

It is not difficult to see how these nonfoundationalist and antiessentialist standpoints could lend support to their proponents' view that the two truths are inseparable. The understanding that all phenomena lack any ontic or epistemic grounding or determinate essences exposes the futility and danger of creating an unbridgeable gulf between true reality and false appearance.

Truth on the Spectrum

Rongzompa's definition of nonfoundationalism reveals the philosophical underpinning of his view that the two truths are best regarded as a distinction by degree rather than kind. While a binary bright-line distinction *by kind* of the two truths treats them as two discrete classes of phenomena (true and

23. Longchenpa subsumed both Apratiṣṭhānavāda and Māyopamādvayavāda under the Svātantrika Madhyamaka tradition, thus implicitly granting a higher status to Prāsaṅgika Madhyamaka. See Almogi 2010, 165–70. This may have had something to do with the fact that Nyingma masters traced their teachings to a period two or three centuries before the Indian Māyopama and Apratiṣṭhāna distinction was introduced, though this apparently did not discourage Rongzompa from favoring the Apratiṣṭhāna viewpoint.

24. For Longchenpa, the Prāsaṅgika philosophy plays something of a propaedeutic role in Nyingma soteriology, though he does regard it as a complete and *reliable* system of liberation, with its own efficacious aims, views, and practices. In strictly doxographical terms, however, the place of Madhyamaka systems within the Nyingma ninefold *yāna* scheme is the third *yāna* up from the bottom, the highest of the Bodhisattvayāna approaches, with outer and inner Mantrayāna systems stretching up and beyond. See Higgins 2013, 111–15.

false), the more fluid distinction *by degree* treats them as markers on a *spectrum of veridicality*, the ultimate being maximally veridical (maximally free of superimpositions) and the conventional spanning many shades of grey. Rongzompa explains that the unity of truth is realized to the extent that realist convictions, including the belief in the two truths as different in nature and kind, are relinquished. In his *Black Snake Discourse*, the wayfarer's progress through the hierarchy of views and vehicles from realist to antirealist to nonfoundational unity is fueled by the progressive attenuation of the ingrained attachment to appearances as being real, independently existent entities. From this perspective, Buddhist doxography—its ascending hierarchy of philosophical viewpoints—reflects the progressive relinquishment of realist aims and aspirations. As Rongzompa explains in his *Entering the Way of Mahāyāna*, "The lower to higher views merely represent greater to lesser degrees of habituation to appearances as real entities."[25] The idea here is that one naturally ascends the doxographic ladder from the substance realism of the *śrāvaka* schools through the progressively antiessentialist views of Madhyamaka, the lower and higher tantras, and up to the nonfoundationalist Dzogchen view of equality, as the gravitational pull of realist goals and assumptions weakens. In Rongzompa's words, "To the extent that one's understanding of the view of equality increases, views based on inequality decrease. In short, this is simply the progressive attenuation of one's habituation to realist views."[26]

Rongzompa's *Black Snake Discourse*, read alongside Mikyö Dorjé's commentarial overview of it,[27] offers a cogent illustration of how the understanding of the inseparability of the two truths unfolds as one proceeds from lower to higher Buddhist vehicles. This is illustrated by the example of varying Buddhist philosophical responses to their perceptions of a reflection in water that resembles a black snake. To summarize, (1) *śrāvaka*s (Mikyö Dorjé adds worldly *tīrthika*s) see the black-snake reflection as real and causally efficacious. They are afraid to touch it but want desperately to get rid of it, so they trample it underfoot. It is explained that their fearful reaction and *renunciate* response to appearance stem from their ontological belief in existence both on the ultimate and conventional levels and in the substantial existence (*dravyasat*) of both. Hence they believe the conventional and ultimate consist in separate types of truth or reality. (2) Mahāyāna Mādhyamikas see the reflected snake and appearances in general as illusion-like since they are

25. *Theg chen tshul 'jug*, 459.4–5.

26. *Theg chen tshul 'jug*, 502.21–23.

27. For a critical edition and translation of Mikyö Dorjé's synopsis of Rongzompa's *Black Snake Discourse*, see Higgins and Draszczyk 2019, 2:264 and 2:268.

not substantially established as something real on the ultimate level. Still, they are deemed efficacious given that even unreal things (such as dream images or hallucinations) can produce harmful or beneficial effects and are thus to be accepted or rejected. Retaining a belief in substantial existence on the conventional level, the Mādhyamikas too are afraid to touch the snake reflection and instead take steps to repel it by applying appropriate antidotes such as compassion. This fearful reaction and *remedial* response to appearance stem from their intransigent ontological beliefs in conventional and nominal existence (*prajñaptisat*), though existence on the ultimate level has been refuted. Hence they too believe in two separate truths or realities but view the conventional as illusion-like. (3) Adepts of the outer tantras (*kriyā* and *yoga* for Rongzompa; *kriyā* and *caryā* for Mikyö Dorjé) perceive the snake reflection as an illusion having no substantial existence, even on the conventional level. However, due to the "power of previous fears," they too are afraid to touch it, and they summon a divine hero having the power to vanquish it. This fearful reaction and *supplicatory* response to appearance are based on their residual ontological belief in nominal existence on the conventional level, though existence on the ultimate level and substantial existence on the conventional level have been refuted. It is at this stage that the inseparability of truth is first realized to a small extent. (4) Adepts of the lower inner tantras (*mahāyoga* for Rongzompa; Mikyö Dorjé adds *niruttarayoga*) see the snake reflection as unreal and nonefficacious but nonetheless engage in religious observances (*vrata*) aimed at removing the last traces of lingering fear and reification due to former conditioning. This reaction and *yogic* response to appearance are based on their "nearly extinguished" yet still operative ontological belief in nominal existence on the conventional level. Here, the inseparability of truth is realized to a medium extent. (5) Finally, Great Perfection adepts see the snake reflection as completely unreal, insubstantial, and nonefficacious and thus find nothing at all to accept or reject. Since there is no longer any basis for fear, there are no logical or ontological grounds (*gzhi med*) whatsoever for accepting or rejecting anything. Since all phenomena are without foundation, there is no need to respond at all. Beyond all hope and fear, acceptance and rejection, the understanding of the inseparability of truth here finds its culmination.

For Rongzompa and Mikyö Dorjé, the final realization of the inseparability of truth marks the concluding stage in the de-reification of phenomena, the point where one can no longer adduce any grounds of justification for bivalent truth conceptions. Rongzompa here explains that all impulses to shun or destroy the snake reflection stem from a view based on clinging to real entities (*dngos por zhen pa'i lta ba*). Concluding that what is illusory provides no grounds (logical or empirical) to justify efforts of any kind, the adept attempts

Metaphysical View	Perception of Black Snake's Reflection	Reaction and Conduct	Ontological Commitment (4 Existences)	Inseparability of Truth View
*śrāvaka*s; M + worldly *tīrthika*s	real and causally efficacious	afraid; want to get rid of it (renunciate)	ultimate conventional substantial (2)	two separate truths
Mahāyāna Mādhyamikas	unreal yet causally efficacious	afraid to touch; apply counteragents (*thabs*) (remedial)	conventional substantial nominal	two truths but conventional is illusion-like
kriyā and *yoga*; M: *kriyā* and *caryā* (outer tantras)	unreal and nonphysical yet efficacious	afraid to touch; summon "hero" (supplicatory)	conventional nominal	attained to a small degree
mahāyoga; M + *niruttara* (inner tantras)	unreal and nonefficacious	last trace of fear and reification removed by yogic practices (*vrata*)	nominal	attained to a medium degree
Dzogchen	unreal, nonefficacious, nothing to accept/reject	no basis for fear; no need to accept or reject anything	none	understanding reaches fullest extent

Buddhist metaphysical views and ontological commitments according to the *Black Snake Discourse*. (Key: M = Mikyö Dorjé; + = adds)

neither to reject or to achieve anything at all, and the realization of the illusion-like nature of things reaches its fullest measure: "Recognizing that appearances have no essential characteristics, adepts are freed of even the most subtle belief in ultimate and conventional truths and are thus liberated from all metaphysical views. This is conventionally termed 'the purport of basic equality,' 'the view of the inseparability of the ultimate and conventional.'"[28]

Echoing Rongzompa's remarks, Mikyö Dorjé says that "practitioners of *atiyoga*, the Great Perfection, realize that all avoiding, fearing, touching, or trampling anything amid the joys and sorrows pertaining to the illusion-like

28. Rong zom pa, *Sbrul nag po'i stong thun*, in 67.23–68.5.

phenomena of the two truths derive from the realist view regarding the merely illusory conventional." With this realization, they "relinquish all deeds based on fear and heroism" and "proceed spontaneously without deliberate activity, without trying to achieve, establish, or reject anything." Awakening to buddhahood, they "no longer view the phenomena of the two truths as existing, either nominally or conventionally."[29]

Cognitive Sources of the Two Truths

As a rule, the unity-of-truth theorists were inclined to reinterpret the two truths of Indian Buddhist philosophy as objects (*viṣaya*) or spheres of activity (*gocara*) of these modes of cognition. I have elsewhere examined how the reframing of the two truths in terms of these two cognitive styles provided Nyingma thinkers with a standard Buddhist philosophical framework for articulating their own disclosive conception of the path as the progressive revelation of primordial knowing (*ye shes*).[30] This is no less true of Kagyü thinkers who align the two truths with their key distinction between consciousness (*rnam shes*) and primordial knowing (*ye shes*). Central to this viewpoint is the insight that how things appear is a feature both of how things are and of how we stand in relation to what is.

This way of interpreting the two truths was hardly unprecedented. Indeed, in correlating the two truths with the two different modes of cognition that make them possible, Nyingma and Kagyü philosophers claimed allegiance to the Prāsaṅgika tradition. On this view, ultimate truth is the sphere of primordial knowing, whereas conventional truth is the provenance of dualistic mind. Not only is this held to be consistent with the Prāsaṅgika approach, it is also said to have been emphasized by its leading thinkers, such as Śāntideva and Candrakīrti.[31] For the unity theorists, this distinction of truth in terms of cognitive styles was also consistent with their own disclosive view of the Buddhist path. On this view, the *conventional* ("concealing") is simply a blanket term for the set of dualizing and distorting mental acts that are collectively called *mind* (*sems*). The goal, then, is to give up mistaken identifications

---

29. *Sku gsum ngo sprod rnam bshad* (Vajra Vidya ed.), 1:113.19–114.3.

30. See Higgins 2013, 111–19.

31. Two oft-quoted examples are Candrakīrti's *Madhyamakāvatāra* 11.17, which states that suchness (*tathatā*) is made manifest by the *kāyas* due to the cessation of mind, and Śāntideva's *Bodhicāryāvatara* 9.2cd, which states "Ultimate reality is not the domain of the intellect (*buddhi*). / Mind is said to be conventional/concealing (*saṃvṛti*)."

of appearance, including illegitimate attributions of truth and falsity thereof, and leave appearance be. As Longchenpa explains in his *Wish-Fulfilling Treasury* autocommentary:

> Since this luminous primordial knowing is not touched by cloud-like conventional saṃsāric phenomena, not the slightest mistaken appearance is established. If that is not established, then one also does not establish an "ultimate" evaluated as the emptiness of all that is perceived. Since neither of these is established, none of the distinctions between two truths as evaluated by the philosophical systems are established. Given that these do not exist, one goes beyond the two truths as they are intellectually imputed in terms of what is "true" and "false." With this quelling of all discursive elaborations, imputed truth is no longer established; hence we speak of the "inseparability of truth." Since there is nothing describable as *conventionally* established but *ultimately* unestablished, this luminous primordial knowing as the basic expanse is called "great utterly pure spontaneity." However, since it does not exist as anything like the two truths of appearance and emptiness acknowledged in the philosophical systems, it is, in this sense also, called the "inseparability of truth."[32]

What is at stake in this reframing of "truth" is something akin to the Heideggerian distinction between *truth as correspondence*, the agreement (confirmation or disconfirmation) between propositions and states of affairs, and a more elementary form of *truth as disclosure*, which is simply the *display* of a state of affairs and therefore the condition of possibility of propositional truth.[33] For unity theorists more generally, this alethic shift from propositional

---

32. *Yid bzhin mdzod 'grel*, 1396.4–1397.4.

33. In *Being and Time*, Heidegger (1962, 218–19) famously distinguishes the traditional Aristotelian conception of truth as *correspondence*—i.e., the agreement between thought and thing (*adequatio intellectus et rei*)—from a deeper sense of truth as *disclosure* (ancient Greek *aletheia*, "unconcealment"), the original *clearing* or opening onto a world that makes any knowing of things qua things possible. Heidegger significantly shifts the locus of truth from the thought, belief, or statement to the original disclosure-discovering of what shows itself. It is important to recognize that in doing so, Heidegger does not question the validity of the claim that propositional truth (or "correctness," as he sometimes called it) consists in the correspondence between our beliefs or utterances and states of affairs. What he does criticize is the way in which such correspondence is typically construed as an agreement between representations and objects, the assumption underlying all meditational epistemologies. Heidegger's notion of

to pre-propositional models of truth coincides with the soteriological move from representational thought to primordial knowing. With this reformulation, as we can also glean from the spectrum of truth views delineated in Rongzompa's *Black Snake Discourse*, truth turns out to be a contingent and contextual theme whose sense, scope, and significance are shaped by variable epistemic and normative interests.

Summing Up: What Truth in View?

What implications does the unity-of-truth thesis have for our understanding of the two truths? When it is recognized that propositional truths depend on perception as a condition of their possibility, and this in turn upon phenomena,[34] it becomes understandable how readily cognitive judgments of truth and falsity can be tacitly reenlisted to distinguish *ontologically* the way things appear to be from the way things *really* are. All too easily, a model of reality slides into the reality of the model. We may recall that for Rongzompa, the real bone of contention for wayfaring Buddhists is not appearance *simpliciter*—the naïve evidence of things available to from everyone from beginners to tenth-level bodhisattvas—but rather how appearances are characterized—that is, reified.[35] In his conclusion to the *Black Snake*, he clarifies the conditions for the genesis and transcendence of this reification of appearance: "Because directly perceived appearance has arisen due to the power of latent tendencies, it is not quickly overcome. Because habituation to such appearance is produced by adventitious erroneous notions, it can be quickly overcome." Rongzompa adds that "this habituation, moreover, arises from belief in characteristics. That in turn arises from the view of real entities. But when these three conceptions subside, then even if appearance based on the essentialist conception has not ceased, there will still not arise the metaphysical view of truth as dual."[36]

disclosure/unconcealment is not intended to replace or revise propositional truth but rather to articulate the condition of its possibility.

34. This point was made by Maurice Merleau-Ponty: "We never cease living in the world of perception, but we go beyond it in critical thought—almost to the point of forgetting the contribution of perception to our idea of truth. For critical thought encounters only bare propositions which it discusses, accepts or rejects. Critical thought has broken with the naïve evidence of things, and when it affirms, it is because it no longer finds any means of denial. However necessary this activity of verification may be, specifying criteria and demanding from our experience its credentials of validity, it is not aware of our contact with the perceived world which is simply there before us, beneath the level of the verified true and the false" (1964, 3).

35. *Sbrul nag po'i stong thun*, 66.5–7.

36. *Sbrul nag po'i stong thun*, 68.5–10.

Rongzompa is unsparing in his diagnosis: Buddhist philosophers from Sarvāstivādins to Mādhyamikas remain, to varying degrees, wedded to the dichotomy between erroneous conventional appearance and veridical ultimate reality, with the resulting bifurcation between the worlds of human beings and āryas. The upshot of his critique is that traditional bivalent views of truth, with their putative dichotomy between *false* appearance (total error) and *true* reality (total absence, emptiness), serve more to reinforce than resolve these pernicious metaphysical dichotomies. As Rongzompa explains, "A person in whose mind defining characteristics of the two truths are intellectually posited as something truly established and are thus determined to be objects of knowledge will never be able to relinquish dualistic mind. For when that person has determined that 'the two truths are inseparable,' with this deeply held belief, he also has not let go of holding that the conventional exists as mere illusion. That being so, even when he establishes the nondual nature of reality, he still harbors thoughts associated with dualism."[37]

This brings us, finally, to the question of whether, in the Buddhist project of dispelling the manifold forms of self-deception and ignorance that are thought to prevent human beings from seeing things as they are (*yathābhūta*), the two truths doctrine is part of the solution or part of the problem. In other words, is this distinction best regarded as a remedy for dualistic perceptions or rather the "illness for which it purports to be the cure" (as the Austrian satirist Karl Kraus famously said of psychoanalysis)? Rongzompa, for one, seems to side with the latter alternative:

> Determining objects of knowledge by fixating the mind on the subdivision of the two truths was declared to be a remedy for people who cling excessively to real entities. However, phenomena are essentially without such bivalent characteristics. Indeed, one in whom the belief in such characteristics has ceased is free from such clinging and therefore no longer craves or wishes for anything that appears. In that instance, the term "view of great equality" is employed.[38]

Mikyö Dorjé signals agreement when he comments that the mind will never be able to settle in the lofty state of the unity of the two truths so long as it has not let go of objectifying them by means of conceptual analysis.

The problem with bivalent truth theories is that they ontologize a useful

37. *Sbrul nag po'i stong thun*, 68.11–16.
38. *Sbrul nag po'i stong thun*, 69.1–4.

phenomenological distinction and embed it in the nature of things. Because unity theorists argue that the conventional and ultimate are not categorically distinct—that appearance is not different in kind and essence from reality—it follows that the unity of truth is a matter of discovery rather than of achievement. Simply put, the original unity of presence and emptiness is a precondition for any distinction between them. For Mikyö Dorjé, the unity of truth revealed in Mahāmudrā meditation is not a conjunction of two disparate phenomena (as the term *yuganaddha*, "yoked together," would seem to imply), but neither is it a commensurability established between two equally existent states of affairs or objects of knowledge. Rather, the two truths are inseparable in the specific sense that they stand to one another in a relationship of asymmetrical priority such that the ultimate (emptiness, the unconditioned) is the condition of possibility of conventional (dependent, the conditioned) but is not itself a conditioned product.

On this view, the barrier separating the ultimate and conventional collapses to the extent that the reifying thought that erected it subsides. This type of unity, as Mikyö Dorjé elsewhere argues, diverges from a metaphysically monist idea of unity that treats the ultimate as having a reality of its own (*rang bden pa*) independently of how, or whether, we perceive and ponder it, while downgrading the conventional to mere epiphenomenon. Unity proponents propose an alternative to the "two worlds" view presupposed by traditional Buddhist truth theories: appearances are not *apart from* reality but *a part of* reality, being modes of its manifestation. The unity doctrine was in this regard intended not as revision or replacement of traditional Buddhist truth theories but rather as a way to articulate the condition of their possibility. For its advocates, there is only one world that is disclosed more fully and clearly to the extent that the conceptual superimpositions that distort and obscure it are dispelled.

Bibliography

Almogi, Orna. 2009. *Rong-zom-pa's Discourses on Buddhology: A Study of Various Conceptions of Buddhahood in Indian Sources with Special Reference to the Controversy Surrounding the Existence of Gnosis (jñāna : ye shes) as Presented by the Eleventh-Century Tibetan Scholar Rong-zom Chos-kyi-bzang-po*. Tokyo: The International Institute for Buddhist Studies.

———. 2010. "Māyopamādvayavāda versus Sarvadharmāpratiṣṭānavāda: A Late Indian Subclassification of Madhyamaka and Its Reception in Tibet." *Journal of the International College for Postgraduate Buddhist Studies* 14: 135–212.

Candrakīrti. *Madhyamakāvatāra*. In La Vallée Poussin [1907–12] 1992.

Dol po pa Shes rab rgyal mtshan. *Ri chos nges don rgya mtsho*. Full title: *Ri chos nges don rgya mtsho zhes bya ba mthar thug thun mong ma yin pa'i man ngag.* Beijing: Mi rigs dpe skrun khang, 1998.

Heidegger, Martin. 1962. *Being and Time.* Translated by John Macquarrie and Edward Robinson. New York: Harper & Row.

Heil, John. 2021. *Appearance in Reality.* Oxford: Oxford University Press.

Higgins, David. 2013. *The Philosophical Foundations of Classical rDzogs chen in Tibet: Investigating the Distinction Between Dualistic Mind (sems) and Primordial Knowing (ye shes).* Wiener Studien zur Tibetologie und Buddhismuskunde 78. Vienna: Arbeitskreis für Tibetische und Buddhistische Studien Universität Wien.

Higgins, David, trans. 2023. *Black Snake Discourse.* Rong zom Chos kyi bzang po. Introduction by Patrick Dowd. Lotsawa House Translations. https://www.lotsawahouse .org/tibetan-masters/rongzom-chokyi-zangpo/black-snake-discourse. Accessed July 26, 2023.

Higgins, David, and Martina Draszczyk. 2016. *Mahāmudrā and the Middle Way: Post-Classical Kagyü Discourses on Mind, Emptiness, and Buddha Nature.* 2 vols. Vienna: Arbeitskreis für Tibetische und Buddhistische Studien Universität Wien.

———. 2019. *Buddha Nature Reconsidered: The Eighth Karma pa's Middle Path.* 2 vols. Vol. 1, *Introduction and Analysis.* Vol. 2, *An Anthology of His Writings: Critical Texts and Annotated Translations.* Wiener Studien zur Tibetologie und Buddhismuskunde 95. Vienna: Arbeitskreis für Tibetische und Buddhistische Studien Universität Wien.

Klong chen rab 'byams pa. *Chos dbyings mdzod 'grel.* Full title: *Chos dbyings rin po che'i mdzod kyi 'grel pa lung gyi gter mdzod.* From A 'dzom chos sgar blocks. Gangtok: Dodrup Chen, 1964–69.

———. 1999. *Yid bzhin mdzod.* Full title: *Theg pa chen po'i bstan bcos yid bzhin rin po che'i mdzod.* In *Mdzod bdun: The Famed Seven Treasures of Vajrayāna Buddhist Philosophy by Kun mkhyen Klong chen pa Dri med 'od zer,* 7:1–137. Chengdu: Bum skyabs. (Oddiyana Institute edition published by Tarthang Tulku. BDRC: purl.bdrc.io/resource /MW22920.)

———. 1999. *Yid bzhin mdzod 'grel.* Full title: *Theg pa chen po'i bstan bcos yid bzhin rin po che'i mdzod kyi 'grel pa padma dkar po.* In *Mdzod bdun: The Famed Seven Treasures of Vajrayāna Buddhist Philosophy by Kun mkhyen Klong chen pa Dri med 'od zer,* 7:139–1591. Chengdu: Bum skyabs. (Oddiyana Institute edition published by Tarthang Tulku. BDRC: purl.bdrc.io/resource/MW22920.)

La Vallée Poussin, Louis de, ed. (1907–12) 1992. *Madhyamakāvatāra par Candrakīrti.* Bibliotheca Buddhica 9. Delhi: Motilal Banarsidass.

Merleau-Ponty, Maurice. 1964. "An Unpublished Text by Maurice Merleau-Ponty: Prospectus of His Work." Translated by Arleen B. Dallery. In *Primacy of Perception,* edited by James M. Edie, 3–11. Evanston, IL: Northwestern University Press.

Mi bskyod rdo rje, Karma pa VIII. *Dwags grub shing rta.* Full title: *Dbu ma la 'jug pa'i rnam bshad dpal ldan dus gsum mkhyen pa'i zhal lung dwags brgyud grub pa'i shing rta.* Reproduced from a Dpal spungs edition of Zhwa dmar Chos kyi blo gros. Gangtok: Rumtek Monastery 1974. Also consulted: *Dbu ma la 'jug pa'i kar tīk: Dwags brgyud grub pa'i shing rta.* Varanasi: Vajra Vidya Library, 2006.

———. *Mi bskyod rdo rje gsung 'bum.* Full title: *Dpal rgyal ba karma pa sku 'phreng brgyad pa mi bskyod rdo rje gsung 'bum.* Editions used: [1] From a computer generated *dbu can* edition of the *Mi bskyod rdo rje gsung 'bum.* 26 vols. Lhasa: 2004. [2] Dpe rnying bris ma edition. From a xylographic copy of a handwritten manuscript *dbu med* edition of *Karma pa Mi bskyod rdo rje gsung 'bum.* 14 vols. Varanasi: Vajra Vidya Institute Library.

———. *Sku gsum ngo sprod rnam bshad* (*Embodiments*). Full title: *Sku gsum ngo sprod kyi rnam par bshad pa mdo rgyud bstan pa mtha' dag gi e vaṃ phyag rgya.* Editions used: [1] Varanasi: Vajra Vidya Institute Library, 2013, vols. 1–3. [2] In *Mi bskyod rdo rje gsung 'bum*, vols. 21–22.

Padma dkar po, 'Brug chen IV. 1974. *Phyag chen rgyal ba'i gan mdzod. Phyag rgya chen po'i man ngag gi bshad sbyar rgyal ba'i gan mdzod.* In *Padma dkar po gsung 'bum = Collected Works (gsung 'bum) of Kun-mkhyen Padma-dkar-po*, 21:7–370. Darjeeling: Kargyud sungrab nyamso khang.

Putnam, Hilary. 1999. *The Threefold Cord: Mind, Body, and World.* New York: Columbia University Press.

Rescher, Nicholas. 2010. *Reality and Its Appearance.* New York: Continuum Publishing Corporation.

Rong zom pa Chos kyi bzang po. 1999. *Lta ba'i brjed byang.* In *Rong zom chos bzang gi gsung 'bum*, 2:1–26. Chengdu: Si khron mi rigs dpe skrun khang.

———. *Sbrul nag po'i stong thun.* In *Rong zom chos bzang gi gsung 'bum*, 2:66–69. Chengdu: Si khron mi rigs dpe skrun khang, 1999.

———. *Theg chen tshul 'jug = Theg pa chen po'i tshul la 'jug pa zhes bya ba'i bstan bcos.* In *Rong zom chos bzang gi gsung 'bum*, 1:415–555. Chengdu: Si khron mi rigs dpe skrun khang, 1999.

Śāntideva. 1960. *Bodhicaryāvatāra.* Edited by Vidhushekhara Bhattacharya. Bibliotheca Indica. Calcutta: The Asiatic Society.

Tauscher, Helmut. 2003. "Phya pa chos kyi seng ge as a Svātantrika." In *The Svātantrika-Prāsaṅgika Distinction: What Difference Does a Difference Make?* edited by Georges B. J. Dreyfus and Sara L. McClintock, 207–55. Studies in Indian and Tibetan Buddhism. Boston: Wisdom Publications.

Thakchoe, Sonam. 2004. "How Many Truths? Are There Two Truths or One in the Prāsaṅgika Madhyamaka?" *Contemporary Buddhism* 5.2: 31–51.

Tillemans, Tom. 1984. "On a Recent Work on Tibetan Buddhist Epistemology." *Asiatische Studien / Études Asiatiques* 38.1: 59–66.

———. 2016. *How Do Mādhyamikas Think? And Other Essays on the Buddhist Philosophy of the Middle.* Studies in Indian and Tibetan Buddhism. Somerville, MA: Wisdom Publications.

Tillemans, Tom, and Guy Newland. 2011. "An Introduction to Conventional Truth." In *Moonshadows: Conventional Truth in Buddhist Philosophy*, by the Cowherds, 3–22. New York: Oxford University Press.

Part 4
Reflections and Responses from Tom

On Truth, Knowledge, Typical/Atypical Madhyamaka Philosophies, and the Science of Tuesdays

Tom J. F. Tillemans

I HAVE on various occasions advanced the now controversial idea that the Prāsaṅgika-Madhyamaka Buddhism ("Consequentialist Middle Way Philosophy") of Tsongkhapa (Tsong kha pa blo bzang grags pa, 1357–1419) is significantly different from that conveyed in Candrakīrti's *oeuvre* read naturally and straightforwardly. The historical Candrakīrti's thought on issues of truth and knowledge is, by and large, more credibly captured by a dominant Indo-Tibetan interpretation that I called "typical Prāsaṅgika." It presents a particular negative stance about knowledge and truth—namely, that the Madhyamaka philosophy of emptiness (*śūnyavāda*), the stance that all things lack intrinsic natures, implies that ordinary people never actually know any truths about anything at all. Atypical thinkers like Tsongkhapa and his Gelukpa (*dge lugs pa*) followers disagree and categorically deny any such implication. While their atypical position is essentially an innovation, I maintain that in some crucial issues about truth and knowledge, it turns out to be a markedly better philosophy.

The terminology "typical/atypical" is my own. It is not traditional and reflects no particular Sanskrit or Tibetan expression used in indigenous classifications of Madhyamaka branches. Nonetheless, I think it can serve to distinguish a major traditional divide concerning issues of truth and knowledge in Indo-Tibetan Madhyamaka and is hence relevant to the focus of this volume.[1] That divide, as I will try to show, is also philosophically relevant in a modern context where truth is increasingly regarded with suspicion or is

---

1. Note that there are Tibetan Mādhyamikas that could be said to be "atypical" in other ways. David Higgins, in this volume, for example, lays out a Tibetan Madhyamaka philosophy that seems to me atypical in promoting a strong version of the inseparability of the two truths (*bden gnyis dbyer med*).

under attack. I have already had my say in some previous publications on various aspects of Madhyamaka. In what follows I'll refer to those publications to avoid repetition. I'll lay out a few new ideas, stress or rethink some old ones, and respond along the way to some of my fellow contributors to this volume. Although I'm well aware that my views are difficult to categorize and not a ringing endorsement of *any* particular Indo-Tibetan author or his school, I also think that this is how things should be. The textual and philosophical issues are complex, with various tensions between them. They should be thought through well beyond traditional partisan monologues and hagiography.

First, the basics. We need a working idea of how the typical interpretation was traditionally presented and whether it actually turns on a credible, close reading of source texts. I am calling "typical Prāsaṅgikas" those that thought that ordinary people (*pṛthagjana*)—that is, those people who are not among the "nobles," or "exalted ones" (*ārya*), who have a direct insight into emptiness—can have no sources of knowledge (*pramāṇa*), or at least no genuine *pramāṇa*s, about any of the matters to which they direct their attention. (Sources of knowledge, for Buddhists, are understandings. While they are not just *simply* any and all true understandings, they are true; to take the usual Buddhist position of Dharmakīrti, they are "understandings that are nonbelying" (*avisaṃvādi jñānam*)—reliable/justified and true. The connection between *pramāṇa*s and truth is thus direct. In what follows, I'll use the Sanskrit technical term for economy.) More generally, all customary truths (*saṃvṛtisatya*)—those concerning the objects making up the world—are said to be false and deceptive (*mṛṣāmoṣadharmaka*), as the Madhyamaka argumentation in major Indian texts supposedly shows that every object is riddled with internal contradictions. Customary truths thus cannot (and should not) be seriously thought about or analyzed; one shouldn't oneself endorse or defend positions about them; one acquiesces instead to what is in fact acknowledged by the world (*lokaprasiddha*). The recurrent Tibetan catchphrase says it all: the customary just exists in the perspective of mistaken minds (*blo 'khrul ba'i ngor yod pa*).

The broad direction of this exegesis of Madhyamaka is very credible as a philologically sound reading of Indian source texts and certainly isn't to be dismissed out of hand. Error theories, with their appeals to humans' collective ignorance (*avidyā*), shared mistakes (*bhrānti*), and supposedly beginningless karmic tendencies (*anādikālavāsanā*) to get things wrong over and over, are the most frequent Mahāyānist way to account for worldlings' consensus about customary truths, from selves to macroscopic objects to properties, relations, and absences. Abhidharma, Yogācāra, and Madhyamaka are similar in overwhelmingly weighting error as explanatory, although they differ as to what specifically is erroneous and what, if anything, is real. Error and ignorance, with varying reliance on more or less sophisticated causal accounts, then, are what makes most Buddhist metaphysics tick.[2] The particularity of the Madhyamaka is that it pushes that error theory about as far as it can go to apply to everything in ordinary people's understanding and construes enlightenment equally radically. To cite a phrase of John Dunne (this volume), "one's seemingly indubitable perception of a coherent lifeworld . . . is actually like a nightmare from which one must awake" (201). Below we will look more specifically at how this idea of radical awakening is expressed in Candrakīrti's *Yuktiṣaṣṭikāvṛtti*.

Not everyone will agree with me about the predominance of error theories in Indian Madhyamaka. My longtime friend and partner in dialogue Mark Siderits, for example, has consistently seen pragmatism where I see error. Ordinary people supposedly accept wholes, like chariots—and indeed are responsible for them existing—because they present a gain in efficiency or convenience, so that people do not always have to think about, or speak long-windedly of, chariot parts such as wheels, axles, felloes, spokes, and so on. Chariots (and all other such things) should thus be seen as the results of a kind of conceptual and linguistic shorthand. The Madhyamaka dialectic supposedly shows us that they cannot be anything more.

Now, philosophically speaking, pragmatism might well be more tempting than an error theory as an explanation of the world, and it will probably resonate more with a modern biological perspective as to how our species evolved. It is sometimes built into modern translations of Buddhist terms like *prajñapti* ("designation") by adding adjectives like "convenient" and "useful." The texts, however, don't actually bear it out. There is a striking paucity of textual support for introducing the adjectives. There are, of course, many passages that say that various Buddhist teachings are nonliteral and only pedagogically useful to specific people in specific contexts. Fictions and white lies were supposedly taught by the Buddha because of his "skill in means" (*upāyakauśalya*) in guiding disciples on the religious path, and they were rationalized by commentators as pertaining to successive levels of analysis (see Dunne, this volume). But while the Buddha and the great paṇḍits may

---

2. Many Buddhist theories turn almost exclusively on what John Haldane and Crispin Wright term "metaphysical superstition"—error and misbelief *tout court* about what there is. Not all do. See Tillemans 1999, 7–11, 209–13, and Tillemans 2011b, 55–57, on the "theory of unconscious error" in Dharmakīrtian philosophies of language and metaphysics. Dharmakīrtian explanations are not reliant on mere metaphysical superstition but also rely on a complex causal account linking thought and the world.

have been skillful in selectively introducing fictions, *we* are not. The usual
Buddhist account is that our lifeworld came about more or less blindly, stuck
as we are in ignorance and a chain of repeated mistakes. Indeed, there does
not seem to be any direct, or even indirect, basis in the Indian source texts
for a pragmatic (or evolutionary) origin story about how *we* populated our
world with fictional things of daily life—like chariots, blueness, absences,
and selves—because of the efficiency in language and thought we gained by
developing concepts of them.[3] Like it or not, the Buddhists generally say that
people proceed through bewilderment (*moha*) and not by a rationally expli-
cable pursuit of utility and convenience or in a quasi-Darwinian fashion.

What about the "atypical"? What can we understand by that term? The
essential point is that Tsongkhapa and the Gelukpa, in contrast to much
mainstream Madhyamaka, did *not* accept that ordinary, worldly people have
no *pramāṇas* because of their global mistakenness. Indeed, Tsongkhapa is
exceptional in that he is not much of an error theorist about the customary
at all, and certainly not like most of his coreligionists, although, of course, as
a Mahāyānist he inherited extensive talk of error and had to locate where the
error was. While his adversaries generally held that customary things, like
vases and such, were *themselves* contradictory and thus only products of error,
Tsongkhapa took the exceptional position that, for Mādhyamikas, vases and
the like are *not* themselves internally contradictory and are *not* only existent
for mistaken minds (Tillemans 2021). The error is elsewhere. It is the intrinsic nature (*rang bzhin = svabhāva*) that people superimpose (*sgro btags pa =
samāropita*) that is the "object to be denied" (*dgag bya*). Superimpositions, or
reified versions of things, are thus the culprits. Vases and the like are themselves left untouched, and there are right views and *pramāṇas* concerning what
they are.

So much, then, for the working ideas. Let me now sketch out a few
reflections and responses on the question of where Candrakīrti himself
stood before we go deeper into the details and merits of typical and atypical
interpretations of his thought in Tibet. Clearly other contributors to this
volume, Jay Garfield and Sonam Thakchoe, have a quite different position
on Candrakīrti from mine. Theirs is, I think, a version of Tsongkhapa back-
read onto Candrakīrti for philosophical reasons. I'll make a philological case
that this approach does not work very well as an account of the historical

---

3. People sometimes cite Dharmakīrtian talk of *arthakriyāsthiti* ("confirmation of practical
efficacy") as evidence of a Buddhist pragmatic theory of truth. I think it is not a theory of truth
(pragmatic or otherwise) but is the Dharmakīrtian account of justification. See Tillemans 1999,
6–8.

Candrakīrti, even though I would be the first to endorse some key parts of Tsongkhapa's position for its philosophical interest. Some of what I have to say will also apply to Dan Arnold's critical analysis of my depiction of Candrakīrti's acquiescence in *lokaprasiddha*.

What About Candrakīrti Himself?

In an article (Tillemans 2011a) published in another collaborative volume, I had said that typical Prāsaṅgika philosophy—with its all-encompassing error theory of the customary, acquiescence in people's going beliefs, and rejection of any overlap in the understandings of noble (*ārya*) and ordinary beings— was "a very natural reading of Candrakīrti's texts," albeit one with potentially "dismal" philosophical consequences, like the adoption of populism and uncritical relativism. My 2011 article, with its specter of a stultifying Madhyamaka, no doubt had shock value. It conveyed a cautionary tale, inspired in part by the eighth-century writer Kamalaśīla, about what Candrakīrtians' talk of *lokaprasiddha* can reasonably suggest. It is, in short, what Candrakīrti looks like to someone unenthralled by a philosophy that seems too lukewarm in its commitment to truth-telling, preferring instead to defer to surface-level opinions. We will see below whether typical Prāsaṅgika is *inevitably* to be saddled with all the dismal consequences of extreme populism and relativism. One of the many good results of the dialogue with Dan Arnold, Jay Garfield, and Sonam Thakchoe is that it has pushed me to reexamine whether a no-*pramāṇa* stance—and especially its modern variants—entails everything that has been said against it, traditionally or recently.

That is for later. For now, let us see how the typical Prāsaṅgika interpretation fares as a straightforward, natural reading of Candrakīrti, the kind that would be favored by philology in that it passes grammatical muster, fits in with antecedent literature and contexts, takes the author at his word, and is without the strain of elaborate hedges added to account for what people think the text *must* or *should* mean. I think the typical Prāsaṅgika interpretation of Candrakīrti fares well on this kind of reading. It reflects the understanding of *lokaprasiddha* by Nāgārjuna, who, in verse 1 of his *Śūnyatāsaptati*, contrasts the customary usage of the world (*lokavyavahāra*) with what the Buddha understands rightly—the Buddha, in short, preached in skillful ways that the mistaken world would accept without himself subscribing to their truth.[4] It was also how an Indian Svātantrika adversary—

---

4. *Śūnyatāsaptati* verse 1 (ed. Erb 1997): *gnas pa'am skye 'jig yod med dam / dman pa'am mnyam dang khyad par can / sangs rgyas 'jig rten snyad dbang gis / gsungs kyi yang dag dbang gis min //*

Kamalaśīla, in his *Sarvadharmaniḥsvabhāva(tā)siddhi*—took Candrakīrti, or Candrakīrtians, in their talk of acquiescence in (all or most?) going beliefs. This Svātantrika took Candrakīrtians as advocating *pratijñāmātreṇa siddha* ("establishment through mere belief/acceptance"), rather than *pramāṇasiddha* ("establishment by *pramāṇas*"), and saw them as weakening critical thought in favor of duplications of popular belief (Tillemans 2011a, 153–54). And, yes, this typical Prāsaṅgika interpretation has considerable textual backing in Candrakīrti's texts[5] and in the Mahāyāna sūtras he cites.[6] Candrakīrti's use of *loka* in *lokaprasiddha* as meaning ordinary, ignorant worldlings, as opposed to āryas or buddhas, is a normal Buddhist Sanskrit usage: *loka* is regularly to be contrasted with *lokottara* ("supra-worldly", i.e., awakened beings). The Ratnakūṭa collection of sūtras' version of the famous (unnamed) scriptural passage (*āgama*) Candrakīrti cites about *lokaprasiddha* takes *loka* as the "world of beings" (*sems can gyi 'jig rten = sattvaloka*), not surprisingly understanding those beings to be "infantile, ordinary beings" (*byis pa so so so'i skye bo = bālapṛthagjana*)—in short, the common folk, who do not actually know anything but all wrongly think they do.[7] There seems little reason

"Abiding, arising, perishing, existence, nonexistence, low, same, and higher: the Buddha spoke [of them] because of the world's customary usage (*lokavyavahāra*) but not because of what is correct."

5. For example, *Madhyamakāvatāra* 6.23, taken straightforwardly and in keeping with Candrakīrti's *Madhyamakāvatārabhāṣya*, promotes the idea that customary truth is simply widespread error by ordinary people due to their ignorance; only āryas understand reality rightly: *samyaṅmṛṣādarśanalabdhabhāvaṃ rūpadvayaṃ bibhrati sarvabhāvāḥ / samyagdṛśāṃ yo viṣayaḥ sa tattvaṃ mṛṣādṛśāṃ saṃvṛtisatyam uktam //* "All things bear two natures constituted through correct and false views. The object (*viṣaya*) of those who see correctly is said to be the 'real' (*tattva*), and the object of those who see falsely is said to be a 'customary truth' (*saṃvṛtisatya*)."

6. On sūtra sources for there being no overlap in ordinary and *ārya* ways of understanding, see, for example, the *Satyadvayāvatārasūtra*, which Candrakīrti cites in *Madhyamakāvatārabhāṣya* ad 6.29. It characterizes the ultimate as "completely beyond all customary usage" (*sarvavyavahārasamatikrānta*) and "free from [any customary distinctions like] the signified, signifiers, the cognized, and cognition" (*abhidheyābhidhānajñeyajñānavigata*). The Sanskrit of the sūtra is cited in Prajñākaramati's commentary to Śāntideva's *Bodhicaryāvatāra* 9.2, which (read straightforwardly) is itself a source for typical Prāsaṅgika: "the true [way things are] is not an object of understanding; understanding is said to be customary" (*buddher agocaras tattvaṃ buddhiḥ saṃvṛtir ucyate*). See also the quotation from *Yuktiṣaṣṭikāvṛtti* below and note 8.

7. *Trisaṃvaranirdeśaparivarta*, the first sūtra of the Ratnakūṭa collection, D 45, ka, 9b. On the Sanskrit of the *āgama* Candrakīrti quotes to ground his idea of *lokaprasiddha*, see Tillemans 2022, 224–26. The Pāli version of the Saṃyutta Nikāya (22.94) is significantly different and speaks of "what is accepted by experts in the world" rather than just what is "accepted by worldlings."

to think that Candrakīrti's own understanding of *loka* was significantly different when he quoted the (unnamed) *āgama* in *Prasannapadā* ad 18.8 and *Madhyamakāvatārabhāṣya* ad 6.81.

I think it is thus undeniable that many of Candrakīrti's usual formulations and the rhetorical thrust of his unhedged words go toward the typical, even though his complete *oeuvre* sends some mixed messages here and there and shows itself to be malleable on occasion. The jury will probably stay out on *precisely* how typical he was. In a recent publication (Tillemans 2023), I have philosophically expanded upon a few passages from his *Catuḥśatakaṭīkā* that present dependent designation (*upādāya prajñapti*) as the needed alternative to the semantic theory of realism (*dngos po smra ba*) and metaphysics. With a strong interpretative hand, they could also provide for some customary truths being right and not just widely believed. Dan Arnold, too, in the present volume, argues that with a more charitable reading of various passages from Candrakīrti, one can find evidence of normativity and not mere duplication of ordinary people's beliefs.

The cautionary tale in my 2011 article, however, should remain. It originates in what I see as a fundamental ambiguity in Candrakīrti's texts, a gray zone that doesn't easily go away by citing more textual passages. Taking his *oeuvre* as a whole, it is unclear, on balance, whether his own acquiescence in worldly acceptances is a kind of disengagement from metaphysical controversies over issues like the nature of causation and the existence of an external world, universals, realism, and so on in favor of ordinary accounts of these customary matters, or whether it is a disengagement from other conflicts with what ordinary people accept, especially their folk beliefs on empirical matters. Answering a metaphysical inquiry about the nature of causation by reproducing ordinarily used formulae like "This did that," "Rice comes from rice," or "When wood, strings, and manual effort are present, sounds arise from musical instruments" could well be the best responses to a metaphysician's misguided questions about nature writ large. Those formulae, however, obviously cannot be proper responses to legitimate causal enquiries in genetics, botany, or the physics of sound production, where one should not respond by reading off the surface of ordinary beliefs and usage (see Tillemans 2011a, 155 and 159–60).

The *Catuḥśatakaṭīkā* passages I took up may, exceptionally, provide a way to valorize the customary and make the needed distinction. My impression, however, is that Candrakīrti did not by and large prioritize discrimination between appropriate and inappropriate ways to acquiesce in *lokaprasiddha*. Nor did he attach much importance to investigating nonobvious physical objects in the world profoundly or in a difficult, theoretical fashion in contrast to surface-level investigations. He instead prioritized enlightenment and thought of it as the way out of *all* customary matters whatsoever. He says as much in his *Yuktiṣaṣṭikāvṛtti* to verse 4cd, in which enlightenment is depicted as a gnosis without any intentionality—that is, without any object (*dmigs pa = ālambana*) whatsoever, certainly none to which ordinary people, "the infantile," direct their attention.

> Therefore, because they abide in an objectless gnosis (*ye shes = jñāna*) that radically goes beyond the infantile people, they are superior [to them] and so are called *superior individuals* (*bdag nyid chen po = mahātman*).[8]

Candrakīrti thus clearly saw superior people—that is, enlightened buddhas and what Thakchoe calls the "exalted" (= *ārya*)—as having a thoroughly different sort of understanding. The customary lifeworld is, on the whole, treated perfunctorily, with relatively little interest on his part in the intricacies of worldlings' knowledge or, for that matter, in exalted people's knowledge of the customary either. When it came to all such understanding, he himself (much like a typical Prāsaṅgika) had little epistemology to speak of.

Tibetans on Candrakīrti

Ironically, although the atypical Prāsaṅgika of Tsongkhapa, Khedrup Jé (Mkhas grub rje), Jamyang Shepa ('Jam dbyangs bzhad pa), and followers is promising philosophically to many of us largely because it *does* clarify the gray zone and valorize the customary, it is nevertheless at crucial points demonstrably unwarranted by the Indian textual sources that are cited as its support. Among the most problematic uses of Indian sources are Tsongkhapa's citing of Śāntideva's *Bodhicaryāvatāra* 9.140 to anchor his idea of the "object to be denied" (*dgag bya*), as well as his exegesis of passages from Bhāviveka's *Prajñāpradīpa* to show an Indian source for Svātantrikas accepting that things are customarily established via their intrinsic characteristics (*tha snyad du rang gi mtshan nyid kyis grub pa*). Textually, all this turns out to be strained

---

8. *De'i phyir de dag skye bo byis pa rnams las shin tu 'das pa dmigs pa med pa'i ye shes la gnas pas de dag nyid che ba'i phyir bdag nyid chen po zhes bya ste* (Scherrer-Schaub 1991, 32). MacDonald 2009 starkly, but not inaccurately, characterizes this kind of Madhyamaka awakening from error as a nonrational gnosis that knows nothing. Note that an objectless gnosis beyond all the customary is not just a Prāsaṅgika goal; it is also what Kamalaśīla advocates in his *Madhyamakāloka*. See Keira 2004, 85: "the nonperception of all dharmas has indeed the nature of cognition, since it is yogins' *clear perception where nothing appears*" (italics in original).

and implausible. Back-reading Tsongkhapa onto Candrakīrti's words is therefore extraordinarily complex and, in the end, unconvincing. He disguises his originality. Indeed, despite his ideological insistence upon textual grounding in Indian sources (*khungs*), on a number of important matters, his readings seem to have turned Candrakīrti into a more subtle philosopher than he actually was.[9]

But did Candrakīrti himself even have a clear-enough position on *pramāṇa*s, for or against, so that the philosophically significant debate on truth could be pursued exclusively, or even primarily, on the basis of his own words? Likely he did not, or at least we're not going to find it articulated for all to see in an as-yet-undiscussed or underappreciated passage.[10] That being said, philosophers and Buddhologists investigating Madhyamaka are, fortunately, not obliged to stick with Candrakīrti's own words either. Other fruits are within reach. We can do a lot better by looking directly at two philosophies that rival Tibetan Prāsaṅgikas attribute to Candrakīrti concerning *pramāṇa*s and evaluate their merits. I propose, then, to shift the focus away from what Candrakīrti *himself* meant in his statements about truth and knowledge. I think we can more profitably evaluate philosophically what principal Tibetan actors *say* he meant.

Let me, then, take up a philosophically significant debate that the Sakyapa cleric Taktsang Lotsāwa Sherab Rinchen (Stag tshang Lo tsā ba Shes rab rin chen, 1405–77) had with Tsongkhapa on the issue of *pramāṇa*s that divides typical and atypical Prāsaṅgikas. I am indebted in what follows to a recent two-volume study, *Knowing Illusion*, by a collective of ten authors, the Yakherds, three of whom are contributors to this volume. While I have nothing to add to their excellent documentation and translations of key textual sources in a debate that raged in Tibet over centuries, I may be able to put the fundamental oppositions in a different light by bringing in issues of warranted assertibility versus truth.[11] Of course, it is slightly anachronistic to have Tsongkhapa debating with Taktsang—or, for that matter, with twentieth-century Americans and Australians, as I do. But the key positions that Tsongkhapa attacks are also the same ones Taktsang espouses a little bit later. Richard

9. See Williams 1995 on the misreading of *Bodhicaryāvatāra* 9.140, Eckel 2003 on Tsongkhapa's implausible reading of the *Prajñāpradīpa* passages, and Tillemans 2003 on the philosophical merits of the ideas.

10. On more than a few major issues concerning early Indian Mādhyamikas (including Candrakīrti), there is sobering truth in Paul Griffiths's remark (2000, 24): "Nāgārjuna's works are, in this reviewer's judgment, insufficiently precise and systematic to make debates about what he really meant, philosophically speaking, very useful."

11. See also the review article on *Knowing Illusion* by Matthew Kapstein (Kapstein 2023).

Rorty and Huw Price will turn out to be relevant, too. Time travel is not going to vitiate our discussion.

Taktsang versus Tsongkhapa

In his *Grub mtha' kun shes nas mtha' bral sgrub pa*, Taktsang Lotsāwa, whom I'll focus upon as a representative of the typical Prāsaṅgika no-*pramāṇa* position, took the Indian passages about customary truth being false and deceptive categorically. Falsity simply precluded any genuinely alethic distinctions: the customary is *completely* erroneous, with no possible distinction into right and wrong and no *pramāṇa*s ensuring customary truth.[12] Indeed, his underlying position on customary truth was that everything ordinary people believe could be seen to be false on "slight analysis" (*cung zad dpyod pa*) using Madhyamaka reasonings. In effect, a Mādhyamika *śūnyavādin* ("exponent of emptiness") can never make affirmations about what *is* customarily but only describe what people misbelieve to be so by their own mistaken lights—full stop. I think Jayānanda and other interpreters of Candrakīrti, like Taktsang and sympathizers in the Karma Kagyü or Jonang schools, held these basic ideas by and large.

Let's now go to the other side of the ledger in this Tibetan debate. Here are two samples of Tsongkhapa's atypicality on truth and knowledge. First, in *Dbu ma dgongs pa rab gsal*, his commentary on Candrakīrti's *Madhyamakāvatāra*, he argued directly against rival (unnamed) Mādhyamikas who thought that because different life forms perceived things in opposing ways, there were no *pramāṇa*s at all—nobody thought truly.[13] (Significantly, Taktsang held exactly the ideas Tsongkhapa attacks.) The reply looks like a fairly usual (East-West) reply to a global denial of truth: if someone wrongfully denied all *pramāṇa*s (*tshad ma thams cad la skur ba 'debs pa*), they would be utterly incoherent (*shin tu mi 'thad*), as they could never make any reliable assertions nor know anything at all, not even their own negative positions. The argument is, in effect, a transcendental argument: truth is presupposed by rational deliberation and thus cannot be globally denied by rational thinkers.

Second, in *Drang nges legs bshad snying po*, Tsongkhapa polemicized against coreligionists who held that customary things "just exist in a mistaken perspective" (*'khrul ngor yod pa tsam*). He said that on such a criterion, a proposition like "God (*īśvara*) is responsible for our happiness or pain" would be as

---

12. "Taktsang also argues that it makes no sense to distinguish—as Tsongkhapa and his followers do—between true and false in a world in which everything is deceptive" (Yakherds 2021, 2.17).

13. See *Dbu ma dgongs pa rab gsal*, 278–79 (Sarnath edition), 338–39 (*Collected Works*).

customarily true as "Karma is responsible for our happiness and pain." After all, each of these propositions was believed to be true by respective groups of (supposedly) mistaken people.[14] Tsongkhapa's point, of course, is that, customarily speaking, karma *is* responsible, and God is not—the former proposition alone is true. A more robust conception of truth and knowledge was thus needed in Tsongkhapa's eyes: in effect, truth is what *should* be believed through *pramāṇa*s, often correcting what is believed at any given time and place by individuals or groups of people.

Tsongkhapa's position is a composite, with elements that are promising, both philosophically and exegetically, and others that are less so. Contrary to Taktsang, he held that human understanding has recurrent right and wrong parts, or facets (*cha*); they appear mixed (*'dres pa*) and inseparable (*dbyer med*) to ordinary people but not to nobles.[15] Nuanced discrimination is thus needed to leave the customary unassailed but tease out the superimposed error—the object of negation, the *dgag bya*.

I have argued that this nuancing of Madhyamaka is a remarkable innovation. It shifts the focus from questionable metaphysical proofs of the general, unnuanced incoherence of all concepts and the unreality of things that fall under them to a more targeted investigation of our deep-seated quest for

14. *Drang nges legs bshad snying po*, 233 (Sarnath edition), 697–98 (*Collected Works*): *de dag zhib tu 'byed pa'i dpyad pa ma rdzogs par rigs pa ltar snang res don dam du grub pa bkag cing / kun rdzob tu yod pa rnams 'khrul shes res yod par bzung na de'i ngor yod pa tsam gyis 'jog nus te / de'i don ni 'khrul ngor yod pa tsam yin pa'i phyir ro snyam du bsams na ni / dbang phyug dang gtso bo la sogs pa las bde sdug skye ba dang dkar nag gi las gnyis las skye ba gnyis 'thad na 'thad mnyam dang ma 'thad na ma 'thad mnyam du 'gro ste / sngar bzhin dpyad na ni dpyod byed kyis phyi ma yang mi rnyed la 'khrul ngor ni snga ma yang yod pa'i phyir ro //* "Suppose that without fully analyzing such things, one negates their ultimate existence through a bogus reasoning and holds that customary existents exist because of some mistaken cognitions. If one were to think that one could establish them merely because of their existence from the perspective of this [mistaken cognition]—that is to say, because that [cognition's] object just exists in a mistaken perspective—then it would be just as correct [customarily] or incorrect [ultimately to say] that God or Primordial Matter (*gtso bo = pradhāna*) and the like are responsible for producing [our] happiness and pain as to say that it is white and black karma that are responsible. This is because if we analyze them along the previous lines [i.e., in terms of their ultimate status], then the second [state of affairs, karma being responsible for producing happiness and pain,] would also be unfindable by the analyzer, while the first [state of affairs, that God is responsible,] would also exist from the perspective of mistaken cognition."

15. See, e.g., *Dbu ma dgongs pa rab gsal*, 222 (Sarnath edition), 273 (*Collected Works*): *sngon po rang gi mtshan nyid kyis grub par snang na yang / sngon po'i steng nas rang bzhin gyis grub par snang mi snang gi cha gnyis dbyer med par snang la.* "Also, in the case of blue, which appears as established by its own characteristics, then with regard to the blue, the facet (*cha*) [of blue] that appears to be established by its intrinsic nature and the [facet] that does not appear [in this way] both appear inseparably (*dbyer med*)."

"superlative facts" and reifications, which *are* incoherent (see Tillemans 2016, 39ff.). It also helps resolve the fundamental ambiguity I spoke about above and thus would allow Mādhyamikas to actively promote sophistication and progress in the pursuit of nonobvious customary truths while remaining disengaged from all that is reified.

However, it's also a long way from Indian Madhyamaka, and it seems much easier said than done. Indeed, Tibetans to this day tell us that teasing out the needed distinctions between the true and the superimposed is a daunting task that cannot be accomplished by simply relying on, or restating, the traditional five arguments (*gtan tshigs lnga*) in Indian treatises, like inter alia the *ekānekaviyogahetu*—the "neither one nor many" proofs for mereological nihilism (see Kellner [this volume] on that recurrent argument).[16] José Cabezón, in this volume, has examined the development of the idea of "recognition of the object to be refuted" (*dgag bya ngos 'dzin*) in the Geluk tradition and shows how it significantly moves Madhyamaka in the direction of an introspective and contemplative approach. I can only agree. It doesn't look like the content of this recognition is just the proposition figuring as the conclusion to a metaphysical argument in Indian philosophy. Nor is recognition, if taken seriously, a finite undertaking limited to the handful of exercises devised by later Gelukpa authors. It seems to me more like an ever-evolving work in progress.

Tsongkhapa, however, went much further than just stressing the importance of disengaging the true from the superimposed. He maintained that there are innate *pramāṇa*s (*lhan skyes kyi tshad ma*) possessed by all people.[17] A whole set of innocuous customary matters were thus immediately known, innately, in the same untheoretical, neutral way, so that a set of phenomenal objects

---

16. See Keira 2004, 10–13n32, for an extensive footnote on the five arguments. Note that the first Indian text to use this schema, the *Madhyamakārthasaṃgraha* (attributed to Bhāviveka), speaks of four arguments (*gtan tshigs bzhi*) instead of five, without entering into any details. That seems a classificational issue of relatively little importance.

17. See his *Rtsa ba'i shes rab kyi dka' gnad chen po brgyad*, 8a–b (*Collected Works* 581–82), where he summarizes his interpretation of the Candrakīrti-Bhāviveka debate: *mdor na lhan skyes kyi tshe tshad ma* mthun snang du grub pa dngos smra ba dang [dbu ma pa] gnyis ka'i rgyud la yod pas / de kho na nyid kyi rtogs pa bskyed du rung ba yin la / grub mthas bzhag pa'i mthun snang med pa la rang rgyud mi rung ba yin no //*. *Sarnath edition: *lhan skyes kyi tshad ma*. "In summary, innately (*lhan skyes kyi tshe*) there are *pramāṇa*s established as having similar appearances [of customary things] in both the realist's and [the Mādhyamika's] mindstreams, and therefore a realization of the [ultimate] truth can be properly produced. However, there are no similar appearances that would be established [in common] by the [two rival] philosophical systems (*grub mtha' = siddhānta*), and [thus] there cannot properly be an autonomous [inference, contrary to what Svātantrikas maintain]."

that "similarly appear" (*mthun snang ba*) and are commonly acknowledged—a given or phenomenological foundation, if you will—would ensure that understandings of the customary can indeed be truths. It should be clear that this is a major step beyond Candrakīrti's oft-quoted talk about accepting "things that are acknowledged by [everyone] starting with uneducated people like cowherds, women, and the like on up."[18] It is no doubt true that there is a wide consensus on basic "house and garden variety" matters among people. But wide consensus doesn't imply an innate knowledge of truths. Consensus could just as easily show the near universality of shared errors.

Taktsang Read Differently

None of these main ideas of Tsongkhapa on the customary was accepted by Taktsang, neither the right and wrong parts that appear inseparable to ordinary people nor the innate *pramāṇa*s to which things appear similarly. Did Taktsang and typical Prāsaṅgikas then—as Tsongkhapa certainly suggests they did—counsel the outright elimination of all customary alethic distinctions, replacing them with uncritical, unanalyzed adoption of going ideas? That would indeed be the dismal, populist stance I argued against in 2011. But is it, after all, inevitable? What are the alternatives for *śūnyavādin*s who stick with a typical Prāsaṅgika philosophy like that of Taktsang? What might Taktsang and typical Prāsaṅgikas have *intelligently* meant in saying that customary truth was not to be examined nor analyzed (*ma brtag pa ma dpyad pa*), that it was somehow only acceptance, and that there were no *pramāṇa*s establishing it? I think that an interpretation that avoids the most problematic, stultifying consequences is available and is certainly worth getting clear on, even if it, too, will come up short in the end. Here are a few new reflections on the mire of uncritical duplication of popular belief—or, to use current Madhyamaka shoptalk, the dismal slough.

Roger Jackson, in his recent book on Mahāmudrā, made an important remark about Kagyüpa thinkers:

> [They] are more inclined to see the ultimate as thoroughly transcending the conventional, which does not, in the end, have real status as a "truth." (Jackson 2019, 357)

I think that this is on the right track. What is more, it applies to all, or at least

---

18. *Madhyamakāvatārabhāṣya* ad 6.26, D 3862, 254a: *skye bo ma byang ba gnag rdzi dang bud med la sogs pa yan chad la grags pa'i dngos po.* Instead of *yan cad*, I read *yan chad.*

most, typical Prāsaṅgikas: Taktsang counsels transcendence but not outright elimination, even if all is only error. In short, the customary is not *worthy* of analysis, and there are no *pramāṇas worthy* of the name. To see it as *unworthy*, however, leaves open the possibility that it is a "truth" in scare quotes, one that is not full-fledged or well founded but nonetheless integral to ordinary life in the world.[19]

This reading provides a way, too, for typical Prāsaṅgikas to square Candrakīrti's repeated characterizations of everything customary as *mṛṣāmoṣadharmaka* ("false and deceptive") with his perfunctory concession, in the first chapter of his *Prasannapadā*, that the four *pramāṇas* of the non-Buddhist Naiyāyikas are an adequate account of observed worldly usage:

> So, in this way, the world's understanding of objects is established as proceeding from a fourfold set of sources of knowledge (*pramāṇa*). Now, those *pramāṇas* and their objects are established in mutual dependence [and hence are not really established]. The upshot: just let the worldly matter be as we observe it. Enough of this digression.[20]

Prāsaṅgikas, thus, could even concede that ordinary beings make a whole panoply of analyses of various degrees of complexity using the Naiyāyika-style *pramāṇas* they regularly do. However, they would take those *pramāṇas* as only providing "truths" (in scare quotes) by people's own present lights. To put it another way, in this scenario, our entrenched alethic practices would proceed in a rule-guided fashion but with only the limited normativity internal to going beliefs and practices. We might say what people would or would not consistently have to believe by extrapolating from what they presently believe and their presently entrenched practices, but anything else would run afoul of Madhyamaka *śūnyavāda*. In what remains, I want to look deeper at the matter of the normative force of *pramāṇas*, thinking alongside Tsongkhapa and Taktsang on issues of truth and truth-telling that are, in my opinion, as important now as they were seven centuries ago.

19. Cf. Yakherds 2021, 1:78: "Taktsang argues that . . . no Mādhyamika rejects truth and falsity, right and wrong, etc., within the world of convention."

20. *Tad evaṃ pramāṇacatuṣṭayāl lokasyārthādhigamo vyavasthāpyate // tāni ca parasparāpekṣayā sidhyanti / tasmāl laukikam evāstu yathādṛṣṭam ity alaṃ prasaṅgena.* La Vallée Poussin [1903–13] 1970a, 75.9–12, and MacDonald 2015, §123. I have followed MacDonald's edition here. La Vallée Poussin has two additional sentences.

Warranted Assertibility and Truth

Let's take a few steps outside the purely Indo-Tibetan conceptual apparatus. Since John Dewey, many Anglo-American philosophers, the best known being perhaps Richard Rorty, have thought that truth could be identified with a type of assertibility, one that is warranted in that it is in keeping with epistemic standards and procedures of justification. In so doing, philosophers often seek to avoid a realist, metaphysical account of truth, according to which the truth of a proposition <*p*> would be as it is, irrespective of all epistemic matters and evidential constraints, because the corresponding state of affairs is as it is intrinsically. Opting for truth *qua* warranted assertibility rather than metaphysically loaded truth, then, could also seem an intelligent move for a Mādhyamika to avoid reliance on real entities with intrinsic natures, correspondence theories, and the like. What is more, it could account better for at least some of the alethic distinctions that the world makes—what I'm calling "truth" and "falsity" in scare quotes—in that it would recognize the importance of worldly practices of criticism and selection and steer clear of pure duplication of going beliefs. Perhaps it could, for example, make sense of passages like *Madhyamakāvatāra* 6.26, where Candrakīrti maintains that non-Buddhist fictions—God (*īśvara*), the Sāṃkhya's three qualities (*guṇa*), and the like—do not exist from the point of view of the world's customary truth (*lokasaṃvṛtisatya*), despite the fact that in various places and times, many people have professed belief in them. I think that an intelligent version of Taktsang's thought can, indeed, be developed along these lines: he identified customary truth with a type of warranted assertibility.

Which type of warranted assertibility? Some modern writers, like Hilary Putnam, have felt they had to add the qualifying proviso "ideally," so that a statement's being warrantedly assertible, or rationally justified, would mean that it is ideally assertible/justified—that is, assertible under "epistemically ideal conditions" (Putnam [1981] 1993, 55–56). Such a qualification would supposedly guarantee that a true statement is not simply one that is warrantedly assertible *now* or was so in the past but, rather, would be assertible if our epistemic powers and other conditions were ideal. Understandably the proviso has its critics, for it is far from clear what is epistemically ideal or how one is to gauge greater or lesser proximity to it. Richard Rorty, for one, had nothing to do with the ideal, opting instead for what is actual and ethnocentric: "the way *we* live now, what *we* do now, how *we* talk now."[21] And I don't think

---

21. Rorty [1991] 1996, 158: "The question of whether there is anything for philosophers to appeal to save the way *we* live now, what *we* do now, how *we* talk now—anything beyond *our*

idealization has any place in the typical Prāsaṅgika no-*pramāṇa* philosophy, either. When Taktsang maintains that Madhyamaka reasonings show that worldly understandings are always thoroughly erroneous and could never be right, a corollary would be that there cannot be any ideal assertibility of the customary at all. Idealization doesn't mesh with all-pervasive and inevitable mistakenness.

Tsongkhapa's idea of truth, as we saw above, is strongly normative and contrasts with what I am calling "truths" in scare quotes, which are essentially descriptions of existing societal facts. I think that truth for him, thus, would not be reducible to *de facto* warranted assertibility. Here is where I want to bring in Huw Price's article "Truth as Convenient Friction" (2003) to see more clearly the difference truth makes beyond assertibility. Price's position is shrewd: he sees a distinct and necessary place for truth as a norm—that is, as an obligation governing assertoric discourse (with censure when not fulfilled)—but rejects the need for a theoretically satisfying theory of truth. In effect, we should be truth-tellers taking clashes between truth claims seriously, but, in a deflationary spirit, we need not say what truth essentially *is*.

Price sees three distinct norms governing assertoric discourse. They go like this. First, opposing parties regularly recognize that they should speak sincerely in accordance with their more-or-less deeply held views and not just lie or deliberately obfuscate. Second, they also regularly recognize that they should justify their views in keeping with their epistemic standards. And third, their assertoric discourse—and not just talk about preferences and feelings—is governed by a norm about truth-telling. Price formulated that third norm as follows:

> (Truth) If not-*p*, then it is incorrect to assert that *p*; if not-*p*, then there are prima facie grounds for censure of an assertion that *p*. (Price 2003, 175)

This is not a definition or a theory of truth, such as philosophers have typically sought. Nor does it in any way dictate *how* we determine truth and falsity and justify claims. It is, rather, an essential regulative feature of our practices of truth-telling in assertoric discourse so basic that it is rarely made explicit: claiming a proposition to be true, prima facie, involves incompatibility with contradicting claims and censure when the claimed proposition is not the case.

The norm may at first sight look bland, but it is actually not. It has teeth.

own little moment of world-history—is the decisive issue between representationalist and social-practise philosophers of language."

Indeed, Price argues that both sides can be sincere, both can make assertions that are warranted by their own lights, and yet one is asserting falsehoods and should be censured. Requiring only sincerity and warranted assertibility, on the other hand, would be a recipe for immobilism, in that we would limit rational discussion to a series of juxtaposed *merely opinionated assertions*, or MOAs. While distinct MOAs of p and of not-p coexist without any impact on each other, the norm of truth says that if p is not so—i.e., is false—assertions of p *should* be avoided and repudiated, on pain of censure.

F. P. Ramsey in 1925 had similarly characterized what happens when a type of discourse has no norm of truth (as is, according to him, the case in talk of literature and art). As he put it, discussants would just "compare notes."[22] A distinct norm of truth, then, incentivizes speakers to do *more* than compare notes—that is, to speak truth, avoid falsity, and go beyond merely producing coexisting comparisons. It thus differentiates assertoric discourse from sincere, justified expressions of preferences, purely personal beliefs, and feelings—like reasoned justifications of one's choice of wine or the kinds of people one likes. Assertoric discourse involves incompatible competing propositions and censure when a proposition turns out to be false, whereas reasoned talk of preferences does not and is thus, in a sense, conflict free.

Some will nevertheless say that there need be no norm of truth in assertoric discourse and that we are charging warranted assertibility—and hence Taktsang and company—with faults they do not have. It will probably be argued that while substituting *personal* warranted assertibility for truth will lead to endless excessively tolerant comparisons of notes, *communally* warranted assertibility will fare better. Yes, it is so that communal standards and epistemic procedures allow us to say that what certain individuals put forth as justified by solely *their* lights is not justified by current communal lights.[23]

Nonetheless, there is a problem in dispensing with a minimal norm of truth in this admittedly more sophisticated way, too. Again, what Price has to say is important. Communal standards frequently do come to the rescue to revise personally warranted assertions, provided that we actually recognize a Price-style norm of truth and thus take clashes seriously—if we do not recognize that norm, then a clash with communal standards could just as well be greeted

22. Ramsey [1925] 1990, 248: "There still are literature and art; but about them one cannot argue, one can only compare notes." To be clear, I do not subscribe to Ramsey's particular views on art and literature. I am concerned with what it means for a discourse to lack a Price-style norm of truth.

23. Crowd sizes at presidential inaugural addresses in the United States, for example, can be determined accurately in keeping with going procedures of observation and communally accepted elementary arithmetic.

with an indifferent yawn. And, if we recognize such a norm and the possibility of censure that goes with it, then just as individuals' views may be correctable by the community and not just remain MOAs, so too any given community's views, epistemic standards, and justificatory procedures may also be correctable by those of a better-informed future community. Our recognition of the norm of truth in question means that we do not just rely on assertions justified by compliance with *de facto* beliefs or epistemologies, be they personal or communal. In effect, it is integral to our alethic practices to accept that any given claim (relying on personal or communal justification) may turn out to be one that people should not make and indeed should never have made. MOAs (or, to put things in more Buddhist terms, acceptance of what the world acknowledges by its own present lights) without some version of Price's norm to provide friction would not be enough for us to continue to reason and debate in the basic ways we do.

Let me make two final reflections on the implications and advantages of acknowledging a strong norm of truth. The first concerns the relativism that Mahāyāna Buddhists wrestle with. The second is the issue as to whether truth-telling, as demanded by the norm, needs backing by truth theories. On both, what Tsongkhapa thought is significant. It is also, in my opinion, essentially right.

Madhyamaka Relativism? No, Thank You

Here's the background. Indo-Tibetan Mādhyamikas, of all stripes, frequently discuss an example cited in idealist works like Asaṅga's *Mahāyānasaṃgraha* and Vasubandhu's *Viṃśikā* and then alluded to in Candrakīrti's *Madhyamakāvatāra* 6.71ab: A stream is perceived differently by the six different classes of being—that is, as pus and blood by ghosts, drinking water by humans, a home by fish, and space by gods.[24] The example figures prominently in Taktsang, Tsongkhapa, and other authors mentioned in *Knowing Illusion*, and although the formulation is in terms of the Buddhist cosmology and reincarnation, there is nothing that limits the issues purely to Buddhism. Anthropologists, historians, and Wittgensteinian philosophers examining different cultures, historical periods, or forms of life (*Lebensformen*) with radically different worldviews can also prick up their ears and construe the debate accordingly.

---

24. There is also a well-known example in Dharmakīrti's *Pramāṇavārttikasvavṛtti* of a woman's body being perceived as desirable by a lover, as a skeleton by an ascetic yogin, and as a meal by a dog.

Relativism, then, loomed large in India and Tibet just as it does now. Tibetan Mādhyamikas like Gorampa Sönam Senge (Go rams pa Bsod nams seng ge, 1429–89) did indeed take the example of the stream as showing a form of ontological relativism—namely, that the objects understood by the respective classes of beings were in contradiction (*'gal ba* = *viruddha*) and that customary truths and *pramāṇa*s were thus internal to, and relative to, specific worlds (*loka*).[25] Others, like Taktsang, thought that the contradictions showed that there were never any *pramāṇa*s anywhere establishing ontologies, only misbeliefs and assertible propositions that varied with worlds and were relative to them. Tsongkhapa, on the other hand, agreed with neither move and had, at most, a very weak type of relativism. In his *Dbu ma dgongs pa rab gsal*, he criticized the "[wrongful] denial of all *pramāṇa*s" and argued that there were *no* contradictions between the objects perceived by different life forms, nothing that necessitated the ontological relativism his opponents cultivated. He describes the water, blood, and so on as compatible, noncontradictory, facets (*cha shas*) of one and the same stream that flows in all six worlds—being drinking water in the human world, thus, does not oppose being a home in the animal world, blood and pus in the ghost world, and so on.[26]

What kind of position is this? It's odd, prima facie. I suspect that Tsongkhapa wanted to take differences as due to a type of *seeing as*. He says that they were due essentially to varying perceptions or karmically conditioned mindsets concerning a same object and not due to there being incompatibilities between objects populating worlds. There are, of course, numerous banal cases

25. Yakherds 2021, 2:323: "So, Gorampa's conclusion is that there are never six substances in the same place and that one cannot say that the perceptions of all of the six kinds of beings are authentic; authenticity is relative to each perspective. From the perspective of human beings, what is conventionally true is what appears to humans; from the perspective of hungry spirits, what is conventionally true is what appears to hungry spirits."

26. Tsong kha pa, *Dbu ma dgongs pa rab gsal*, 279 (Sarnath edition), 339–40 (*Collected Works*): *de bzhin du gzhi gang du chu klung 'bab pa'i gzhi der chu klung de'i cha shas shig yi dwags rnams la sngon las kyi dbang gis rnag khrag tu skyes pa dang / chu klung gi cha shas gzhan zhig mi la sngon las kyi dbang gis rnag khrag tu mi snang ba'i btung ba dang / khrus kyi chur skye ba na de gnyis ka chu klung gcig gi cha shas re yin pas / yi dwags kyi mig shes tshad mas grub pa'i don dang / mi'i mig shes tshad mas grub pa'i don gnyis kyang dngos po so so ba yin pas de gnyis gcig gis grub pa'i don de nyid / cig shos kyis de'i bzlog phyogs su grub pa ga la yin /* "One facet (*cha shas*) of the stream that is [located] in the place where a river flows is what arises as pus and blood to hungry ghosts due to their previous karma. When another facet of the stream arises as drinking and washing water to people due to their previous karma and not appearing as pus and blood, then both of them are each facets of the one stream. Therefore the object that is established by hungry ghosts' ocular *pramāṇa*s and the object established by people's ocular *pramāṇa*s are different things. So, for those two [facets], why would it be that the very object established by one [type of being] would be established in the opposite fashion by another?"

of *seeing as*, *hearing as*, and so on, and they do not establish incompatibilities that lead to ontological relativism. It is not, for example, an indicator of anything metaphysically interesting if we say that Canadians hear the same dog's bark as "bow wow" whereas Japanese hear it as "wan wan."

I'm doubtful, however, that the specifics of the Buddhist canonical example can actually work as *seeing as*. It is obvious that H_2O can rightly be seen as drinking water and as a home for fish, but it is not at all obvious that pure H_2O can be rightly seen as drinking water and as blood, for blood and pure water have significantly different chemical compositions. We would, rather, say that one party is wrong about what the liquid is and say that the genuine difference between water and blood shows that we should not confine ourselves to potentially ambiguous perceptual phenomena but should be chemists instead.

There is, however, a general lesson here in *Dbu ma dgongs pa rab gsal* that *is* important. Tsongkhapa goes a considerable distance in endorsing what, I think, is a basic regulative principle of rationality—namely, that one should not sanguinely accept "incompatible realities," nor promote and multiply them as grist for a relativist mill. Some incompatibilities may indeed turn out, on investigation, to be only *prima facie* clashes—for example, cases of *seeing as* or deeper agreements. But they may also be due to wrong understandings by one side. What a rational thinker should not do is to eliminate clashes and censure by adopting the blanket position that, *in any case*, truth and reality are relative to worlds, or societies, historical periods, power elites, religious or political institutions, what have you. Not sanguinely dismissing opposition between claims is thus a natural consequence of the norm of truth that Price formulated, one that is, I think, integral to assertoric discourse, be it Tsongkhapa's or ours. Advocates of warranted assertibility, by contrast, will see nothing censurable in letting several rival MOAs coexist without friction and even embrace those rivalries relativistically. Perhaps, like Richard Rorty, they will say that concern with truth is *passé*, to be replaced by solidarity with the broad community with which we identify. Advocates of the norm of truth will not say that. They hold, rightly I think, that rationality demands a lot more.

Truth-Telling, Substantive Theories of Truth, and a Science of Tuesdays

Tsongkhapa, in practice, followed a strong norm of truth and truth-telling that set him apart not only from Taktsang but also, arguably, from most proponents of relativism. Did he then have a substantive theory of truth that explained or somehow grounded that norm? I don't think he did. I also think he was right in decoupling the norm from substantive theories.

Now, Georges Dreyfus, in discussion, raised the important question as to whether Tsongkhapa's triple characterization of customary truth in the last chapter of his *Lam rim chen mo* was itself a substantive theory of truth. It's clear enough that Candrakīrti himself did not put forward a substantive theory of truth—that is to say, an account promoting a recurring property that explains nontrivially what customary truth is and whose discernible presence ensures that certain propositions are customarily true. Indeed, in *Madhyamakāvatāra* 6.25, he again acquiesces in what he saw as the ways of the world. He thought that the world simply accepts ordinary people's understandings of customary matters by default when we see no impairments and other such customarily recognized conditions that vitiate those understandings.[27] This is a far cry from a theoretical quest for an explanatory property (like correspondence to reality) that would be common to all true propositions and nontrivially account for why they are true.

I think Tsongkhapa, in his *Lam rim chen mo*, also favored a type of default acceptance rather than a substantive truth-making property. He did, however, come up with the refinement that such acceptance of customary matters be subject to a threefold set of conditions: they must be "acknowledged by customary understanding" (*tha snyad pa'i shes pa la grags pa yin pa*); there must be "no opposition [to them] by another customary *pramāṇa*" (*tha snyad pa'i tshad ma gzhan gyis gnod pa med pa*); and they must "not be subject to opposition by reasoning that correctly analyzes the [ultimate] truth—that is, whether they have intrinsic natures" (*de kho na nyid dam rang bzhin yod med tshul bzhin du dpyod pa'i rigs pas gnod pa mi 'babs pa*).[28] What is striking is that *pramāṇas* play an essential role here, too, in what is a complex set of provisos limiting default acceptance. Tsongkhapa's proviso that there be no opposition (*gnod pa = bādhā*) by *pramāṇas* suggests more than just not seeing any vitiation here and now. Nonetheless, there is in Geluk Prāsaṅgika philosophy no informative characterization of what a *pramāṇa* is and what makes an understanding true; *pramāṇas* are simply characterized as "nonbelying" (*mi bslu ba = avisaṃvādin*) but without the special Dharmakīrtian type of correspondence theory and explanatory metaphysics of grounding in

---

27. *Madhyamakāvatāra* 6.25: *vinopaghātena yad indriyāṇām ṣaṇṇām api grāhyam avaiti lokaḥ / satyaṃ hi tal lokata eva śeṣaṃ vikalpitaṃ lokata eva mithyā //* "What the world considers to be grasped by the six sense faculties without impairment, that is true purely from the perspective of the world. The rest, purely from the world's perspective, is thought to be false."

28. *Lam rim chen mo*, 376b. See also Cutler and Newland 2002, 178.

particulars (*svalakṣaṇa*), both of which had been so crucial in the thought of Mahāyānist realist philosophers (see Tillemans 1999, 6–12). There is a strong dose of normativity built in practically but no truth-making property that lies behind it.

I've long thought that Mādhyamika Buddhists and the rest of us could profitably use the technical possibilities and clarity offered by a deflationist version of truth (see Tillemans 2016, 6–7, Tillemans 2022, chap. 7, and Cowherds 2011, chap. 8) to remain passionate about the obligation to pursue truths while also abandoning the quest for substantive theories about what truth is. A proposition $<p>$ is true if and only if p—no more no less. That is a deliberately austere and theoretically shallow account, but it will do technically and may well be all there is to truth, or to the connection between *pramāṇa*s and the world. We need not pursue a more substantive *pramāṇavāda*, the theory of *pramāṇa*s, to steer clear of the global error theory of typical Prāsaṅgikas and Candrakīrti.

Look at it this way. There is not the requisite unity underlying various truths for the theoretical quest to have a point. Jerry Fodor once had a catchy saying about how some longstanding philosophical quests—such as theories about the nature of representation and meaning—could turn out to be like the pursuit of a "science of Tuesdays" (2000). He himself attributed that critique of theory to Wittgensteinians and did not embrace much of it. But I do suspect that something similar applies to truth and that it reinforces deflationism. There likely is no single, theoretically satisfying explanation for propositions about diverse subjects—from particle physics to ethics to daily life—all being true, just as there is no single good explanation for events—from the 1929 stock market crash to my dentist appointment—all happening on the same day of the week, i.e., Tuesday. Nonetheless, truths can each be explained and are not arbitrary or purely subjective—there are also good but differing explanations why the stock market crash and my dentist appointment each happened when they did. If that is right, then Buddhist *śūnyavādin*s, too, would not need to settle for a scaled-down alternative to truth (be it "truth" in scare quotes or one of the current varieties of post-truth substitutes) because of there being no substantive theory of truth. There just is no science of Tuesdays.

Bibliography

Candrakīrti. *Madhyamakāvatāra* and *Madhyamakāvatārabhāṣya*. P 5262 and 5263, D 3861 and 3862. Editions in La Vallée Poussin [1907–12] 1970b.

———. *Prasannapadā Madhyamakavṛtti*. P 5260, D 3860. Editions in La Vallée Poussin [1903–13] 1970a, and MacDonald 2015.

———. *Yuktiṣaṣṭikāvṛtti*. P 5265, D 3864. See Scherrer-Schaub 1991.

Cutler, Joshua, and Guy Newland, eds. 2002. *The Great Treatise on the Stages of the Path to Enlightenment*: Lam rim chen mo of Tsong kha pa, vol. 3. Translated by The Lamrim Chenmo Translation Committee. Ithaca, NY: Snow Lion.

Cowherds, the (= Georges Dreyfus, Bronwyn Finnigan, Jay Garfield, Guy Newland, Graham Priest, Mark Siderits, Koji Tanaka, Sonam Thakchoe, Tom Tillemans, and Jan Westerhoff). 2011. *Moonshadows: Conventional Truth in Buddhist Philosophy*. New York: Oxford University Press.

Eckel, Malcolm David. 2003. "The Satisfaction of No Analysis: On Tsong kha pa's Approach to Svātantrika-Madhyamaka." In *The Svātantrika-Prāsaṅgika Distinction: What Difference Does a Difference Make?* edited by Georges B. J. Dreyfus and Sara L. McClintock, 173–203. Boston: Wisdom Publications.

Erb, Felix. 1997. *Śūnyatāsaptativṛtti: Candrakīrti's Kommentar zu den 'Siebzig Versen über die Leerheit' des Nāgārjuna [Kārikās 1–14]*. Tibetan and Indo-Tibetan Studies 6. Stuttgart: Franz Steiner Verlag.

Fodor, Jerry. 2000. "A Science of Tuesdays." *London Review of Books* 22.14.

Griffiths, Paul. 2000. "Book Review: *Emptiness Appraised: A Critical Study of Nagarjuna's Philosophy* by David F. Burton." *Journal of Buddhist Ethics* 7: 22–25.

Jackson, Roger R. 2019. *Mind Seeing Mind: Mahāmudrā and the Geluk Tradition of Tibetan Buddhism*. Studies in Indian and Tibetan Buddhism. Somerville, MA: Wisdom Publications.

Kapstein, Matthew. 2023. "Illusions of Knowing." *Philosophy East and West* 71.4: 1023–46.

Keira, Ryusei. 2004. *Mādhyamika and Epistemology: A Study of Kamalaśīla's Method for Proving the Voidness of All Dharmas*. Wiener Studien zur Tibetologie und Buddhismuskunde 59. Vienna: Arbeitskreis für Tibetische und Buddhistische Studien Universität Wien.

La Vallée Poussin, Louis de, ed. (1903–13) 1970a. *Mūlamadhyamakakārikās (Mādhyamikasūtras) de Nāgārjuna, avec le Commentaire de Candrakīrti*. Bibliotheca Buddhica 4. Osnabrück: Biblio Verlag.

———. (1907–12) 1970b. *Madhyamakāvatāra par Candrakīrti: Traduction Tibétaine*. Bibliotheca Buddhica 9. Osnabrück: Biblio Verlag, 1970.

MacDonald, Anne. 2009. "Knowing Nothing: Candrakīrti and Yogic Perception." In *Yogic Perception, Meditation and Altered States of Consciousness*, edited by Eli Franco in collaboration with Dagmar Eigner, 113–68. Vienna: Austrian Academy of Sciences Press.

———. 2015. *In Clear Words: The Prasannapadā, Chapter One*. 2 vols. Beiträge zur Kultur- und Geistesgeschichte Asiens 86. Vienna: Verlag der Österreichischen Akademie der Wissenschaften.

Price, Huw. 2003. "Truth as Convenient Friction." *Journal of Philosophy* 100.4: 167–90.

Putnam, Hilary. (1981) 1993. *Reason, Truth, and History*. New York: Cambridge University Press.

Ramsey, Frank P. (1925) 1990. "Epilogue." In *F. P. Ramsey: Philosophical Papers*, edited by D. H. Mellor, 245–50. New York: Cambridge University Press.

Rorty, Richard. (1991) 1996. *Objectivity, Relativism, and Truth*. Philosophical Papers 1. New York: Cambridge University Press.

Scherrer-Schaub, Cristina. 1991. *Yuktiṣaṣṭikāvṛtti: Commentaire à la soixantaine sur le raisonnement ou Du vrai enseignement de la causalité par le Maître indien Candrakīrti*. Brussels: Institut Belge des Hautes Études Chinoises, 1991.

Tillemans, Tom J. F. 1990. *Materials for the Study of Āryadeva, Dharmapāla and Candrakīrti: The Catuḥśataka of Āryadeva, Chapters XII and XIII, with the Commentaries of Dharmapāla and Candrakīrti. Introduction, Translation, Sanskrit, Tibetan and Chinese Texts, Notes*. 2 vols. Wiener Studien zur Tibetologie und Buddhismuskunde 24.1 and 24.2. Vienna: Arbeitskreis für Tibetische und Buddhistische Studien.

———. 1999. *Scripture, Logic, Language: Essays on Dharmakīrti and His Tibetan Successors*. Studies in Indian and Tibetan Buddhism. Boston: Wisdom Publications.

———. 2003. "Metaphysics for Mādhyamikas." In *The Svātantrika-Prāsaṅgika Distinction: What Difference Does a Difference Make?* edited by Georges B. J. Dreyfus and Sara L. McClintock, 93–123. Boston: Wisdom Publications.

———. 2011a. "How Far Can a Mādhyamika Buddhist Reform Conventional Truth? Dismal Relativism, Fictionalism, Easy-Easy Truth, and the Alternatives." In *Moonshadows: Conventional Truth in Buddhist Philosophy*, by the Cowherds, 151–65. New York: Oxford University Press. Reprinted in Tillemans 2016, 47–63.

———. 2011b. "How to Talk about Ineffable Things: Dignāga and Dharmakīrti on Apoha." In *Apoha: Buddhist Nominalism and Human Cognition*, edited by Mark Siderits, Tom Tillemans, and Arindam Chakrabarti, 50–63. New York: Columbia University Press.

———. 2016. *How Do Mādhyamikas Think? And Other Essays on the Buddhist Philosophy of the Middle*. Studies in Indian and Tibetan Buddhism. Somerville, MA: Wisdom Publications.

———. 2021. "Reversing Śāntarakṣita's Argument: Or Do Mādhyamikas Derive Part-Whole Contradictions in All Things?" In *A Road Less Traveled: Felicitation Volume in Honor of John Taber*, edited by Vincent Eltschinger, Birgit Kellner, Ethan Mills, and Isabelle Ratié, 443–70. Wiener Studien zur Tibetologie und Buddhismuskunde 100. Vienna: Arbeitskreis für Tibetische und Buddhistische Studien Universität Wien.

———. 2022. *Views from Tibet: Studies on Tibetan Buddhist Logic, the Philosophy of the Middle, and the Indigenous Grammatico-Linguistic Tradition*. Vienna: Austrian Academy of Sciences Press.

———. 2023. "Is Metaphysics Madness? A Sixth-Century Polemic Unpacked." In *To the Heart of Truth: A Felicitation Volume for Eli Franco on the Occasion of His 70th Birthday*, edited by Hiroko Matsuoka, Shinya Moriyama, and Tyler Neill, 1–31. Wiener Studien zur Tibetologie und Buddhismuskunde 104.1. Vienna: Arbeitskreis für Tibetische und Buddhistische Studien Universität Wien.

Tsong kha pa blo bzang grags pa. *Collected Works of Tsong kha pa*, or *Khams gsum chos kyi rgyal po Tsong kha pa chen po'i gsung 'bum*. Tashi Lhunpo edition. Geden sungrab minyam gyunphel series 79–105. Delhi: Ngag dbang dge legs bde mo, 1975–79.

———. *Dbu ma dgongs pa rab gsal = Bstan bcos chen po dbu ma la 'jug pa'i rnam bshad dgongs pa rab gsal.* In *Collected Works*, vol. *ma.* Modern textbook edition. Sarnath: Pleasure of Elegant Sayings Press, 1973.

————. *Drang nges legs bshad snying po* = *Drang ba dang nges pa'i don ram par phye ba'i bstan bcos legs bshad snying po.* In *Collected Works*, vol. *pha.* Modern textbook edition. Sarnath: Pleasure of Elegant Sayings Press, 1973.

————. *Lam rim chen mo* = *Byang chub lam rim chen mo.* In *Collected Works*, vol. *pa.*

————. *Rtsa ba'i shes rab kyi dka' gnad chen po brgyad kyi bshad pa.* In *Collected Works*, vol. *ba.* Modern textbook edition. Sarnath: Pleasure of Elegant Sayings Press, 1970.

Williams, Paul. 1995. "Identifying the Object of Negation: On *Bodhicaryāvatāra* 9:140 (Tib. 139)." *Asiatische Studien / Études Asiatiques* 49.4: 969–86.

Yakherds, the (= José Cabezón, Ryan Conlon, Thomas Doctor, Douglas Duckworth, Jed Forman, Jay Garfield, John Powers, Sonam Thakchoe, Tashi Tsering, and Yeshes Thabkhas). 2021. *Knowing Illusion: Bringing a Tibetan Debate into Contemporary Discourse.* 2 vols. New York: Oxford University Press.

About the Contributors

Dan Arnold is the John Henry Barrows Professor of Philosophy of Religions at the University of Chicago Divinity School. He is the author of *Buddhists, Brahmins, and Belief: Epistemology in South Asian Philosophy of Religions* (2005), and of *Brains, Buddhas, and Believing: The Problem of Intentionality in Classical Buddhist and Cognitive-Scientific Philosophy of Mind* (2012). His *Madhyamaka Reader: The Middle Way in Indian Buddhist Philosophy* will appear in the fall of 2026.

José Ignacio Cabezón is Distinguished Research Professor and Dalai Lama Professor Emeritus at the University of California, Santa Barbara. A scholar of Indian and Tibetan Buddhism, he has published numerous books and articles on themes as diverse as Madhyamaka philosophy, Buddhist monasticism, sexuality in South Asian Buddhism, and Tibetan ritual. Cabezón is currently working on the "synoptic" literature of late Indian Buddhism and on the life and works of the early Kadampa masters of Tibet. He was elected to the American Academy of Arts and Sciences in 2019 and served as president of the American Academy of Religion in 2020.

John Dunne (PhD 1999, Harvard University) serves on the faculty of the University of Wisconsin-Madison, where he holds the Distinguished Chair in Contemplative Humanities at the Center for Healthy Minds. He is also distinguished professor in the Department of Asian Languages and Cultures, where he recently served as department chair. John's work is guided by the motivation to reduce suffering and enhance flourishing, and he brings that intention to his research, writing and teaching on Buddhist philosophy and contemplative practice, especially in dialogue with cognitive science and psychology. His diverse research agenda includes collaborations around Buddhist philosophy, contemplative education, meditation-based interventions, psychedelics, and consciousness, and his publications appear in venues ranging across both the humanities and the sciences. He is a member of Mind and Life Europe and a Fellow of the Mind and Life Institute, where he previously served on the board of directors. His academic collaborations include a senior advisory role at the Rangjung Yeshe Institute in Kathmandu, Nepal.

Jonardon Ganeri is the Bimal K. Matilal Distinguished Professor of Philosophy at the University of Toronto. His work draws on a variety of philosophical traditions to construct new positions in the philosophy of mind, metaphysics, and epistemology. His books include *The Self: Naturalism, Consciousness and the First-Person Stance* (2010); *Attention, Not Self* (2017), a study of early Buddhist theories of attention; *The Concealed Art of the Soul* (2012), an analysis of the idea of a search for one's true self; *Virtual Subjects, Fugitive Selves* (2020), an analysis of Fernando Pessoa's philosophy; and *Inwardness: An Outsiders' Guide* (2021), a review of the concept of inwardness in literature, film, poetry, and philosophy. His latest book, *Fernando Pessoa: Imagination and the Self* (2024), brings the ideas of the Portuguese poet into dialogue with Indian philosophical poetics. He joined the Fellowship of the British Academy in 2015 and won the Infosys Prize in the Humanities the same year, the only philosopher to do so. He delivered the 2024 John Locke Lectures at the University of Oxford, entitled *Seeing & Subjectivity* (forthcoming).

Jay L. Garfield previously served as Doris Silbert Professor in the Humanities and professor of philosophy and Buddhist studies at Smith College, visiting professor of Buddhist philosophy at Harvard Divinity School, and professor of philosophy at Melbourne University before retiring to Tasmania in 2024. Garfield's research addresses topics in the philosophy of mind, metaphysics, the history of modern Indian philosophy, epistemology, ethics, and topics in Buddhist philosophy, particularly Indo-Tibetan Madhyamaka and Yogācāra. He is the author or editor of over thirty books and over two hundred articles, chapters, and reviews. Garfield's most recent books are *Norms and Nature: A Humean Account of the Sources of Normativity* (2025), *By the Light of the Moon: Candrakīrti's Prāsaṅgika Madhyamaka*, with Sonam Thakchöe (2025), *Subject as Freedom: A Contemporary Translation* with Nalini Bhushan (2025), *How to Be Caring: An Ancient Guide to a Compassionate Life* (2025), and *How to Lose Yourself* (with Maria Heim and Robert Sharf 2025).

David Higgins received his doctorate in 2012 from the University of Lausanne, Switzerland, and subsequently held a position as a postdoc research fellow at the University of Vienna. His research interests include Indo-Tibetan Buddhist philosophy and epistemology, with a particular focus on

Bka' brgyud Mahāmudrā and Rnying ma Rdzogs chen doctrines and practices. His recent publications include *Mahāmudrā and the Middle Way: Post-Classical Kagyü Discourses on Mind, Emptiness and Buddha Nature* (2016) and *Buddha Nature Reconsidered: The Eighth Karmapa's Middle Path* (2019), both coauthored with Martina Drazczyk, and *Heartfelt Advice: Yang dgon pa's Song of the Seven Direct Introductions with Commentary by 'Ba' ra ba Rgyal mtshan dpal bzang* (2022). He is currently a Research Fellow at the Tsadra Foundation, finalizing a translation of the Eighth Karmapa's commentary on the *Madhyamakāvatāra*.

Pascale Hugon studied Indology and Tibetology at the University of Lausanne. She is a senior research associate at the Institute for the Cultural and Intellectual History of Asia, Austrian Academy of Sciences. Her primary research focus is the philosophical literature of Buddhism: its transmission to Tibet, Tibetan interpretations, and indigenous elaborations. Based on recently surfaced sources, she investigates the development of Tibetan scholasticism in the eleventh to thirteenth centuries. Her publications include editions, translations, and thematic studies based on Sanskrit and Tibetan materials. Together with Jonathan Stoltz, she published the first monograph on Phya pa Chos kyi seng ge (*The Roar of a Tibetan Lion*, 2019).

Shōryū Katsura, professor emeritus of Hiroshima and Ryukoku Universities, earned his BA and MA degrees in Buddhist philosophy at Kyoto University and his PhD at the University of Toronto for his study of Harivarman's **Tattvasiddhi*. He was later granted the degree of DLitt by Kyoto University for his study of the concept of pervasion (*vyāpti*) in Indian philosophy. He has edited *Dharmakīrti's Thought and Its Impact on Indian and Tibetan Philosophy* (1999) and *The Role of the Example (dṛṣṭānta) in Classical Indian Logic* (coedited with Ernst Steinkellner, 2004) and published *Nāgārjuna's Middle Way* (with Mark Siderits, 2013), *Indian Logic (Indojin no Ronrigaku)* (2021), the complete Japanese translation of the *Gaṇḍavyūha-sūtra* (with Yūichi Kajiyama and others, 2021), *Candrakīrti's Middle Way: Madhyamakāvatāra Chapter 6* (with Mark Siderits, 2026), and many books and articles on various aspects of Indian and Buddhist philosophy. He is the recipient of the Japanese Association of Indian and Buddhist Studies Award (1977) and the Nakamura Hajime Eastern Academic Award (2010).

Birgit Kellner is Distinguished Researcher at the Austrian Academy of Sciences in Vienna. She works primarily on the history of Indian and Tibetan Buddhist logic and epistemology, with the knowledge of absences and theories of reflexive awareness as main areas of research. She is the author of two monographs, *Nichts bleibt Nichts* (1997) and *Jñānaśrīmitra's Anupalabdhirahasya and Sarvaśabdābhāvacarcā* (2007), and has coedited several edited volumes and journal issues on various subjects in Buddhist philosophy. Her most recent article deals with Dharmakīrti and nonduality (*Bloomsbury Research Handbook of Non-duality in Indian Thought*).

Kenneth Liberman is professor emeritus of sociology at the University of Oregon, where he taught for thirty years. He trained as a phenomenologist and ethnomethodologist and has undertaken sociological research among Australian Aboriginal people and Tibetans. He is author of *Dialectical Practice in Tibetan Philosophical Culture* and translator of *The Panchen Lama's Debate Between Wisdom and the Reifying Habit*. Two of his books, *More Studies in Ethnomethodology* and *Tasting Coffee: An Inquiry into Objectivity*, have won Best Book awards from the American Sociological Association. In 2025, he received a Distinguished Career Award from the American Sociological Association.

Sara McClintock is a Buddhist philosopher and scholar of religion whose interests converge at the intersections of ethics, metaphysics, truth, and story. They received a BA in fine arts from Bryn Mawr College in 1983, an MTS from Harvard Divinity School in 1989, and a PhD in the study of religion from Harvard University in 2002. They have studied and conducted research at the Central University for Higher Tibetan Studies in Sarnath, India, and the University of Lausanne, Switzerland. They now serve as associate professor in the Department of Religion at Emory University. Their publications include articles on Buddhist philosophy and narrative; a monograph, *Omniscience and the Rhetoric of Reason* (2010); several edited volumes, including *The Svātantrika-Prāsaṅgika Distinction* coedited with Georges Dreyfus (2003); and an award-winning translation of Nāgārjuna's *Ratnāvalī* with John Dunne (2024). They are currently working on a book on truth.

Mark Siderits retired from Seoul National University in 2012, having taught previously at Illinois State University. His research interests lie in the intersection between classical Indian philosophy on the one hand and analytic metaphysics and philosophy of language on the other. Among his more recent publications are *Personal Identity and Buddhist Philosophy: Empty Persons* (2nd ed., 2015), *How Things Are: An Introduction to Buddhist Metaphysics* (2021), *Buddhist Physicalism?* (2025), and *Candrakīrti's Middle Way: Madhyamakāvatāra Chapter 6* (with Shōryū Katsura, 2026). A collection of his papers on Buddhist philosophy, *Studies in Buddhist Philosophy*, was published in 2016.

Sonam Thakchoe is a senior philosophy lecturer at the University of Tasmania, where he has served since 2003. His unique academic background combines traditional Indo-Tibetan philosophical training (ācārya degree from Central University of Tibetan Studies, 1997) with Western philosophical expertise (PhD from University of Tasmania, 2003). This dual foundation, along with his native fluency in Tibetan and other Asian languages, positions him as an exceptional bridge between Eastern and Western philosophical traditions. Thakchoe has established himself as a prolific scholar, with eight authored books and with articles in leading journals such as *Philosophy East & West* and the *Journal of Indian Philosophy*. His latest work, a collaboration with Jay Garfield, is *By the Light of the Moon: Candrakīrti's Prāsaṅgika Madhyamaka* (2025). His current research explores how contemplative practices can inform rigorous philosophical methodology and contribute to addressing fundamental questions about consciousness, ethics, and meaning in contemporary life.

Tom J. F. Tillemans is a Canadian and Dutch citizen. Educated as a philosopher and philologist, he became a professor of Buddhist studies at the University of Lausanne in Switzerland and subsequently emeritus professor there. His interests range from comparative metaphysics and logic to Tibetan poetry. He has long resided on a smallish island off the west coast of Canada. For more about Tom, see the introduction to this volume.

Jan Westerhoff was educated at the University of Cambridge and the School of Oriental and African Studies at the University of London. After teaching at Oxford and Durham for several years, he is now professor of Buddhist philosophy at the University of Oxford and a fellow of Lady Margaret Hall. His publications include *Nāgārjuna's Madhyamaka: A Philosophical Introduction* (2009), *The Golden Age of Buddhist Philosophy in India* (2018), *The Non-Existence of the Real World* (2020), and *Candrakīrti's "Introduction to the Middle Way": A Guide* (2024).

Chizuko Yoshimizu is a professor emerita of Buddhist studies and Tibetology at the University of Tsukuba as well as a Tibetan studies researcher at the Toyo Bunko (Oriental Library) in Tokyo. She specializes in Madhyamaka philosophy and Buddhist epistemology. Her publications on Buddhist philosophy include numerous articles and books, including recently *Zhang Thang* *sag pa 'Byung gnas ye shes, dBu ma tshig gsal gyi ti ka,* Part I (2013) and Part II (2018), "Revisiting the Tenth Chapter of the *Saṃdhinirmocanasūtra*: A Scripture on Rational Reflection," in *Evolution of Scriptures, Formation of Canons: The Buddhist Case* (2022), and "The Negation of Arising from Other in the *Mūlamadhyamakakārikā* and Beyond" in *Burlesque of the Philosophers: Indian and Buddhist Studies in Memory of Helmut Krasser* (2023).

Studies in Indian and Tibetan Buddhism
Titles Previously Published

Among Tibetan Texts
History and Literature of the Himalayan Plateau
E. Gene Smith

Approaching the Great Perfection
Simultaneous and Gradual Methods of Dzogchen Practice in the Longchen Nyingtig
Sam van Schaik

Authorized Lives
Biography and the Early Formation of Geluk Identity
Elijah S. Ary

The Buddha's Single Intention
Drigung Kyobpa Jikten Sumgön's Vajra Statements of the Early Kagyü Tradition
Jan-Ulrich Sobisch

Buddhism Between Tibet and China
Edited by Matthew T. Kapstein

The Buddhist Philosophy of the Middle
Essays on Indian and Tibetan Madhyamaka
David Seyfort Ruegg

Buddhist Teaching in India
Johannes Bronkhorst

A Direct Path to the Buddha Within
Gö Lotsāwa's Mahāmudrā Interpretation of the Ratnagotravibhāga
Klaus-Dieter Mathes

The Essence of the Ocean of Attainments
The Creation Stage of the Guhyasamāja Tantra according to Paṇchen Losang Chökyi Gyaltsen
Translated by Yael Bentor and Penpa Dorjee

Foundations of Dharmakīrti's Philosophy
John D. Dunne

Freedom from Extremes
Gorampa's "Distinguishing the Views" and the Polemics of Emptiness
José Ignacio Cabezón and Geshe Lobsang Dargyay

Reasons and Lives in Buddhist Traditions
Studies in Honor of Matthew Kapstein
Edited by Dan Arnold, Cécile Ducher, and Pierre-Julien Harter

Remembering the Lotus-Born
Padmasambhava in the History of Tibet's Golden Age
Daniel A. Hirshberg

Resurrecting Candrakīrti
Disputes in the Tibetan Creation of Prāsaṅgika
Kevin A. Vose

Saraha's Spontaneous Songs
With the Commentaries by Advayavajra and Mokṣākaragupta
Klaus-Dieter Mathes and Péter-Dániel Szántó

Scripture, Logic, Language
Essays on Dharmakīrti and His Tibetan Successors
Tom J. F. Tillemans

Sexuality in Classical South Asian Buddhism
José I. Cabezón

Splitting the Middle
A Natural History of Middle Way Reasoning
Kevin A. Vose

The Svātantrika-Prāsaṅgika Distinction
What Difference Does a Difference Make?
Edited by Georges Dreyfus and Sara McClintock

The Vajrabhairava Tantra
A Study and Annotated Translation
Aleksandra Wenta

Vajrayoginī
Her Visualizations, Rituals, and Forms
Elizabeth English

Available October 2026

Buddhist Minds and Bodies
Essays in Honor of José Ignacio Cabezón
Edited by Rory Lindsay and Vesna Wallace

About Wisdom Publications

Wisdom Publications is the leading publisher of classic and contemporary Buddhist books and practical works on mindfulness. To learn more about us or to explore our other books, please visit our website at wisdom.org or contact us at the address below.

Wisdom Publications
132 Perry Street
New York, NY 10014 USA

We are a 501(c)(3) organization, and donations in support of our mission are tax deductible.

Wisdom Publications is affiliated with the Foundation for the Preservation of the Mahayana Tradition (FPMT).